Dr. (John) Doran

Table Traits with something on them

Dr. (John) Doran

Table Traits with something on them

ISBN/EAN: 9783743329966

Manufactured in Europe, USA, Canada, Australia, Japa

Cover: Foto ©ninafisch / pixelio.de

Manufactured and distributed by brebook publishing software (www.brebook.com)

Dr. (John) Doran

Table Traits with something on them

BILL OF FARE

	PAGE
The Legend of Amphitryon—A Prologue.	7
Diet and Digestion	14
Water	18
Breakfast	29
Materials for Breakfast	33
Corn, Bread, &c.,	37
Tea	48
Coffee	56
Chocolate	62
The Old Coffee House	65
The French Cafés	76
The Ancient Cook and his Art	81
The Modern Cook and his Science	92
Pen and Ink Sketch of Carême	105
Dinner Traits	113
The Materials for Dining	124
A Light Dinner for Two	152
Sauces	171
The Parasite	196
Table Traits of Utopia and the Golden Age	206
Table Traits of England in the Early Times	218
Table Traits of the Last Century	232
Wine and Water	251
The Birth of the Vine, and what has come of it	256
The Making and Marring of Wine	271
Imperial Drinkers and Incidents in Germany	380
An Incident of Travel	280
A few odd Glasses of Wine	290
The Tables of the Ancient and Modern Egyptians	305
The Diet of Saints of Old	316
The Bridal and Banquet of Ferques	333
The Support of Modern Saints	338
The Cæsars at Table	353
Their Majesties at Meat	368
English Kings at their Tables	395
Strange Banquets	417
The Castellan Von Coucy	423
Authors and their Dietetics	436
The Liquor-loving Laureates	454
Supper	459

TABLE TRAITS

WITH SOMETHING ON THEM.

THE LEGEND OF AMPHITRYON.

A PROLOGUE.

"*Le véritable Amphitryon est l'Amphitryon où l'on dine.*"—Molière.

AMONG well-worn illustrations and similes, there are few that have been more hardly worked than the above line of Poquelin-Molière. It is a line which tells us pleasantly enough, that he who sits at the head of a table is among those "respectable" powers who find an alacrity of worship at the hands of man. I say, "at the hands;" for what is "adoration" but the act of putting the hand to the mouth (as expressed by its components *ad* and *os*, or *oris*)? and what worship is so common as that which takes this form, especially when the Amphitryon is amiable, and his altar well supplied?

But such a solution of the question affords us, after all, no enlightenment as to the mystery of the reality or Amphitryon himself, whose name is now worn, and sometimes usurped, by those who preside at modern banquets. Was he real? is he a myth? was he ever in the body? or is his name that of a shadow only employed for purposes of significance? If real, whence came he? What does classic story say of the abused husband of Alcmena.

Amphitryon was a Theban gentleman, who had two nephews, fast young men, who were slain by the Teleboans. This is a myth. They were extravagant individuals, of the class of those who count the chimes at midnight. Their father could not help them; and so the uncle, a bachelor, was expected to do his avuncular office, spend his substance for the benefit of his brother's children, and get small thanks for his trouble. His brother, however, had an article of small value,—a daughter named Alcmena; and this lady was given in marriage to her uncle, without any scruple about the laws of affinity. As soon as the ceremony of the betrothal was over, Amphitryon departed to punish the Teleboans; and he had not been long absent, when Jupiter presented himself in the likeness of the absent husband, set up a household with the readily-convinced Alcmena, and became the father of Hercules. When Amphitryon returned, his surprise was natural, and his ill-temper not to be wondered at. But Jupiter explained the imbroglio in a very cavalier way, as was his custom, and which they who are curious may see in the liveliest of the lively comedies of the miller's man, Plautus.

An incident connected with the story shows us that Amphitryon, fond of good living generally, and of beef in particular, made a razzia among the Teleboan herds, and brought back all the cows and oxen he found amongst them. He was exhibiting the cattle to his brother Electryon, when one of the animals strayed from the herd; and Amphitryon, in order to bring it back, flung a stick at it, but with such violence, that the weapon, falling on the horns, rebounded as violently upon Electryon, who died upon the spot. But this, too, is a myth; and I have no doubt but that Electryon died of indigestion; for the Teleboan beef was famous for its toughness. Indeed, many of the Teleboës themselves were so disgusted with it, that they abandoned their Ætolian homes, and settled in the island of Capreæ.

The Egyptians claim Amphitryon for their own. They boast

that his dinners at Memphis were divine, and that Hercules, his son was among the last-born of gods; for Hercules was more than a hero among the leek-worshippers of Egypt. But the truth is, that the story of Amphitryon, his strength, his good fare, and his hard fate, belongs to a more distant period and land. It is a Hindoo story, the actors are children of the sun, and Voltaire declares that the tale is to be found in Dow's "Hindostan;" but that is as much of a fable as the legend itself of Amphitryon, whose name, by the way, may be as easily "Indicized" as that of Pythagoras.

In Scotland, the crime of child-stealing is distinguished by the title of "plagiary;" and an instance of the latter is here before us. When Plautus sat in his master's mill, and thought over the subject of his lively comedy, founded on the story of Amphitryon, he took for granted all that he had been told of his hero's birth and parentage. But the classical Amphitryon is, as I have said, but a stolen child. His home is in the far East; and his history was calling up smiles upon the faces of listeners by the Indus long before the twin founders of Rome had been intrusted, by their nurse Lupa, to walk alone. The Hindoo Amphitryon was a fellow of some renown, and here is his story.

A Hindoo, whose name, indeed, has not descended to us,—but he was the individual whom the Greeks stole, and called Amphitryon,—lived many years ago. He was remarkable for his gigantic strength and stature; and he not only found the former a good thing to possess, but he used it *like* a giant. He had for the wife of his bosom a fair, but fragile girl, who lay in his embrace, as she sang to him at sunset, "like Hebe in Hercules' arms." It was not often, however, that such passages of peace embellished the course of their daily life. The Hindoo was jealous, and his little wife was coquettish. The lady had smiles for flatterers; and her monster of a husband had a stick, which showered blows upon her when he detected her neglecting her household work. Cudgelling took its turn with carressing, as it did in the more modern and consequently more vulgar, case of Captain Wattle and Miss

Roe; and finally there was much more of the first than there was of the last. One summer eve, the husband, in a fit of frantic jealousy, assaulted his wife so ferociously, that he left her insensible on the threshold of their house, and threatened never again to keep up a *ménage* with so incorrigible a partner.

A Hindoo deity, of an inferior order,—not the King of gods and men, as in the Grecian legend,—had witnessed the whole proceeding from his abiding place in a neighbouring cloud. He smiled as the husband disappeared; and, gradually descending in his little palace to the ground, he lightly leaped on to the firm set earth, gave a hurried glance at the unconscious and thickly-bruised beauty, and then, in testimony of his ecstatic delight, he clapped his hands, and commenced revolving on one leg, as D'Egville used to do, when Venua's violin led the orchestra, and gave him strength.

The spirit having subsided into repose, thought for a while, and speedily arrived at a resolution. It infused itself into a human body, which was found without difficulty, and it clothed the whole under the counterfeit presentment of the errant husband. These feats of transmutation were common among the eastern deities; and I take for granted that my readers are aware that Pythagoras himself—who is connected with Table Traits, on the subject of beans—was no other than Buddha Goroos, who slipped into a vacant body, and taught the metempsychosis to wondering Europe.

The wife of the Hindoo giant was something astonished, on recovering herself, to find that she was seated, without any sense of pain, on a bench in the little garden, with her apparent husband at her feet, pouring out protestations of love and assurances of fidelity. She accepted all, without questioning; for it was all too pleasant to be refused. A new life commenced. The married pair became the admiring theme of the village; and when a son was born to them, there ensued such showers of felicitations and flowers as had never fallen upon married lovers since the Hindoo world first started on its career, on the back of the self-supporting elephant. Their moon never ceased to shed honey; and this was flowing, sweetly and copiously as ever, when, one sultry noon, the vagrant husband returned home, and, confronting the counterfeit at the inner door, bitterly satirized the vanity of women who indulged in capricious tempers and Psyche glasses. In an instant, however, he was conscious that his other self was not a reflection, but only the cause of many that began crowding into the brain of the true man. The cool complacency of the counterfeit irritated the bewildered and legitimate husband, and an affray ensued, in which the mortal got all the blows, and his rival all the advantage. The wife was herself perplexed, but manifested a leaning towards the irresistible divinity. In vain did the gigantic original roar forth the tale of his wrongs, and claim his undoubted rights; and it was only during a lull in the storm that he heeded a suggestion made, to the effect, that all the parties should submit their case to the judgment of an inspired Brahmin.

This eminent individual speedily perceived that, of the doubleman that stood before him, one was a dupe, and the other a deity,—something, at all events, above humanity. The question was, how to discover the divinity. After much cogitation, this was the judgment pronounced by the dusky Solomon: "Madam," said he to the perplexed lady, "your husband was known as being the most robust man ever made out of the red earth, of which was composed the father of us all. Now, let these two litigants salute you on the lips; and we pronounce him to be the true man who comes off with the loudest report." The trial took place forthwith in presence of the assembled multitude. The Indian mortal first approached the up-raised lips of his wife; and he performed the required feat with an echo that was as half a hundred culverins to the "pistol shot" kiss recorded of Petruchio. The Judge and the people looked curiously to the defendant, as wondering how, on the pretty instrument before him, he could strike a note higher than his rival. The Indian god addressed him to what seemed a rose-bud wet with dew; and therewith ensued a sound as though all the artillery of the skies were saluting, too, in honour of the achievement. The multitude and the Brahmin looked, for all the world, as if they had lost their hearing; and it was calculated that the astounding din might have been heard by the slumbering tortoise below the antipodes. At length, the assembly hailed the deity as the undoubted Simon Pure, and looked towards the Brahmin for confirmation of their award; but the Brahmin merely remarked to them, with urbanity, that they were the sons and fathers of asses, and were unable to distinguish between the almost invisible seed which diets the bird of Paradise, and the gigantic palm of the garden of the gods, each leaf of which is of such extent that an earthly courser, at his utmost speed, could not traverse it in fifty millions of mortal-measured years. "Here is the true husband," added the Judge, putting his hand on the shoulder of the Indian, "who has done all that human being, in the particular vocation required, could do; and here," added he, turning reverentially to the other, "is some supreme being, who has been pleased to amuse himself at the expense of his servants."

The god smiled, and confessed to the excellence of the Judge's perspicuity by revealing himself in his true, and somewhat operatic, form. He ascended the cloud, which appeared in waiting for him like an aërial cab, and, looking from over its side, laughingly bade the edified multitude farewell, adding, that he was the deity appointed to preside at tables that were not ungraced by the fair;—and, "if these have a cause for complaint, it is my privilege to avenge them according to my good pleasure." The ladies thereupon flung flowers to him as he rose, and the husbands saluted his departure with rather faint cheers; but throughout India, while orthodoxy lasted, there never was a table spread, but the master thereat, prince or peasant, invoked the Hindoo deity to cast the beams of the sun of his gaiety upon the board. Heresy, however, in this matter, has crept in; and, if Hindoo feasts lack real brilliancy, it is because the sunlight of the god no longer beams from the eyes of the fair, who are no longer present sharers in the banquet. It is otherwise in Europe, whither, perhaps, the god came, and aped Jupiter, as well as Amphitryon, when he perplexed the household of Alcmena. He sits presiding at our feast, ensconced within a rose; from thence his smiles urge to enjoyment, and the finger on his lip to discretion; and every docile guest whispers *sub rosâ*, and acknowledges the present god.

It is said, in India, that this divinity was the one who gave men diet, but forgot digestion. It was like giving them philosophical lectures, without power to understand them; and the case is still common enough upon earth. These subjects demand brief notice, were it only by way of appendix to this prolegomenical chapter.

DIET AND DIGESTION.

" No digest of law's like the law of digestion."—Moore.

Our good neighbours the French, or rather, the philosophers among them, have asserted that the perfecting of man and his species depends upon attention to diet and digestion; and, in a material point of view, they are not far wrong; and, indeed, in a non-material point of view, it may be said that the spirit, without judgment, is very likely to be exposed to indigestion; and perhaps ignorance complete is to be preferred to an ill-digested crudition. With diet and patience, Walpole thought all the diseases of man might be easily cured. Montesquieu, on the other hand, held that health purchased by rigorously watching over diet, was but a tedious disease. But Walpole was nearly correct, while Montesquieu was not very distant from the truth. Dieting, like other things, must be undertaken on common-sense principles; for, though there be multitudes of mad people in the world, society generally is not to be put up on the *régime* of "Bedlam."

We live, not by what we eat, but by what we digest; and what one man may digest, another would die of attempting. Rules on this subject are almost useless. Each man may soon learn the powers of his stomach, in health or disease, in this respect; and this ascertained, he has no more business to bring on indigestion than he has to get intoxicated or fall into debt. He who offends on these three points, deserves to forfeit stomach, head, and his electoral franchise!

Generally speaking, fat and spices resist the digestive power, and too much nutritious food is the next evil to too little. Good cookery, by developing flavour, increases the nutritiousness of food, which bad cookery would perhaps render indigestible. Hence a good cook rises to the dignity of "artist." He may rank with the chemists, if not with the physicians.

Animal food, of mild quality, is more digestible than vegetable, and fresh meats are preferable to salted. In the latter the salt is a different composition from that which is taken at meals, and which is indispensable to health. Fish fills rather than feeds; but there are exceptions to this. Vegetables are accounted as doing little to maintain stamina; but there have been races and classes of men who have been heroes upon bread, fruit, and vegetables. The poor cannot live upon "curry," it is true; but in England, with less drink and more vegetable food, they would be an improved race. Not that they could live like a Lazzaroni on maccaroni and the open air. Layard says the Bedouin owes his health and strength to his spare diet. But even a Bedouin swallows lumps of butter till he becomes bilious: and were he to live in England instead of the desert, he would not keep up his strength by living on dishes which support him in Arabia Felix. The golden rule is "moderation and regularity," he who transgresses the rule, will pay for it by present suffering and a "check after Christmas."

A false hunger ought not to be soothed, nor a false thirst to be satisfied; for satisfaction here is only adding fuel to a fire that would otherwise go out. On the other hand, the bilious and sedentary man need not be afraid of beer; it is a better stomachic than wine. For him, and for all the lords of that heritage of woe, a weak stomach, the common-sense system of cookery, as it is called, is most required. It is something between the hard crude system of the English, and the juice-extracting method of the French; with a leaning, however, towards the latter, (with whom it is common to reduce food to a condition of pulp), but uniting with it so much of the English custom as to allow the gelatinous matter to be retained, especially in the meats. "*Festina lente*," is "*Latin de cuisine*," for "Eat slowly," and it is of first-rate value. He who does so, gives best chance for healthy chyle; and that wanting, I should like to know where the *post-prandial* enjoyment would be. Without it, digestion is **not; and when digestion is away, Death is always peering about to profit by his absence** "See to it!" as the Chinese "chop" says.

There are upwards of seventeen hundred works extant on the subject of diet and digestion. Sufferers may study the question till they are driven mad by doubt and dyspepsia, and difference of opinions among the doctors. Fordyce saw no use in the saliva, and Paris maintains that without it digestion is not. "*Quot homines, tot sententiæ,*" is as applicable here as in every other vexed question. But Paris's book on Diet is the safest guide I know for a man who, being dyspeptic, wants to cure himself, or simply to discover the definement of his degree of suffering. On the other hand, every man may find comfort in the reflection, that with early hours, abundant exercise, generous diet, but not too much of it, and occupation,—without which a worse devil than the former enters on possession of the victim,—dyspepsia cannot assume a chronic form. It may be a casual visitor, but it will be the easiest thing possible to get rid of him. But philosophy has said as much from the beginning, and yet dyspepsia prevails and physicians ride in carriages. Exactly! and why? Because philosophers themselves, like the Stoic gentleman in Marmontel, after praising simplicity of living, sink to sleep, on heavy suppers and beds of down, with the suicidal remark, that "*Le Luxe est une jolie chose.*"

We must neither act unreservedly on the *dictum* of books, nor copy slavishly the examples of others, if we would have the digestion in a healthy condition. There is a self-monitor that may safely be consulted. Of his existence there can be no doubt; for every man who wakes with a head-ache most ungratefully blames that same monitory "self."

If any class may fairly complain of others in this respect, rather than of themselves, it is the "babies." The Rajpoots do not slay half so many of their infants out of pride, as we do by indiscreet dieting; or, to speak plainly, over-feeding. The New Zealand mother is not more foolish, who thrusts stones down the throat of her babe, in order to make him a stern and fearless warrior, and only mars him for a healthy man. And Christian matrons have been quite as savage without intending it. Brantome's uncle, Chastargnerage, was no sooner weaned than, by the advice of a

Neapolitan physician, he took gold, steel and iron, (in powders,) mixed up with all he ate and drank. This regimen he followed until he was twelve years old, by which time (we are asked to believe) it had so strengthened him that he could stop a wild bull in full course. This diet, however, seems little likely to have produced such an effect. As soon might one expect that the Bolton ass, which chewed tobacco and took snuff, was made swift as a race-horse by so doing. I think that it is of Dean Nowell it is said, that he grew strong by drinking ale. He was the accidental inventor of bottled ale. He was out fishing with a bottle of the freshly-drawn beverage at his side, when intelligence reached him touching the peril his life was in, under Mary, which made him fly, after flinging away his rod, and thrusting his bottle of ale under the grass. When he could again safely resort to the same spot, he looked for his bottle, which, on being disturbed, drove out the cork like a pellet from a gun, and contained so creamy a fluid, that the Dean, noting the fact, and rejoicing therein, took care to be well provided with the same thenceforward. As Henry II. was the first King who acted as sewer, and placed the boar's head on the table of his young son, just crowned, so Dean Nowell was the first church dignitary who laid the foundation of red noses, by bringing bottled ale to the notice of the clergy. There is an old tradition, that what this ale used to do for churchmen, cider used to effect for Africans.

As we have said, "moderation" is the first principle of digestion; and as, according to the Latin proverb, "water gives moderation," it behoves us to look for a few minutes into the much praised, and little appreciated, *aqua pura*.

WATER.

A Kentucky man, who was lately at one of the great tables in an hotel in the States, where the bill of fare was in French, after sorely puzzling himself with descriptions which he could not comprehend, "*cotelettes à la Maintenon*" and "*œufs à la braise;*" exclaimed, "I shall go back to first principles: give me some roast beef!" So, after speaking of the birth of him, whose putative father has lent a name to liberal hosts, let us also fall back upon first principles, and contemplate the uses of water.

There is nothing in nature *more* useful; but, commonly speaking, you can neither buy any thing with it, nor get any article for it in exchange. Adam Smith strikingly compares with it the uselessness and the value of a diamond: the latter has scarcely any value in use, but much that is valuable may be had in exchange for it. In the desert a cup full of water is worth one full of diamonds; that is, in certain emergencies. The diamond and the water illustrate the difference between value in use and value in exchange.

If water be not, according to Pindar and the legend over the Bath Pump-room, the best of things, few things would attain to excellence without it. Greek philosophy was not wrong which made it the principle of life, and the popular belief scarcely erred in seeing in every stream, spring and fountain a resident deity. Water was so reverenced by certain ancient nations, that they would never desecrate it by purifying themselves therewith! The ancient Persians and Cappadocians exemplified their devotion by personal dirtiness. In presence of the visible power of the stream, altars were raised, and adoration paid to the god whose existence was evidenced by such power. The Egyptians gave their divine river more than prayers, because their dependence on it was more absolute than that of other nations on their respective streams. The Nile, swelling beneficently, bestowed food, health, and therewith content on the Egyptians; and they, in return, flung gratefully into the stream corn, sugar, and fruit. When human sacrifices were made to rivers, it was probably because the river was recognised as giving life, and was worthy of being paid in kind. We may smile superciliously at this old reverence for the "liquid good," but there was connected therewith much that we might profitably condescend to copy. Greece had her officers appointed to keep her streams pure. Had those officials exposed the people to drink such indescribable matter as we draw from the Thames, they would have been thrown into it by popular indignation. In Rome, Ancus Martius was long remembered, not for his victories, but for his care to supply the city with salubrious and sufficient water; and if people generally cursed Nero for his crimes, they acknowledged that he had at least not damaged the public aqueducts; and that in his reign ice-houses were first built, the contents of which enabled thousands to quaff the cool beverage which is so commendably spoken of by Aristotle.

The fountains were the ornaments of the public places, as the crystal *ampulla*, with its slender neck and its globular body, was of the side-boards of private houses in Rome. The common people drank to excess, both of hot water and cold: the former they drank in large measures;—this was in winter, and in taverns where they fed largely upon pork, and drank the water as a stimulant! The Emperor Claudius looked upon this regimen as an immoral indulgence, and he closed the taverns where proprietors injured the public stomach by such a diet. Some Romans were so particular as to boil the water they intended to drink, in vessels at their own table. They were like the epicures who never intrust the boiling of an egg to their own cooks. We may notice that Augustus employed it lavishly, both as a bather and drinker. The "faculty" were unanimous in recommending a similar use of it, and some of these gentlemen made considerable fortunes by the various methods of applying it. For instance, patients resorting to Charmis, to take cold baths in winter under his directions, were required to pay him a consulting fee of £800! He was the first "water-cure" Doctor that ever practised, and he realized a fortune such as his successors may aim at in vain.

Horace Walpole, forgetting what he had once before said, namely, that diet and patience formed the universal panacea, declared that his "great nostrum was the use of cold water, inwardly and outwardly, on all occasions, and that with disregard of precaution against catching cold. I have often," he continues, "had the gout in my face and eyes, and instantly dip my head in a pail of cold water, which always cures it, and does not send it anywhere else." And again, alluding to another use of water, he says sneeringly, "Whether Christianity will be laid aside I cannot say. As nothing of the spirit is left, the forms, I think, signify very little. Surely, it is not an age of morality and principle; does it import whether profligacy is baptized or not?"

With regard to the sanitary application of water, as noticed by Walpole, there can be no doubt but that diet and digestion proceed the more perfectly, as the ablution of the body is general and daily, and made with cold water. But discretion must be used; for there are conditions of the body which cannot endure cold bathing without palpitation of the heart following. In such case, tepid water should be used for a time, when the palpitations will soon cease, unless the heart be organically affected.

The same writer's remarks on the Christian uses of water, remind me of what is said of some such uses in Weever's "Funeral Monuments." He cites the inscriptions that used to be placed over the holy water in ancient churches. Some deposed that the sprinkling of it drove away devils:—

"*Hujus aquæ tactus depellit dæmonis actus.*"

Others promised a blessing, as, for example:—

"*Asperget vos Deus cum omnibus sanctis suis ad vitam æternam.*"

Another implied, that six benefits arose from its use; namely,—

> "*Sex operantur aquâ benedictâ:*
> *Cor mundat, accidiam (?) fugat, venalia tollit,*
> *Auget opem, removetque hostem, phantasmata pellit.*"

Homer, too, it will be recollected, speaks of the sound of water inspiring consolatory thoughts, in the passage where he describes one "suffering cruel wounds from a diseased heart, but he found a remedy; for, sitting down beneath a lofty rock, looking down upon the sea, he began to sing."

The dormitories of many of the old convents were adorned with inscriptions recommendatory of personal cleanliness; but the inmates generally were more content with the theory than the practice: they were, in some degree, like the man at Bishop-Middleham, who died with the reputation of a water-drinker, but who really killed himself by secret drunkenness. He praised water in public, but drank brandy in private, though it was not till after death that his delinquency was discovered.

The use of water against the spells of witchcraft lingered longer in Scotland than elsewhere. The Strathdown Highlander even now, it is said, is not ashamed to drink "the water of the dead and living ford," on New Year's Day, as a charm to secure him from sorcery until the ensuing New Year.

St. Bernard, the Abbot, made application of water for another purpose. Butler says of him, that he *once* happened to fix his eyes on the face of a woman; but immediately reflecting that this was a temptation, he ran to a pond, and leaped up to the neck into the water, which was then as cold as ice, to punish himself, and to vanquish the enemy!

There is a second incident connected with water, that will bear to be told as an illustration, at least, of old times. When Patricius was Bishop of Prusa, the Proconsul Julius resorted thither to the famous baths, and was restored to such vigorous health thereby, that he not only made sacrifice of thanksgiving to Esculapius and Health, but required the Bishop to follow his example. The Prelate declined, and the Proconsul ordered him to be thrown into a caldron of boiling water, by which he was no more affected than if he had been enjoying a bath of tepid rose-water. Whereupon he was taken out and beheaded. The power that kept the water cool did not interfere to blunt the axe.

We have seen the reverence paid by certain "ancients of old" to the supposed divinities whose crystal thrones were veiled beneath the waves. Men under a better dispensation have shown, perhaps, a worse superstition. Bede makes mention of a Monk who thought he would purify his sin-stained spirit by actual ablution. He had, the church-historian tells us, a solitary place of residence assigned him in the monastery, adjacent to a river: into the latter he was accustomed to plunge, by way of penance to his body. He went manfully to the bottom, and his mouth was no sooner again in upper air, than it was opened to give utterance to lusty prayer and praise. He would sometimes thus stand for hours, up to the neck, and uttering his orisons aloud. He was in full dress when this penance was performed, and, on coming from the stream, he let his wet, and sometimes frozen, garments dry upon his person. A Friar, once seeing him break the ice, in order that he might make his penitential plunge, expressed shiveringly his wonder at the feat: "It must be so *very* cold," said the Friar. "I have seen greater cold," was the sole remark of the devotional diver. "Such austerity *I* never beheld," exclaimed another spectator. "*I* have beheld far greater," replied the Monk. "And thus," adds the historian, as simply as any of them, "thus he forwarded the salvation of many by his words and example."

Connected with a pious man of our own time, I may mention an incident touching water, which is rather remarkable:—the person to whom I allude is Bishop Gobat, of Jerusalem. He states, in his last Annual Letter, that he is building a school which will cost him about £600; the school is not yet finished: but the water used for mixing the mortar has already cost the enormous sum of £60. It is, in fact, a luxury which must be paid for. Where it is so dear, it were well if the people never were thirsty; and there were such people of old.

The late Vice-Chancellor of England, Sir Lancelot Shadwell

was as indefatigable a bather as the Monk noticed by Bede. Every morning throughout the year, during his residence at Barnes Elms, he might be seen wrestling joyously with the Thames. It is said that, on one occasion, a party, in urgent need of an injunction, after looking for the Judge in a hundred places where he was not to be found, at length took boat, and encountered him as he was swimming in the river. There he is said to have heard the case, listening to the details as the astonished applicants made them, and now and then performing a frolicsome "summersault," when they paused for want of breath. The injunction was granted, it is said; after which the applicants left the Judge to continue his favourite aquatic sport by himself.

If the late amiable and able Vice-Chancellor was a water-lawyer, so was the late Archdeacon Singleton a water-divine. When tutor to the young Lords Percy, he, and the eldest of the sons of the then Duke of Northumberland,—Hugh, Earl Percy,—were expert swimmers, and often, by their achievements, excited the admiration of less daring venturers. The Archdeacon was accustomed to float away for miles from Sion, depending upon the tide to float him back again. At first, many a boatman looked inquiringly at the motionless body carrying on with the stream; but, when he was better known, his appearance thus excited no more surprise than if he had been in an outrigger, calmly taking a pull before the hour of dinner.

With respect to water-drinkers, they seem to have abounded among the good old Heathens, of whom so many stories are told that we are not called upon to believe.

Aristotle, who, like Dr. Macnish, wrote an "Anatomy of Drunkness," (Περὶ Μέθης,) states therein, that he knew, or had heard, of many people who never experienced what it was to be thirsty. Archonides, of Argos, is cited by him as a man who could eat salt beef for a week without caring to drink, therewith or thereafter. Mago the Carthaginian, is famous for having twice crossed the Desert without having once tasted water, or any other beverage. The Iberians, wealthy and showy people as they were, were water-drinkers; and it was peculiar to some of the Sophists of Elis, that they lived upon nothing but water and dried figs. Their bodily strength, which was great, is said to have been the result of such diet; but, it is added, that the pores of their skin exuded any thing but a celestial ichor, and that, whenever they went to the baths, all the other bathers fled, holding their offended noses between their fingers! Matris, of Athens, lived all his life upon myrtle-berries and water; but, as nobody knows how long he *did* live, it would be rather rash to imitate him in hopes of obtaining extension of existence. Lamprus, the musician, was a water-drinker, as were Polemon, the Academician, and Diocles, of Peparethus; but, as they were never famous for any thing else, they are hardly worth citing. It is different when we contrast Demosthenes with Demades. Demosthenes states, in his second Philippic, that he was a water-drinker; and Phytheas was right, when he bade the Athenians remark, that the sober demagogue was, like Dr. Young, in fact, constantly engaged in solemn Night Thoughts. "Not so your other demagogue, Demades," said Pytheas; "*he* is an unclean fellow, who is daily drunk, and who never comes into your assemblies but to exhibit his enormous paunch." Such was the style of election speeches in Greece; and it has a smack of the hustings, and, indeed, of the market, too, in Covent Garden.

To turn from old to modern Mythology, I may notice that water entered into the old sports of St. Distaff's Day, or the morrow after Twelfth Day. It is thus alluded to by one whose "mind was jocund, but his life was chaste,"—the lyric Parson of Dean Priors:—

> "Partly work and partly play
> Ye must, on St. Distaff's Day.
> From the plough soon free your team,
> Then come home and fother them.
> If the maids a-spinning go,
> Burn the flax, and fire the tow,
> Scorch their plackets, but beware
> That you singe no maiden-hair.

> Bring in pails of water then,
> Let the maids bewash the men.
> Give St. Distaff all the right,
> Then bid Christmas sport 'Good night;'
> And next morrow ev'ry one
> To his own vocation.'

When Herric wrote these lines, I do not know how it may have been at Dean Priors, but London was but indifferently supplied with water. But *now* London is supplied with water from eight different sources. Five of them are on the north, or Middlesex, side of London, three on the Southwark and Surrey side. The first comprise the New River, at Islington; the East London, at Old Ford, on the Lea; the West Middlesex, on the Thames, at Brentford and Hammersmith; and the Chelsea and Grand Junction, on the same river, at Chelsea. The south side is entirely supplied from the Thames, by the Southwark, Lambeth, and Vauxhall Waterworks, whose names are descriptive of their locality.

The daily supply amounts to about 35,000,000 of gallons, of which more than a third is supplied by the New River Company. The original projector of this Company was Sir Hugh Myddelton, who proposed to supply the London conduits from the wells about Amwell and Ware. The project was completed in 1613, to the benefit of posterity and the ruin of the projector. The old hundred-pound shares are now worth ten times their original cost.

In 1682 the private houses of the metropolis were only supplied with fresh water twice a-week. Mr. Cunningham, in his "Handbook of London," informs us that the old sources of supply were the Wells, or Fleet River, Wallbrook and Langbourne Waters, Clement's, Clerk's, and Holy Well, Tyburn, and the River Lea. Tyburn first supplied the City in the year 1285, the Thames not being pressed into the service of the City conduits till 1568, when it supplied the conduit at Dowgate. There were people who stole water from the pipes then, as there are who steal gas now. "This yere," (1479,) writes an old chronicler of

London, quoted by Mr. Cunningham, "a wax-chandler in Flete Strete had bi craft perced a pipe of the condite withynne the ground, and so conveied the water into his selar, wherefore he was judged to ride thurgh the Citee with a condite upon his hedde." The first engine which conveyed water into private houses, by leaden pipes, was erected at London Bridge, in 1582. The pipes were laid over the steeple of St. Magnus; and the engineer was Maurice, a Dutchman. Bulmer, an Englishman, erected a second engine, at Broken Wharf. Previous to 1656, the Strand and Covent Garden, though so near to the river, were only supplied by water-tankards, which were carried by those who sold the water, or by the apprentice, if there were one in the house, whose duty it was to fill the house-tankard at the conduit, or in the river. In the middle of the seventeenth century, Ford erected water-works on the Thames, in front of Somerset House; but the Queen of Charles II.—like the Princess Borghese, who pulled down a church next to her palace, because the incense turned her sick, and the organ made her head ache—ordered the works to be demolished, because they obstructed a clear view on the river. The inhabitants of the district depended upon their tankards and water-carriers, until the reign of William III., when the York-buildings Waterworks were erected. The frequently-occurring name of Conduit-street, or Conduit-court, indicates the whereabouts of many of the old sources whence our forefathers drew their scanty supplies.

Water is not necessarily unhealthy, because of a little earthy matter in it; mineral, or animal, or vegetable matter held in it, by solution, or otherwise, renders it decidedly unwholesome. Rain water is the purest water, when it is to be had by its natural distillation in the open fields. When collected near towns, it should never be used without being previously boiled and strained.

The hardness of water is generally caused by the presence of sulphate of lime. Horses commonly refuse to drink hard water, —a water that can make neither good tea, nor good beer, and which frequently contains many salts. Soft water, which is a powerful solvent of all vegetable matters, is to be preferred for all domestic purposes. River water is seldom pure enough for drinking. Where purest, it has lost its carbonic acid from long exposure; and in the neighbourhood of cities it is often a slow poison, and nothing more, scarcely to be rescued from the name by the process of filtration. London is still supplied, at a very costly price, with water which is "offensive to the sight, disgusting to the imagination, and destructive to the health." Thames water, as at present flowing into our houses, is at once the jackal and aide-de-camp of cholera. People are apt to praise it, as being the water from which is made the purest porter in the world; but it is a well-known fact, that the great London brewers never employ it for that purpose.

The more a spring is drawn from, the softer the water will become; hence old wells furnish a purer water than those which are more recent; but a well of soft water is sensibly hardened by a coating of bricks. To obviate this, the bricks should be coated with cement. Snow water deserves a better reputation than it has acquired. Lake water is fitted only for the commonest household detergent purposes. But the salubrity of water is converted into poison by the conveyances which bring it almost to our lips; and we have not yet adopted in full the recommendation of Vitruvius and Columella to use pipes of earthenware, as being not only cheaper, but more durable and more wholesome, than lead. We still convey away refuse water in earthenware, and bring fresh water into our houses in lead! The noted choleraic colic of Amsterdam, in the last century, was entirely caused by the action of vegetable matter in the water-pipes.

Filtration produces no good effect upon hard water. The sulphate of lime, and still more the super-carbonate of lime, are only to be destroyed by boiling. Boiled water, cooled, and agitated in contact with the atmosphere, before use, is a safe and not an unpleasant beverage. It is essential that the water be boiling when "toast and water" is the beverage to be taken.

Water, doubtless, is the natural drink of man—in a natural state. It is the only liquid which truly appeases thirst; and a small quantity is sufficient for that effect. The other liquids are, for the most part, palliatives merely. If man had kept to water, the saying would not be applicable to him, that "he is the only animal privileged to drink without being thirsty." But, then, where would the medical profession have been?

But he does well who, at all events, commences the day with water and prayer. With such an one we go hand in hand, not only in that service, but, as now, to Breakfast.

BREAKFAST.

Swift lent dignity to this repast, and to laundresses partaking of it, when he said, in illustration of modern Epicureanism, that "the world must be encompassed before a washerwoman can sit down to breakfast."

Franklin, who made a "morality" of every sentiment, and put opinions into dramatical action, has a passage in some one of his Essays, in which he says, that "Disorder breakfasts with Plenty, dines with Poverty, sups with Misery, and sleeps with Death." It is an unpleasant division of the day, but it is truly described, as far as it goes. On the other hand, it is not to be concluded that Disorder is the favourite guest of Abundance; and I do not know any one who has described a plentiful breakfast, with regularity presiding, better than another essayist, though one of a less matter-of-fact quality than Franklin,—I mean Leigh Hunt. In the "Indicator" he invites us to a "Breakfast in Cold Weather." "Here it is," he says, ready laid. "*Imprimis*, tea and coffee; secondly, dry toast; thirdly, butter; fourthly, eggs; fifthly, ham; sixthly, something potted; seventhly, bread, salt, mustard, knives, forks, &c. One of the first things that belong to a breakfast, is a good fire. There is a delightful mixture of the lively and the snug, in coming down to one's breakfast-room of a cold morning, and seeing every thing prepared for us,—a blazing grate, a clean table-cloth and tea-things; the newly-washed faces and combed heads of a set of good-humoured urchins; and the sole empty chair, at its accustomed corner, ready for occupation. When we lived alone," he adds, "we could not help reading at meals; and it is certainly a delicious thing to resume an entertaining book, at a particularly interesting passage, with a hot cup of tea at one's elbow, and a piece of buttered toast in one's hand. The first look at the page, accompanied by a co-existent bite of the toast, comes under the head of 'intensities.'" Under the head of "&c." in the above list, I should be disposed to include "sunshine;" for sunshine in a breakfast-room in winter, is almost as glorious a thing as the fire itself. It is a positive tonic; it cheers the spirits, strengthens the body, and promotes digestion. As for breakfast in hot weather, all well-disposed persons who have gardens take that meal, of course, in "the arbour," and amid flowers. Breakfasts *al fresco* are all the more intensely enjoyed, because so few may be discussed in the open air in a country whose summer consists of "three hot days and a thunder-storm;" and in a climate wherein, according to Boerhave, people should not leave off their winter clothing till Midsummer-Day, resuming the same next morning when they are dressing for breakfast! Walpole and Boerhave are right; our summers do sometimes set in with extraordinary severity.

The breakfast of a Greek soldier, taken at dawn of day, required a strong head to bear it. It consisted of bread soaked in wine. If Princes were in the habit of so breaking their fast, we hardly need wonder at the denunciation in Ecclesiastes against those who eat in the morning. The Greek patricians sat daily down to but one solid meal. Soldiers and plebeians had less controllable appetites, and these could not be appeased with less than two meals a-day. They were accounted peculiarly coarse people who consumed three. The Romans were in this respect, similar to the Greeks. Fashionable people ate little or nothing before the hour when they compensated for a long fast by a daily meal, where they fed hugely. A simple breakfast, as soon as they awoke, of "bread and cheese," has a very unclassical sound; but good authority assures us that it was a custom duly honoured with much observance. Not of such light fare, however, was the breakfast of Galba. Suetonius says that the old Emperor used to cry for his morning repast long before day-break. This was in winter time. He took the meal in bed, and was probably induced to do so by indisposition; for he was a huge, ogre-like supper-eater,—eating much, leaving more, and ordering the remains to be divided among the attendants, who duly, rather than dignifiedly, scrambled for the same.

Modern epicures would hardly approve of some of the dishes half-consumed by the hungry Galba at breakfast; but potentates of our own days have made their first meal upon very questionable matter.

When Clapperton, the African traveller, breakfasted with the Sultan of Baussa, which is a collection of straggling villages on the banks of the Quorra, among the delicacies presented were a large grilled water-rat, and alligators' eggs, fried or stewed. The company were much amazed at the singularity of taste which prompted the stranger to choose fish and rice in preference to those savoury viands. The Prince, who gave this public breakfast in honour of a foreign commoner, was disgusted at the fastidious super-delicacy of his guest. In the last century, our commoners used to give similar entertainments in honour of Princes.

"Ælia Lælia" Chudleigh, as Walpole calls the famous lady who was still more famous as Duchess of Kingston, gave splendidly untidy entertainments of this sort in a splendidly untidy mansion. Her suppers will be found noticed in another page. In 1763, she gave a concert and vast cold collation, or "breakfast," in honour of Prince Edward's birthday. The *scene* is admirably painted by Walpole. "The house is not fine, nor in good taste, but loaded with finery. Execrable varnished pictures, chests, cabinets, commodes, tables, stands, boxes, riding on one another's backs, and loaded with terrines, figures, filligrees, and every thing upon earth! Every favour she has bestowed is registered by a bit of Dresden China. There is a large case full of enamels, eggs, ambers, lapis-lazuli, cameos, tooth-pick cases, and all kinds of trinkets, things she told me were her playthings. Another cupboard full of the finest japan, and candlesticks, and vases of rock-crystal, ready to be thrown down in every corner. But of all curiosities are the conveniencies in every bed-chamber; great mahogany projections, with brass handles, cocks, &c. I could not help saying it was the loosest family I ever saw."

There was a philosopher of the same century, at whom even Walpole dared not have sneered. I allude to Dr. Black, whom Lavoisier called "the Nestor of the Chemical Revolution." Dr. Black was famous for the frugality of his breakfasts, and for the singularity of his death, when seated at that repast. His usual fare was a little bread, a few prunes, and a measured quantity of milk and water. One morning in November, 1799, he was seated at this modest meal. His cup was in his hand, when the Inevitable Angel beckoned to him, and the Christian philosopher calmly obeyed. He placed the cup on his knees, "which were joined together, and kept it steady with his hand, in the manner of a person perfectly at his ease; and in this attitude he expired, without a drop being spilt, or a feature in his countenance changed, as if an experiment had been required, to show to his friends the facility with which he departed." There was neither convulsion, shock, nor stupor, we are told, to announce or retard the approach of death. This was a more becoming end than that of another chemist, the younger Berthollet, although in the latter there was something heroical, too. He had taken his last breakfast, when he calmly proceeded to a sacrifice which he made to the interests of science. He destroyed his life by enclosing himself in an atmosphere of carbonic acid. There he began registering all the successive feelings he experienced, which were such as would have been occasioned by a narcotic;—"a pause, and then an almost illegible word occurred. It is presumed that the pen dropped from his hand, and he was no more."

I have spoken of winter and of summer breakfasts. I must have recourse to Mr. Forrester's "Norway in 1848 and 1849," to show what a breakfast for a traveller should be; namely, oatmeal porridge, or stir-about, with a slice of rye or wheaten bread. Such a breakfast, he says, will not only fortify the traveller for a lengthened period, but to the sedentary, the bilious, and the dyspeptic, its adoption will afford more relief than the best prescription of a physician. But this breakfast must be prepared with due care, and this is the fashion of it: "Take two or three handsfull of oatmeal; I prefer it of mixed coarse and fine meal, in the proportion of one third of the latter to two of the former. Mingle the meal in a basin of cold water, and pour it into a saucepan containing about a quart of boiling water; add a small portion of salt. Set the saucepan over the fire, and keep stirring it, sprinkling, from time to time, small quantities of the meal, till the composition boils, and has acquired the proper consistency. That may be known by its glutinous state as it drops from the spoon. Let it simmer for ten minutes, and then pour it, not into a deep dish, but into common dinner plates, and it will form a soft, thin, jellied cake; spoon out portions of this, and float it in new milk, adding moist sugar, to your taste." For the benefit of others, I may add my testimony touching this recipe, I have strictly followed the instruction given, and I certainly never tasted any thing to equal the dish. It was execrable! But it has the double recommendation of being easy to digest, and of keeping off the sensation of hunger for a very long time. Use alone is needed to make it a popular breakfast, and he is a hero who uses it till he likes it. But it is time to consider the various

MATERIALS FOR BREAKFAST.

AND first, of milk. If Britons really have, what they so much boast of,—a birth-right,—the least disputable article of that class, is their undoubted right to that lacteal treasure which their mother holds from Nature, on trust, for their use and advantage.

It is a curious fact that aristocratic infants are those who are most ordinarily deprived of this first right of their citizenship, and are sent to slake their thirst and fortify their thews and sinews at ochlocratic breasts. Jean Jacques Rousseau was not often right, but he was triumphantly so when he denounced the young and healthy mother, let her rank be what it might, who made surrender of what should be one of the purest of a young mother's pleasures, and flung her child to the bosom of a stranger. Who can say what bad principles may not have been drawn in with these "early breakfasts?" Certainly this vicarious exercise of the office of maternity is an abomination; and the abomination of having one's child suckled by a mercenary stranger can only be next in intensity to that of having him——but let us keep to "Table Traits."

Milk is too popularly known to need description; but it is not all that is sold under that name that comes from the cow. The cow with one arm, that produces what fresh medical students call the *aqua pumpaginis*, has very much to do with the dairies of London. Metropolitan milk-maids are not as unsophisticated as the milk-maids of the olden time; if, indeed, maids or milk were particularly pure even then; for milk was a propitiatory offering to Mercury, and if ever there was a deity who loved mischief, why, Dan Mercury was the one.

In Rome milk was used as a cosmetic, and for baths as well as beverage. Five hundred asses supplied the bath and toilette-vases of the Empress Poppæa; and some dozen or two were kept to maintain the decaying strength of Francis I. Of course, asses' milk became fashionable in Paris immediately, just as bolster cravats did with us, when the Regent took to them in order to conceal a temporary disease in the neck.

"Oil of milk" and "cow-cheese" were classical names for butter,—a substance which was not known in either Greece or Rome until comparatively late periods. Greece received it from Asia, and Rome knew it not as an article of food until the legionaries saw the use to which it was applied by the German matrons. The Scythians, like the modern Bedouins, were great butter-consumers. Their churners were slaves, captured in war, and blinded before they were chained to the sticks beside the tub, at which, with sightless orbs, they were set to work.

There have been seasons when, as now in Abyssinia, butter has been burned in the lamps in churches, instead of oil. The "butter-tower" of the cathedral at Rouen owes its distinctive appellation to its having been built from the proceeds of a tax levied in return for permissions to eat butter at uncanonical times; so that the tower is a monument of the violation of the ecclesiastical canons.

But there is great licence in these matters; and chapels in Ireland have been constructed with money raised by putting up Moore's erotic works to be raffled for, at half-a-crown a ticket!

Goats, cows, sheep, asses, and mares have all contributed their milk towards the making of cheese; and national prejudice has run so high on the question of superiority, that as many broken heads have been the result, as there have been rivulets of blood spilt at Dinant, on the question of copper kettles. The Phrygian cheese is said to have owed its excellence to the fact, that it was made of asses' and mares' milk mixed together. I doubt, however, if the strong-smelling Phrygian cheese was equal to our Stilton,—which, by the way, is not made *at* Stilton,—and whose ripeness has been judiciously assisted by the addition of a pint of Madeira. Delicate persons at Rome breakfasted on bread and cheese,—principally goat cheese. It was administered, on the same principle that we prescribe rump-steak, as strengthening. People in rude health flourished in spite of it, and therefore ailing people *must*, it was thought, be invigorated because of it. However, our own system is less open to objection than that of the ancient faculty.

I do not know whether mothers will consider it complimentary or not; but it is a fact, that the milk of asses more nearly resembles human milk than any other. Like the human milk, it contains more saccharine matter than that of the cow, and deposits a large proportion of curd by mere repose.

Milk is easily assimilated, nourishes quickly, and but slightly excites to vascular action. It is stringent, however, and has a tendency to create acidity; but an addition of oatmeal gruel will correct both these matters. Suet, inserted in a muslin bag, and simmered with the milk, is of highly nourishing quality; but it is sometimes more than weak stomachs can bear. Lime-water with milk is recommended as sovereign against the acidity which milk alone is apt to create in feeble stomachs.

Eggs have been as violently eulogized as they have been condemned, and both in extremes. In some parts of Africa, where they are very scarce, and the Priests are very fond of them, it has been revealed to the people, that it is sacrilege for any but clerical gentlemen to eat eggs! The lay scruple, if I may so speak, is quieted by the assurance, that, though the sacred hens produce only for the servants at the altar, the latter never address themselves to the food in question, without the whole body of the laity profiting thereby! I suppose that Dissenters naturally abound in this part of Africa. There is nothing so unsatisfactory as vicarious feeding. Feeding is a duty which every man is disposed to perform for himself, whether it be expected of him or not. All the eggs in Africa, passing the œsophagus of a Priest, could hardly nourish a layman, even though the eggs were as gigantic as those which an old author says are presented by ladies in the moon to their profoundly delighted husbands, and from which spring young babies, six feet high, and men at all points.

If the matrons in the moon were thus remarkable in this respect, the Egyptian shepherds on earth were not less so in another: they had a singular method of cooking eggs, without the aid of fire. They laid them in a sling, and then applied so violent a rotatory motion thereto, that they were heated and cooked by the very friction of the air through which they passed!

Diviners and dreamers dealt largely in eggs. Livia was told, just before the birth of Tiberius, to hatch one in her bosom, and that the sex of the chick would foretell that of the expected little stranger. In Rome and Greece eggs were among the introductory portions of every banquet. But Rome knew only of twenty different manners of cooking them. What an advance in civilization has been made in Paris, which, according to Mr. Robert Fudge, boasts of six hundred and eighty-five ways to dress eggs!

Eggs, filled with salt, used to be eaten by curious maidens, after a whole day's fasting, on St. Agnes' Eve: the profit of such a meal was, that she who partook of it had information, in her after-dreams, of that very interesting personage, her future husband!

There is a story narrated of a Welsh weaver, that he could tell, by the look of the egg, whether the bird would be worth anything or not. He reminds me of an old Monk I heard of, when in Prague, who, on a man passing him, could tell whether he were an honest man, or a knave, by the smell! But the Welsh weaver was even more clever than this. He could not only judge of eggs but hatch them. A badger once carried off his sitting-hen, and no plumed nurse was near to supply her place. The weaver, thereupon, took the eggs (there were six of them) to bed with him, and in about two days hatched them all! Of this brood he only reared a cock and a hen. The cock was a gallant bird, that used to win flitches of bacon for his master at cock-fights; and the hen was as prolific as Mrs. Partlett could have desired. The result was, that they kept their step-mother, the weaver, in bacon and eggs for many a month; and the two days spent in bed were not so entirely thrown away as might, at first sight, appear.

Let it be understood that eggs may lose their nourishment by cooking. The yolk, raw, or very slightly boiled, is exceedingly nutritious. It is, moreover, the only food for those afflicted with jaundice. When an egg has been exposed to a long continuance of culinary heat, its nature is entirely changed. A slightly-boiled egg, however, is more easy of digestion than a raw one. The best accompaniment for a hard egg is vinegar. Raw eggs have a laxative effect; hard-boiled, the contrary. There is an idiosyncrasy in some persons, which shows itself in the utter disgust which they experience, not only against the egg itself, but also against any preparation of which it forms an ingredient, however slight. Eggs should always be liberally accompanied by bread; of which I will now say a few words, and first of

CORN.

Our first parents received the mission to cultivate the garden which was given them for a home. Their Hebrew descendants looked upon tillage of all descriptions with a reverence worthy of the authority which they professed to obey. The sons of the tribes stood proudly by the plough, the daughters of the patriarchs were gleaners, warriors lent their strength in the threshing barn, Kings guided oxen, and Prophets were summoned from the furrows to put on their mantles, and go forth to tell of things that were to come. What Heaven had enjoined the law enforced. The people were taught to love and hold by the land which was in their own possession. To alienate it was to commit a crime. And it is from this ancient rule, probably, that has descended to us the feeling which universally prevails,—that he alone is aristocratic, has the best of power, who is lord of the land upon which he has built his earthly tabernacle.

The fields of Palestine were fertile beyond what was known elsewhere; her cattle produced more abundantly, and the very appellations of many of her localities have reference to the beauty and the blessings showered down upon them by the Lord.

Next to it, perhaps, in richness and productiveness, was Egypt, the home of fugitives from other homes where temporary famine reigned. Egypt was long the granary of the Roman empire, and twenty million bushels of corn was the life-sustaining tribute she annually poured into the store-houses of Imperial Rome. That territory could hardly be more productive, of which an old Latin author speaks, and touching which he says, that a rod thrust into the soil at night would be found budding before morning. And this ancient story, I may notice, has been the venerable father of a large family of similar jokes among our Transatlantic cousins.

The Egyptians recognised Osiris as their instructor how to subdue and use the earth. The Greeks took the teaching from Ceres. Romulus, too, acknowledged the divine influence; and his first public act, as King, was to raise the twelve sons of his nurse into a priesthood, charged with watching over the fields, and paying sacrifice and prayer to Jove for yearly increase of harvests.

It was a selfish wish: but no more so than that of the Italian peasants, who, when one who was a native of their district had been raised to the tiara, sent a delegation to request an especial favour at his hands. The new Pope looked on his old acquaintances benevolently, and bade them express their wish. "They wanted but a modest boon," they replied: "nothing more than a declaration from the Pontiff that their district should be henceforth distinguished by its having *two* harvests every year!" And the obliging "successor of the Fisherman" smiled, and not only granted their request, but promised more than he was petitioned for. "To do honour to my old friends," said he, "not alone shall they have two harvests every year, but henceforth the year in their district shall be twice as long as it is in any other!" And therewith the simple people departed joyously.

The older Romans honoured agriculture, as did the Jews. Their language bore reference to this, their coin was stamped with symbols in connection therewith, and their public treasury "*pascua*" showed, by its name, that "pasturage" was wealth. So he who was rich in minted coin enjoyed the *pecunia*, or "money," for which "flocks" (*pecus*) were bought or sold. The owner of an "estate" (*locus*) was *locuples*, a term for a man well endowed with worldly goods; and he was in possession of a "salary," who had his *salarium*, his allowance of salt-money, or of salt, wherewith to savour the food by which he lived.

The Greeks refreshed the mouths of their ploughing oxen with wine. The labour was considerable; for, although the plough was light, it lacked the conveniencies of the more modern implement. Like the Anglo-Norman plough, it had no wheels: the wheeled plough is the work of the inventive Gauls.

The French Republicans made a show of paying honour to agriculture by public demonstrations, the chief actors in which were the foremost men in the Land of Equality. They, absurdly enough, took their idea from the example presented them by a Monarch, all of whom they pronounced execrable; and by one, too, who was the most despotic upon earth,—the Emperor of China.

And, in the case of the Emperor, there probably was more ostentation than any better motive for the act. Grimm, in his "Correspondence," says, truly enough, that the ceremony is a fine one, which places the Emperor of China, every year, at the tail of the plough; but, as he adds, it is possible that, like much of the etiquette of European Courts, such a custom may have sunk into a mere observance, exercising no influence on the public mind. "I defy you," he says, "to find a more impressive ceremony than that by which the Doge of Venice yearly declares himself the husband of the Adriatic Sea. How exalting!—how stimulating!—how proudly inspiring for the Venetians, when their nation was, in reality, sovereign of the seas! But now it is little more than a ridiculous sport, and without any other effect than that of attracting a multitude of people to the Fair of the Ascension."

Charles IX., infamous as he was in most respects, was honourable in one; namely, in exempting from arrest for debt all persons engaged in the cultivation of land, "with intent to raise grain and fruit necessary for the sustenance of men and beasts." All the property of such husbandmen was alike exempted from seizure; and it strikes us, that this was a much more reasonably-founded exemption than that with which we endow *roué* Members of Parliament, who have no excuse for exceeding their income. They are free from arrest for six weeks from the prorogation of Parliament; and this is the cause of the farce which is so often played in the autumn and winter, when Parliament is "further prorogued." The Great Council would be all the better for the absence of men who so far forget their duty as to cheat her Majesty's lieges by exceeding their own income. The Senate could better spare the spendthrifts, than the land could spare the presence of him whose mission is to render it productive.

Wheat is a native of Asia,—some say, of Siberia; others, of Tartary; but it is a matter of doubt, whether it can now be found there growing in a wild state. The Romans created a corn-god, and then asked its protection. The powerful deity was called Robigus, and he was solemnly invoked, on every 25th of April, to keep mildew from the grain. The Romans had a reverence for corn, but barley was excepted from this homage; and to threaten to put an offending soldier on rations of barley, was to menace him with disgrace. The Italian antipathy still exists, if we may believe the Italian Professor, who, being offered a basin of gruel, (made from barley,) declared its proper appellation to be "*acqua crudele.*" He accounted of it, as Pliny did of rye, that it was detestable, and could only be swallowed by an extremely hungry man. Oats were only esteemed a degree higher by Virgil. The poet speaks of them almost as disparagingly as Johnson did, when he described them as "food for horses in England, and for men in Scotland." The grain, however, found a good advocate in him who asked, "—— where did you ever see such horses and such men?" The meal is, nevertheless, of a heating quality, and certain cutaneous diseases are traced to a too exclusive use of it. But oatmeal cakes are not bad eating,—where better is not to be procured,—though they are less attractive to the palate than those sweet buns made from sesame grain, and which the Romans not only swallowed with delight, but used the name proverbially. The lover who was treating his mistress to sugared phrases, was said to be regaling her with "sesame cakes." This sort of provision was very largely dealt in by Latin lovers. It was to be had cheaply; and nymphs consumed as fast as swains presented.

If lovers gave the light bread of persuasion to win a maiden's affection, the Government distributed solid loaves, or corn to make them with, to the people, in order to gain the popular esteem, and suppress sedition. In some cases, it was as a "poor's rate" paid by the Emperors, and costing them nothing. In too many cases, it was ill applied; and if Adrian daily fed all the children of the poor, other imperial rulers showered their tens of thousands of bushels daily on an idle populace and a half-dressed soldiery. It was easily procured. Sixty millions of bushels—twenty times that number of pounds' weight—were supplied by Africa; and those "sweet nurses of Rome," the islands of the Mediterranean, also poured into the imperial granaries an abundant tribute of the golden seed. It is a fact, however, that neither Romans nor Gauls were, till a late period, acquainted with **the method of making fermented bread.**

Ambrosia, nine times sweeter than honey, was the food of the gods; the first men existed on more bitter fare,—bread made from acorns. Ceres has the honour of having introduced a better fare. Men worshipped her accordingly; and, abandoning acorns, took also to eating the pig, now allowed to fatten on them at his leisure. Ceres and King Miletus dispute the renown of having invented grinding-stones. The hand-mill was one of the trophies which the Roman eagles bore back with them from Asia. Mola, the goddess charged therewith, looked to the well-being of mills, millers, and bread. In Greece, Mercury had something to do with this. It was he, at least, who sent to the Athenian market-women, selling bread, their customers; and, as he was the God of Eloquence, it is, doubtless, from this ancient source that all market-women are endowed with shrewdness and loquacity.

The Athenian bread-sellers are said to have possessed both. Our ladies of the Gate, in Billing's Ward, are, probably, not behind them; and I am inclined to think that a true old-fashioned Bristol market-woman would surpass both. Let me cite an instance.

Some years ago, an old member of this ancient sisterhood was standing at her stall, in front of one of the Bristol banks. She had a £10 Bank-of-England note in her hand; and as, in her younger days, she had been nurse-maid in the family of one of the partners, she thought she might venture to enter, and ask for gold for her note. She did so; but it was at a time when guineas were worth five-and-twenty shillings a-piece, and gold was scarce, and——in short, she met with a refusal. The quick-witted market-woman, without exhibiting any disappointment, thereupon asked the cashier to let her have ten of the bank's £1 notes in exchange for her "Bank-of-Englander." The cashier was delighted to accommodate her in this fashion. The exchange being completed, the old lady, taking up one of the provincial notes, read aloud the promise engraved upon it, to pay the bearer in cash. "Very good!" said she, with a gleesome chuckle, "now gi' me goold for *your* notes, or I'll run to the door, and call out, 'Bank's broke!'" There was no resisting this, and the market-woman departed triumphantly with her gold. Light-heeled Mercury could not have helped her better than she helped herself, by means of her own sharp wit.

Despite what Virgil says of oats, the Roman soldiery, for many years, had no better food than gruel made from oatmeal, and sharpened for the appetite by a little vinegar. The vinegar was an addition suggested by Numa, who also not only improved the very rude ideas which previously prevailed with regard to the making of bread, but turned baker himself, and sent his loaves to the ovens which he had erected, and to the bakers whom he had raised into a "guild," placed under the protection of the goddess Fornax;—and a very indifferent, nay, disreputable, deity she was! The public ovens were to the people of Rome what a barber's shop is to a village in war time,—the temple of gossip. It had been well had they never been anything worse! The vocation of baker was hereditary in a family; the son was compelled to follow his father's calling. Occasionally, a member of the fraternity was offered a senatorship; but then he was required to make over his property, realized by baking, to his successors; and, consequently, the honour was as deeply declined as the London mayoralty would be by the Governor of the Bank of England.

If Fornax was the goddess to whose patronage the bakers were consigned by the State, she suffered by the religious liberty exercised by the bakers themselves, who chose to pay adoration to Vesta. Vesta was the very antipodes in character and attributes to Fornax; and the selection of the former would seem to show, that the generally reviled bakers could not only praise virtue, but practice it.

Endless were the varieties of bread sold in the markets at Rome. There was Cappadocian bread for the wealthy; pugilistic loaves for the athletæ; batter-bread for the strong, and Greek rolls for the weak, of stomach: and there were the prepared bread poultices, which people who, like Pompey's young soldiers, were afraid of injuring their complexion, were wont to keep applied to their cheeks during the hours of sleep. Anadyorene so slumbering, with Adonis at her side similarly poulticed, can hardly be said to be a subject for a painter; and yet many a blooming Caia slept on the bosom of her Caius, and more *panis madidus* than blushes on the cheeks of either.

Pliny ventures on a strange statement with regard to oats. He says that oats and barley are so nearly allied, that when a man sows the one, he is not sure that he may not reap the other! He also illustrates the prolificness of millet, by asserting that a single grain produced " innumerable ears of corn; and that a bushel (twenty pounds' weight) of millet would make more than sixty pounds of wholesome bread!" The Romans and the Greeks also appear to have been acquainted with Indian corn.

Jean Jacques Rousseau, much as he affected to love nature,—and he was himself one of the most artificial of characters,—knew very little about her, or her productions. Some of our great men are described as being in much the same condition of ignorance. Three poets of the last century were one day walking through a field, promising a glorious harvest of grain. One of them extolled the beauty of the wheat. "Nay," said the second, "it is rye." "Not so," remarked the third, "it is a field of barley." A clown, standing by, heard and marvelled at the triple ignorance. "You are all wrong, gentlemen," said he; "those be oats." The poets were town-bred; or were of that class of people who go through a country with their eyes open, and are unable to distinguish between its productions. I have seen Londoners contemplating, with a very puzzled look, the "canary" crops growing in the vicinity of Herne Bay; and I was once gravely asked if it was "teazle!"

These crops are, as I was told by a grower, "capricious." They will grow abundantly upon certain land having certain aspects; but where the aspect is changed, although the land be chemically the same, the canary will scarcely grow at all. It is shipped in large quantities from Herne Bay for London, where it is used for many purposes. None of its uses are so singular as one to which corn was applied, some thirty years ago, in the western settlements of America, namely, for stretching boots and shoes. The boot or shoe was well filled with corn, and made secure by such tight tying that none could escape. It was then immersed for several hours in water; during which the leather was distended by the gradual swelling of the grain. After being taken from the water, a coating of neat's-foot oil, laid on and left to dry, rendered the boot or shoe fit for wear.

A more interesting anecdote in connexion with corn, and illustrative of character, is afforded us by Dr. Chalmers in his Diary. The Doctor, as is well known,—and he was ever ready to confess his weakness,—occasionally let his warm temper get the better of his excellent judgment. Here is an instance, which shows, moreover, how Christian judgment recovered itself from the influence of human nature: "Nov. 20th, 1812.—Was provoked with Thomas taking it upon him to ask more corn for my horse. It has got feebler under his administration of corn, and I am not without suspicion that he appropriates it; and his eagerness to have it strengthens the suspicion. Erred in betraying anger to my servant and wife; and, though I afterwards got my feelings into a state of placidity and forbearance, upon Christian principles, was moved and agitated when I came to talk of it to himself. Let me take the corn into my own hand, but carry it to him with entire charity. O, my God, support me!" Was it not to Socrates that some one said?—"To judge from your looks, you are the best-tempered man in the world." "Then my looks belie me," replied the philosopher; "I have the worst possible temper, by nature; with the strongest possible control over it, by philosophy." Chalmers was, in one sense, like Socrates; but the control over his stubborn infirmity had something better "than your philosophy" for its support.

Reverting to the feeding of horses, I may notice, that, according to the Earl of Northumberland's "Household Book," the corn was not thrown loose into the manger, but made into loaves. It has been conjectured, that the English **poor** formerly ate the same bread. There can be no question about it; and even at the present time it is no uncommon sight, in some towns of the Continent, to see a driver feeding his horse from a loaf, and occasionally taking a slice therefrom for himself.

There is no greater consumer of corn in England than the pigeon. Vancouver, in laudable zeal for the hungry poor, calls pigeons " voracious and insatiate vermin." He calculates the pigeons of England and Wales at nearly a million and a quarter ; " consuming 159,500,000 pints of corn annually, to the value of £1,476,562. 10s." It is impossible for calculation to be made closer. Darwin says of pigeons, that they have an organ in the stomach for secreting milk. And it is not alone in the way of devouring corn that they are destructive. In the " Philosophical Transactions," it is mentioned that pigeons for many ages built under the roof of the great church of Pisa. Their dung spontaneously took fire, at last, and the church was consumed.

I have said that the Roman soldiers marched to victory under the influence of no more exciting stimulant than gruel and vinegar. A little oatmeal has often sustained the strength of our own legions in the hour of struggle. The Germans, brave as they are, sometimes require a more substantial support. Thus, after a defeat endured by the Great Frederick, hundreds of respectable burgesses of the province of Mark set out as volunteers for the royal army,—the Hellengers in white, the Sauerlanders in blue jackets,—each man with a stout staff in his hand, and a rye loaf and a ham on his back. " Fritz " glared with astonishment when they presented themselves at his head-quarters. " Where do you fellows come from ?" said he. " From Mark, to help our King." " Who doesn't want you," interrupted Fritz. " So much the better; we are here of our own accord." " Where are your officers ?" " We have none." " And how many of you deserted by the way ?" " Deserted !" cried the Markers indignantly : " if any of us had been capable of *that*, we should not be what we are,—volunteers." " True !" said the King, " and I can depend upon you. You shall have fire enough soon to toast your bread and cook your hams by."

When Henri IV. was besieging Paris, held by the Leaguers, the want most severely felt by the famished inhabitants was that of bread. The Guise party, who held the city,—and the most active agent of that party was the Duchess of Montpensier, the sister of Duke Henri of Guise,—endeavoured to keep life in the people by means that nature revolts at. When every other sort of food had disappeared, the Government within the walls distributed very diminutive rolls made of a paste, the chief ingredient in which was human bones ground to powder. The people devoured them under the name of "Madame de Montpensier's cakes;"—no wonder that they soon after exultingly welcomed the entry of a King, who declared that his first desire was to secure to every man in France his "*poule au pot.*" But enough of bread. Let us examine briefly the subject of

BUTTER.

The illustrious Ude, or some one constituting him the authority for the nonce, has sneered at the English as being a nation having twenty religions, and only one sauce,—melted butter. A French commentator has added, that we have nothing polished about us but our steel, and that our only ripe fruit is baked apples. Guy Pantin traces the alleged dislike of the French of his day for the English, to the circumstance that the latter poured melted butter over their roast veal. The French execration is amusingly said to have been further directed against us, on account of the declared barbarism of eating oyster-sauce with rump-steak, and "poultice," as they cruelly characterize "bread-sauce," with pheasant. But, to return to butter:—the spilling of it has more than once been elucidative of character. When, in the days of the old *régime*, an English servant accidentally let a drop or two of melted butter fall upon the silk suit of a French *petit-maître*, the latter indignantly declared that "blood and butter were an Englishman's food." The conclusion was illogical, but the arguer was excited.

Lord John Townshend manifested better temper and wit, when a similar accident befell him, as he was dining at a friend's table, where the coachman was the only servant in waiting. "John," said my Lord, "you should never grease anything but your coach-wheels."

It was an old popular error that a pound of butter might consist of any number of ounces. It is an equally popular error, that a breakfast cannot be, unless bread and butter be of it. Marcus Antoninus breakfasted on dry biscuits; and many a person of less rank, and higher worth, is equally incapable of digesting any thing stronger. Solid breakfasts are only fit for those who have much solid exercise to take after it; otherwise heartburn may be looked for. Avoid new bread and spongy rolls; look on muffins and crumpets as inventions of men of worse than sanguinary principles, and hot buttered toasts as of equally wicked origin. Dry toast is the safest morning food, perhaps, for persons of indifferent powers of digestion; or they may substitute for it the imperial fashion set by Marcus Antoninus. Of liquids I may next speak; and in this our ancient friend, Tea, takes the precedence.

TEA.

THE origin of tea is very satisfactorily accounted for by the Indian mythologist. Darma, a Hindoo Prince, went on a pilgrimage to China, vowing he would never take rest by the way; but he once fell asleep, and he was so angry with himself, on awaking, that he cut off his eye-lids, and flung them on the ground. They sprang up in the form of tea-shrubs; and he who drinks of the infusion thereof, imbibes the juice of the eye-lids of Darma. Tea, however, is said to have been first used in China as a corrective for bad water; and *that* not at a remote date.

In the seventeenth century, half the physicians of Holland published treatises in favour of tea. It was hailed as a panacea, and the most moderate eulogizers affirmed that two hundred cups a day might be drunk without injury to the stomach of the drinker. In the ninth century, Tea was taken in China simply as a medicine; and it then had the repute of being a panacea. The early Dutch physicians who so earnestly recommended its use as a common beverage, met with strenuous opposition. France, Germany, and Scotland, in the persons of Patin, Hahnemann, and Duncan, decried tea as an impertinent novelty, and the vendors of it as immoral and mercenary. Nor was Holland itself unanimous in panegyrizing the refreshing herb. Some, indeed, eulogized the infusion as the fountain of health, if not of youth; but others again, and those of the Dutch faculty, indignantly derided it as filthy " hay-water." Olearius, the German, on the other hand, recognised its dietetic virtues as early as 1633; while a Russian Ambassador, at about the same period, refused a pound or two of it, offered him by the Mogul as a present to the Czar, on the ground that the gift was neither useful nor agreeable.

The Dutch appear to have been the first who discovered the value of the shrub, in a double sense. They not only procured it for the sake of its virtues, but contrived to do so by a very profitable species of barter. They exchanged with the Chinese a pound of sago for three or four pounds of tea; and it is very possible that each party, preferring its own acquisition, looked on the opposite party as duped.

Tea is supposed to have been first imported into England, from Holland, in 1666, by Lords Arundel and Ossory. We cannot be surprised that it was slow in acquiring the popular favour, if its original cost was, as it is said to have been, 60s. per pound. But great uncertainty rests as well upon the period of introduction, as upon the original importers, and the value of the merchandise. One fact connected with it is well ascertained; namely that European Companies had long traded with China, before they discovered the value and uses of tea.

It is said to have been in favour at the Court of Charles II., owing to the example of Catherine, his Queen, who had been used to drink it in Portugal. Medical men thought, at that time, that health could not be more effectually promoted than by increasing the fluidity of the blood; and that the infusion of Indian tea was the best means of attaining that object. In 1678, Bontekoe, a Dutch physician, published a celebrated treatise in favour of tea, and to his authority its general use in so many parts of Europe is to be attributed.

The first tea-dealer was also a tobacconist, and sold the two weeds of novelty together, or separately. His name was Garway, ("Garraway's,") and his *locale*, Exchange-alley. It was looked upon chiefly as a medicinal herb; and Garway, in the seventeenth century, not only "made up prescriptions," in which tea was the sole ingredient, but parcels for presents, and cups of the infusion for those who resorted to his house to drink it over his counter. Its price then varied from 11s. to 50s. per pound. The taking tea with a visitor was soon a domestic circumstance; and, towards the end of the century, Lord Clarendon and Père Couplet supped together, and had a cup of tea after supper, an occurrence which is journalized by his Lordship without any remark to lead us to suppose that it was an extraordinary event.

Dr. Lettsom has written largely, and plagiarized unreservedly, on the subject of tea; adding, as Mr. Disraeli remarks, his own dry medical reflections to the sparkling facts of others; but he was the first, perhaps, who established the unwholesomeness of green tea. He "distilled some green tea, injected three drachms of the very odorous and pellucid water which he obtained, into the cavity of the abdomen and cellular membrane of a frog, by which he paralysed the animal. He applied it to the cavity of the abdomen and ischiatic nerves of another, and the frog died; and this he thought proved green tea to be unwholesome"—to the frogs, and so applied, as it undoubtedly was. Such experiments, however, are unsatisfactory. *Nux vomica*, for instance, deadly poison to man, may be taken, almost with impunity, by many animals.

The first brewers of tea were often sorely perplexed with the preparation of the new mystery. "Mrs. Hutchinson's great grandmother was one of a party who sat down to the first pound of tea that ever came into Penrith. It was sent as a present, and without directions how to use it. They boiled the whole at once in a bottle, and sat down to eat the leaves with butter and salt, and they wondered how any person could like such a diet."

"Steele, in "The Funeral," laughs at the "cups which cheer but not inebriate." "Don't you see," says he, "how they swallow gallons of the juice of the tea, while their own dock-leaves are trodden under foot?"

What Bishop Berkeley did with "Tar Water," when he made his Essay thereupon a ground for a Dissertation on the Trinity, Joseph Williams—"the Christian merchant" of the early and middle part of last century, whose biography is well known to serious readers—did, when he wrote to his friend Green upon the necessity of "setting the Lord always before us." When treating of this subject, the pious layman adverts to a present of that new thing called "tea," which Green had sent him, and which had lost some of its flavour in the transit. There is something amusing in the half sensual, half spiritual way in which worthy Joseph Williams mixes his Jeremiad upon tea with one upon human morals. "The tea," he says, came safe to hand, but it had lost the elegant flavour it had when we drank of it at Sherborne, owing, I suppose, to its conveyance in paper, which, being very porous, easily admits effluvia from other goods packed up with it, and emits effluvia from the tea. Such are the moral tendencies of evil communications among men, which nothing will prevent, (like canisters for tea), but taking to us the whole armour of God. Had the tea been packed up with cloves, mace, and cinnamon, it would have been tinctured with these sweet spices; so 'he that walks with wise men shall be wise.' He that converses with heaven-born souls, whose conversation is in heaven, whose treasure and whose hearts are there, will catch some sparks from their holy fire; but 'evil communications corrupt good manners.' I have put the tea into a canister, and am told it will recover its original flavour, as the pious soul which hath received some ill impressions from vicious or vain conversation will, by retiring from the world, by communing with his own heart, by heavenly meditation, and fervent prayer, recover his spiritual ardour." The simile, however limps a little; for if every man canistered himself, and a good example, from the world, the wide-spreading aroma of that example would never seductively insinuate itself into the souls of men. It is by contact we brighten, and sometimes suffer. We must not canister our virtue as Mr. Williams did his tea: the latter was for selfish enjoyment. A guinea may be kept for ever unstained by the commerce of the world, in the very centre of the chest of avarice; but what good does it there? Let it circulate merrily through the hundred hands of the giant Industry, and there will be more profit than evil effected by the process. But good Joseph Williams would not have agreed with us, and he *would* take his saintly similes from traits of the table. "O that I may walk humbly," he says, "and look on myself, when fullest of divine communications, but as a drinking-glass without a foot, and which, consequently, cannot stand of itself, nor retain what may be put into it." A very tipsy-like simile!

I may be permitted to add that, after all, religion happily proved stronger than tea, but not without still stronger opposition; and we are told by the disgusted *Connoisseur*, that "persons of fashion cannot but lament that the Sunday evening tea-drinkings in Ranelagh were laid aside, from a superstitious regard to religion." A remark which shows how very poor a *connoisseur* this writer was in matters of propriety. Not, indeed, that diet and divinity could not be seated at the same table. On Easter-day, for instance, the first dish that used to be placed before the jubilant guest was a red-herring on horseback, set in corn salad. Some hundred and fifty years ago, too, there was a semi-religious, semi-roystering club held at the "Northern Ale-house in St. Paul's Alley," every member of which was of the name of Adam. It was formed in honour and remembrance of the first man. The honour was more than Adam deserved; for the first created man not only betrayed his trust, but he shabbily sought to lay the responsibility upon the first woman. And as for "remembrance," he has managed to survive even the memory of the club founded by his namesakes, and long since defunct. The members were hard drinkers, but not of saffron posset, which Arabella, in "The Committee," recommends as "a very good drink against the heaviness of the spirits." The Adamites mostly died, as the legend says Adam himself did, of hereditary gout,—an assertion which would seem to indicate that the author of it was of Hibernian origin!

There are various passages of our poets which tend to show that "tea" and "coffee" became, very early, fixed social observances. Pope, writing, in 1715, of a lady who left town after the coronation of George I., says that she went to the country—

"To part her time 'twixt reading and Bohea,
To muse, and spill her solitary tea;
Or o'er cold coffee trifle with the spoon,
Count the slow clock, and dine exact at noon."

At the same period, the fortunate belles who remained in town made of tea a means for other ends than shortening time. Dr. Young, in his "Satires," says of Memmia, that—

"Her two red lips affected zephyrs blow,
To cool the Bohea and inflame the beau;
While one white finger and a thumb conspire
To lift the cup and make the world admire."

Dr. Parr's delicate compliment is well-known; but I may be pardoned, perhaps, for introducing it here. He was not very partial to the *Thea Sinensis*, though lauded so warmly by a French writer, as "*nostris gratissima Musis;*" but once being invited to take tea by a lady, he, with a mixture of wit and gallantry, exclaimed, "*Ne ctea-cum possum vivere, nec sine te!*" The Christchurch men at Oxford were remarkable, at an early period, for their love of tea; and, in reference to it, they were pleasantly recommended to adopt as their motto: "*Te veniente die, te decedente notamus.*" In 1718, Pope draws an illustration from tea, when writing to Mr. Digby: "My Lady Scudamore," he remarks jocosely "from having rusticated in your company too long, really behaves herself scandalously among us. She pretends to open her eyes for the sake of seeing the sun, and to sleep because it is night; drinks tea at nine in the morning, and is thought to have said her prayers before; talks, without any manner of shame, of good books, and has not seen Cibber's play of 'The Nonjurer.'" This is a pleasant picture of the "good woman" of the last century. She drank tea at nine in the morning, not sleeping on till noon, to be aroused at last, like Belinda, by—

"Shock, who thought she slept too long,
Leap'd up and waked his mistress with his tongue."

Tea is little nutritious; it is often injurious from being drunk at too high a temperature, when the same quantity of the fluid at a lower temperature would be beneficial. It is astringent and narcotic; but its effects are various on various individuals, and the cup which refreshes and invigorates one, depresses or unnaturally excites and damages the digestive powers of others. Green tea can in no case be useful, except medicinally, in cases where there has been excessive fatigue of the mind or body; and even then the dose should be small. Tea, as a promoter of digestion, or rather as a comforter of the stomach when the digestive process has been completed, should not be taken earlier than from three to four hours after the principal meal. Taken too early, it disturbs digestion by arrested chymification, and by causing distension. The astringency of tea is diminished by adding milk, and its true taste more than its virtue is spoiled by the addition of sugar.

These remarks are applicable to tea in its pure state, and not to the adulterated messes which come from China, or are made up in England. If sloe leaves here are made to pass for Souchong, so also is many an unbroken chest of "tea" landed, which is largely composed of leaves that are not the least akin to the genuine shrub. Black teas are converted into green, some say by means of a poisonous dye, others by roasting on copper; but I do not think this process is extensively adopted. At one time the chests were rendered heavy by an adulterated mixture of a considerable quantity of tea, and a not inconsiderable quantity of earthy *detritus*, strongly impregnated with iron. But our searchers soon put a stop to this knavery. They just dipped a powerful magnet into the chest, stirred it about, and, when drawn out, the iron particles, if any, were sure be found adhering to the irresistible "detective." I have heard that Lady Morgan's tea-parties, in Dublin, were remarkable for the excellent qualities both of the beverage and the company; and also for her Ladyship's stereotyped joke, of "Sugar yourselves, gentlemen, and I'll milk you all."

Tea-parties, I may observe in conclusion, are not confined in China to festive occasions. Tea is solemnly drunk on serious celebrations, with squibs to follow. Thus, for instance, at the funeral of a Buddhist Priest, there is thought taken for the living as well as for the dead, for the appetites of mortals as well as for the gratification of the gods. The latter are presented with various sorts of food, save animal. It is placed on the altar, and is eaten at night by the deities, of course. While the ceremonies preliminary to the interment are proceeding, a servant enters the temple, and hands tea round to the reverend gentlemen who are officiating! The interment usually takes place in the morning, and it is numerously attended; but if, as the long procession is advancing, the hour of breakfast should happen to arrive, the corpse is suddenly dropped in the highway, the entire assembly rush to their respective homes, and not till they have consumed their tea and toast, or whatever materials go to the constituting of a Chinese *déjeûner*, do they return to carry the corpse to its final resting-place, and fire no end of squibs over it, in testimony of their affliction. Which done, more refreshment follows; and perhaps some of the mourners retire to Chinese taverns, where inviting placards promise them "A cup of tea and a bird's nest for 4*d*.!"

COFFEE.

The English and French dispute the honour of being the first introducers of coffee into Western Europe. The Dutch assert that they *assisted* in this introduction; and, although coffee was not drunk at Rome, until long after it had been known to, and tasted by, Italian travellers at Constantinople, the Church looked with pleasure on a beverage, one effect of which was to keep both Priests and people awake.

An Arab author of the fifteenth century—Sherbaddin—asserts, that the first man who drank coffee was a certain Muphti of Aden, who lived in the ninth century of the Hegira, about A.D. 1500. The popular tradition is, that the Superior of a Dervish community, observing the effects of coffee-berries when eaten by some goats, rendering them much more lively and skittish than before, prescribed it for the brotherhood, in order to cure them of drowsiness and indolence.

It was originally known by the name of *cahui* or *kauhi*,—an orthography which comes near to that of the ingenious Town-Councillor of Leeds, who, writing out a public bill of fare for a public breakfast, contrived to spell "coffee" without employing a single letter that occurs in that word,—to wit, *kauphy!*

Sandys, a traveller of the seventeenth century, gives it no very attractive character. Good for digestion and mirth, he allows it to be; but he says that in taste as in colour it is nearly as black as soot.

The coffee-houses of England take precedence of those of France, though the latter have more enduringly flourished. In 1652, a Greek, in the service of an English Turkey merchant, opened a house in London. "I have discovered his hand-bill," says Mr. Disraeli, "in which he sets forth the virtue of the coffee drink, first publiquely made and sold in England, by Pasqua Rosee, of St. Michael's Alley, Cornhill, at the sign of his own head." Mr.

Peter Cunningham cites a MS. of Oldys in his possession, in which some fuller details of much interest are given. Oldys says, "The first use of coffee in England was known in 1657, when Mr. Daniel Edwards, a Turkey merchant, brought from Smyrna to London one Pasqua Rosee, a Ragusan youth, who prepared this drink for him every morning. But the novelty thereof drawing too much company to him, he allowed his said servant, with another of his son-in-law's, to sell it publicly; and they set up the first coffee-house in London, in St. Michael's Alley, Cornhill. But they separating, Pasqua kept in the house; and he who had been his partner obtained leave to pitch a tent, and sell the liquor, in St. Michael's church-yard." Aubrey, in his Anecdotes, states that the first vendor of coffee in London was one Bowman, coachman to a Turkey merchant, named Hodges, who was the father-in-law of Edwards, and the partner of Pasqua, who got into difficulties, partly by his not being a freeman, and who left the country. Bowman was not only patronized, but a magnificent contribution of one thousand sixpences was presented to him, wherewith he made great improvements in his coffee-house. Bowman took an apprentice, (Paynter,) who soon learned the mystery, and in four years set up for himself. The coffee-houses soon became numerous: the principal were Farres', the Rainbow, at the Inner-Temple Gate, and John's, in Fuller's Rents. "Sir Henry Blount," says Aubrey, "was a great upholder of coffee, and a constant frequenter of coffee-houses."

The frequenters of these places, however, were considered as belonging to the idle and dissipated classes; and the reputation was not altogether undeserved. Respectable people denounced the coffee-drinking evils, illustriously obscure and loyal people dreaded the politics that were discussed at the drinking, and tipsy satirists hurled strong contempt and weak verse at the new-fangled fashion of abandoning Canary wine for the Arabian infusion. The fashion, however, extended rapidly; the more so, that cups were soon to be had at so low a price, that the shops where they were sold went by the name of "Penny Universities." The ladies, who were excluded from public participation in the bitter enjoyment, made some characteristic complaints against the male drinkers, and intimated that the indulgence of coffee-drinking would in time deteriorate, if not destroy, the human race; but the imbibers heeded not the complaint, their answer to which was that of Béranger's gay martial philosopher:—

> "*Nous laisserions finir le monde,*
> *Si nos femmes le voulaient bien.*"

While the ladies, through their poetical representatives, were complaining, male philanthropists quickly discerned the social uses of the cup; and Sir Henry Blount acknowledges, with grateful pleasure, that the custom, on the part of labouring men and apprentices, of drinking a cup of coffee in the morning, instead of their ordinary matinal draught of beer or wine, was chiefly owing to Sir James Muddiford, "who introduced the practice hereof first in London."

The Government of the Stuarts, hating free discussion and not particularly caring for wit, watched the coffee-houses with much jealousy, and placed as much restriction upon them as they possibly could strain the law to. The vexatious proceeding did not secure the desired result; and the coffee-house wits laughed at the Government. The wits, however, were not always successful either in their praise of, or satire against, coffee. Pepys, on the 15th of October, 1667, went to the Duke's House, to see the comedy of "Taruga's Wiles; or, the Coffee-House," of which he says, "The most ridiculous, insipid play that ever I saw in my life; and glad we were that Betterton had no part in it." But Pepys was probably not in the true vein to decide critically that night; for his pretty maid Willett was sitting at his side; and his wife, who was on the other, spoiled the effect of the play by her remarks on the girl's "confidence." Perhaps one of the most curious apologies for coffee-houses was that of Aubrey, who declared that he should never have acquired so extensive an acquaintance but for the "modern advantages of coffee-houses in this great city, before which men knew not how to be acquainted but with their own relations *and societies*." And Aubrey, who has been called the small Boswell of his day, " was a man who had more acquaintances than friends."

Yemen is the accepted birth-place, if we may so speak, of the coffee tree. Pietro de la Vallé introduced it into Italy, La Royne into Marseilles, and Thevenot brought it with him to Paris. In 1643, a Levantine opened a coffee-house in Paris, in the Place du Petit Chatelet; but it was Soleiman Aga, Turkish Ambassador in Paris, in 1689, who was the medium through which coffee found its way into the realm of fashion. Had it been really what some have supposed it to have been,—the black broth of the Lacedæmonians,—he could have made it modish by his method of service. This was marked by all the minute details of oriental fashion,—small cups and foot-boys, gold-fringed napkins and pages, coffee wreathing with smoke, and Ganymedes wreathed with garlands, the first all aroma, and the hand-bearers all otto of roses; the whole thing was too dazzling and dramatic to escape adoption. But the intolerable vulgar would imitate their betters, and coffee became as common at taverns as wine, beer, and smoking. It would have inevitably been abandoned to coarse appetites only, but for François Procope, a Sicilian, who, in the Rue de l'Ancienne Comédie, exactly opposite to the old play-house in the Faubourg St. Germain, opened an establishment expressly for the sale of coffee, but with such innocent additional articles as ices, lemonade, and the like harmless appliances, to make pleasant the seasons in their change. The *Café Procope* became the immediate resort of all the wits, philosophers, and refined *roués* of Paris. There Rousseau wrote or repeated the lines which brought him into such frequent trouble. There Piron muttered the verses with which the incitement of devils inspired him. There Voltaire tried to rule supreme, but found himself in frequent bitter contest with Palissot and Freron. The *Café Procope* was the morning journal, the foreign news-mart, the exchange,—literary, witty, and emphatically charming. There Lamothe renewed the contest between the ancient and modern, the classical and the romantic, drama. There the brilliant Chevalier de St. Georges gave lessons in fencing to the men of letters; and thence Dorat addressed his amorous missives to Mademoiselle Saunier. There Marmontel praised Clairon, and the Marquis de Bièvre tried his calembourgs; and there Duclos and Mercier made their sketches of society, at once serious and sarcastic. The universal favour in which coffee is still held in Paris, and the crowds which still wait on "Andromaque," sufficiently belie the famous prophecy of Madame de Sévigné, that "coffee and Racine would have their day." The dark infusion reigns without a rival, the *demi-tasse* follows dinner oftener than "grace," Rachel helps to keep Racine alive, and *café*, in its turn, has the reputation of being *one* of the favourite stimulants of the great *tragédienne*.

With regard to the making of coffee, there is no doubt that the Turkish method of pounding the coffee in a mortar is infinitely superior to grinding it in a mill, as with us. But after either method the process recommended by M. Scyer may be advantageously adopted; namely, "Put two ounces of ground coffee into a stew-pan, which set upon the fire, stirring the coffee round with a spoon until quite hot, then pour over a pint of boiling water; cover over closely for five minutes, pass it through a cloth, warm again, and serve."

The chemist Laplace explained to Napoleon the results of various methods of manipulation. "How is it, Sir," said the Emperor, "that a glass of water in which I melt a lump of sugar, always appears to me to be superior in taste to one in which I put the same quantity of powdered sugar?" "Sire," said the sage, "there exist three substances, whose elements are precisely the same; namely, sugar, gum, and starch. They only differ under certain conditions, the secret of which Nature has reserved to herself; and I believe that it is possible, that, by the collision caused by the pestle, some of the portions of the sugar pass into the condition of gum or starch, and thence arises the result which has been observed."

Medical men are widely at issue as to the merits of coffee. All however, are agreed that it stimulates the brain, and banishes somnolency. Voltaire and Buffon were great coffee-drinkers; but I do not know that we are authorized to attribute the lucidity of the one or the harmony of the other to the habit in question. Ability would be cheaply purchased if that were the case; and the "royal road" would have been discovered where it had never been looked for.

The sleeplessness produced by coffee is not one of an unpleasant character. It is simply a painless vigilance; but, if often repeated, it may be exceedingly prejudicial. Brillat de Savarin illustrates the power of coffee by remarking, that a man may live many years who takes two bottles of wine daily; but the same quantity of strong coffee would soon make him imbecile, or drive him into consumption.

Taken immediately after dinner, coffee aids the dyspeptic, especially to digest fat and oily aliment, which, without such stimulant, would undoubtedly create much disturbance. The Turks drink it to modify the effects of opium. *Café au lait*, that is, three parts of milk to one of coffee, is the proper thing for breakfast; but the addition of milk to that taken after dinner is a cruelty to the stomach. A Dutchman, named Nieudorff, is said to have been the first who ventured on the experiment of mixing milk with coffee. When he had the courage to do this, the two liquids together were considered something of such an abomination as we should now consider brown sugar with oysters.

I must not omit to mention, that the favourite beverage of Voltaire, at the *Café Procope*, was "*choca*,"—a mixture of coffee (with milk) and chocolate. The Emperor Napoleon was as fond of the same mixture as he was of Chambertin; and, in truth, I do not know a draught which so perfectly soothes and revives as that of hot, well-frothed "*choca*."

Substances mixed with coffee, or substitutes for the berry altogether, have been tried with various degrees of success. Roasted acorns have been made to pass for it when ground. There is more chicory than coffee consumed at the present time in France; and the infusion of the lupin does duty for it at the poor hearths in Flanders; as that of roasted rye (the nearest resemblance to coffee) does in America. Experimentalists say, that an excellent substitute for coffee may be made from asparagus; and Frankfort, alarmed lest the complications of the "Eastern Question" should deprive it of the facilities for procuring the berry as heretofore, is gravely consulting as to whether asparagus coffee may be a beverage likely to be acceptable as a substitute for the much prized "*demi-tasse.*"

CHOCOLATE.

FERDINAND CORTEZ went to Mexico in search of gold; but the first discovery he made was of chocolate. The discovery was not welcomed ecclesiastically, as coffee was. This new substance was considered a sort of wicked luxury, at least for Monks, who were among the earliest to adopt it, but who were solemnly warned against its supposed peculiar effects. The moralists quite as eagerly condemned it; and in England Roger North angrily asserted, that "the use of coffee-houses seems much improved by a new invention, called 'chocolate-houses,' for the benefit of rooks and cullies of quality, where gambling is added to all the rest, and the summons of W——— seldom fails; as if the devil had erected a new university, and these were the colleges of its Professors, as well as his schools of discipline." The Stuart jealousy of these localities, where free discussion was amply enjoyed, seems to have influenced the Attorney-General of James II.; for, although they may not have been frequented, he says, by "the factious gentry he so much dreaded," he adds, "This way of passing time might have been stopped at first, before people had possessed themselves of some convenience from them of meeting for short dispatches, and passing evenings with small expenses." Of what chiefly recommended these places, the stern official thus made a grievance.

CHOCOLATE.

Chocolate (or, as the Mexicans call it, *chocolatl*) is the popular name for the seeds of the cocoa, or, more properly, the *cacao*, plant, in a prepared state, generally with sugar and cinnamon. The Mexicans improve the flavour of the inferior sorts of cacao seeds by burying them in the earth for a month, and allowing them to ferment. The nutritious quality of either cacao or chocolate is entirely owing to the oil or butter of cacao which it contains. Cacao-nibs, the best form of taking this production, are the seeds roughly crushed. When the seed is crushed between rollers, the result is flake cacao. Common cacao is the seed reduced to a paste, and pressed into cakes. The cheap kinds of chocolate are said to be largely adulterated with lard, sago, and red-lead,—a pernicious mixture for healthy stomachs; but what must it be for weak stomachs craving for food at once nutritious and easy of digestion? The "patent" chocolates of the shops are nothing more than various modes of preparing the cacao seeds.

The ladies of Mexico are so excessively fond of chocolate, that they not only take it several times during the day, but they occasionally have it brought to them in church, and during the service. A cup of good chocolate may, indeed, afford the drinker strength and patience to undergo a bad sermon. The Bishops opposed it for a time, but they at length closed their eyes to the practice. I am afraid there is no chance of the fashion being introduced into England. The advantages would be acknowledged; but then there would be a savour of Popery detected about it, that would inevitably cause its rejection. The Church herself found a boon in this exquisite supporter of strength. The Monks took it of a morning before celebrating Mass, even in Lent. The orthodox and strong-stomached raised a dreadful cry at the scandal; but Escobar metaphysically proved, that chocolate made with water did not break a fast; thus establishing the ancient maxim, "*Liquidum non frangit jejunium.*"

Spain welcomed the gift of chocolate made her by Mexico with as much enthusiasm as she did that of gold by Peru; the metal she soon squandered, but chocolate is still to be found in abundance in the Peninsula; it is an especial favourite with ladies and Monks, and it always appears on occasions when courtesy requires that refreshments be offered. The Spanish Monks sent presents of it to their brethren in French monasteries; and Anne of Austria, daughter of Philip II. of Spain, when she brought across the Pyrenees her hand, but not her heart, to the unenergetic Louis XIII., brought a supply of chocolate therewith; and henceforth it became an established fact. In the days of the Regency it was far more commonly consumed than coffee; for it was then taken as an agreeable aliment, while coffee was still looked upon as a somewhat strange beverage, but certainly akin to luxury. In the opinion of Linnæus it must have surpassed all other nutritious preparations, or that naturalist would hardly have conferred upon it, as he did, the proud name of *Theobroma*, "food for the Gods!"

Invalids will do well to remember, that chocolate made with vanilla is indigestible, and injurious to the nerves. Indeed, there are few stomachs at all that can bear chocolate as a daily meal. It is a highly concentrated aliment; and all such cease to act nutritiously if taken into constant use.

We will now look into some of those famous resorts of by-gone days, where coffee and chocolate were prepared, and wit was bright and spontaneous.

THE OLD COFFEE-HOUSES.

The "Grecian" appears to have been the oldest of the better-known coffee-houses, and to have lasted the longest. It was opened by Constantine, a Grecian, "living in Threadneedle-street, over against St. Christopher's Church," in the early part of the last half of the seventeenth century. Its career came to a close towards the middle of the nineteenth century; namely, in 1843, when the Grecian Coffeehouse, then in Devereux-court, Strand, where it had existed for very many years, was converted into the "Grecian Chambers," or lodgings for bachelors.

Constantine not only sold "the right Turkey coffee berry, or chocolate," but gave instructions how to "prepare the said liquor gratis." The "Grecian" was the resort rather of the learned than the dissipated. The antiquarians sat at its tables; and, despising the news of the day, discussed the events of the Trojan war, and similar lively, but remote, matters. The laborious trifling was ridiculed by the satirists; and it is clear that there were some pedants as well as philosophers there. It was a time when both sages and sciolists wore swords; and it is on record that two friendly scholars, sipping their coffee at the "Grecian," became enemies in argument, the subject of which was the accent of a Greek word. Whatever the accent ought to have been, the quarrel was acute, and its conclusion grave. The scholars rushed into Devereux-court, drew their swords, and, as one was run through the body and killed on the spot, it is to be supposed that he was necessarily wrong. But the duel was the strangest method of settling a question in grammar that I ever heard of. Still it was rather the scholars than the rakes who patronized the "Grecian;" and there were to be found the Committee of the Royal Society, and Oxford Professors, enjoying their leisure and hot cups, after philosophical discussion and scientific lecturing; and even the Privy Council Board sometimes assembled there to take coffee after Council.

The "coffee-houses," which were resorted to for mere conversation as well as coffee, began on a first floor; they were the seed, as it were, whence has arisen the political and exclusive "club" of the present day. The advantages of association were first experienced in coffee-houses; but at the same time was felt the annoyance caused by intrusive and unwelcome strangers. The club, with its ballot-box to settle elections of members, was the natural result.

William Urwin's Coffee-house, known as "Will's," from its owner's name, and recognized as the "Wits'," from its company, was on the first floor of the house at the west corner of Bow-street and Russell-street, Covent Garden. In the last half of the seventeenth century, it was at the height of its good fortune and reputation. The shop beneath it was kept by a woollen-draper.

Tom Brown says that a wit was set up at a small cost; he was made by "peeping once a day in at Will's," and by relating "two or three second-hand sayings." It was at Will's that Dryden "pedagogued" without restraint, accepted flattery without a blush, and praised with happy complacency the perfection of his own works. He was the great attraction of the place, and his presence there of an evening filled the room with admiring listeners, or indiscreet adulators. Dryden had the good sense to retire early, when the tables were full, and he knew he had made a favourable impression, which the company might improve in his absence. Addison, more given to jolly fellowship, sat late with those who tarried to drink. Pepys, recording his first visit, in February, 1663-4, says that he stepped in on his way to fetch his wife, "where were Dryden the poet, (I knew at Cambridge,) and all the wits of the town, and Harris the player, and Mr. Hoole of our College. And had I had time then, as I could at other times, it will be good coming thither; for there I perceive is very witty and pleasant discourse. But I could not tarry; and, as it was late, they were all ready to go away."

The reign of Dryden at Will's was not, however, without its pains. Occasionally, a daring stranger, like young Lockier, raw from the country, would object to the *dicta* of the despot. Thus when Dryden praised his "Mac Flecknoe," as the first satire "written in heroics," the future Dean timidly suggested that the "Lutrin" and the "*Secchia Rapita*" were so written; and Dryden acknowledged that his corrector was right. The London beaux would have been afraid, or incapable, of setting Dryden right; they were sufficiently happy if they were but permitted to dip their fingers into the poet's snuff-box, and, at a separate table, listen to the criticisms uttered by the graver authorities who were seated round another, at the upper end of the room. Of the disputes that there arose, "glorious John" was arbiter; for his particular use a chair was especially reserved; therein enthroned, he sat by the hearth or the balcony, according to the season, and delivered judgments which were not always final.

No man was better qualified to do so, for the "specialty" of Will's Coffee-house was poetry. Songs, epigrams, and satires, circulated from table to table; and the wits judged plays, even Dryden's, until the play-wrights began to satirize the wits. With Dryden, "Will's" lost some of its dignity. Late hours, card-playing, and politics; poets more didactic in their verse, and essayists more instructive in their prose, than in their daily practice; "dissipateurs" like Addison, and peers who shared in Addison's lower tastes, without either his talent or occasional refinement,—spoiled the character of "Will's," where, by the way, Pope had been introduced by Sir Charles Wogan, though, years before, in his youth, he had been proud to follow old Wycherley about from coffee-house to coffee-house; and then "Button's" attracted the better portion of the company, and left Will's to the vulgar and the witless.

"Button's" Coffee-house was so named from its original proprietor, who had been a servant of the Countess of Warwick, the wife of Addison. It was situated in Great Russell-street, on the south side, about two doors from Covent Garden. What Dryden had been at "Will's," Addison was at "Button's." There,—after writing during the morning at his house in St. James's Place, where his breakfast-table was attended by such men as Steele, Budgell, Philips, Carey, Davenant, and Colonel Brett, with some of whom he generally dined at a tavern,—he was to be found of an evening, until the supper hour called him and his companions to some other tavern, where, if not at Button's, they made a night of it. Pope was of the company for almost a year, but left it because the late hours injured his health; and furthermore, perhaps, for the reason, that his irritable temper had rendered him unpopular, and that he had so provoked Ambrose Philips, that the latter suspended a birchen rod over Pope's usual seat, in intimation of what the ordinary occupant would get if he ventured into it. The Buttonians were famous for the fierceness of their criticism, but it appears to have been altogether a better organized establishment than Will's; for while the parish registers show that the landlord of the latter was fined for misdemeanour, the vestry-books of St. Paul (Covent Garden), prove that Button paid "for two places in the pew No. 18, on the south side of the north aisle, £2. 2s.;" and charity leads us to conclude that Daniel and his wife occupied the places so paid for, and were orthodox, as well as loyal. The "Lion's Head" of the "Guardian," which was put up at Button's, over the box destined to receive contributions for the editor, is now at Woburn, in the possession of the Duke of Bedford.

Of coffee-houses that went by the name of "Tom's" there were three. At the one in Birchin-lane, Garrick occasionally appeared among the young merchants; and Chatterton, before despair slew even ambition, more than once dined. At the second house so called, in Devereux-court, many of the scholars, critics, and scientific men of the last century used to congregate. There Akenside essayed to rule over the tables as Dryden had done at "Will's," and Addison at "Button's;" but his imperious rule was often overthrown by "flat rebellion." *The* "Tom's" was opposite "Button's," and stood on the north side of Great Russell-street, No. 17. It received its name from the Christian appellation of its master, Thomas West, who committed suicide in 1722. If guests gained celebrity in the latter days at "Will's" for writing a "posie for a ring," so at "Tom's" Mr. Ince was held in due respect, for the reason that he had composed a solitary paper for the "Spectator." It was a place where the tables were generally crowded from the time of Queen Anne to that of George III. Seven hundred of the nobility, foreign Ministers, gentry, and geniuses of the age, subscribed a guinea each, in 1714, for the erection of a card-room; and this fact, with the additional one that, only four years later, an enlarged room for cards and conversation was constructed, may serve to show by what sort of people, and for what particular purposes "Tom's" was patronized.

At the time that White's Chocolate-house was opened at the bottom of St. James's-street,—the close of the last century,—it was probably thought vulgar; for there was a garden attached, and it had a suburban air. At the tables in the house or garden more than one highwayman took his chocolate, or threw his main, before he quietly mounted his horse and rode slowly down Piccadilly towards Bagshot. Before the establishment was burned down, in 1733, it was famous rather for intensity of gaming than excellence of chocolate. It arose from its ashes, and settled at the top of the street, into a fixedness of fashion that has never swerved. Gallantry, pleasure, and entertainment were the characteristics of the place. The celebrated Lord Chesterfield there "gamed and pronounced witticisms among the boys of quality.' Steele dated all his love-news in the "Tattler" from White's. It was stigmatized as "the common rendezvous of infamous sharpers and noble cullies;" and bets were laid to the effect that Sir William Burdett, one of its members, would be the first Baronet who would be hanged. The gambling went on till dawn of day; and Pelham, when Prime Minister, was not ashamed to divide his time between his official table and the picquet-table at White's. Selwyn, like Chesterfield, enlivened the room with his wit. As a sample of the spirit of betting which prevailed, Walpole quotes "a good story made at White's." A man dropped down dead at the door, and was carried in; the club immediately made bets whether he was dead or not, and, when they were going to bleed him, the wagerers for his death interposed, and said it would affect the fairness of the bet!

Some of the old rules of the houses are rich in "table traits."

Thus, in 1736, every member was required to pay an extra guinea a year "towards having a good cook." The supper was on table at ten o'clock; the bill at twelve. In 1758, it was agreed that he who transgressed the rules for balloting should pay the supper reckoning. In 1797 we find, "Dinner at 10s. 6d. per head, (malt liquor, biscuits, oranges, apples, and olives included,) to be on table at six o'clock; the bill to be brought at nine." "That no hot suppers be provided, unless particularly ordered; and then to be paid for at the rate of 8s. per head. That in one of the rooms there be laid every night (from the Queen's to the King's birthday) a table, with cold meat, oysters, &c. Each person partaking thereof to pay 4s., malt liquor only included."

Colley Cibber was a member, but, as it would seem, an honorary one only, who dined with the Manager of the Club, and was tolerated afterwards by the company for the sake of his wit. Mr. Cunningham states, that at the supper given by the Club in 1814, at Burlington House, to the Allied Sovereigns, there were covers laid for 2,400 people, and that the cost was "£9,849. 2s. 6d." "Three weeks after this, (July 6, 1814,) the Club gave a dinner to the Duke of Wellington, which cost £2,840. 10s. 9d." The dinner given in the month of February of the present year, to Prince George of Cambridge, was not one to welcome a victorious warrior, but to cheer an untried, about to go forth to show himself worthy of his spurs. White's ceased to be an open Chocolate-house in 1736, from which period it has been as private an establishment as a Club can be said to be.

The politicians had their coffee-houses as well as the wits. The "Cocoa Tree," in St. James's-street, was the Tory house in the reign of Queen Anne. The "St. James's" was the Whig house. It was a well-frequented house in the latter days of George II., when Gibbon recorded his surprise at seeing a score or two of the noblest and wealthiest in the land, seated in a noisy coffee-room, at little tables covered by small napkins, supping off cold meat or sandwiches, and finishing with strong punch and confused politics.

The St. James's Coffee-house ranked Addison, Swift, Steele, and, subsequently, Goldsmith and Garrick, among its *habitués*. It had a more solid practical reputation than any of the other coffee-houses; for within its walls Goldsmith's poem of "Retaliation" originated. But politics was its "staple;" and poor politicians seem to have been among its members, seeing that many of them were in arrears with their subscriptions; but these were probably the outer-room men; for the magnates, who were accustomed to sit and watch the line of Bourbon, within the steam of the great coffee-pot, were doubtless punctual in their payments ere they could have earned the privilege. And yet their poetical acumen was often more correct than their political discernment; for while the company at Button's ascribed the "Town Eclogues" to Gay, the coffee-drinkers at St. James's were unanimous in giving them to a lady of quality.

Of the coffee-houses of a second order, the "Bedford," in Covent Garden, was probably the first; but, for good fellowship, it equalled any of the more exclusive houses; for Garrick, and Quin, and Murphy, and Foote, were of the company. Wit was the serious occupation of all its members; and it never gave any of them serious trouble to produce in abundance. Quin, above all, was brilliant in the double achievements of Epicureanism and sparkling repartee. Garrick, in allusion to the sentiments often expressed here by his brother actor, wrote the epigrammatic lines, supposed to be uttered by Quin, in reference to a discussion on embalming the dead, and which will be found in a subsequent chapter, under the head of "Table Traits of the last Century."

Æsopus, the actor, who was to Cicero what Quin was to George the Third,—he "taught the boy to speak,"—Æsopus was as great an epicure, in his way, as Quin himself. It is related of him, that one day he dined off a costly dish of birds, the whole of which, when living, had been taught either to sing or speak. Æsopus was as fond of such a dish as his fellow-comedian, Quin, was of mullet; for which, and for some other of his favourite *morceaux*, he used to say that a man ought to have a swallow as long as from London to Botany Bay, and palate all the way! When the fish in question was in season, his first inquiry of the servant who used to awaken him was, "Is there any mullet in the market this morning, John?" and if John replied in the negative, his master's reported rejoinder was, "Then call me at nine to-morrow, John."

The Bedford coffee-house had its disadvantages, as when bullies, like Tiger Roach, endeavored to hold sovereignty over the members. But usurpers like the Tiger were deposed as easily by the cane as by the sword; but such occurrences marred the peace of the coffee-house, nevertheless. It was, indeed, a strange company that sometimes was to be found within these houses. At Batem's, the City House, patronized by Blackmore, the brother of Lord Southwell was to be found enacting the parasite, and existing by the aid of men who thought his wit worth paying for. Child's Coffee-house, St. Paul's Church-yard, was patronized by the Clergy, who assembled there, especially the younger Clergy, in gowns, cassocks, and scarfs, smoked till they were invisible, and obtained the honorary appellation of "Doctor" from the waiters. Clerical visitants were also to be found at the "Smyrna," in Pall Mall. Swift was often there with Prior; and the politics of the day were so loudly discussed, that the chairman and porters in waiting outside used to derive that sort of edification therefrom which is now to be had in all the cheap weekly periodicals. "Garraway's" takes us once more into the City. Garway, as the original proprietor was called, was one of the earliest sellers of tea in London; and his house was frequented by nobles who had business in the City, who attended the lotteries at his house, or who wished to partake of his tea and coffee. Foreign Bankers and Ministers patronized "Robin's;" the buyers and sellers of Stocks collected at "Jonathan's;" and the shipping interest went, as now, to "Lloyd's." All these places were in full activity of business and coffee-drinking in the reign of Queen Anne. Finally the lawyers crowded "Squire's," in Fulwood's Rents; and there, it will be remembered, Sir Roger de Coverley smoked a pipe, over a dish of coffee, with the Spectator. But enough of these places, whose names are more familiar to us than their whereabout, but whose connexion with what may be called the table-life of past times gives me warrant for the notice of them, with which, perhaps, I have only troubled the reader. I will only add, that the ceremony of serving chocolate was never such a solemnity in England as in France. In the latter country, as late as the days of Louis XVI., a "man of condition" required no less than four footmen, each with two watches in his fob, according to the fashion, to help him to take a single cup of chocolate. One bore the tray, and one the chocolate-pot, a third presented the cup, and a fourth stood in waiting with a napkin!—and all this coil to carry a morning draught to a poor wretch, whose red heels to his shoes were symbols of the rank which gave him the privilege of being helpless.

The old coffee-houses were not simply resorts for the critics, the politicians, and the fine gentlemen. Gay, writing to Congreve, in 1715, says, "Amidst clouds of tobacco, at a coffee-house, I write this letter. There is a grand revolution at Will's. Moira has quitted for a coffee-house in the City; and Titcomb is restored, to the great joy of Cromwell, who was at a great loss for a person to converse with upon the Fathers and church history. The knowledge I gain from him is entirely in painting and poetry; and Mr. Pope owes all his skill in astronomy to him and Mr. Whiston." Pope learnt his astronomy by the assistance of what Moore calls, "the sun of the table;" for, adding a postscript to Gay's letter to Congreve, he says, "I sit up till two o'clock, over Burgundy and Champagne." Ten years before, the coffee-house and London life had less charms for him. Witness the paragraph in the letter to Wycherley, in 1705, to this effect: I have now changed the scene from town to country,—from Will's coffee-house to Windsor Forest. I found no other difference than this betwixt the common town wits and the downright country fools,— that the first are partly in the wrong, with a little more flourish and gaiety; and the last, neither in the right nor the wrong, but confirmed in a stupid settled medium, betwixt both." But, ten years later than the period of Pope's postscript to Congreve, in which he boasted of sitting over wine during the "wee short hours ayont the twal'," as Burns calls them, we find the toaster stricken. Swift, writing to him, in 1726, remarks, "I always apprehend most for you after a great dinner; for the least transgression of yours, if it be only two bits and one sup more than your stint, is a great debauch, for which you certainly pay more than those sots who are carried drunk to bed."

In England, the chocolate and coffee-houses were not confined to the metropolis and its rather rakish inhabitants. The Universities had their coffee-houses, as London had; and the company there, albeit *alumni* of the various colleges, do not appear to have been remarkable for refinement. Dr. Ewins, at Cambridge, in the last century, acquired the ill-will both of Town and Gown for exercising a sort of censorship over their conduct. According to Cole, the Antiquary, they needed it; for he says, with especial allusion to the Undergraduates, that "they never were more licentious, riotous, and debauched. They often broke the Doctor's windows," he adds, "as they said he had been caught listening on their staircases and (at their) doors." The Doctor, like his adversaries, was in the habit of visiting the Union Coffee-house, opposite St. Radigund's (or Jesus) lane,—a fashionable rendezvous. He was there one night about Christmas, 1771, or January, 1772, "when some Fellow-Commoners, who owed him a grudge, sitting in a box near him, in order to affront him, pretended to call their dog 'Squintum,' and frequently repeated the name very loudly in the coffee-house; and, in their jovialty, swore many oaths, and caressed their dog. Dr. Ewin, as did his father, squinted very much, as did Whitefield, the Methodist teacher, who was vulgarly called Dr. Squintum, from the blemish in his eyes. Dr. Ewin was sufficiently mortified to be so affronted in public. However, he carefully marked down the number of oaths sworn by these gentlemen, whom he made to pay severely the penalty of five shillings for each oath, which amounted to a good round sum." The next week, ballad-singers sang, in the streets of Cambridge, a ballad, which they gave away to all who would accept a copy, and from which the following verses are extracted. They will show—if nothing else—that the University coffee-house poet was less elegant than Horace, and that the "well of English" into which he had dipped was not altogether "undefiled :"—

> "Of all the blockheads in the Town,
> That strut and bully up and down,
> And bring complaints against the Gown,
>   There's none like Dr. Squintum.
>
> "With gimlet eyes and dapper wig,
> This Justice thinks he looks so big ;
> A most infernal stupid gig
>   Is this same Dr. Squintum.
>
> "What pedlar can forbear to grin,
> Before his Worship that has been,
> To think what folly lurks within
>   This Just Ass Dr. Squintum ?"

Old René d'Anjou used to say, that, as soon as a man had breakfasted, it was his bounden duty to devote himself to the great business of the day,—think of dinner. We will in some wise follow the instructions given,—first, however, saying a word or two upon French coffee-houses, and then upon those who naturally take precedence of "dinners,"—the cooks by whom dinners are prepared.

THE FRENCH CAFÉS.

In the reign of Louis XV. there were not less than six hundred *cafés* in Paris. London, at the same period, could not count as many dozens. Under Louis Napoleon, the *cafés* have reached to the amazing number of between three and four thousand. All these establishments acknowledge the *Café Procope* as the founder of the dynasty, although, indeed, there were coffee-vendors in Paris before the time of the accomplished Sicilian. " *Vixerunt fortes ante Agamemnona*."

The consumption of coffee in Paris, at the period of the breaking out of the Revolution, was something enormous. The French West-Indian Islands furnished eighty millions of pounds annually, and this was irrespective of what was derived from the East. The two sources together were not sufficient to supply the kingdom. Thence adulterations, fortunes to the adulterers, and that supremacy of chicory, which has destroyed the well-earned reputation of French coffee.

I have already spoken of the *Café Procope*, and here I will only add an anecdote illustrative of the scenes that sometimes occurred there, and of the national character generally in the reign of Louis XV. One afternoon that M. de Saint Foix was seated at his usual table, an officer of the King's Body-Guard entered, sat down, and ordered " a cup of coffee, with milk, and a roll," adding, " It will serve me for a dinner!" At this Saint Foix remarked aloud, that " a cup of coffee, with milk, and a roll, was a confoundedly poor dinner." The officer remonstrated; Saint Foix reiterated his remark, and again and again declared, that nothing the gallant officer could say to the contrary, would convince him that a cup of coffee with milk, and a roll, was *not* a confoundedly poor dinner. Thereupon a challenge was given and accepted, and the whole of the persons present adjourned as spectators of a fight which ended by St. Foix receiving a wound in the arm. " That is all very well," said the wounded combatant; " but I call you to witness, gentlemen, that I am still profoundly convinced, that a cup of coffee, with milk, and a roll, is a confoundedly poor dinner!" At this moment, the principals were arrested, and carried before the Duke de Noailles, in whose presence Saint Foix, without waiting to be questioned, said, "Monseigneur, I had not the slightest intention of offending the gallant officer, who, I doubt not, is an honourable man; but Your Excellency can never prevent my asserting, that a cup of coffee, with milk, and a roll, is a confoundedly poor dinner." "Why, so it is," said the Duke. "Then I am not in the wrong," remarked St. Foix; "and a cup of coffee,"—— at these words Magistrates, delinquents, and auditory, burst into a roar of laughter, and the antagonists became friends. It was a more bloodless issue than that which occurred to Michel Lepelletier, in later years, at the *Café Février*. He was seated at dinner there, when an *ex-garde-du-corps*, named Paris, approached him, inquired if he were the Lepelletier who had voted for the death of Louis XVI., and, receiving an affirmative reply, drew forth a dagger, and swiftly slew him on the spot.

Before Procope, the Armenian, Pascal, sold coffee at the Fair of St. Germain, at three-halfpence a cup; and the beverage was sung by the poet Thomas in terms not exactly like those with which Delille subsequently sang the virtues of the tree. The French coffee-houses at once gained the popularity to which they aspired. To Pascal succeeded Maliban, and then Gregoire opened his establishment in the Rue Mazarin, in the vicinity of players and play-goers. At the same time, there was a man in Paris, called "the lame Candiot," who carried ready-made coffee about from door to door, and sold it for a penny per cup, sugar included. The *café* at the foot of the bridge of Notre-Dame was founded by Joseph; that at the foot of the bridge of St. Michel, by Etienne; and both of these are more ancient than that of Procope, who was the first, however, who made a fortune by his speculation. The *Quai de l'École* had its establishment, (the *Café Manoury*,) which I believe still exists, as does the *Café de la Régence*, which dates from the time of the Regent Duke of Orleans, and where Rousseau used to play at chess, and appear in his Armenian costume. It was also frequented *incog.*, by the Emperor Joseph. The oldest *café* in the Palais Royal is the celebrated *Café de Foy*, so called from the name of its founder. Carl Vernet was one of its most constant patrons. He was there on one occasion, when some repairs were going on, and, in his impatience, he flung a wet colouring brush from him, which struck the ceiling and left a spot. He immediately ascended the ladder, and with a touch of his finger converted the stain into a swallow; and his handy-work was still to be seen on the ceiling, when I was last in Paris. It was before the *Café de Foy* that Camille Desmoulins harangued the mob, in July, 1789, with such effect, that they took up arms, destroyed the Bastille, and inaugurated the Revolution.

The *Café de Valois* will long be remembered for its aristocratic character; that of Montansier, on the other hand, was remarkable for the coarseness of its frequenters, and the violence with which they discussed politics, especially at the period of the Restoration. The *Café du Caveau* was more joyously noisy with its gay artists and broad songs. The Empire brought two establishments into popular favour, both of which appealed to the lovers of beauty as well as of coffee. The first was the *Café du Bosquet*, and the second the *Café des Mille Colonnes*. Each was celebrated for the magnificent attractions of the presiding lady,—the *belle limonadière*, as she was at first called, or the *dame du comptoir*, as refinement chose to name her. Madame Romain, at the *Mille Colonnes*, had a longer reign than her rival; and the lady was altogether a more remarkable person. In the reign of Louis XVIII., her seat was composed of the throne of Jerome, King of Westphalia,—which was sold by auction on the bankruptcy of his Majesty. Madame Romain descended from it like a weary Queen, to take refuge in a nunnery; and, curiously enough, the ex-King has recovered his "throne," which now figures, in the reduced aspect of a simple arm-chair, in the *salon* of his residence at the Palais Royal. After the abdication of Madame Romain, the *Mille Colonnes* endeavoured to secure success by very meretricious means. Girls of a brasen quality of beauty bore through the apartments flaming bowls of punch, usually taken after the coffee; and the beverage and the bearers were equally bad.

As the *Café Chrétien* was once thoroughly Jacobin, so the *Café Lemblin* became entirely imperial, and was the focus of the Opposition after the return of the Bourbons. It was famous for its chocolate, as well as for its coffee. When the allies were at Paris, it was hardly safe for the officers to enter the *Café Lemblin*, and many scenes of violence are described as having occurred there, and many a duel was fought with fatal effect, after a *café* dispute between French and foreign officers,—and all for national honour. The Bourbon officers were far more insulting in the *cafés* to the ex-imperial "braves," than the latter were to the invading captains,—and they generally paid dearly for their temerity. Finally,—for to name all the *cafés* in Paris, would require an encyclopædia,—it is worthy of notice that Tortoni's, which is now a grave adjunct to the *Bourse*, first achieved success by the opposite process of billiard-playing. A broken-down provincial advocate, Spolar of Rennes, came to Paris with a bad character, and a capital cue; and the latter he handled so wonderfully at the *Café Tortoni*, that all Paris went to witness his feats. Talleyrand patronized him, backed his playing, and gained no inconsiderable sum by the cue-driving of Spolar, whose star culminated when he was appointed "Professor of Billiards to Queen Hortense,"—an appointment which sounds strange, but which was thought natural enough at the time; and, considering all things, so it was.

There is one feature in the French *cafés* which strikes an observer as he first contemplates it. I allude to the intensity, gravity, and extent of the domino-playing. A quartett party will spend half the evening at this mystery, with nothing to enliven it but the gentlest of conversation, and the lightest of beer, or a simple *petit verre*. The Government wisely thinks that a grave domino-player can be given to neither immorality nor conspiracies. But a British Government proudly scorns to tolerate such insipidities in Britons. British tradesmen, at the end of the day, may be perfectly idle, spout blasphemy, and get as drunk as they please, in any London tavern, provided they do not therewith break the peace; *but*, let the reprobates only remain obstinately sober, and play at dominoes, then they offend the immaculate justice of Justices, and landlords and players are liable to be fined. Lo, on Sabbath nights, the working-classes have thrown open to their edification the gin-palaces, which invite not in vain; but if one of these same classes should, on the same Sunday evening, knock at the religiously-closed door of a so-called free library, the secretary's maid who answers the appeal would be pale with horror at the atrocity of the applicant. And what is the bewildered Briton to do? He looks in at church, where, if there be a few free seats, they have a look about them so as to make him understand that he is in his fustian, and that he and the miserable sinners in their fine cloth are not on an equality in the house of God; and so he turns sighingly away, and goes where the law allows him,—to the house of gin

But, leaving the further consideration of these matters to my readers, let us now address ourselves to the sketching of a class whose most illustrious members have borne witness to their own excellency, not exactly according to the fashion spoken of by Shakspeare; namely, by putting a strange face on their own perfection.

THE ANCIENT COOK, AND HIS ART.

It is an incontestable fact, that he who lives soberly does not depend upon his cook for the pleasure which he derives from his repast. Nevertheless, the cook is one of the most important of personages; and even appetite, without him, would not be of the value that it is at present. A great *artiste* knows his vocation. When the cook of Louis XVIII. was reproached, by His Majesty's Physician, with ruining the royal health by savoury juices, the dignitary of the kitchen sententiously remarked, that it was the office of the cook to supply His Majesty with pleasant dishes, and that it was the duty of the doctor to enable the King to digest them. The division of labour, and the responsibilities of office, could not have been better defined.

From old times the cook has had a proper sense of the solemn importance of his wonderful art. The *Coquus Gloriosus*, in a fragment of Philemon, shows us what these artists were in the very olden time. He swears by Minerva that he is delighted at his success, and that he cooked a fish so exquisitely, that it returned him admiring and grateful looks from the frying-pan! He had not covered it with grated cheese, not disguised it with sauce; but he had treated it with such daintiness and delicacy, that, even, when fully cooked, it lay on the dish as fresh-looking as if it had just been taken from the lake. This result seems to have been a rarity; for, when the fish was served up at table, the delighted guests tore it from another, and a running struggle was kept up around the board to get possession of this exquisitely prepared *morceau*. "And yet," says the cook, "I had nothing better to exhibit my talent upon than a wretched river fish, nourished in mud. But, O Jupiter Saviour! if I had only had at my disposal some of the fish of Attica or Argos, or a conger from pleasant Sicyon, like those which Neptune serves to the gods in Olympus, why, the guests would have thought they had become divinities themselves. "Yes," adds the culinary boaster, "I think I may say that I have discovered the principle of immortality, and that the odour of my dishes would recall life into the nostrils of the very dead." The resonant vaunt is not unlike that of Bechamel, who said that, with the sauce he had invented, a man would experience nothing but delight in eating his own grandfather!

Hegesippus further illustrates the vanity of the *genus coquorum* of *his* days. In a dialogue between Syrus and his *chef*, the master declares that the culinary art appears to have reached its limit, and that he would fain hear something novel upon the subject. The cook's reply admits us to an insight into ancient manners. "I am not one of those fellows," says the personage in question, "who are content to suppose that they learn their art by wearing an apron for a couple of years. My study of the art has not been superficial: it has been the work of my life; and I have learned the use and appliances of every herb that grows—for kitchen purposes. But I especially shine in getting up funeral dinners. When the mourners have returned from the doleful ceremony, it is I who introduce them to the mitigated affliction department. While they are yet in their mourning attire, I lift the lids of my kettles, and straightway the weepers begin to laugh. They sit down with their senses so enchanted, that every guest fancies himself at a wedding. If I can only have all I require, Syrus," adds the artist, "if my kitchen be only properly furnished, you will see renewed the scenes which used to take place on the coasts frequented by the Syrens. It will be impossible for any one to pass the door; all who scent the process will be compelled, despite themselves, to stop. There they will stand, mute, open-mouthed, and nostrils extended; nor will it be possible to make them 'move on,' unless the police, coming to their aid, shut out the irresistible scent by plugging their noses."

Posidippus shows us a classical master-cook instructing his pupils. Leucon is the name of the teacher; and the first truth he impresses on his young friend is, that the most precious sauce for the purpose of a cook is impudence. "Boast away," he says, "and never be tired of it." For, as he logically remarks, "if there be many a Captain under whose dragoon-embossed cuirass lies a poor hare, why should not we, who kill hares, pass for better than we are, like the Captains? "A modest cook must be looked on," he says, "as a contradiction in nature. If he be hired out to cook a dinner in another man's house, he will only get considered in proportion to his impudence and overbearing conduct. If he be quiet and modest, he will be held as a pitiful cook."

Alexis, another artist, takes other and higher ground. He says, that in all the arts the resulting pleasure does not depend solely on those who exercise the art; there must be others who possess the science of enjoyment. This is true; and Alexis further adds, that the guest who keeps a dinner waiting, or a master who suddenly demands it before its time, are alike enemies to the art which Alexis professes.

The earthly paradise of the early cooks was, unquestionably, among the Sybarites,—the people to whom the crumpling of a rose under the side on which they lay, gave exquisite pain. They were as self-luxurious as though the world was made for them alone, and they and the world were intended to last for ever. They would not admit into their city any persons whose professions entailed noise in the practice of them: the trunkmaker at the corner of St. Paul's would have been flogged to death with thistledown, if he had carried on his trade in Sybaris for an hour, and if a Sybarite could have been found with energy enough to wield the instrument of execution! The crowing of one of the proscribed race of cocks once put all the gentlemen of the city into fits; and, on another occasion, a Sybarite telling a friend how his nerves had been shaken by hearing the tools of some labouring men in another country strike against each other, at their work, the friend was so overcome, that he merely exclaimed, "Good gracious!" and fainted away.

Athenæus, borrowing, if I remember rightly, from one of the authors whose works were in that Alexandrian library, the destruction of which by the Caliph Omar, Dr. Cumming tells us in his

"Finger of God," is a circumstance at which he is rather glad than sorry,—Athenæus mentions the visit of a Sybarite to Sparta, where he was invited to one of the public dinners, at which the citizens ate very black broth, in common, out of wooden bowls. Having tasted the national diet, he feebly uttered the Sybaritic expression for "Stap my vitals!" and convulsively remarked, that "he no longer wondered why the Lacedæmonians sought death in battle, seeing that such a fate was preferable to life with such broth!"

Certainly the public repasts of the Sybarites were of another quality. The giver of such repasts was enrolled among the benefactors of their country, and the cook who had distinguished himself was invested with a golden crown, and an opera ticket; that is, free admission to those public games where hired dancers voluptuously perverted time and the human form divine.

I am afraid that all cooks in remote ages enjoyed but an indifferent reputation, and thoroughly deserved what they enjoyed. The comic Dionysius introduces one of the succulent brotherhood, impressing upon a young apprentice the propriety of stealing in houses where they were hired to cook dinners. The instruction is worthy of Professor Fagan of the Saffron-Hill University. "Whatever you can prig," says the elder rogue, "belongs to yourself, as long as you are in the house. When you get past the porter into the street, it then becomes *my* property. So fake away! (Βάδιζε δεῦρ ἅμα,) and look out for unconnected trifles."

And yet Athenæus asserts that nothing has so powerfully contributed to instil piety into the souls of men, as good cookery! His proof is, that when men devoured each other, they were beasts,—which is a self-evident proposition; but that when they took to cooked meats, and were particular with regard to these, why, then alone they began to live cleanly,—which is a proposition by no means so self-evident. In his opinion, a man to be supremely happy only needed the gift of Ceres to Pandora,—a good appetite, and an irreproachable indigestion. These are, doubtless, great portions of happiness; and if felicity can do without them,—

which is questionable,—where they are not, comfort is absent, and a good conscience is hardly a sufficient compensation.

If Sybaris was the paradise of cooks, Lacedæmon was their purgatory. They were blamed if men grew fat on their diet, and plump children were legally condemned to get spare again upon their gruel. The Romans, again, restored the cook to his proper place in society. He might still be a slave, and so were greater men than he; but he was the confidant of his master, and there were not a few who would have exchanged their liberty for such a post and chains. And who dare affirm that the *coquus* was not an officer of distinction? He who knows how to prepare food for digestion and delight, is a greater man, in one particular at least, than Achilles, who could go no farther in culinary science than turning the spit; than Ulysses, who could light fires and lay cloths with the dexterity of a Frankfort waiter; or than Patroclus, who could draw wine and drink it, but who knew no more how to make a stew, than he did how to solve the logarithms of Napier.

When it is asserted that it was Cadmus, the grandfather of Bacchus, who first taught men how to eat as civilized beings should, it is thereby further intimated that good eating should be followed by good drinking.

We have heard of cooks in monasteries who made dissertations on eternal flames by the heat of their own fires: so Timachidas, of Rhodes, made patties and poetry at the same stove, and both after a fashion to please their several admirers. Artemidorus was the Dr. Johnson of his own art, and wrote a Kitchen Lexicon for the benefit of students. Sicily especially was celebrated for its literary cooks, and Mithœcus wrote a treatise on the art; while Archestratus, the Syracusan, looking into causes and effects, meditated on stomachs as well as sauces, and first showed how digestion might be taught to wait on appetite. Then theoretical laymen came in to the aid of the practical cook, and gastronomists hit upon all sorts of strange ideas to help them to renewed enjoyments. Pithyllus, for instance, invented a sheath for the tongue, in order that he might swallow the hottest viands faster than other guests, who wisely preferred rather to slowly please the palate than suddenly satisfy the stomach. It is of Pithyllus the Dainty, that it is related how, after meals, he used to clean his tongue by rubbing it with a piece of rough fish-skin; and his taking up hot viands with his hand, like that of Götz von Berlichingen, encased in a glove, is cited as proof that the Greeks used no forks. The spoons of the Romans had a pointed end, at the extremity of the handle, for the purpose of picking fish from the shell.

Then came the age when, if men had not appetites of nature's making, they were made for them by the cooks; and the latter, in return, were crowned with flowers by the guests who had eaten largely, and had no fears of indigestion. The inventor of a new dish had a patent for its exclusive preparation for a year. But ere that time it had probably been forgotten in something more novel discovered by a Sicilian rival; for the Greeks looked on Sicily as the Parisians of the last century used to look on Languedoc,—as the only place on earth where cooks were born and bred, and were worth the paying. The artists of both countries, and of the opposite ages mentioned, were especially skilled in the preparation of materials which were made to appear the things they were not; and a seemingly grand dinner of fish, flesh, and fowl, was really fashioned out of the supplies furnished by the kitchen garden. The Greeks, however, never descended to the bad taste of which the diarists of the last century show the French to have been guilty; namely, in having wooden joints, carved and painted, placed upon their tables for show. Artificial flowers may be tolerated, but an artificial sirloin, made of a block of deal, would be very intolerable board indeed, particularly to the hungry guests, who saw the seemingly liberal fare, but who could make very little of the deal before them.

In Sicily, the goddess of good cheer, Adephagia, had her especial altars, and thence, perhaps, the estimation in which the Sicilian cooks were held, who prayed to her for inspiration. Her ministers were paid salaries as rich as the sauces they invented. Something like £800 *per annum* formed the *honorarium* of the learned and juicy gentleman. But he was not always to be had, even at that price; and the disgusted Languedocien who would not remain in the *cuisine* of the Duke of Richmond, when Governor of Ireland, for the sufficient reason that there was no Opera in Dublin, had his prototype among his Sicilian predecessors. The jealousy of the culinary bondsman in Greek households against the free cook from Sicily, must have been sometimes deadly in its results.

The best-feed cook on record is the happy mortal to whom his master Antony gave a city, because he had cooked a repast which had called forth encomium from that dreadful jade, Cleopatra.

But money was the last thing thought of by the wearied epicures of Rome, especially when what they gave belonged to somebody else. When Lucullus spent £1,000 sterling on a snug dinner for three,—himself, Cæsar, and Pompey,—he doubtless spent his creditors' money; at least, extravagant people generally do. Claudius dined often with six hundred guests, and the Roman people paid the cooks. The dinners of Vitellius cost that sacrilegious feeder upwards of £3,000 each, but the bills were discharged by a levy on the public pocket. When Tiberius ordered several thousands sterling to be bestowed on the author of a piece wherein everything eatable was made to speak wittily, the author was really paid out of the popular pocket; and when Geta insisted on having as many courses at each repast as there were letters in in the alphabet, and all the viands at each course so named that their initials should be the same as that of the course itself, he was the last person to trouble himself about the payment for such extravagance.

The cooks of such epicures must necessarily, however, have been as despotic in the kitchen as their lord was in the saloon. The slaves there, who hurried to and fro, bearing their tributes of good things from the market-place, or distributing them according to his bidding, obeyed the cook's very nod, nay, anticipated his very wishes. They were, in fact, the ministers of an awful Sovereign. The cook was their Lord paramount. The stewards possessed no little power; but when the fires were lighted, and the dinner had to be thought of, the head cook was the kitchen Jupiter; and when he spoke, obedience, silence, and trembling followed upon his word.

From his raised platform, the *Archimagirus*, as he was called, could overlook all the preparations, and with his tremendous spoon of office he could break the heads of his least skilful disciples, and taste the sauces seething in the remotest saucepans. The effect must have been quite pantomimic; and to complete it, there was only wanted a crash of discordant music to accompany the rapid descent of the gigantic spoon upon the skull or ribs of an offender. The work was done in presence of the gods, and scullions blew the fires under the gaze of the *Lares*,—sooty divinities to whom, the legend says, inferior cooks were sometimes sacrificed in the month of December. "But," as Othello says, "that's a fable!"

Great Roman kitchens were as well worth seeing, and perhaps were as often inspected by the curious and privileged, as that of the Reform Club. "Order reigned" there quite as much as it did, according to Marshal Sebastiani, at Warsaw, amid the most abject slavery. Art and costliness were lavished upon the vessels, but the human beings there were exactly the things that were made the least account of.

No doubt that the triumph of the art of the cook consisted in serving up an entire pig at once roasted and boiled. The elder Disraeli has shown from Archestratus how this was done. "The animal had been bled to death by a wound under the shoulder, whence, after copious effusion, the master-cook extracted the entrails, washed them with wine, and hanged the animal by the feet. He crammed down the throat the stuffings already prepared. Then, covering the half of the pig with a paste of barley thickened with wine and oil, he put it in a small oven, or on a heated table of brass, where it was gently roasted with all due care. When the skin was browned, he boiled the other side, and then, taking away the barley paste, the pig was served up, at once boiled and roasted." And such was the way by which the best of cooks spoiled the best of pigs.

According to Plautus, cooks alone were privileged in the old days to carry knives in their girdles. In the "*Aulularia*," old Euclio says to Congrio, the cook, "*Ad tres viros jam ego deferam tuum nomen*,"—" I'll go and inform against you to the Magistrates." "Why so?" asks Congrio. "Because you carry a knife," —"*Quia cultrum habes*." "Well," says the artist, standing on his rights, "*cocum decet*," "it is the sign of my profession." From another of the many cooks of Plautus we learn, in the "*Menæchmei*," that, when a parasite was at table, his appetite was reckoned as equivalent to that of eight guests; and when Cylindrus is ordered to prepare a dinner for Menæchmus, his "lady," and the official parasite, "Then," says the cook, "that's as good as ten; for your parasite does the work of eight:"—

"*Jam isti sunt decem,
Nam parasitus octo hominum munus facile fungitur.*"

The musicians would appear to have lived as pleasantly as the parasites. Simo remarks to Tranio, in the "*Mostellaria*," that he lives on the best the cooks and vintners can procure for him,—a real fiddler's destiny:—

"*Musice hercle agitis ætatem: ita ut vos decet.
Vino et victu, piscatu probe electili,
Vitam colitis.*"

Stalino complains in the "*Casina*," that, clever as cooks are, they cannot put a little essence of love into all their dishes,—a sauce, he says, that would please everybody. Their reputation in Rome for stealing was much the same as that enjoyed by their Grecian brethren. The scene of the "*Casina*," indeed, is in Athens; but Olympio utters a Roman sentiment when he says, that cooks use their hands as much for larceny as cookery, and that wherever they are they bring double ruin, through extravagance and robbery, upon their masters: "*Ubi sunt, duplici damno dominos multant.*" This is further proved by the speech of *Epidicus*, in the comedy so called, where that slave-cook speaks of his master's purse as if it were game, to disembowel which, he says, he will use his professional knife:—

"*Acutum cultrum habeo, senis qui exenterem
Marsupium.*"

We learn something of the pay of a cook from a speech of one of the craft, in the "*Pseudolus.*" Ballio, seeing a single practitioner remaining in the square to be hired, asks how it is that he has not been engaged. "*Eloquar*," says the cook, "here is the reason :—

"He who, now-a-days, comes here to hire cooks,
No longer seeks the best, that is, the dearest,
But some poor spoil-sauce who for nothing works.
Therefore you see me here alone to-day.
A poor drachma hath my brethren purchased;
But under a crown I cook a dish for no man.
For 'twixt the common herd and me, you see,
There is a diff'rence : they into a dish
Fling whole meadows, and the guests they treat, Sir,
As though they were but oxen out at grass.
Herbs season they with herbs, and grass with grass;
And in the mess, garlic, coriander, fennel,
Sorrel, rochet, beet-root, leeks and greens,
All go together, with a pound of benzoin,
And mustard ditto, that compels the tears
From out the eyes of those that have to mix it.
* * * * *
If men are short-lived now, the reason's plain:
They put death into their stomachs, and so
Of indigestion and bad cookery die.
Their sauces but to think of, makes me shudder:
Yet men would eat what asses would not bend to.
* * * * *
Who of *my* dishes eats, obtains at least
Two hundred happy years of life renew'd.
I season Neptune's fishes with a juice
Made up of Cicilindrum, Muscadel,
Sipolindrum, and Sancapatides.
The odour of my mutton, nicely stuffed
With Cicimandrum, Nappalopsides,
And of Cataractaria a pinch,
Feeds Jupiter himself, who, when I rest,
Sleeps on Olympus, sad and supperless.

> As for my potions, he who deeply drinks,
> Gulps with the draught the gift of endless youth."

Finally after inventing the above names unpronounceable of sauces that do not exist, the boaster adds, that his fee is a crown, provided he is not overlooked; but that if there be supervision to check him in his perquisites, he is not to be hired under a mina:—

> "Si credis, nummos; si non, ne mina quidem!"

I do not know if cooks more especially used different fingers in mingling their sauces, according as they were employed on wedding banquets, martial feasts, senatorial entertainments, *al-fresco déjeûners,* or commercial suppers; but certain it is, that the fingers were sacred to diverse deities. The thumb was devoted to Venus, the index finger to Mars, the longest finger to Saturn, the next to the Sun, and the little finger to Mercury.

I conclude with a remark that I hope will be gratifying to all culinary artists who respect themselves and their calling, and who are anxious to prove that their vocation is of ancient and honourable descent. Cadmus, who introduced letters into Greece, had formerly been cook to the King of Sidon. Thus learning ascended to us from the kitchen; and to the ex-cook of the King of Sidon we perhaps owe all the epics that have ever been written. By this genealogy, even "Paradise Lost" may be traced to the patties of Cadmus. But cooks in England may boast of a *noblesse de cuisine,* which dates from the Norman Conquest. When William, who wooed his wife Matilda by knocking her down, had established himself in England, he gave a banquet, at which his cook, Tezelin, served a new white soup of such exquisite flavour, that William sent for the artist, and inquired its name. "I call it *Dillegrout,*" said Tezelin. "A scurvy name for so good a soup," said the Conqueror; "but let that pass. We make you Lord of the Manor of Addington!" Thus modern cooks may boast of a descent from the landed aristocracy of the Conquest! Some of their masters cannot do as much; and this, perhaps, accounts for the pride of the one, and the simplicity of the other.

THE MODERN COOK AND HIS SCIENCE.

If it were necessary that the cook of the ancient world should be a Sicilian, and that the *cuisinier* of the ancient *régime* should be of Languedoc, (the native place of "*blanc manger*,") so in these modern times he alone is considered a true graduate in the noble science *de la gueule* who is a Gaul by birth, or who has gone through his studies in the University of French Kitchens. In England, it must be confessed that great cooks have formed the exception rather than the rule; and that our native culinary literature, however interesting in certain national details, is chiefly based upon a French foundation. And yet we may boast of some native professors who were illustrious in their way. Master John Murrel, for instance, wrote a cookery book in 1630, and dedicated it to the daughter of the Lord Mayor. He starts by asserting that cookery books generally mar rather than make good meats; and then shows what good meats were in his estimation, by teaching how to dress " minced bullock's kidney, a rack of veal, a farced leg of mutton, an umble pie, and a chewit of stockfish." He is succulently eloquent on a compound production, consisting of marrow-bones, a leg of mutton, fowls and pullets, and a dozen larks, all in one dish.

The Duke of Newcastle, in the last century, had a female cook of some renown, named " Chloe." General Guise, at the siege of Carthagena, saw some wild fowl on the wing, and amid the din of war, he thought of " Chloe " and her sauces. She was famous for her stewed mushrooms, and there is an anecdote connected therewith that will bear repeating. " Poor Dr. Shaw," writes Horace Walpole, " being sent for in great haste to Claremont, (it seems the Duchess had caught a violent cold by a hair of her own whisker getting up her nose, and making her sneeze,) the poor Doctor, I say, having eaten a few mushrooms before he set out, was taken so ill that he was forced to stop at Kingston; and, being carried to the first apothecary's, prescribed a medicine for himself which immediately cured him. This catastrophe so alarmed the Duke of Newcastle, that he immediately ordered all the mushroom-beds to be destroyed; and even the toad-stools in the park did not escape scalping in this general measure. And a voice of lamentation was heard at Ramah in Claremont, '*Chloe* weeping for *her* mushrooms and they are not!" But, let us turn to trace lightly the genealogy of the cooks of modern times.

The descent of the barbarians from the north was the ruin of cooks as well as Kings, of kitchens as well as of constitutions. Many of the cooks of the classic period were slain like the Druid Priests at the fire of their own altars. A patriotic few fled rather than feed the invader; and the servile souls who tremblingly offered to prepare a *fricassée* of ostrich brains for the Northmen, were dismissed with contempt by warrior princes, who lived on under-done beef, and very much of it!

But as sure as the Saxon blood beats out the Norman, so does good cookery prevail over barbarous appetites. The old cooks were a sacred race, whose heirs took up the mission of their sires. The mission was so far triumphant, that, at the period of Charlemagne, the imperial kitchen recognised in its *chef* the representative of the Emperor. The oriental pheasant and the peacock, in all the glories of expanded tail, took the place, or appeared at the side, of coarser viands. The dignity and the mirth of Charlemagne's table were heightened by the presence of ladies. Brillat de Savarin states, that since that period the presence of the fair sex has ever been a law of society. But in this he errs; for the Marquis de Bouillé, in his admirable work on the Dukes of Guise, affirms that the good civilizing custom had fallen into disuse, but that a permanent improvement was commenced in the reign of Francis I., when the Cardinal of Lorraine induced that Monarch to invite ladies to be present at all entertainments given at Court. Society followed the fashion of the Sovereign; and as it used to be said, "No feast, no Levite," so now it was felt that where there was no lady, there was no refined enjoyment.

At whatever period the emancipation of the ladies from their forced seclusion took place, from that period the tone of social life was elevated. They went about, like Eve, "on hospitable thoughts intent." The highest in rank did not disdain to supervise the kitchen; they displayed their talents in the invention of new dishes, as well as in the preparation of the old; and they occasionally well-nigh ruined their lords by the magnificence of their tastes, and their sublime disregard of expense. All the sumptuary laws of Kings to restrain this household extravagance were joyously evaded, and banquets became deadly destructive to men's estates.

The French Kings granted corporate rights to the different trades connected with the kitchen and the table; and perhaps the most valued privilege was that conceded by Charles IX. to the pastry-cooks, who alone were permitted to make bread for the service of the Mass.

Montaigne, in his pleasant way, recounts a conversation he had with an Italian *chef* who had served in the kitchen of Cardinal Caraffa, up to the period of the death of his gastronomic Eminence. "I made him," says the great Essayist, "tell me something about his post. He gave me a lecture on the science of eating, with a gravity and magisterial countenance as if he had been determining some vexed question in theology. He deciphered to me, as it were, the distinction that exists between appetites:—the appetite at fasting; that which people have at the end of the second or third service; the means of awaking and exciting it; the general 'police,' so to speak, of his sauces; and then particularized their ingredients and effects. The differences of salads, according to the seasons, he next discoursed upon. He explained what sorts ought to be prepared warm, and those which should always be served cold; the way of adorning and embellishing them, in order to render them seductive to the eye. After this he entered on the order of table-services,—a subject full of fine and important considerations; and all this was puffed up with rich and magnificent terms; phrases, indeed, such as are employed by statesmen and diplomatists, when they are discoursing on the government of an empire." We see by this what the "*art de la gueule*" was in the days of Charles IX., whose mother, Catherine de Medicis, had introduced it into France, as a science whereby men should enjoy life. The same lady introduced also poisoning, as a science whereby men might be deprived of life. Her own career was full of opposing facts like these,—facts which caused a poetic cook to write the epitaph upon her, which says:—

"Here lieth a Queen, who was angel and devil,
Admirer of good, and a doer of evil;
She supported the State, and the State she destroyed;
She reconciled friends, and she friendships alloyed;
She brought forth three Kings, thrice endanger'd the Crown,
Built palaces up, and threw whole cities down;
Made many good laws, many bad ones as well,
And merited richly both heaven and hell."

The mention of Cardinal de Caraffa, by Montaigne, reminds me that, for a gastronome, the Cardinal was singularly sanguinary in spirit. I know no one to compare with him, except Dr. Cahill, who is not averse to good living, and who has earned so gloomy a notoriety by his terrible sentiment of the massacre of Protestants being "a glorious idea." Caraffa was enabled to enjoy both his propensities, of swallowing good things and slaughtering heretics. "Having obtained leave from the Pope to establish the Inquistion at Rome, at a time when the resources of the State ran low, he turned his private property to the use of his zeal, and set up a small Inquisition at his own expense." Thus he could dine within hearing of the groans of his victims; his cook could inform him that the hares and heretics had both been roasted; and he *may* have been occasionally puzzled to know whether that smell of burning came from the patties or the Protestants.

The Italian cooks were, for a season, fashionable in France; but they had a passion for poetry as well as for pies, and were given to let their sauces burn while they recited whole pages of "Orlando

Furioso." They were critics as well as cooks, and the kitchens resounded with their denunciations of all who objected to the merits of the divine Ariosto. But even the Papal ennobling of a cook could not compensate for an indifferent dinner; and though Leo X., in a fit of modest delight at a sauce made by his cook during Lent, named him from that circumstance "Jack o' Lent," or "Jean de Carême," the French would not allow that such an event authorized the *artiste* to be dreaming over epics, when he should be wide awake to the working of his proper mystery. But the mystery itself was much obstructed by the political events of the times. There were the bloody wars of the Guises, the troubles of the League, the despotic reign of Richelieu, the cacochymical temperament (as the editor of the *"Almanach des Gourmands"* would call it) of Louis XIII., and the ridiculous war of the Fronde. The glory of the French kitchen rose with that of the *Grand Monarque*, and Vatel and Louis XIV. were contemporaries. Vatel slew himself to save his honour! The King had come to dine with Condé: but the cod had not arrived in time to be dressed for the King, and thereupon the heroic artist fell upon his sword, like an ancient Roman, and is immortalized for ever by his glorious folly!

But there was nothing really heroic in the death of Vatel, whose sword was pointed at his breast by wounded vanity. Far more heroic was the death of the cook of the Austrian Consul, in the late cruel massacre, by the cowardly Russian fleet, at Sinope. The Consul's cook was a young woman of thirty years of age. The Muscovite murderers were at the very height of their bloody enjoyment, and sending shots into the town, when the cook attempted to cross a garden, to procure some herbs; for Consuls *must* dine, though half the world be dying. She had performed her mission, and was returning, when a thirty-six pounder shot cut her completely in two. Rather than give up the parsley for her master's soup, she thus encountered death. What was Vatel and his bodkin, to this more modern cook and the thirty-six pounder, loaded by the Czar for her destruction?

The cooks "looked up" in the nights and suppers of the Regency, and the days and dinners of Louis XV. It would be difficult to say whether under the Regent, or under the King, the culinary art and its professors most flourished. I am inclined, however, to think, that, during the tranquil and voluptuous period of the reign of Louis XV., the cooks of France rose to that importance from which they have never descended. They became a recognised and esteemed class in society, whose spoiled children they were; and in return, it was very like spoiled children that they behaved. But how could it be otherwise, when the noble, the brave, and the fair girded aprons to their loins, and stood over stew-pans, with the air of alchymists over alembics? It is to the nobility and other distinguished persons in high life, yet not noble, in France, that gastronomy owes many a dish, whose very name betrays to ecstasy. And here are a few of these droll benefactors of mankind.

The Marquis de Béchamel immortalized his name, in the reign of Louis XIV., by his invention of cream-sauce, for turbot and cod. Madame de Maintenon imagined the "cutlets in curlpapers" which go by her name, and which her ingenuity created in order to guard the sacred stomach of the Grand Monarque from the grease which he could not digest. The "*Chartreuse à la Mauconseil*" is the work, and the most innocent one, of the free and easy Marchioness of that name. A woman more free and easy still, the Duchess of Villeroy, (Maréchale de Luxembourg,) produced, in her hours of reflection, the dish known as the *poulets à la Villeroy*. They were eaten with bread *à la Régent*, of which the author was the *roué* Duke of Orleans. His too "well-beloved" daughter, the Duchess of Berry, had a gastronomic turn of mind, like her illustrious father. She was an epicurean lady, who tasted of all the pleasures of life without moderation, whose device was, "Short and sweet," and who was contented to die young, seeing that she had exhausted all enjoyment, and had achieved a renown, that should embalm her name for ever, as the inventor of the *filets de lapereau*. The *gigot à la Mailly* was the result of much study, on the part of the first mistress of Louis XV., to rid herself of a sister who was a rival. Madame de Pompadour, another of the same King's "ladies," testified her gratitude for the present which the Monarch made her of the Château de Bellevue, by the production of the *filets de volaille à la Bellevue*. The Queen of Louis was more devout, but not less epicurean, than his mistresses; and the *petites bouchées à la Reine*, if they were not of her creating, were named in honour of Maria Leczinzka. Louis himself had a contempt for female cooks; but Madame Du Barry had one so well-trained, that with a charming dinner of *coulis de faisans, croustades de la foie de lottes, salmis de bécassine, pain de volaille à la suprême, poularde au cresson, écrevisses au vin de Sauterne, bisquets de pêches au Noyau*, and *crême de cerneaux*, the King was so overcome with ecstasy, that, after recovering from the temporary disgust he experienced at hearing that it was the handywork of a woman, he consented to ennoble her by conferring upon her the *cordon bleu*,—which phrase, from that time, has been accepted as signifying a skilled female cook.

With respect to other dishes and their authors, the *vol au vent à la Nèsle* owns a Marquis for its father; and the *poularde à la Montmorency* is the offspring of a Duke. The *Bayannoise*, or the *Mabonnoise* rather, recalls one of the victories of the Duke de Richelieu; and *veau à la Montgolfier*, well inflated, was the tribute of a culinary artist to the hero who first rode the air at the tail of a balloon. The *sorbet à la Donizetti* was the masterpiece of the Italian confectioner of the late Duke of Beaufort. He had been to the Opera; and one of the composer's charming airs having given him an idea, he brooded over it, till an hour or so before dawn, it was hatched into reality, when he rushed to the Duke's bed-chamber, and, "drawing Priam's bed curtains in the night," announced to his startled Grace the achievement of a new *sorbet*.

The *tendrons d'agneaux au soleil*, and the *filets de poulets à la Pompadour*, were two of the dishes invented by the famous lady of that name. The *carbonnade à la Soubise*, and the *carré de veau à la Guemenée*, date—the first from the reign of Louis XV., the last from that of Louis XVI.,—periods when the people were famishing. The Pompadour was a great patron of the arts, and especially of the culinary art; and the *cuisine des petits appartemens*, during *her* reign, was at the very height of its savoury reputation. The Prince of Soubise was a poor General, but a rich glutton; and his son-in-law, the Prince de Guemenée, was famous for his invention of various *ragoûts*, his inordinate extravagance, and his bankruptcy, with liabilities against him amounting to twenty-eight millions of francs. Madame la Maréchale de Mirepoix was the authoress of *cailles à la Mirepoix;* and her descendants live on the reputation acquired thereby by their epicurean ancestress. The Bourbons vied with the aristocracy in taxing their genius, and cudgelling their brains, in order to produce new dishes. Thus, the *potage à la Xavier* was the production of Louis XVIII., in the days of his early manhood; while the *soupe à la Condé* was a rival dish invented by his princely cousin, —a cousin, by the way, who, when a refugee in England, used to pass his evenings at Astley's, with his pockets full of apples, which he gallantly presented to ladies as highly, but not as naturally, coloured as the fruit. Perhaps the reputation of the Maréchal de Richelieu rests more on his *boudins à la carpe*, than on his battles and *billets-doux*. Finally, a mysterious obscurity conceals from us the name of the inventor of the *petites bouchées de foie gras*. He is the Junius of gastronomic literature; but if he be guessed at in vain, he is blessed abundantly, as one who has concentrated paradise, (an Epicurean's paradise,) and given an antepast thereof, in a single mouthful.

The Prince de Soubise was famous in the reign of Louis XV. for giving great dinners, and paying nobody but his cooks, and the young ladies of the opera. He once varied his extravagance by a splendid fête, which was to terminate by a supper. His *chef* waited on him with the bill of fare for the banquet, and the first article which attracted his attention was "fifty hams." "Half a hundred hams!" said the Prince, "that's a coarse idea, Bertrand. You have not got to feed my regiment of cavalry." "Truly,

Prince! and only one ham will appear on the table; I want the remaining forty-nine for adjuncts, seasonings, flavourings, and a dozen other purposes." "Bertrand," replied the Prince, "you are robbing me, and I cannot allow this article to pass." "Monseigneur!" exclaimed the offended *artiste*, "you doubt my morals, and libel my merit. You do not know what a treasure you possess in me; you have only to order it, and those fifty hams which so terribly offend you, why, I will put them all into a phial not bigger than my thumb!" The Prince smiled, and Bertrand triumphed.

The cooks of the young King Louis XVI. remarked, with mingled terror and disgust, that his appetite was rather voracious than delicate. He cared little what he ate, provided there was enough of it; and he looked to nutrition rather than niceness. A succulent joint with him had more merit than the most singular of dishes, the invention of which had perhaps caused three nights of wakefulness to its author. But the aristocracy, the law, and finance, maintained tables which ought to have been the pride of Versailles. Late dinners, or gorgeous suppers, were indulged in to such a degree by the moneyed classes, that it was familiarly said, that of an evening the chimneys of the Faubourg Saint Honoré made fragrant with their incense the entire capital. It was reckoned that, at this period, twenty thousand men had no other profession than that of "diner out," which they carried on, like the parasites of old, by retailing anecdotes and news in return for the repast. It was a time when "Monseigneur" thought nothing of dispatching his cook to London to procure a turtle; which, after all, was less extravagant than the process of Cambacérès, who had his Périgord pies sent to him through the post, "On his Majesty's Service." The Languedocien cooks in France were paid the quadruple of the salary of the family tutor, good eating being so much more essential to life than mere instruction; and, besides, could the family tutor have accomplished any thing that could equal the achievement of the family cook who could bring to table *entire* a "*sanglier à la crapaudine?*" The cooks of the age of Louis XVI. invented the "*bouillie*" and the "*con-*

sommé," because mastication was considered by them a vulgar process; and the royal cooks, during Passion Week, manipulated the vegetables placed before the King into the forms of ocean-dwelling fish, and gave to the semblance the taste of the reality for which it passed to the eye.

The glory of gastronomy was again rising when it was suddenly quenched by the revolutionary torrent, and the nation was put on a three years' meagre dietary by the Jacobins and the Directory. But the Revolution which affected to hate cooks as aristocratic appendages that ought to be suppressed, sometimes made, where it hoped to mar. The case of Ude is one in point.

Monsieur Ude, like Prince Eugene, was originally intended for the Church. At the breaking out of the French Revolution, he was residing, for instruction, with an Abbé, and master and pupil had to fly before the popular indignation, which, for a time, assailed the Church, and all therewith connected. Ude's life was in peril in the public streets, and he just saved it, by rushing into the shop of a pastry-cook, where he found a permanent asylum. The "house of Ude," like other great houses, nearly perished in the great political shipwreck of the day, and this particular scion thereof took to the study of practical gastronomy, and became chief supreme in various great kitchens, from that of royalty down to that of Crockford.

When the sluices of the French Revolution were opened, how diverse were the fortunes of those who fled from before it! It was the same with the gentlemen who had followed the fortunes of Napoleon. They were scattered like the Generals of Alexander, without being able, like them, to retire upon independent sovereignties, and rear dynasties of barbaric splendour. Some went to Greece to crush despotism, some went to Lahore to aid it. A few, like Latour d'Auvergne, took to the Church; but, saving that portly person himself, none had the good luck to reach the archiepiscopate. Those who failed to procure employment in foreign armies, and yet could not lay aside their propensity for killing, went to the East, and prescribed as Physicians. Such of the rest as were absolutely fit for nothing, and willing to do it, inundated

England, and undertook the light and irresponsible office of Private Tutors!

But it was the earlier Revolution that afforded examples of the greatest contrasts. Many young men, intended for the Church, changed their profession and became popular, useful and rich, in the households of European royalty, as civilizers of the kitchen, who raised cookery from its barbarous condition to a matter of science and taste. Perhaps the most curious of the waifs and strays of the Revolution flung upon our shores, was the Chevalier D'Aubigné, who contrived to live, as so many French gentlemen of that time did, in bitter poverty, without a sacrifice of dignity. He had one day been invited by an English friend to dine with the latter at a tavern. In the course of the repast, he took upon himself to mix the salad; and the way in which he did this, attracted the notice of all the other guests in the room. Previous to the period of which I am speaking, lettuces were commonly eaten, by tavern frequenters at least, *au naturel*, with no more dressing than Nebuchadnezzar had to his grass when he dieted daily among the beasts. Consequently, when D'Aubigné handled the preparation for which he had asked, like a chymist concocting elixir in his laboratory, the guests were lost in admiration; for the refreshing aroma of a *Mayonnaise* was warrant to their senses, that the French Knight had discovered for them a new pleasure. One of them approached the foreign magician, and said, "Sir, it is universally known that your nation excels all others in the making a salad. Would it be too great a liberty to ask you to do us the favour to mix one for the party at my table?" The courteous Frenchman smiled, was flattered, performed the office asked of him, and put four gentlemen in a state of uncontrollable ecstasy. He had talked cheerfully, as he mixed gracefully and scientifically, and, in the few minutes required by him to complete his work of enchantment, he contrived to explain his position as emigrant, and his dependence on the pecuniary aid afforded by the English Government. The guests did not let the poor Chevalier depart without slipping into his hand a golden fee, which he received with as little embarrassment, and as much dignity, as though he had been the Physician De Portal taking an *honorarium* from the hands of the Cardinal de Rohan.

He had communicated his address, and he, perhaps, was not very much surprised when, a few days after, he received a letter in which he was politely requested to repair to a house in Grosvenor Square, for the purpose of mixing a salad for a dinner-party there to be given. D'Aubigné obeyed the summons; and, after performing his mission, returned home richer by a five-pound note than when he went out.

Henceforth he became the recognised "fashionable salad-maker;" and ladies "died" for his salads, as they do now for Constantine's simulative bouquets. The preparer was soon enabled to proceed to his responsible duties in a carriage; and a servant attended him, carrying a mahogany case, containing the necessary ingredients for concocting various salads, according to the respective tastes of his employers. At a later period, he sold, by hundreds, similar mahogany cases, which he had caused to be made, and which were furnished with all matters necessary for the making an irreproachable salad, and with directions how to administer them. The Chevalier, too, was, like old Carré,—whose will was so cleverly made by the very disinterested friends who had never before spoken to him,—a prudent and a saving man; and by the period which re-opened France to the *émigrés*, he had realized some eighty thousand francs, upon which he enjoyed a dignified retirement in a provincial town. He invested sixty thousand francs in the Funds; with the other twenty thousand he purchased a little estate in the Limousin, and, if he lacked a "legend" to his device, I would have helped him to one in "*Sal adfert.*"

A Knight over a salad-bowl is not a chivalrous picture; but the stern necessity of the case gave it dignity and the resulting profits quieted the scruples of the gentleman. When Booth pounced upon Captain Bath, sitting in a dirty flannel gown, and warming his sister's posset at the fire, the noble and gaunt Captain was taken something aback, and said, in a little confusion, "I did not expect, Sir, to be seen by you in this situation." Booth told him "he thought it impossible he could appear in a situation more becoming his character." The compliment was equivocal; but the Captain said, "You do not? By G— I am very much obliged to you for that opinion; but I believe, Sir, however my weakness may prevail on me to descend from it, no man can be more conscious of his own dignity than myself." The apology of good Captain Bath in Fielding's "Amelia," would have served the Chevalier who made salads, had he needed one.

If a salad made the fortune of a Chevalier, it on one occasion made that of a female cook, with whose dexterity in this respect a learned English Judge was so enchanted, that he raised the lucky maiden to the quality of wife. If we discuss the traits of life at table, we have nothing to do with the secrets of household; but an incident, illustrative of the consequences of this match, may be mentioned. The Judge ever after was famous for protracting the sittings of court beyond all precedent and patience; and when weary Barristers were aghast at hearing a new cause called on, when the night was half spent, and fairly remonstrated against the judicial cruelty, the learned husband of his cook would remark with a sigh, "Gentlemen, we *must* be somewhere; we cannot be better any where than where we now are,"—the half of which assertion was stoutly denied by his hearers.

Our aristocracy are not quite so famous for their invention of dishes as that of France; but their love for good dinners, and their knowledge of what they ought to be, are not inferior to the affection and science of our neighbours. When Lord Marcus Hill officiated as whipper-in to the Whig Government, it was part of his office to order the fish dinner at which Ministers regale themselves when sectional cares no longer molest them. The fish dinners of Lord Marcus are remembered with satisfaction and gratitude; for they were first-rate in their way. The reputation of the Carlton *cuisine* and cellar is said to be chiefly owing to Sir Alexander Grant, of whom a gastronomic critic says, "No living Amphitryon has given better dinners in his time; and few can boast of having entertained more distinguished guests." His name, as a patron, reminds me of that of Carême, as a practitioner.

PEN AND INK SKETCH OF CARÈME.

It would be as easy to compile a Dictionary of Cooks, as of Musicians or Painters; but it would not be so amusing or so edifying, except perhaps to those who think more of their stomach than of their mind. But it *would* then be attractive and useful to the majority of readers; for the sages themselves are not unmindful of their stomachs, and, according to a sage, they would be unworthy of the name if they neglected that vital matter. Johnson, you know, lived in an age when things were called by their real names. '*J'appelle un chat un chat*,' was the device of the plain-spoken, when not only men, but ladies, bold as the Thalestris of Young's pungent satire, loudly dared to name what nature dared to give. Dr. Johnson, then, says, "Some people have a foolish way of not minding, or pretending not to mind, what they eat. For my part, I mind my *belly* very studiously; for I look upon it that he who does not mind his *belly*, will hardly mind any thing else!"

To the world, then, even a Biographical Dictionary of Cooks might be captivating; but as my present mission is not to write an Encyclopædia, but rather deferentially to offer my little sketches to gentle, and not too critical, readers, with leisure half-hours at their command, so do I offer them a sketch of Carème, as the knowledge of the individual may stand for that of the class.

He was illustrious by descent; for one of his ancestors had served in the household of a Pope, who himself made more sauces than saints, Leo X. But Carème was one of so poor and so numerous a family, that when he came into the world, he was no more welcome than Oliver Goldsmith was: the respective parents of the little-cared-for babes did not know what future great men lay in naked helplessness before them. One wrote immortal poetry, and starved: the other made delicious pastry, and rode in a chariot! We know how much Oliver received for his "Vicar;" while Antnony Carème used to receive twice as much for merely writing out a recipe to make a "*pâté*." Nay, Carême's untouched patties, when they left royal tables, were brought up at a cost which would have supported Goldsmith for a month; and a cold sugared *entremet*, at the making of which Carême had presided, readily fetched a higher price than the publi now pay for the "Complete Works" of the poet of Green-Arbour-court!

Carême studied under various great masters, but he perfected his studies under Boucher, *chef des services* of the Prince Talleyrand. The glory of Carême was co-eval with that of Napoleon: those two individuals were great men at the same period; but the glory of one will, perhaps, be a little more enduring than that of the other. I will not say *whose* glory will thus last the longer; for as was remarked courteously by the Oxford candidate for honours, who was more courteous than "crammed," and who was asked which were the minor Prophets, "I am not willing to draw invidious distinctions!"

In the days of the Empire,—the era of the greatness, of the achievements, and of the reflections of Carême,—the possession of him was as eagerly contested by the rich as that of a nymph by the satyrs. He was alternately the glory of Talleyrand, the boast of Lavalette, and the pride of the Saxon Ambassador. In their houses, too, his hand was as often on his pen as on the handle of his *casserole;* and inspiration never visited his brain without the call being duly registered in his note-book, with reflections thereon highly philosophical and gastronomic.

But Carême was capricious. It was not that he was unfaithful, but he was *volage;* and he passed from kitchen to kitchen, as the bee wings from flower to flower. The Emperor Alexander dined with Talleyrand, and forthwith he seduced Carême: the seduction money was only £100 sterling per month, and the culinary expenses. Carême did not yield without much coyness. He urged his love for study, his desire to refine the race of which he made himself the model, his love for his country; and he even accompanied, for a brief moment, "Lord Stewart" to Vienna; but it was more in the way of policy than pastry: for Count Orloff was sent after him on a mission, and Carême, after flying, with the full intention of being followed, to London and Paris, yielded to the golden solicitation, and did the Emperor Alexander the honour of becoming the head of the imperial kitchen in whatever palace His Majesty presided. But the delicate susceptibility of Carême was wounded by discovering that his book of expenses was subjected to supervision. He flung up his appointment in disgust, and hastened across Europe to England. The jealous winds wished to detain him for France, and they blew him back on the coast between Calais and Boulogne, exactly as they did another gentleman, who may not be so widely known as Carême, but who has been heard of in England under the name of William Wordsworth. Carême accepted the omen, repaired to Paris, entered the service of the Princess Bagration, and served the table of that capricious lady, *en maître d'hotel*. As the guests uttered ecstatic praises of the fare, the Princess would smile upon him as he stood before her, and exclaim, "He is the pearl of cooks!" Is it a matter of surprise that he was vain? Fancy being called a "pearl" by a Princess! On reading it we think of the days when Lady Mary Wortley Montague put nasty footmen into eclogues, and deified the dirty passions of Mrs. Mahony's lacquey.

The Princess, however, ate herself into a permanent indigestion, and Carême transferred his services to the English Ambassador at the Court of Vienna. There, every morning, seated in his magnificent kitchen, Carême received the visit of "Milor Stewart," who seldom left him without presents and encouragements. Indeed, these rained upon the immortal artist. The Emperor Alexander had consented to have Carême's projects in culinary architecture dedicated to him, and, with notice of consent, sent him a diamond ring. When Prince Walkouski placed it on his finger, the cook forgot his dignity, and burst into tears. So did all the other cooks in the Austrian capital,—out of sheer jealousy.

Carême, two years before George IV. was King, had been for a short period a member of the Regent's household. He left Vienna to be present at the Coronation; but he arrived too late; and he does not scruple to say, very ungenerously, that the banquet was spoiled for want of his presence, nor to insinuate that the colleagues with whom he would have been associated were unworthy of such association,—an insinuation at once base and baseless. After being the object of a species of semi-worship, and yielding to every new offer, yet affecting to despise them all, Carême ultimately tabernacled with Baron Rothschild in Paris; and the super-human excellency of his dinners, is it not written in the "Book without a name" of Lady Morgan? And was not his residence there the object of envy, and cause of much melancholy, and opportunity for much eulogy, on the part of George IV.? Well, Anthony Carême would have us believe as much with respect to himself and the King; but we do not believe a word of it; for the royal table was never better cared for by the royal officers, whose duty lay in such care, than at this very period. George IV. is said to have tempted him by offering triple salaries; but all in vain; for London was too *triste* an abiding place for a man whose whole soul, out of kitchen hours, was given to study. And so Carême remained with his Jewish patron until infirmity overtook his noble nature, and he retired to dictate his immortal works (like Milton, very!) to his accomplished daughter. *Les beaux restes* of Carême were eagerly sought after; but he would not heed what was no longer a temptation; for he was realizing twenty thousand francs a year from the bookseller, besides the interest of the money he had saved. Think of it, shade of Milton! Eight hundred pounds sterling *yearly*, for writing on kitchen-stuff! Who would compose epics after that? But Carême's books were epics after their sort, and they are highly creditable to the scribe who wrote them from his notes. Finally, even Antony Carême died, like cooks of less degree; but he had been the imperial despot of European kitchens, had been "be-ringed" by Monarchs, and been smiled on by Princesses; he had received Lords in his kitchen, and had encountered ladies who gave him a great deal for a very little knowledge in return; and finally, as Fulke Greville had inscribed on his tomb that he had been the friend of Sir Philip Sidney, so the crowning joy of Carême's life might have been chiselled on his monument, indicating that he had been the friend of one whom he would have accounted a greater man than the knightly hero in question,—namely, *il Maestro Rossini!* Carême's cup was thereat full; and he died, perfectly convinced that paradise itself would be glad at his coming.

The celebrated Danvers was *chef* to the as celebrated financier Grimoud de la Reynière, in the last century. Grimaud died a martyr to his epicurean tastes. He was dining on a *pâté de foies gras*, when he allowed his appetite to overpower his digestion, and he died of the excess. Barthe, the author of *"Les Fausses Infidélités,"* also fell on the field of the dining-room. He was extremely short-sighted, and ate of every thing on the table. He did not consult his appetite, but his servant, asking him, "Have I eaten of that?" "Have I had any of this?" It was after partaking too freely, both of "this" *and* "that," that poor M. Barthe let his temper get the better of him in an argument, and a stroke of apoplexy sent him under the table. His cook deplored in him the loss of a man of taste.

The cook of the Count de Tessé, Master of the Horse to Marie Antoinette, was famous for dressing artichokes. The great Morillian surpassed him, however; but this feat did not save the artist from ending his days in poverty. The elder Robert was, perhaps, equal to either of them in this or in any other respect connected with his art. The great Carême, ignorant of every thing else, was at least an accomplished cook. There is, as I have said, a tradition that his *petits pâtés*, when they left the Regent's table, were sold, like the second-hand pies from the royal table at Versailles, for fabulous prices. As I have before intimated, it was for Leo X. that Carême the First invented those succulent, but orthodox, dishes, which pleased the pontifical palate at a season when gratification by gravy would have been scandalous! It was in the Baron Rothschild's household that Carême the Second invented his famous *sauce piquante*, the result of his studies under Richaut,

Asne, and the elder Robert. It was in and for France that Carême published the learned and curious work of which he is the reputed author, and which he may have dictated, but which he could not have written. It is marked by philosophical inquiry, instruction and pleasant trifling; and neither book nor reputed author has been excelled by any artist, or any example of kitchen literature, that has appeared since that period.

Before the age of Carême, the popular kitchen in France was not very superior to our own; and the patrons of *tavernes* and *traiteurs* were as coarsely fed as our frequenters of ordinaries. But as royalty fell, the *restaurateurs* rose; and when, in 1786, the cooks of Louis XVI. began to augur badly of their prospects, three provincial brothers, Barthélemy, Mannielles and Simon, opened their famous *restaurant*, "*Les Trois Frères Provençaux*," in the Palais Royal, and constituted themselves the cooks of another King,—the sovereign people. The new establishment created an era in the history of cookery, and men of all shades of politics and Generals of all grades of reputation, resorted to the tables of the Brothers. General Bonaparte and Barras were to be seen there daily, before they took their cheap pleasure at the theatre of Mdlle. Montansier. During the wars of the Empire it was the chosen stage for the farewell banquets of brethren in arms, and at this period the receipts amounted to not less than £500 sterling daily. The triumvirate of proprietors endured longer than any such union in the political world; and it was not till the reign of Louis Philippe that the establishment of "*Les Trois Frères*" descended, under a new proprietary, into a more unpretending position than that which it had proudly sustained during half a century. The *casseroles* of the savoury brothers had remained unshaken, while Kings and constitutions had fallen around them.

The fortune of the Provincial Brothers tempted another country cook from his obscurity; and some four years after the former had set up their tables in the Palais Royal, the immortal Véry thrust his feet into wooden clogs, and trudged from a village on the Meuse up to the capital, to give it a taste of his quality. He enchanted

Marshal Duroc with some of his *plats*, and henceforth his fortune was secure. He married a beautiful woman, whose pen kept his books, whose face attracted customers, and whose heart was devoted to her husband. A quarter of a century sufficed to enable Véry to die immensely rich, after working excessively hard, and to be magnificently entombed in the *Cimetière Montmartre*, under a marble column, which bore the engraved assurance that "his whole life was devoted to the useful arts."

Beauvilliers appeared in Paris about the same time as "the Three Brothers;" he made and unmade his fortune three or four times, and died poor, three years after Véry died so rich. Beauvilliers was the author of "*L' Art du Cuisinier*," a book almost as interesting as "The Art of Dining;" and one cannot name either without standing mentally *chapeau bas!* before the author.

Beauvilliers was famous for his splendid wines and heavy bill. The *Veau qui tette* was renowned for its sheep-trotters. The reputation of others was built upon kidneys; that of Véry, on his *entrées truffées*. The "Three Provincial Brothers" enjoyed a wide esteem for the way in which they dressed cod with garlic. Baleine kept a house that was crowded by the admirers of fish; while that of Robert was distinguished for the graceful attention with which previously ordered dinners were served; and that of Henneveu for the splendid *boudoirs* in which shy couples, too modest to encounter the public gaze could dine in private, and cease to find their modesty oppressive. Beauvilliers', as I have intimated, was a costly house; but it was not *therefore* the most excellent in Paris. The excellence of a dinner is not to be determined by its price. Four years ago an illustrious party dined at Philippe's, in the Rue Montorgueil, at a far lower cost, and after a far more exquisite fashion, than if they had joined the Epicureans of the Clarendon, at £5 per head. The party consisted of Lords Brougham and Dufferin the Honourable W. Stuart, two other "Britishers," and Count D'Orsay and M. Alexandre Dumas. The dinner on this occasion was a *recherchée* affair. It had been as anxiously meditated upon as an epic poem; and it was a far pleasanter thing. "The most successful dishes," says the author of "The Art of Dining," "were the *bisques* the *fritures à l' Italienne*, and the *gigot à la Bretanne*. Out of compliment to the world-wide fame of Lord Brougham and Alexandre Dumas, M. Philippe produced some *Clos de Vougeot*, which, (like his namesake in 'High Life Below Stairs,) he vowed, should never go down the throat of a man whom he did not esteem and admire; and it was voted first-rate by acclamation."

The French repasts are not always good, even when they are rather costly. In 1807, a party of twenty-two sat down to a repast at the younger "Robert's," in Paris. The Amphitryon of the feast was M. Daolouis; and the bill, exclusive of wine, amounted to thirty louis. There were but three or four great dishes, and two or three sauces. The discontent of the guests was general, and the giver of the feast allowed that the dinner was not near so good as that of the "*Société des Mercredis*," at *Le Gacque's*, which cost only seven francs per head, ordinary wine, liqueurs, and coffee included. "*Mais, à dîner, Messieurs, à dîner!*"

DINNER TRAITS.

"For these and all His mercies"——once began Dr. Johnson, whose good custom it was always to thank Heaven for the good things set before him; but he almost as invariably found fault with the food given. And of this see-saw process Mrs. Johnson grew tired; and on the occasion alluded to, she stopped her husband by remarking that it was a farce to pretend to be grateful for dishes which, in two minutes, he would pronounce to be as worthless as the worst of Jeremiah's figs! And so there was no blessing. Mrs. Johnson might have supplied the one employed by merry old Lady Hobart at a dinner where she looked inquiringly, but vainly, for a grace-sayer. "Well," remarked the good ancient dame, "I think I must say as one did in the like case, 'God be thanked!—nobody will say grace!'" It is seldom that "grace" is properly said or sung. The last is a terribly melodious mockery at public dinners; but then every man should silently and fervently make thanksgiving in his own heart. He is an ungracious knave who sits down to a meal without at least a silent acknowledgment of gratitude to Him, without whom there could have been no spreading of the banquet. Such a defaulter deserves to be the bound slave of dyspepsia, until he learn better manners. "Come, gentlemen," Beau Nash used to say, "eat, and welcome!" It was all his grace; and had he said, "Come, gentlemen, be thankful and eat," it would have been more like the Christian gentleman, and less like the "beau."

It was a good old rule that prescribed as a law of numbers at the dinner table, that the company should not be more than the Muses nor less than the Graces. There was not always unlimited freedom of action in the matter; for, by the *Lex Faunia*, a man was forbidden to invite more than three strangers (not of his family) to dinner, except on market days, (three times a month,) when he might invite five. The host was restricted to spending only two and a half *drachmas;* but he might consume annually one hundred and twenty Roman pounds of beef for each person in his house, and eat at discretion of all plants and herbs that grew wild; and, indeed, little restriction was put upon vegetables at all. One consequence was, that this law against luxury begot a great deal of it, and ruined men's stomachs in consequence. When the French Mayor ordered all good citizens in his dark district to carry lanterns at night, he forgot to say a word about candles, and the wits walked about with the lanterns unfurnished. The official rectified the mistake by ordering the candles; but as he omitted to say that these were to be lighted, the public did not profit by the decree. So the *Lex Faunia,* when it allowed unrestrained liberty in thistles, forgot to limit sauces; and vegetables generally were eaten with such luscious aids to which the name of "sauce" was given, that even the grave Cicero yielded to the temptation, spoiled his digestion, and got a liver complaint! After all, it is said that only three Romans could be found who rigorously observed the *Faunia* Law, according to their oaths. These were men more easily satisfied than Apicius, who cried like a child, when, of all his vast fortune, he had only about £250,000 sterling that he could devote to gluttony; or than Lucullus, who never supped in the "Apollo" without its costing him at least ten thousand pounds.

Notwithstanding this, the *Faunia* Law was an absurd impertinence. It was like the folly of Antigonus, who one day, seeing the poet Antagoras in the camp, cooking a dish of congers for his dinner, asked, "O Antagoras, dost thou think that Homer sang the deeds of heroes while he boiled fish?" "And you, O King," returned the poet, "thinkest thou that Agamemnon gained renown for his exploits, by trying to find out who had boiled fish for dinner in his camp?" The moral is, that it is best to leave men at liberty to eat as they like. Society is strong enough to make laws on these matters for itself; and no one now could commit the crime of the greedy Demylos, who, to secure a superb dish of fish for himself, ἐνέπτυσεν εἰς αὐτήν, "spat in it;" and if my readers refer to the chapter illustrating "Their Majesties at Meat," they will find that so dirty a trick was not the reserved privilege of Heathenism.

The Pythagoreans were clean eaters, and dined daily on bread and honey. On the smell of the latter Democritus did not indeed dine, but died. He had determined to commit suicide, and had cut down his allowance to such small rations, that his death was expected daily. But the fun and the festival of Ceres was at hand; and the ladies of his house begged him to be good enough not to spoil the frolic by dying at such a mirthful moment. He consented, asked for a pot of honey, and kept himself alive by smelling at it, till the festival was over, when his family hoped that he would die whenever he found it convenient. He took one sniff more at the pot, and in the effort his breath passed away for ever. There was nothing reprehensible in the conduct of those ladies. They did not outrage the spirit of their times. I think worse of Madame du Deffand, who went out to dine on the day her old lover died, remarking, as she entered the room, how lucky it was that he had expired before six o'clock, as otherwise she would have been too late for the gay party expecting her. The brilliant society who played cards by the side of the bed of the dying Mlle. de l'Espinasse, and counted their tricks while they commented upon her "rattles," may be pronounced as being twice as Pagan as the ladies of the household of Democritus.

A small portion of soup is a good preparative to excite the digestive powers generally for what is to follow. Oysters form a far less commonly safe introduction to the more solid repast, their chill, which even Chablis cannot always rectify, paralysing rather than arousing the stomach. The French *bouilli* after soup is a dangerous vulgarity; for it is simply, as a distinguished professor has styled it, "meat, all but its nourishing juice."

"Poultry," says M. Brillat, "is to the sick man who has been floating over an uncertain and uneasy sea, like the first odour or sight of land to the storm-beaten mariner." But a skilful cook ran render almost any dish attractive to any and every quality of appetite. In this respect, the French and Chinese cooks are really professional brethren; much more so than a general practitioner and a veterinary surgeon!

The Chinese are exceedingly skilful cooks, and exhibit taste and judgment in the selection of their food. With a few beans, and the meal of rice and corn, they will make a palatable and nutritious dish. They eat horse-flesh, rats, mice, and young dogs. Why not? All these are far cleaner feeders than pigs and lobsters. A thorough-bred horse is so nice in his appetite, that he will refuse the corn which has been breathed upon by another horse. The Tonquin birds' nests eaten in China may be described as young Mr. Fudge describes the Paris *grisettes:* "Rather eatable things, those *grisettes*, by the bye!" So are the birds' nests, composed as they are of small shell-fish and a glutinous matter, supplied by the plumed inhabitant of the edible houses. Bears' paws, rolled in pepper and nutmeg, dried in the sun, and subsequently soaked in rice-water, and boiled in the gravy of a kid, form a dish that would make ecstatic the grave Confucius himself.

There are some men for whom cooks toil in vain. The Duke of Wellington's cook had serious doubts as to his master being a great man,—he so loved simple fare. Suwarrow was another General who was the despair of cooks. His biographer says of him, that he was at dinner when Col. Hamilton appeared before him to announce an Austrian victory over the French. The General had one huge plate before him, a sort of Irish stew, with every thing for sauce, from which he ate greedily, spitting out the bones, "as was his custom." He was so delighted with the message and the messenger that he received him as Galba did Icelus, the announcer of Nero's death: with his unwiped mouth, he began kissing the latter, (as the half-shaven Duke of Newcastle once did the bearer of some welcome intelligence,) and insisted on his sitting down and eating from the General's plate, "without ceremony." The great Coligny was, like Suwarrow, a rapid eater; but he was more nice in his diet. The characteristic of Coligny was, that he always used to eat his tooth-picks!

According to ancient rule, an invitation not replied to within four-and-twenty hours was deemed accepted; and from an invitation given and accepted, nothing releases the contracting parties but illness, imprisonment, or death! Nothing suffers so much by delay as dinner; and if punctuality be the politeness of Kings, it should also be the policy both of guests and cooks. Lack of punctuality on the part of the former has been illustrated in the cases of men, of whom it is said that they never saw soup and fish but at their own tables. The late Lord Dudley Ward used to cite two brothers as startling examples of want of punctuality: "If you asked Robert for Wednesday, at seven, you got Charles on Thursday, at eight!" On the other hand, an unpunctual cook is scarcely to be accounted a cook; and an unpunctual master is no worthy of a cook whose dinner is ready to be served at the moment it has been ordered. The great "*artiste*" who dismissed his patron because he never sat down to dinner until after he had kept it waiting for an hour, was thoroughly acquainted with the dignity of his profession.

At the beginning of the present century, it was the custom in France to serve the soup immediately before the company entered the dining-room. The resulting advantage was a simultaneous operation on the part of the guests. The innovation was introduced by Mlle. Emilie Contat, the actress; but it was tolerated only for a season. It was, at the same period, of rigorous necessity, when eggs were eaten at dinner, to crush the empty shell. To allow the latter to leave the table whole was a breach in good manners; but the reason of this prandial law I have never been able to discover. Mlle. Contat was almost as famous for her love of good cheer as our own Foote, and both were, equally often, "on hospitable thoughts intent."

It would appear that in Foote's time Scotland was not famous for a lavish hospitality. The old actor gave some glorious dinners to the first people in the city, and his preliminary proceedings thereto were intended to be highly satirical upon what he considered Scottish parsimony. Every night, before retiring to bed, he used to paper the curls of his wig with Scotch bank-notes,—

promissory paper, as he said, of no value. When his cook waited on him at breakfast-time for orders, "Sam" gravely uncurled his locks, flung the papers to the attendant, as purchase-money for the necessary provisions, and sent her to market in a sedan-chair. But the old actor was as eccentric and ostentatious at his own table in London, as he was any where. When the wines were placed on the board, he solemnly, and as it were with a shade of disgust, inquired, "If any body drank port?" As no one dared to answer in the affirmative at his table, (though the owner took it "medicinally,") he would direct the servant to "take away the ink!"

If Foote dislike port, Bentley, on the other hand, had a contempt for claret, "which," said he, "would be like port, if it could!" The latter individual was not like Flood, the Irishman, who used to raise his glass of claret aloft, with a cry, "If this be war, may we never have peace!"

Comparatively speaking, claret is a very modern wine. Indeed, none of the Bourdeaux wines were fashionable, that is, consumed in large quantities out of the province, before the reign of Louis XV. That Sovereign is said to have asked Richelieu if Bourdeaux wines were "drinkable." "From father to son the Bourbon race," says Bungener, in his incomparable work, "*Trois Sermons sous Louis XIV*," ate and drank with relish; and it was no jest that among the three talents attributed by the old song to Henri IV., (their ancestor,) was numbered that of a "good drinker." "None of them, however, with the exception of the Regent, carried it to excess; but what was not excess for them, would have been so for many others. Louis XIV., at the summit of his glory, and Louis XVI., surrounded by his jailers, submitted equally to the laws of their imperious appetite."

When Louis XV. asked Richelieu if Bourdeaux wines were drinkable, the Duke answered him in terms which I may cite, because of their correctness. "Sire," he replied, "they have, what they call, 'white Sauterne,' which, though far from being so good as that of Monrachet, or that of the little slopes in Burgundy, is still not to be despised. There is also a certain wine from Grave, which smacks of the flint, like an old carbine. It resembles Moselle wine, but keeps better. They have besides, in Medoc and Bazadois, two or three sorts of red wine, of which they boast a great deal. It is nectar fit for the gods, if one is to believe them. Yet it is certainly not comparable to the wine of Upper Burgundy. Its flavour is not bad, however, and it has an indescribable sort of dull, saturnine acid, which is not disagreeable. Besides, one can drink as much as one will. It puts people to sleep, and that is all!" "It puts people to sleep," said the King: "send for a pipe of it!" This is as just a description of good, healthy Bourdeaux, as was that given by Sheridan, I believe, of Champagne: "It does not enter," he said, "and steal your reason; it simply makes a run-away knock at a man's head, and there's an end of it!"

But we are indulging in too much at dinner. Let us return to the solids. Of the self-important personages who daily cross our path, perhaps the most important circumstance of their life is, that they have dined every day of it. But it is a necessity. All men must, or should; and sorrow of the saddest sort is subdued before the anguish of appetite. As Jules Janin says, in his *Gaietés Champêtres*," "Nemorin takes leave of Estelle, and returns home, overcome by hunger. Don Kyrie Eleison de Montauban, after running, all day long, after Mademoiselle Blaisir de-ma-vie, goes and knocks at the door of the neighbouring *château*, and asks to be invited to supper. Niobe herself, in the 'Iliad,' as afflicted as woman can be, does not forget, when night comes, to take a little refreshment." If Seneca derided such doings, it was only after dinner, when appetite failed him. Human nature is made up of sentiment and hunger; and Hood's sentimentalist was not unnatural with his epicurean reminiscences, when he said,—

"'**Twas** at Christmas, I think, that I met with Miss Chase,—
  Yes, for Morris he ask'd me to dine;
And I thought I had never beheld such a face,
  Or so noble a turkey and chine.''

This conglomeration of feeling and feeding is mixed up with all the acts of most importance in our lives; and though Bacchus, Cupid, Comus, and Diana be no longer the deities or the *beati* of the earth, the substantial worship remains; and, as M. Brillat Savarin asserts, under the most serious of all beliefs, we celebrate by repasts not only births, baptisms, and marriages, but even interments.

The last-named writer fixes the era of dinners from the time when men, ceasing to live upon fruits, took to flesh; for then the family necessarily assembled to devour what had been slain and cooked. They know the pleasures of eating, which is the satisfaction of the animal appetite; but the true, refined pleasures of the table date only from the time when Prometheus fired the soul with heavenly flame, from which sprang intellect, with a host of radiant followers in its train. A good dinner sharpens wit, while it softens the heart. A hungry man is as slow at a joke as he is at a favour.

Nelson never knew the sensation of "fear," but when he was asked to dine with a Mayor. He had a horror of great dinners generally: and he was right; for true intellectual enjoyment is seldom there. Horace, with his modest repasts and fair wine, was something of the same opinion as Horatio. Where the wine is indifferent, the guests too numerous and ill-assorted, the spirit heavy, the time short, and the repast too eagerly consumed, there is no dinner, in the legitimate sense of the word. I never so much admired one of the most hospitable of Amphitryons, my friend M. Watier, as when he once prefaced one of his exquisite dinners by saying, with a solemn smile, "*Mes amis, ne nous pressons pas!*" I thought of Talleyrand and his advice to a too willing Secretary:— "*Surtout, pas de zèle!*" The most accomplished professor of his time has laid down, as rules for securing to their utmost degree the prandial pleasures of the table, that the guests do not exceed twelve, so that the conversation be general; that they be of varied occupations, but analogous tastes; that the lighting, cheerful cleanliness, and temperature of the dining-room be carefully considered; that the viands be exquisite rather than numerous, and the wines of the first quality, each in its degree; the progression of the former from the more substantial to the more light; of the latter, from the more brilliant to the more perfumed. It is further enjoined that there be no accelerated movement; all the guests are to consider themselves as fellow-travellers, bound to reach one point at the same time. The rules for the "after dinner" in the drawing room are those more commonly observed in this country, with the exception that "punch" expired when lemons ceased to be dear at the Peace; but the concluding rule is worth noticing:—"That no one withdraw before eleven, and that all be asleep by midnight."

I have spoken of the aids which the French nobility have given to table enjoyment. To them may be added the innovation introduced by Talleyrand, of offering Parmesan with soup, and presenting after it a glass of dry Madeira. Talleyrand had one thing in common with St. Peter,—he was hungry at the hour of mid-day, the dinner time of the Jews; and he would have also come under the anathema in Ecclesiastes which is levelled against the Princes who eat in the morning.

Plato was rather shocked at those people of Italy who made two substantial meals daily; and Seneca was satisfied with one meal,—a dinner of bread and figs. The Roman Priests of Mars dined jollily and sumptuously in a secret room of the temple, and they would not be disturbed. They were like Baillie de Suffren, who, being waited on in India, by a deputation, just as he was sitting down to dine, sent out word that his religion would not allow of his interrupting his repast; and the delegates retired, profoundly struck by the strictness of his conscience. The original dinner hour of the mediæval ages was, as I have elsewhere stated, ten o'clock, the *dixième heure;* hence the name. It was not till the reign of Louis XIV. that so late an hour as noon was fixed for the repast. It is clear, however, that we have not so much changed the hours as changed the names of our meals. A French historian shows us how a Dauphin of France dined (at ten o'clock) in the fifteenth century:—

"As an every-day fare, the Dauphin took for his dinner rice

pottage, with leeks or cabbage, a piece of beef, another of salt pork, a dish of six hens or twelve pullets, divided in two, a piece of roast pork, cheese, and fruit." The supper was nearly as plentiful; but, on particular days, the bill of fare was varied. It is added, that the Barons of the Court had always half of the quantity of the Dauphin; the Knights, the quarter; and the Equerries and Chaplains, the eighth. "Take pride from Priests, and nothing remains," once remarked an Encyclopædist to Voltaire. "Umph!" said Voltaire; "do you, then, reckon gluttony for nothing?" Gluttony, at least, does not seem to have characterized the Dauphin's Chaplains, in the fifteenth century, seeing that they took an eighth where a Baron had half.

But there was a late Prince of Bourbon, who dined after a more singular fashion than that of the Dauphins, his ancestors. I allude to the Prince mentioned by Maurepas, and whose imagination was so sick, that he fancied himself a hare, and would not allow a bell to be rung, lest it should terrify him into the woods, where he might be shot by his own game-keepers, and afterwards served up at his own table. At another time, he had a fancy that he would look well dished up; and, dreaming himself a cauliflower, he stuck his feet in the mould of his kitchen-garden, and called upon his people to come and water him! At last, he pronounced himself dead, and refused to dine at all, as an insult to his spiritual entity. He would have died, had he not been visited by two friends, who introduced themselves as his late father, and the deceased Maréchal de Luxembourg; and who solemnly invited him to descend with them to the shades, and dine with the ghost of Maréchal Turenne. The melancholy Prince accepted with alacrity, and went down with them to a cellar already prepared for the banquet of the departed; and he not only made a hearty meal, but, as long as his fancy made of himself a ghost, he insisted every day on dining with congenial shadows in the coal-cellar! In spite of this monomaniacal fantasy, he was excessively shrewd in all matters of business, especially where his own interests were concerned.

Thus much—briefly and imperfectly, I fear—for Dinner Traits. In the next chapter we will put something on them. And as we have been drawing examples from folly, let us end this section by adding a maxim full of wisdom. "Be not made a beggar," says *Ecclesiasticus,* "by banqueting upon borrowing, when thou hast nothing in thy purse." If this maxim were generally adopted, there might be fewer dinners given, but there would be more dinners paid for. But some people are like the ancient Belgians, who borrowed, and, indeed, lent, upon promises of repayment in the world to come! Many a dinner-giver belongs to the class of the borrowing Belgians of antiquity. After all, there was, perhaps, more intended honesty in the compact than *we* can distinguish. A compact far less honest was made some years ago by an Irish Baronet, who had given so many dinners for which he had not paid, that he was compelled to pledge his plate in order to raise means to satisfy the most pressing of his creditors. Some time subsequently, he induced the pawnbroker to lend him the plate for one evening, on hire; the pawnbroker's men were to wait at the dinner in livery, and convey the silver back as soon as the repast was concluded. The dinner was given and enjoyed, and the company made the attendants drunk, helped the Baronet to pack up his forks, spoons, ladles, and épergnes, with which he set off for Paris, where some of them afterwards visited him at the little dinners he used to give in the Rue de Bourbon, and laughed over the matter as a very capital jest.

I will only add here the record of the fact, that sitting at table to drink, after dinner was over, was introduced by Margaret Atheling, the Saxon Queen of Scotland. She was shocked to see the Scottish gentlemen rise from table before *grace* could be said by her Chaplain, Turgot; and she offered a cup of choice wine to all who would remain. Thence the fashion of hard drinking following the "thanksgiving."

THE MATERIALS FOR DINING.

"All flesh is grass;" and grass has been the foundation of all feasts, in a double sense. It was not only a part of the early repast, in some shape or another, by derivation rather than immediately, but it formed the most ancient seats occupied by primitive and pastoral guests in very remote times. Dr. Johnson approved of asparagus being called "grass." Romulus thought grass a sacred emblem, or he would not have suddenly converted his twelve lay foster-brothers into a priesthood to look after it. When Baber had defeated the Afghans of Kohat, they approached him in despair, and, according to their custom when in extremities, with grass between their teeth, to signify, as the imperial autobiographer says, "We are your oxen." Baber treated them worse than oxen; for the amiable savage says, "All that were taken alive were beheaded by my order, and at the next halting-place we erected a minaret of their skulls.' And the conqueror dined pleasantly in front of the monument.

My friend, Captain Lionel da Costa, tells me, that on accompanying (*en amateur*) a French force on a razzia against an Arab tribe in Algeria, he witnessed the employment of grass as an emblem of defiance rather than of submission. The French officers had assembled the Arab Chiefs, and, telling them that the foreigners had filled up their wells, carried off their cattle, and burned their dwellings, exhorted them to submission, asking them what they would do further against a country so powerful as France? The Arabs, as if impelled simultaneously, stooped to the earth, plucked some scant blades of grass there growing, and began chewing the same in angry silence: this was all their reply, and by it they intimated that they would eat what the earth gave, like the beasts that are upon it, rather than surrender. Their enemies could not refrain from admiring and feeding such adversaries; their mute eloquence was worth more than any thing uttered to tyrants by Power's statue of the Greek Slave, which, according to Mrs. Elizabeth Browning, "thunders white silence,"—a silence that must have been akin to that in the French Tragedy, "*silence qui se fit entendre!*"

Soup, as I have remarked, is not a bad preparation for the stomach. Some one calls it the "preface of a dinner," adding, however, that a good work needs no preface. Soup is of very ancient date. Rebecca and Jacob ate of a potage, in which the meat was cut into small bits *before* the muscular fibres had cooled and become hardened, and stewed in milk, thickened with meal and herbs. The famous French gastronomist, the Marquis de Cussy, was orthodox in his gastronomy, fed well, but heeded the church. His favourite soup in Lent was an onion soup, composed of a score of small bulbs, well cleaned, sliced, and put into a stew-pan, with a lump of fresh butter and a little sugar. They were turned over the fire till they became of a fine golden colour, when they were moistened with broth, and the necessary quantity of bread added. Before the soup was served, its excellence was perfected by the addition of two small glasses of very old Cognac brandy. This Lent fare was, however, only the preface to salmon and asparagus, with which the orthodox epicure mortified his appetite.

The famous Carême did with the soups he discovered, what the most famous navigators have done with the new territories on which they were the first to land; namely, gave them the names of the most illustrious contemporaries then existing. Royalty was honoured in the "*Potage Condé;*" music in that of "Boieldieu;" and the medical faculty, which Carême generally despised, in the "*Soupes à la Broussais, Roques,* and *Segalas;*" poetry was illustrated in the "*Lamartine;*" history in the "*Dumesnil;*" and philosophy in the "*Potage Buffon.*" The last name he thus bestowed, was to his last culinary inspiration just before death, when he conferred on a vegetable soup the name of "Victor Hugo." It was after reading the "*Messéniennes,*" that he created the "*Matelotte à la Delavigne;*" and he paid the doctor who had cured him of an indigestion, by inventing the dish of fish which he called "*Perche à la Gaubert.*" And with this record we will put the fish on our own table.

"It is only the Arabs of the desert that affect to despise fish." This eastern proverb is tantamount to the more homely one of, 'The grapes are sour;" for the Arabs only affect to despise that which they cannot readily obtain. The Jews were prohibited from eating fishes without scales or fins. The Egyptian Priests cared not for fish of any sort, but they generally allowed the people to eat with what appetite they chose, of what the priesthood declined to taste. It is said in the legend, that St. Kevin lived by the fish he caught in the Lake of Glendaloch; and that when the celebrated beauty tempted him, she did it by flattery and suggestion :—

> "'You 're a rare hand at fishing,' says Kate,
> 'It 's yourself, dear, that knows how to hook them;
> But when you have caught them, agrah!
> Don 't you want a young woman to cook them?'"

Gatis, Queen of Spain, was something like Mr. Lover's "Kate;" for, if her subjects caught fish well, she it was who first taught them how to cook what they caught, and how to enjoy what they cooked.

When philosophers were occupied with inquiries touching the soul of an oyster, fish was probably not a popular diet. It certainly was not so in Greece, until a comparatively late period. Then fish became fashionable : the legislature secured their freshness by decreeing that no seller should sit down until he had sold his entire stock; sages discussed their qualities, and tragic writer, introduced heroes holding dialogues on the qualities of fish-sauce. There was a Greek society at that day "against cruelty to fish," by devouring what also, allegedly, made the devourer ferocious and inhuman; but general society did not allow its appetite to be influenced thereby.

The Romans were enthusiastic for the mullet. It was for them *the* fish, *par excellence*. It was sometimes served up six pounds in weight, and such a fish was worth £60 sterling. It was cooked on the table, for the benefit and pleasure of the guests. In a glass vessel filled with brine made from water, the blood of the mackerel, and salt, the live mullet, stripped of its scales, was enclosed; and as its fine pink colour passed through its dying gradations, until paleness and death ensued, the *convives* looked on admiringly, and lauded the spectacle.

The turbot was next in estimation; but as, occasionally, offending slaves were flung into the turbot preserves for the fish to feed upon, some gastronomists have affected to be horror-stricken at the idea of eating a *turbot à la Romaine;* quite forgetting that so many of our sea-fish, in their own domain, feed largely on the human bodies which accident, or what men call by that name, casts into the deep. Our own early ancestors in Britain were said to have entirely abstained from fish. In later days, however, here as in France, the finny tribes were protected by royal decrees; and certain fish were named—the sturgeon was one—as to be caught for the royal table alone. In the same days porpoises and seals were devoured by the commonalty, and the latter knew not the art of the cooks of Louis XIV., who could so dress fish as to give it the taste of any flesh they pleased to fix on as an object of imitation. By this means, the King in Lent, while he obeyed the church, enjoyed the gratification of feeling as though he were cheating Heaven,—and with impunity, too!

The most curious fish of which I have ever read, were those of a lake attached to a Burgundian convent, and which were always of the same number as the monks. If one of these sickened and died, the same circumstance occurred with the fish; and if a new brother appeared in the refectory, there was also sure to be found a new denizen in the pond. These fish were, of course, piously inclined; but they did not come up, in that respect, to the **parrot of** Cardinal Ascanius, which could not only repeat the Creed, but could maintain a thesis! I believe that the Burgundian **fish** were principally perch; and they *are* an eccentric fish. Arthur Young says, that "about the year 1760, perch first appeared in all the lakes of Ireland and in the Shannon at the same time."

As a singularity with respect to the cooking of fish, I may here mention that observed by the Romans with the *sepia*, or "cuttle-fish." They invariably took out the eyes before boiling it. It is in allusion to this custom that Trachalion says, in the *Rudens*,—

" Age nunc jam,
Jube oculos elidere, itidem ut sepiis faciunt coqui.'

I think I have read somewhere, that the cuttle-fish was esteemed a fitting sacrifice to the gods; but I do not know if pious people had their pet *sepiæ*, as they had their pet lambs and pigs, ("*Sunt domi agni et porci sacres*," says the orthodox husband in the *Rudens*,) reared for the purpose of being offered at the altars.

The sturgeon is at this day, in China, reserved for the imperial table. At those of Greece it was introduced by sound of trumpet, and it was almost as esteemed a subject at those of Rome, until Vespasian condescended not to care for it, and to bring other fish into fashion. "It is *caviare* to the general," is a proverb which Shakespeare has popularized. The *caviare* is the roe of the sturgeon dried; that of the larger sturgeon, which produces hundredweights of eggs, and tons of oil, is *caviare* for the general, and is not worth eating. The delicate white *caviare* is the produce of the smaller sturgeon, and it is highly esteemed by gastronomists. It forms a great portion of the food taken by the Greeks during their long Lent.

We have heard of an American who tried to tame an oyster. The Romans were more successful with their sea-eels, which would come when called, and feed from the hands of men, who occasionally fattened them upon live slaves. Vedius Pollio would have grown sick and disgusted, if he had been asked to eat one of these slaves; but he was particularly fond of the fish that had been fed upon such fare; and so he only ate his slaves at second-hand; for *their* flesh was declared by him to have greatly improved the taste of the eel. Epicures with less ferocious appetites preferred the fish that had been fattened upon veal steeped in blood. Vitellius put the fish altogether out of fashion by only eating the roes; which were procured for him at a great expense; and Heliogabalus caused even the roes to cease to be modish, by forcing them upon the Mediterranean peasants, who got as sick of their repasts as English servants in the Scottish Highlands grow weary of the everlasting sameness of their dinners consisting of venison and salmon. The Egyptians placed the sea-eel in their Pantheon; and even the unorthodox cannot deny that he was as good a deity as any to be found there; and we are told that among the Sybarites the fishers and vendors of the eel were exempt from taxation! The origin of these honours is, however, unknown. Nearly as great were offered, even in Rome, to the fish known as the seawolf, which abounded in the most filthy parts of the Tiber, and which some epicures distinguished by the appellation of "child of the gods." The Romans paid high prices for it, as they did for the regicide lamprey,—a fish which killed our first Henry, and which Italian cooks used to kill, as the murderers did maudlin Clarence, in his Malmsey butt, by plunging the victim, decked for the sacrifice with a nutmeg in his mouth, and a clove in either gill, into a pan of Candian wine; after which, covered with almonds, bread crumbs, and spices, he was exposed to a slow fire, and then to the jaws that impatiently awaited him. It was once as popular as the tunny,—a fish, by the way, which once so enriched the city of Sinope, that the coin minted there bore the figure of the fish. Where they are found at all, it is generally in shoals; but these are never to the extent which Pliny speaks of, when he says, that they so obstructed the fleet of Alexander, that the pilots of the Macedonian madman were compelled to shape a different course; and though they are to be found in something like abundance in the Mediterranean, yet tourists who resort thither must not expect to see realized the gay picture of Vernet. It does not appear, however, that the tunny was ever in such favour at ancient tables as the eel, which was greedily eaten where

6*

it was not devoutly worshipped, or where medical ordinances had not been directed against it, as unfavourable to the weak of digestion, and perilous to those affected by pulmonary diseases. The pike, emblem of fecundity and example of lengthened years, was still less popular. The carp, which even surpasses the pike in fecundity, and is a long liver to boot, was, on the other hand, an especial favourite, but it was served up with sauces that would certainly not tempt a modern gastronomist to eat a fish which is seldom worth eating, and which is almost defiant of digestion. Carp, reduced to a pulp, and served up with sows' paps, and yolk of egg, must have been as nasty as gold fish with carrots and myrtle leaves,—the delight of the Roman loungers at their "Blackwall," on the Tiber. So the Greeks spoiled good cod by eating it with grated cheese and vinegar; and the Romans made perch more indigestible than it was before, by swallowing Damascus plums with it. But the ancients had strangely accommodating stomachs: a sauce of honey could induce them to eat cuttle-fish. Garlic and cheese made the swordfish delicacies; the rhombus floated into Greek stomachs on a sauce of wine and brine; the ladies of Rome ate onions with the muzil, and pine-nuts with the pilchard. The more refined Greeks, on the other hand, would not touch the pilchard; and the same difference of taste existed with regard to the loach; while, again, both Rome and Greece united in admiration of the gudgeon. To neither of these countries was the herring known. The Scots found the fish, and the Dutch bought, pickled, and sold, or ate them; and it is said, that Charles V., in 1536, ate a herring upon the tomb of Beuckels, the first salter of that fish, and therewith the friend of the poor and enricher of the State. The profit realized by Holland exceeded two millions and a half sterling, annually. But neither Greece nor Rome felt the want of the herring while there was an abundant supply of the favourite oyster. This shell-fish was easily procured by the Greeks from Pelorus, Abydos, and Polarea; by the Romans, from Brindés, the Lake of Lucrinus, Armorica, and even from Britain. The Romans were hardly worthy of the delicacy, seeing that they abused it by mincing oysters, muscles, and sea hedgehogs together, stewed the whole with pine-almonds and hot condiments, and devoured the mixture scalding! Others, however, ate them raw, when they were opened at table by a slave; and the larger the fish, the more the Roman epicures liked them. They were not only eaten before a feast to stimulate the appetite, but during a banquet, when the appetite began to be palled. They excited to fresh exertion, and it was a cleaner custom (perhaps) than that imperial one of exonerating the stomach by tickling the throat with a peacock's feather. The Bordeaux oyster was the favourite fish of most of the Emperors. It is very inferior to the Whitstable oyster, however, and also to that which goes by the name of "Colchester," and which is not caught there. The passion for the savoury fish is well illustrated in the epitaph which says,—

> "Tom ⸺⸺⸺
> Lies buried in these cloisters;
> If, at the last trump,
> He does not quickly jump,
> Only cry '*Oysters!*'"

If the Emperors affected oysters, the gods themselves patronized mussels, a dish of which was contributed by Jupiter to the wedding banquet of Hebe. The mythological sanction has, however, failed to render the mussel popular, and for good reasons. It is often extremely poisonous, and in certain conditions of the stomach they who eat muscles may reckon for being attacked by violent cutaneous disorders, painfully participated in by the oppressed intestines.

It was otherwise with the tortoise, the blood of which was reckoned good in cases of ophthalmia, and the flesh of which was eagerly devoured. The natural history of the products of those early times seems to have been written by philosophers with very poetical imaginations. We read of shells of tortoises being converted into roofs of cottages, as we are told by Pliny of crawfish measuring four cubits in length. It was then that men ate lobsters *au naturel*, and crabs converted into sausages. But this latter dish was a more dainty one than that afforded by the frog,—the abhorrence of early gastronomists, but the delight of many French and German epicures, who first find delight in angling for these unclean beasts with a bait of yellow soap, and then swallowing, with delight more intense, the hind-quarters of the animal they have caught. But if the moderns swallow frogs, the ancients ate the polypus, and which were the nastiest even I could not tell! The Romans were especially fond of fish; and some "fast" epicures among them not only had preserve ponds of fish on the roofs of their houses, but little rivulets stocked therewith around the dinner-table, whence the guests selected their fish, and delivered them to be cooked.

It was once thought that the prawn, or shrimp, was somehow necessary to the production of soles, acting, it was believed, as a sort of nurse, or foster-parent, to the spawn. But this I suppose to be about as true as that soles always swim in pairs, with three-pennyworth of shrimps behind them, ready for sauce.

I remember two anecdotes connected with fish at table, which a guest may retail when he is next at that period of the repast. Talleyrand was dining, in the year 1805, with the Minister of Finance, who did the honors of his house in the very best style. A very fine carp was on the table opposite to Talleyrand, but the fish was already cold. "That is a magnificent carp," said the financier: "how do you like it? It came from my estate of Vir-sur-Aisne." "Did it?" said Talleyrand, "but why did you not have it cooked *here!*" This reply was not as fatal to the utterer of it, as a remark once made by Poodle Byng at Belvoir Castle. "Ah, ah!" he exclaimed, as he saw the fish uncovered at the Duke of Rutland's board, "my old friend Haddock! I have not seen a haddock, at a gentleman's table, since I was a boy." The implication shut the gates of Belvoir on the unlucky Poodle from that day forward. He was never again the Duke's guest.

Some French writers have asserted, after tracing the "vestiges of creation" according to a fashion of their own, that man origin ally sprang from the ocean; and that his present condition is one of development, the consequence of life ashore, and exposure to atmospheric air! According to this theory, I suppose, Venus Anadyomene was the Eve of our fishy generation, and mermaids show the transition state, when our ancestors were of both land and sea, and yet properly of neither!

As judges of fish, the moderns are inferior to the ancients. A Greek or Roman epicure could, at first sight, tell in what waters the fish before him had been caught. This sort of wisdom is, however, not uncommon to oyster eaters, who swallow so greedily what contains little nourishment, but what may be easily digested. It was not unusual, some years ago, in France, for a gourmand to prepare for dinner by swallowing a gross, or a dozen dozen, of oysters! Twelve of them, including the liquor, will weigh four ounces; and the gross, four pounds (Troy)!—a pretty amount of ballast to take in freight. The skin of such a feeder had need be in a good condition; but so, indeed, ought that of every one who cares for his digestion. When we remember that a person in health, who takes eight pounds of aliment during twenty-four hours of his wakefulness, discharges five of the eight pounds solely through the pores by perspiration, it will at once be seen that to hold the skin clean, and keep the pores unobstructed, is of first-rate necessity for the sake of digestion and comfort.

There are sea-board populations who live almost exclusively on fish. They feed their domestic animals upon it, and with it manure their ground; so that the pork that they may occasionally indulge in, acquires a fish-like flavour, and their bread is but a consequence of the plentiful rottenness of sprats. Such populations are usually lean and sallow, but they are strong-muscled and active-limbed; and altogether they afford good testimony in favour of the efficacy of a fish diet, when no better is to be had. As a diet, fish is only so far stimulating that it augments the lymph rather than renews the blood. It is a puzzle to many gastronomic philosophers that fish was so constant a diet of the monkish orders. Its heating quality hardly suited men who were required to be ever coolly contemplative. But this matter I leave to the philosophers to determine. One of them,—that is, a gastronomic philosopher,—M. Fayot, says, that "if you would have a dinner composed altogether of fish, the meal should consist of a "turbot, a large salmon done in a *court-bouillon*, flanked with aromatic herbs, and covered with a fresh winding-sheet of delicate seasoning. In such dinners, sea-fish have, undoubtedly, the first rank; and among them the Cherbourg lobster, the shrimp of Honfleur, the cray-fish of the Seine, and the smelts of that river's mouth, and numerous fresh-water fish mingle agreeably. Salmon and turbot should be done briskly; drink afterwards a glass of those old wines which give a digestive action to the stomach." With M. Fayot, the turbot is "the king of fish, especially in Lent, as it is then of most majestic size. You may serve up salmon with as much ornament as you will, but a turbot asks for nothing but aristocratic simplicity. On the day after he makes his first appearance, it is quite another affair. It may then be disguised; and the best manner of effecting this is, to dress him *à la Béchamel*,—a preparation thus called from the Marquis de Béchamel, who, in the reign of Louis XIV., for ever immortalized himself by this one *ragoût*."

The *Almanach des Gourmands* speaks of a Lorraine carp which was fed on bread and wine, and which was twice sent to the Paris market, in the care of a courier who travelled by the mail. It returned to its native waters in default of a purchaser willing to give thirty *louis-d'ors* for the monstrous delicacy. This was when fish dinners were much in vogue in Paris. There was then a *table-d'hôte* for a fish repast only, held at a house profanely called, "The Name of Jesus." This house stood in the "Cloitre St. Jacques de l'Hôpital," and every Wednesday and Friday it was crowded by the Clergy, who dined magnificently on *maigre* fare, for about 2s. a head. It is of one of these Fayot recounts a pleasant story, the locality, however, of which was the *Rocher de Cancale*. A certain Abbé dined there so copiously of salmon that a fit of indigestion was the consequence. Some days afterwards, when celebrating Mass, the savoury memories of the fish flocked into his mind; and he was heard to murmur, not the *meâ culpâ* of the "*Confiteor*," but, as he quietly beat his breast, "Ah! that capital salmon! that capital salmon!"

Of the more nutritive species of fish, turbot, cod, whiting, haddock, flounder, and sole, are the least heating. Of these, the cod is the least easy of digestion, though turbot is quite as difficult of digestion when much lobster sauce is taken with it. The crimping of cod facilitates the digestion of the fish. Sole and whiting are easily digested. Salmon is nutritive, but it is oily, heating, and not very digestible; far less so than salmon trout. The favourite parts of most of these fish are the least fit for weak stomachs, and the most trying to strong ones. Salmon, caught after the spawning season has commenced, is almost poisonous; and eels are objectionable at all seasons, from their excessive oiliness. Shellfish generally may be put down as "indigestible," particularly the under-boiled lobsters of the London market. The mussel is especially so; and these are not rendered innocuous by the removal of the beard, which is not more hurtful than any other part. Shellfish, and, indeed, fish generally, affects the skin, by sympathy with the stomach. The effect is, sometimes, as if a poison had been generated: at others it very sensibly affects the odour of the cutaneous secretions. The effect was thoroughly understood when the Levitical Priests, like those of Egypt, were prohibited from eating fish. The prohibition was based upon a just principle.

The Egyptian and Levitical Priests were more obedient to such prohibitions than St. Patrick, who once, overcome by hunger, helped himself to pork chops on a fast-day. An angel met him with the forbidden cutlets in his hand; but the saint popped them into a pail of water, pattered an Ave-Mary over them, and our indulgent Lady heeded the appeal by turning them into a couple of respectable and orthodox-looking trout. The angel looked perplexed, and went away, with his index finger on the side of his nose. And see what came of it! In Ireland, meat dipped into water, and christened by the name of "St. Patrick's Fish," is commonly eaten there even on fast-days, and to the great regret of all those who eat greedily enough to acquire an indigestion.

St. Patrick's fish ought to have fetched as high a price as the four cod which formed the sole supply in Billings-gate-market on one of the great frost-days in January, 1809; they were sold to one dealer for fourteen guineas. During the same month, salmon were sold at a guinea a pound! When fish is so high-priced, it is time to have done with it. So *enlevez!* and let us to the succeeding courses of viands more substantial. While the fish is being removed, I will merely relate that it was the practice of Sir Joshua Reynolds, who gave plentiful dinners to admirable men, in his house in Leicester-square, always to choose his own fish, of which he was a capital judge. He was, on those occasions, ever the first visitor to the fish-shop still existing, in its primitive simplicity, in Coventry-street. He selected the best; and later in the day, his niece, Miss Palmer, used to call, dispute the price, and pay for the fish. Sir Joshua's table is said to have been too crowded, both as to guests and dishes, while there was scant attendance, and a difficulty of getting served; but the hilarity compensated for all. The guests enjoyed themselves with a vulgar delight that would have very much ruffled the dignity of such a pompous president at repasts as the bewigged, bepatched, and bepowdered Sir Peter Lely.

With the introduction of animal food is dated the era of professional cooks; and that era itself is set down by M. Soyer, a competent authority, as having commenced in the year of the world 1656. Other authorities give 2412 as the proper date, when Prometheus, or Fore-thought, as his name implies, taught men the use of fire, and cooked an ox. But I think that both dates and mythology are somewhat loose here, and that the period is easier of conjecture than of determination. Ceres killed the pig that devoured her corn, Bacchus the goat that nibbled at the tendrils of the vine, and Jupiter the ox that swallowed his sacred cakes; and the animals slain by deities were roasted and eaten by men. Another tradition is, that roast meat originally smoked only on the altars of the gods, and that the Priests lived on the pretended sacrifices, until some lean and greedy heretic, having wickedly pilfered the sacred viands, so improved under the diet, that his example was promptly followed, and men took to animal food, in spite of the thunder of gods and the anathemas of Priests. I need not say where there is better authority than all these pretty tales for man's subduing to his use and service the beasts of the earth, the birds of the air, and the fishes of the sea.

A rearer of cattle was, in the olden time, an aristocrat in his way. The gods looked after his herds, and the law gave its protection where Olympian divinity so often proved worthless. Bubona sat the watchful goddess of their fattening; and it was she who blessed the cabbages steeped in vinegar, the straw and wheat-bran, and the bruised barley, wherewith the oxen were prepared for the cattle-show or the market. In the latter, the office of the Roman Prefect fixed the selling price: the breeder could neither ask more nor take less than according to the official tariff. There was a singular custom at one time in Rome, which proves, however, that the seller had a voice in declaring the value of his stock. Purchaser and vendor simultaneously closed, and then suddenly opened one of their hands, or some of the fingers. If the number of fingers on both sides was even, the vendor obtained the price which he had previously asked for his meat; but if the number was uneven, the buyer received the viands for the sum he had just before tendered. This was as singular a custom as, and a more honest one than, that adopted by the first Dutch settlers in America. In their trading with the Indians a Dutchman's fist was established as the standard of weight, with this understanding, that when a Dutchman was selling to an Indian his fist weighed a pound, but that it should only be half that weight when the Hollander was a purchaser!

The Roman markets were well supplied, and the pig seems to have been the national favourite. The Emperors used to distribute thousands of pounds of pork to the poor, as on festive occasions we, less magnificently, divide among the needy our time-honoured English roast beef. There was even an edict against making sausages of any thing *but* pork,—an edict which is much needed in some of our suburbs, where "pork sausages" are made of any thing but pig;—and, after all, they could not be made of a dirtier animal. But the grave Romans strangely reverenced this unclean beast. Pliny places him only one degree below humanity; and certainly the porcine and human stomachs are very much alike! In the East, our ancient friend was a Pariah, and his position among the unclean was fixed by a Jewish doctor, who said, that if ten measures of leprosy were flung into the world, nine of them would naturally fall to the execrated pig. There is no doubt that the eating of the flesh of the pig in hot climates would bring on diseases in the human system akin to leprosy; and this fact may have tended to establish the unpopularity of the animal throughout the East, and to count also for the prohibition. Galen, however, prescribed it as good food for people who worked hard; and there are modern practitioners who maintain that it is the most easily digested of all meats. It is certainly more easy of digestion than that respectable impostor, the boiled chicken, which used so cruelly to test, and defy, the feeble powers of invalids.

Pigs were fatted, both in Greece and Rome, until they had attained nearly the bulk of the elephant. These fetched prices of the most "fancy" description; and they were served up whole, with an entire Noah's-ark collection of smaller animals inside, by way of stuffing. A clever cook could so dress this meat as to make it have the flavour of any other viand; and the first culinary *artistes* of the day prided themselves on the preparation of a *ragoût* composed of young pigs stifled before they were littered. The mother would have had no difficulty in performing this feat herself for her own young, if sows generally had been as huge as the one mentioned by Varro, and which he says was so fat as to be incapable of movement, and to be unconscious that a mouse, with a young family, had settled in the folds of her fat, where they lived like mites in cheese.

In another page, I have spoken of what were called "the sacred pigs and lambs." Menæchmus, in Plautus, asks the price of the "*porci sacres, sinceri.*" "*Sacres*" was applied to all animals intended for immolation. The *sinceri porci* were the white and spotless pigs offered to the Lares on behalf of the insane. The merchant who gives instruction, in the *Pseudolus*, to his servant, as to the splendid repast that is to be served up on his birthday, is very particular on the subject of pork; and he shows us what parts form a dish that might tempt princes,—the ham, and the head: "*Pernam, callum, glandium, sumen, facito in aquâ jaceant.*"

If men were not, anciently, fonder of beef than of pork, the reason, perhaps, was, that the ox was religiously reverenced, because of his use to man, whereas the pig was really of no value at all but for consumption. The excellence of the ox as food was, nevertheless, very early ascertained, and acted on by some primitive people. The Jews were permitted to eat of that of which Abraham had offered a portion to angels; and calf and ox were alike an enjoined food. The Greeks, too, devoured both with much complacency, as they also did tripe, which was deemed a dainty fit for heroes. Indeed, for tripe there was an ancient and long-standing propensity among the early nations. It formed the chief dish at the banquets of men who met to celebrate the victory of mortals and gods over the sacrilegious Titans.

The lamb and the kid have smoked upon divine altars and humble tables. The Greeks were especially fond of both, and the Romans were like them in this respect; but the Egyptians religiously abstained from the kid; and more than one Eastern nation held, as of faith, that the lamb was more fitting as an offering to the gods than as a dish for men. On the other hand, there were people who preferred the flesh of the ass, which was not an uncommon dish at Roman tables, where dogs, too, were served as a dainty; for Hippocrates had recommended them as a refined food; and the Greeks swallowed the diet thus authoritatively described. The Romans, however, are said to have eaten the dog out of vengeance. The curs of the Capitol were sleeping, when the sacred and watchful geese saved it by their cackling; and thence arose, it is believed, the avenging appetite with which puppies, dressed like hares, were tossed into the stomachs of the unforgiving Romans. They were also sacrificed to the Dog-star.

It is worthy of remark, that Mexico was partly conquered by aid of the pig. Cortez was in need of supplies of fresh meat on his march, and he took with him a large herd of swine,—sows as well as pigs,—" these animals being very suitable for a long journey, on account of their endurance of fatigue, and because they multiply greatly." The Indians, on most occasions, however, appear to have been able to have supplied him plentifully: for we read, that at Campeche, for instance, in return for his presents, they placed before him partridges, turtle-doves, goslings, cocks, hares, stags, and other animals which were good to eat, and bread made from Indian corn, and fruits. It was, for all the world, like meeting a burglar at your dining-room door, and asking him to stay and take breakfast, before he went off with the plate!

When the uncle of Job entertained his heavenly visitors, the dish he placed before them was "roasted veal," of a freshly killed calf. It was tender, because the muscular fibres had not had time to become stiff; and its pleasant accompaniments were melted butter, milk, and meal-cakes. Veal is the national dish of Germany, where mutton is scarce, and calves abundant. It is poor food at any time; but the German veal is the most tasteless of meats. There, indeed, is applicable the smart saying of that ardent young experimentalist, who declared that eating veal was as insipid an enjoyment as kissing one's sister! Cardinal Zinzendorf used to denounce pork quite strongly. He deemed pigs to have been of no use but for their blood, of which he himself used to make a bath for his legs, whenever he had the gout. Quixote Bowles, on the other hand, held pig, in any form, to be the divinest of meats, and the animal the happiest of all created things. With true Apician fervour, he would travel any distance to feast on the sight of a fatted porker; and a view of that prize of Prince Albert's, which was so uniformly huge that, at first sight, it was difficult to distinguish the head from the tail, would have made him swoon with gentle ecstasy. Bowles was an epicure in bacon; and, whenever he went out to dinner, he took a piece of it, of his own curing, in his pocket, and requested the cook to dress it. The people of the Society Islands carry respect for pigs even beyond the compass of Bowles. They believe that there is a distinct heaven for the porcine souls; and this paradise of pigs is called by them "Ofatuna." The Polynesian pig is certainly a more highly favoured animal than his cousin in Ireland; for, in a Polynesian farm household, every pig has his proper name, as regularly as every member of the family. Perhaps, the strangest cross of pigs ever heard of, was that of Mr. Tinney's famous breed for porkers,—Chinese, crossed by a half-African boar: the meat was said to be delicious. Finally, with respect to pigs, they are connected with a popular expletive, with which they have, in reality, nothing to do. "Please the pigs!" is shown, I think by Southey in his Espriella, to be a corruption of "Please the pyx!" The pyx is the receptacle which contains the consecrated wafer on Romish altars; and the exclamation is equal to "Please God!" The corruption is as curious a one as that of "tawdry," from "'t Audrey," or St. Audrey's fair, famous for the sale of frippery,—showy, cheap, and worthless.

They who are half as particular about mutton as Quixote Bowles was about pork, would do well to remember, that sheep continue improving as long as their teeth remain sound, which is usually six years; and that, at all events up to this time, the older the mutton, the finer the flavour. A spayed ewe, kept five years before she is fattened, is superior to any wether mutton. Dr. Paris, however, states that wedder mutton is in perfection at five years old, and ewe mutton at two years; but he acknowledges that the older is the more digestible. It is the glory of one locality, famous for its sheep, that the rot was never known to be caught upon the South Downs. It is further said, that a marsh, occasionally overflowed with salt water, was never known to rot sheep. A curious fact is stated by Young, in his "Survey of Sussex;" namely, that Lord Egremont had, in his park, three large flocks of the Hereford, South-Down, and Dishley breeds; and that these three flocks kept themselves perfectly distinct, although each had as much opportunity of mixing with the others as they had with themselves.

I have alluded, in another page, to a circumstance first noticed,

I believe, by Madame Dacier,—that there is no mention of boiled meat, as food, throughout Homer's Iliad. The fair commentator is right; but "boiling" is, nevertheless, used by the poet as a simile. When (in the twenty-first book) Neptune applies his flames to check the swelling fury of Scamander,—

> "The bubbling waters yield a hissing sound,
> As when the flames beneath a caldron rise,
> To melt the fat of some rich sacrifice.
> Amid the fierce embrace of circling fires
> The waters foam, the heavy smoke aspires:
> So boils th' imprisoned flood, forbid to flow,
> And, choked with vapours, feels his bottom glow!"

This is not a very elegant version of the original, it must be confessed, albeit the translation is Pope's. It is, however, the only reference to boiling to be found in Homer, and here the fat of the sacrifice boiled down is that of a pig.

Κνίσσῃ κελδόμενος απαλοτρεφέος σιάλοιο.

I do not know that I can take leave of mutton and the meats by doing them greater honour than by mentioning that Napoleon ate hastily of mutton before he entered on the contest at Leipsic, and he lost the triumph of the bloody day through a fit of indigestion.

Before the era of kitchen gardens, scurvy was one of the processes by which the English population was kept down. Cabbages were not known here until the period of Henry VIII.; and turnips are so comparatively new to some parts of England, that their introduction into the northern counties is hardly a century old. A diet exclusively of animal food is too highly stimulant for such a climate as ours; and an exclusively vegetable diet is far less injurious in its effects. No meat is so digestible as tender mutton. It has just that degree of consistency which the stomach requires. Beef is not less nutritious, but it is rather less easy of digestion, than mutton; much, however, depends upon the cooking, which process may, really not inaptly, be called the first stage of digestion. The comparative indigestibility of lamb and veal arises from the meat being of a more stringy and indivisible nature. Old laws ordained that butchers should expose no beef for sale, but of an animal that had been baited. The nature of the death rendered the flesh more tender. A coursed hare is thus more delicious eating than one that has been shot; and pigs whipped till they die, may be eaten with relish, even by young ladies who pronounce life intolerable. A little vinegar, administered to animals about to be killed, is said, also, to render the flesh less tough; and it is not unusual to give a spoonful of this acid to poultry, whose life is required for the immediate benefit of the consumer. Some carnivorous animals have been very expert at furnishing their own larder. Thus we read, that the eagles in Norway exhibit as much cunning in procuring their beef as can well be imagined; and more, perhaps, than can well be believed. They dive into the sea we are told, then roll in the sand, and afterwards destroy an ox by shaking the sand in his eyes, while they attack him. I think the French eagle tried a similar plan with the English bull, during the wars of the Empire, and very ineffectually. It dived into the sea, and rolled itself in the sand at Boulogne, and shook abundance of it across the Channel; but the English bull more quietly shook it off again from his mane, and the eagle turned to an easier quarry in Austria. Animals not carnivorous have sometimes been as expert. There have been horses, for instance, who have had their peculiar appetite also for meat. Some twenty years ago, we heard of one at Brussels, which, fond of flesh generally, was particularly so of raw mutton, which it would greedily devour whenever it could get, as it sometimes did, at a butcher's shop.

The Jews, it is said, never ate poultry under their old dispensation; and French gastronomists asert that this species of food was expressly reserved to enrich the banquets of a more deserving people. About the merits of the people the poultry, and winged animals generally, would perhaps have an opinion of their own, were they capable of entertaining one; for nowhere, as in France, have those unfortunate races been so tortured, and merely in order to extract out of their anguish a little more exquisite enjoyment for the palled appetites of epicures. The turkey has, perhaps, the least suffered at the hands of the Gallic experimentalists, though *he* has not altogether escaped. The goose has been the most cruelly treated, especially in the case of his being kept caged before a huge fire, and fed to repletion until he dies, the Daniel Lambert of his species, of a diseased liver, which is the most delicious thing possible in a pie. But it is ignoble treatment for the only bird which is said to be prescient of approaching earthquakes. The goose saved Rome, and was eaten in spite of his patriotism. He is skilled in natural philosophy, and his science does not save him from death and sage-and-onions. Nay, even a female Sovereign of England could not hear of the defeat of the Spanish Armada without decreeing "death to the geese," until the time comes when Mr. Macaulay's Huron friend shall be standing on a fragment of Blackfriar's Bridge, sketching the ruins of St. Paul's.

It must be allowed, however, that the scientific ladies of farmyards have improved upon the knowledge of their ancestresses. Formerly, of turkeys alone, full one-half that pierced the shell perished; but now we rear more than fifteen out of twenty. I do not know, however, that that fact is at all consolatory to the turkey destined to be dined upon.

Themistocles ordered his victory over Xerxes to be yearly commemorated by a cock-fight; and the bird itself was eaten out of honour, as dogs in Rome were for reasons of vengeance. At Rome, the hen was the favourite bird; but hens were consumed in such quantities, that Fannius, the Consul, issued a decree prohibiting their being slain for food, during a certain period; and, in the meantime, the Romans "invented the capon." The duck was devoured medicinally, that is, on medical assurance that it was good diet for weak stomachs; and there were great sages who not only taught that duck, as a food, would maintain men in health, but that, if they were ill, the ample feeding thereon would soon restore them again. Mithridates, it is alleged, ate it as a counter-poison; other people, of other times and places, simply because they liked it. The goose was in as much favour as the duck with the digestion-gifted stomachs of the older races. It was *the* royal diet in Egypt, where the Monarch did not, like Queen Elizabeth, recommend it to the people, but selfishly decreed that it was only to be served at his own table. Gigantic geese, with ultra-gigantic livers, were as much the delight of epicures in Rome, as the livers, if not the geese, are now the *voluptas suprema* of the epicure of France, and of countries subject to the French code of diet. A liver weighing as much as the rest of the animal without it, was a *morceau*, in Rome, to make a philosopher's mouth water. This was not proof of a more depraved taste than that exhibited by a Christian Queen of France, who spent sixteen hundred francs in fattening three geese, the delicate livers of which alone Her Majesty intended to dine upon. The pigeon and guinea-hen never attained to such popularity as the goose and duck; while the turkey, and especially the truffled turkey-hen, has its value sufficiently pointed out by the saying of the gastronome, that there must be two at the eating of a truffled turkey,—the eater and the turkey! The turkey, originally from the East, was slowly propagated in Europe, and the breed appears to have gradually passed away, like the bustard in England. It was brought hither again from America, and its first re-appearance is said to have been at the wedding-dinner of Charles IX. of France.

The turkey was not protected, as the peacock was by Alexander, by a decree denouncing death against whomsoever should kill this divine bird, with its devilish note. The decree did not affect Quintus Hortensius, who had one served up at the dinner which celebrated his accession to the office of Augur. Tiberius, however, preserved the peacock with great jealousy, and it was only rich breeders that could exhibit this bird at their banquets.

A man who passes through Essex may see whole "herds" of geese and ducks in the fields there, fattening without thought of the future, and supremely happy in their want of reflection. These birds are "foreigners;" at least, nearly all of them are so. They are Irish by birth, but they are brought over by steam, in order to be perfected by an English education; and when the due state of perfection has been attained, they are, like many other young people partaking of the "duck" or the "goose," transferred to London, and "done for."

Some gastronomic enthusiasts, unable to wait for their favourite birds, have gone in search of them. This was the case with the oily Jesuit, Fabi, who so loved beccaficoes. "As soon as the cry of the bird was heard in the fields around Belley," says the author of the "*Physiologie du Goût*," "the general cry was, 'The beccaficoes are come, we shall have soon Father Fabi among us.' And never did he fail to arrive, with a friend, on the 1st of September. They came for the express purpose of regaling themselves on beccaficoes, during the period of the passage of the bird across the district. To every house they were invited in town, and they took their departure again about the 23rd." This good Father died in our "glorious memory" year of 1688; and one of his choice bits of delirium was, that he had discovered the circulation of the blood before Harvey!

And now do I not hear that gentleman-like person at the lower end of the table remark, that the circulation of the blood was a conceived idea long before Harvey? You are quite right, my dear Sir; and your remark is a very appropriate one, both as to time and theme, for the circulation of the blood is one of the results of cooking. As for preconception of the idea, it is sufficient for Harvey, that he demonstrated the fact. The Doctors of ancient Roman days supposed that the blood came from the liver; and that, in passing through the *vena cava* and its branches, a considerable quantity of it turned about, and entered into the right cavity of the heart. What Harvey demonstrated was, that the blood flows from the heart into all parts of the body, by the arteries, from whence it is brought back to the heart again, by the veins. Well, Sir, I know what you are about to remark,—that Paolo Sarpi, that pleasantest of table-companions, claimed to have made the demonstration before Harvey. True, Sarpi used to say, that he did not dare publish his discovery, for dread of the Inquisition; but that he confided it to brother Fabi da Aqua-pendente, who kept it close for the same reason, but told it in confidence to Harvey, who published it as his own. Well, Sir, Sir George Ent exploded all that, by proving that Sarpi himself had first learned the fact from Harvey's lips. The Italians have the same right in this case, as they have to their boast of having produced what old Ritson used to style, "that thing you choose to call a poem, 'Paradise Lost.'" It was an invention or discovery at second-hand.

What conceits Cowley has in his verses on Harvey! He makes the philosophical Doctor pursue coy Nature through sap, and catch her at last in the human blood. He speaks, too, of the heart beating tuneful marches to its vital heat; a conceit which Longfellow twisted into prettiness, when he said, that our "muffled hearts were beating funeral marches to the grave." You will remember, Sir, that Shakespeare makes Brutus say, that Portia was to him "dear as the drops that visit this sad heart." Brutus himself, would, perhaps, have said "liver;" and, by the way, how very much to the same tune is the line in Gray's "Bard," wherein we find,—

"Dear as the light that visits these sad eyes."

But there is in tuneful Edmund, in our ever-glorious friend Spenser, a stanza which contains something that may pass for the circulation theory. You remember, in the first canto of the Second Book, where the bleeding lady is found by the good Sir Guyon:—

> "Out of her goréd wound the cruel steel
>   He lightly snatch'd, and did the flood-gates stop
> With his faire garment; then 'gan softly feel
>   Her feeble pulse, to prove if any drop
>   Of living blood yet in her veynes did hop;
> Which when he felt to move, he hopéd faire
>   To call back life to her forsaken shop.
> So well he did her deadly wounds repaire,
> That at the last shee 'gan to breathe out living aire."

And now, Sir, I shall be happy to take a glass of wine with you, obsolete as that once honoured custom has become. And allow me to send you a slice of this venison. A little more of the fat? Certainly; but, if you *will* take currant jelly with it, the sin be upon your own head. It has always been the approved plan, you say. Ah, my dear Sir! think what the approved plan was, for years, in the treatment of small-pox. That was not a gastronomic matter, you say? I am not so sure of that; for the patient, swathed in scarlet cloth, had to drink mulled port wine. But, on a question of diet, time and numbers, you think, may be taken for authority. Alas, my dear Sir! did you ever try the once popular receipt of Apicius for a thick sauce to roasted chicken? Never! of course you have not; for, in such case, your young widow would already have touched that pretty life-assurance we wot of. English tastes, you urge? Ah! in that case, if old rule be good rule, you must camp in Kensington Gardens, and eat acorns. In Germany, where venison is a national dish, the idea of currant jelly would ruin the digestion of a whole company. But I see you are incorrigible, and William is at your elbow with the doubtful sauce.

Galen could not appreciate venison as the early Patriarchs and the Jewish people did, and as the Roman ladies did, who ate of it as a preserver of youth, as well as a lengthener of life. A roebuck of Melos would have brought tears of delight into the eyes of Diogenes. The deer was preferred to the roebuck at Rome; but the wild boar was also a favourite; and the Sicilian slave, *chef* to Servilius Rullus, cooked not less than three of different sizes in one. The largest had baskets of dates suspended to its tusks, and a litter of young ones in pastry lying in the same dish. Within the first was a second, within the second a third, and within the third some small birds. Cicero, who was *the* guest for whom the dinner was got up, was as delighted with the culinary slave, as Lucullus had been a few days before, when he had eaten a dish of sows' paps prepared by the same artist; and the enraptured gastronome thought that all Olympus was dissolving in his mouth!

A wild boar was at marriage feasts what our wedding cakes are at those dreadful destroyers of time and digestion,—wedding breakfasts,—an indispensable accompaniment. Caranus, the Macedonian, has the reputation of having exceeded all others in his nuptial magnificence; for, instead of one boar at his banquet, he had twenty. But I have seen more than that at many a breakfast in Britain.

The ancient Britons abstained from the hare, like the Jews. Hippocrates held that, as a food, it thickened the blood, and kept people from sleep; but Galen—and such instances among the faculty are not uncommon—differed from his professional brother. People followed the advice of Galen; and though few, like Alexander Severus, could eat a whole hare at every repast, yet many ate as plentifully as they well could, accounting such diet profitable both to health and good looks.

Hares were nearly as injuriously abundant in Greece as rabbits were in Spain, where the latter animals are said to have once destroyed Tarragona, by undermining it in burrowing! Nay, more: the Balearic Isles were so overrun with them, that the inhabitants, afraid of being devoured, sent an embassy to Rome; and Augustus dispatched a military force, which not only slaughtered the enemy, but ate the half of them! The more refined gluttons of Rome did not dine on the rabbit after this fashion. They only picked a little of the young taken alive from the slaughtered mother, or killed soon after birth. They were preferable to the rabbits of the Parisian *gargottes*, where *fricassée de lapins* is invariably made of cats. And these, perhaps, are as dainty eating as the hunch of the camel, or the feet of the elephant,—pettitoes for Brobdignagian lovers to sup upon.

But we *almost* as villanously disguise our poultry. The latter, if not *now*, used—according to Darwin—to be fed for the London market, by mixing gin, and even opium, with their food, and keeping them in the dark; but "they must be killed as soon as they are fattened, or they become weak and emaciated, like human drunkards."

Game was almost as sacred to the Egyptian Priests, as eggs to the sacerdotal gentlemen of some of the modern tribes of Africa. Under the head of "game," we no longer admit the birds which, according to Belon, figured at the gastronomic tables of France in the sixteenth century. These were the crane, the crow, and the cormorant, the heron, the swan, the stork, and the bittern. The last-named bird was in high estimation, although the taste for it was confessedly an "acquired" one. The larger birds of prey were not then altogether despised by epicures, some of whom could sit down with an appetite to roast vulture, while they turned with loathing from the plump pheasant.

This eastern bird, however, has, with this exception, enjoyed a deserved reputation from the earliest ages. The Egyptian Kings kept large numbers of them to grace their aviaries and their triumphs. The Greeks reared them for the less sentimental gratification of the stomach; and a simple Athenian republican, when giving a banquet, prided himself on having on his board as many pheasants as there were guests invited.

Pheasants' brains were among the ingredients of the dish that Vitellius invented, and which he designated by the name of "Shield of Minerva." They were greedily eaten by many others of the Cæsars; and an offering of them to the statue of Caligula was deemed to be propitiatory of that very equivocal deity. The Emperors generally esteemed them above partridges, which were trained for fighting, as well as fattened for eating. Roman epicures fixed on the breast as the most "eatable" portion of the gallant bird. The Greeks thought of it as we do of the woodcock; and with them the leg of the partridge was the part the most highly esteemed. At a Greek table would not have occurred the smart dialogue which is said to have taken place at an English dinner. "Shall I send you a leg or a wing?" said a carver to a guest he was about to help. "It is a matter of perfect indifference to me," was the reply; and it is *not* a courteous one. "It is a matter of equal indifference to me," said the first speaker, at the same time resuming his own knife and fork, and going on with his dinner.

Quails are variously said either to have recalled Hercules to life, or to have cured him of epilepsy. The Romans, however, rather feared them, as tending to cause epileptic fits. Galen thought so; Aristotle took a different view, and the Greeks devoured them as readily as though they had Aristotle's especial authorization; and the Romans were only slowly converted to the same way of thinking. Quails, like partridges and the game-cock, were long reared for the arena; and legislators thought that youth might learn courage from contemplating the contests of quails!

The thrush was perhaps the most popular bird at delicate tables in Greece. They were kept from the young, lest the taste should give birth to permanent greediness; but when a girl married, she was sure of a brace of thrushes, for her especial eating at the wedding-feast. They were still more popular in Rome, where patrician ladies reared thousands yearly for the market, and made a further profit by selling the manure for the land. The thrush aviary of Varro's aunt was one of the sights of Rome, where men ruined themselves in procuring dishes composed of these birds for their guests. Greatly, however, as they abounded, there was occasionally a scarcity of them; for when the physician of Pompey prescribed a thrush, by way of exciting the wayward stomach of the wayward soldier to enjoyment, there was not one to be found for sale in all Rome. Lucullus, indeed, had scores of them; but Pompey, like many other obstinate people, chose rather to suffer than put himself under an obligation; and he contrived to get well on other diet.

The diet was, nevertheless, held to be exceedingly strengthening; and blackbirds, also, were prescribed as fitting food for weak digestions. It was perhaps for this reason that the celebrated

"Four-and-twenty black-birds baked in a pie,"

were the dainty dish set before the legendary and, presumedly, dyspeptic King! In later times, we have had as foolish ideas connected with them. The oil in which they were cooked was said to be good for sciatica, or hipgout; and Vieillot says that freckles might be instantaneously removed from the skin, if—— but ladies would never try what Vieillot recommends.

The blackbird was not imperially patronized. The stomachs of the gastronomic Cæsars gave more greedy welcome to the flamingo. Caligula, Vitellius, and Heliogabalus ruined their digestions by *ragoûts* of this bird, the tongues of which were converted into a stimulating sauce. Dampier ate the bird, when he could get nothing else; and thought the Cæsars fools for doing so when they could get anything beside. The ancients, whether Greeks or Romans, showed more taste in eating beccaficoes,—that delicate little bird, all tender and succulent, the essence of the juice of the fruits (especially the fig) on which it feeds. The only thing to be compared with it is the ortolan. Had Heliogabalus confined himself to these more savoury birds, instead of acquiring indigestion on ostrich brains and flamingoes, his name would have held a more respectable place in the annals of gastronomy. But master and people were alike barbarous in many of their tastes. Who now would think of killing turtle-doves for the sake of eating their legs "devilled?" and yet *we* eat the lark, that herald of the skies, and earliest chorister of the morn. We eat this ethereal bird with as little compunction as we do the savoury, yet unclean, of the earth, earthy, duck. And this thought reminds me of a story, for which I am indebted to a friend, himself the most amiable of Amphitryons, the good things at whose table have ever wit, wisdom, mirth, and good-fellowship attendant, as aids to digestion.*

A LIGHT DINNER FOR TWO.

MANY years ago, when railways were things undreamt of, and when the journeys from Oxford to the metropolis were inevitably performed on that goodly and pleasant high road which is now dreary and forlorn, a gentleman and his son, the latter newly flushed with College fame and University honours, rode forth over Magdalen Bridge and the Cherwell, purposing to reach London in

---

* Henry Holden Frankum, Esq.

a leisurely ride. A groom, their only attendant, carrying their scanty baggage with him on a good stout cob, had been sent on in advance to order dinner at a well-known road-side hostelry, where Oxford nags baited, and where their more adventurous riders frequently caroused, out of reach of any supervision by Principals or Pro-Proctors.

Pleasant is the spot, well approved by past generations of Freshmen, picturesque and charming to an eye content with rich fields, luxuriant meadows, and pretty streams, tributaries of the now adolescent Thames, whose waters had not at that date been polluted by barge or lighter at that point of its course. The neighbourhood is famous for its plump larks; and whether in a savoury pudding, swimming with beef-steak gravy, or roasted, a round half-dozen together, on an iron skewer or a tiny spit, those little warblers furnished forth a pretty adjunct on a well-spread table, tempting to an appetite somewhat appeased by heavier and more substantial viands. Mine host at our road-side quarters had a cook who dressed them to a nicety; contriving to produce or develope a succulency and flavour which meaner practitioners would scarcely have deemed practicable. Now Martin, pursuant to his master's instructions for securing a repast of ducks and the dainty lark, finding the landlord brought out from his shady porch by the clatter of the horse's hoofs on the well-beaten road, announced the approaching arrival, and ordered dinner. "My master wishes to find a couple of larks, and a dozen of ducks, well roasted, on his arrival at four o'clock." "Did I understand you rightly, young man?" said Boniface. "O!" said the varlet, pettishly, "in Oxford no landlord needs twice telling;"—and betook himself to the stables, looking forward to the enjoyment of a tankard of good house-brewed ale,—no brewer's iniquitous mixture,—and the opportunity of shining with some lustre in the tap, or the kitchen, before country bumpkins, eager to listen to a man like himself, who had seen racing at Newmarket and Doncaster, and high life at Bath and Cheltenham. Meantime, his masters came leisurely along the road, nor thought of applying a

7*

spur, until the craving bowels of the younger horseman, whose digestive organs were unimpaired by College theses and examinations, suggested a lack of provender; and, their watches, when consulted, indicating the near approach of the dinner hour, they broke off their chat, and soon drew rein at their place of temporary sojourn.

Finding the cloth laid, and the busy waiter's preparations nearly complete, they glanced with satisfaction at a table of somewhat unnecessary dimensions, considering the limited extent of the party, which our young Hellenist would have described as a "duality." Just as our travellers were growing impatient, the landlord, having previously satisfied himself, by obsequious inquiry, that his guests were quite ready, re-entered, bearing a dish with bright cover, and heading as good a procession of domestics, each similarly laden, as the limited resources of his modest establishment admitted. The large number of dishes rather surprised the elder of the twain, whose mind was less absorbed by the suggestions of appetite; and, having dispatched the sole attendant left for a bottle of the best Madeira the cellar could supply, and a jug of that malt liquor for which the house had obtained some notoriety, he proceeded to look under the formidable range of covers. Seeing under the first a couple of ducks, he said, "Come, this is all right!" but finding the next, and the next, and still the next, but a repetition of the same, either with or without the odour of seasoning, he fairly stood aghast, when six couple of goodly ducks stood revealed before him. The young collegian's mirth was great, his laugh hearty, at the climax of two pretty little chubby larks which closed the line of dishes. Apple sauce and gravy, broccoli and potatoes, stood sentries, flanking the array. Upon his ringing the bell with no gentle hand, the landlord himself stepped in from the passage, where he appeared to have awaited a summons; and, in answer to a question the reader may easily anticipate, replied that the servant's order was precise, and that it was impatiently repeated upon his own hesitation in accepting it. The respectability of the landlord, and the evident truthfulness of his manner, stayed all further questions. But the elder gentleman said firmly, that he should not pay for what had been so absurdly provided; alleging, that no two, or even three, persons could be found who would do justice to such provisions. The landlord, like Othello, "upon that hint spake;" for he saw a faint chance of righting a somewhat difficult matter. "O, Sir," said he, "I think I could find a man hard by, who would not consider the supplies too much for his own appetite." "Produce him," said the guest, "and settle the point; for, if you do, I will pay for the whole." The anxious landlord said no more; but, bowing, left in search of a neighbouring cobbler, whose prowess with the knife and fork was pre-eminent in the vicinity. Meantime, our hungry travellers sat down to dinner with such good will, that each of them disposed of one of the regiment; and in a joint attack, a third fell mutilated, leaving but fragmentary relics. A lark a-piece was a mere practical joke; and cheese, with celery, left nothing farther wanting to appease those cravings which had prompted them to action. While these little matters were in progress, the landlord had found the shoemaker, and told his story. "Well," said Lapstone, "this is plaguy unlucky, for I've just had a gallon of broth! Such a famous chance, too; for if there is any thing I am particularly fond of, certainly ducks is a weak point, Sir!" Boniface, thinking it his only chance, urged him to try; and the man of bristles, nothing loth, consented. On being duly introduced, orders were given for setting-to on the spot, to insure fair play, and defeat any supplementary aid, or a deposit in any other pocket, save that with which the savage in a nude state finds himself provided,—the stomach. While the travellers sipped their wine, and trifled with their dessert, the voracious cobbler fell heartily to work on the row of eight ducks before him: one having been sent down for the undeserving groom, whose blunder had proved a godsend to the man of leather. Wisely eschewing vegetables, and eating scantily of bread, the *disjecta membra* of the doomed ducks rapidly yielded up their savoury integuments. But flesh is weak, and cobblers' appetites are not wholly unappeasable; so that while the fifth victim was under discussion, a stimulant, in the shape of "a little brandy," was requested; and when the sixth' was but slowly and more slowly disappearing, poor Lapstone, who began to think farther progress impossible, was seen whispering to the landlord. The gentleman loudly demanded what the fellow was saying. "Sir," said the landlord, promptly and cunningly, "he says, he wishes there were half-a-dozen more; for he is just beginning to enjoy them." "Confound the rascal's gluttony," cried the travellers; "not a bit more shall he have. Put the remaining couple by for our supper; for we shall not leave your house till to-morrow:"—an arrangement affording much relief to the shoemaker, and entire satisfaction to the innkeeper.

To return to the lark It is worthy of notice, that London is annually supplied, from the country about Dunstable alone, with not less than four thousand dozen of these succulent songsters. At Leipsic, the excise on larks, for that single city, amounts to nearly £1,000 sterling yearly. The larks of Dunstable and Leipsic are, I presume, "caught napping." They are not, then, like the nightingale, who is said to sing all night, to keep herself awake, lest the slow-worm should devour her.

And this reminds me of a remark which I once heard made by one who disputed the fact, that every thing had its use. Mr. Jerdan could not conjecture what use there could be in the *cimex*, that domestic "B flat," which may be found in old beds and old parchments. So my friend could not divine the utility of a slow-worm, or of that unclean parasite, the "louse," which, by the way, infects birds as well as dirty humanity, and even reaches these same aspiring larks. For the use of the slow-worm I referred him to natural history; for that of the *pediculus*, I could only state that it is swallowed by some country-people as a cure for jaundice! At Hardenberg, in Sweden, it held a position of some importance. When a Burgomaster had to be chosen, the eligible candidates sat with their beards upon the table, in the centre of which was placed a louse; and the one in whose beard he took cover was the Magistrate for the ensuing year. After the ceremony, the company supped upon ducks, and sang like larks.

The household of Job was of a hospitable cast. "His sons went and feasted in their houses, every one on his day; (which is explained as being the *birth*-day;) "and sent and called for their three sisters to eat and drink with them." We know what materials the joyous family had to make a superb feast; and doubtless he who presided thereat was as proud as the Knight who, by virtue of triumphing in the tournament, alone had the right to carve the peacock which was placed before him—plumage, tail, and all—by the fairest "she" to be found in the vicinity. After all, the peacock was inferior to the succulent and sweet-throated thrush. The proper time for eating thrushes, and indeed, much other of the small game of the bird species, is towards the end of November. The reason assigned by a French epicure is, that, after they have been fattened in the fields and vineyards, they then give a biting, bitter aroma to their flesh by feeding on juniper berries. The Romans fed them on a paste made up of figs, wheat, and aromatic grains. The Roman epicures were as fond of them as the Marquis de Cussy was of red partridges, one of which he ate on the day of his death, and after a six months' illness. It was his last act; and, in gastronomic annals, it is recorded, as Nelson's calling for sealing-wax amid the thunders of Copenhagen, or his writing to Horatio before he went to meet death at Trafalgar, is noticed by the biographers of our naval heroes. Statistics, which are as pleasantly void of truth as poetry, generally speaking, set down the enormous total of nearly fifty-two millions of francs as the sum expended yearly in France for fowls of all species. Taking the amount of population into consideration, this would prove that France is a more fowl-consuming nation than any other on the face of the globe.

In a dietetic point of view, it would be well for weak stomachs to remember, that wild birds are more nutritious than their domesticated cousins, and more digestible. But the white breast or wing of a chicken is less healing than the flesh of winged game. Other game—such as venison, which is dark-coloured, and contains a large proportion of fibrine—produces highly stimulating chyle; and, consequently, the digestion is an easy and rapid affair for the stomach. But, though the whiter meats be detained longer in the stomach, furnish less stimulating chyle, and be suffered to run into acetous fermentation, their lesser stimulating quality may recommend them when the general system is not in want of a spur. Meats are wholesome, or otherwise, less with reference to themselves than to the consumer. "To assert a thing to be wholesome," says Van Swieten, "without a knowledge of the condition of the person for whom it is intended, is like a sailor pronouncing the wind to be fair, without knowing to what port the vessel is bound."

Cardinal Fesch would have made an exception in the case of "blackbirds." His dinners at Lyons were reverenced for the excellence and variety of these dishes. The birds were sent to him weekly from Corsica; and they were said to incense half the archiepiscopal city. They were served with great form; and none who ate thereof ever forgot the flavour which melted along his palate. The Cardinal used to say that it was like swallowing paradise, and that the smell alone of his blackbirds was enough to revivify half the defunct in his diocese.

Quite as rich a dish may be found in the pheasant which has been suspended by the tail, and which detaches himself from his caudine appendage, by way of intimation that he is ready. It is thus, we are told, that a pheasant hung up on Shrove Tuesday is susceptible of being spitted on Easter-day! It is popularly said in France of the pheasant, that it only lacks something to be equal to the turkey? A wise saying, indeed! but, the truth is, the two cannot be compared. Our own popular adage regarding the partridge and woodcock has far better grounds for what they assert:—

> "If the partridge had but the woodcock's thigh,
> 'T would be the best bird that ever did fly.
> If the woodcock had but the partridge's breast,
> 'T would be the best bird that ever was dress'd."

The partridge is much on the ground, the woodcock ever on the wing; and these parts, and the immediate vicinity of them, acquire a muscular toughness, not admired by epicures.

The vegetarians may boast of a descent as ancient as that claimed by the Freemasons. In ancient days, if, indeed, flesh meat was not denounced, unmeasured honor was paid to vegetables. Monarchs exchanged them as gifts, wise men and warriors supped on them after study and battle, Chiefs of the noblest descent prepared them with their own hands for their own tables, agricultural chymists tended their planting, and pious populations raised some of them to the rank of gods.

The Licinian Law enacted their use, while it restricted the consumption of meat; and the greatest families in Rome derived their names from them. Fabius was but General *Bean*, Cicero was Vice-Chancellor *Pea*, and the house of Lentilus took its appellation from the slow-growing *Lentil*.

The kitchen-garden of Henry VIII. was worse supplied than that of Charlemagne, who not only raised vegetables, but, as Gustavus Vasa's Queen did with her eggs and milk, made money by them. He was a royal market-gardener, and found more profit in his salads than he did in his sons. A salad, by the way, was so scarce an article during the early part of last century, that George I. was obliged to send to Holland to procure a lettuce for his Queen; and now lettuces are flung by cart-loads to the pigs. Asparagus and artichokes were strangers to us until a still later period.

The bean has, from remote times, held a distinguished place. Isidorus asserts that it was the first food used by man. Pythagoras held that human life was in it. By others the black spot was accounted typical of death; and the *Flamen* of Jupiter would neither look upon it nor pronounce its name. The Priests of

Apollo, on the other hand, banqueted on a dish of beans at one of the festivals of their god. Those of Æsculapius taught that the smell of beans in blossom was prejudicial to health; and farmer's wives, in the days of Baucis and Philemon, maintained that hens reared on beans would never lay eggs.

The "bean" was once the principal feature in the Twelfth-Night cake; and he to whose share fell the piece containing the vegetable was King for the night. The last Twelfth Night observed, with ancient strictness, at the Tuileries, was when Louis XVIII. was yet reigning. Among his guests was Louis Philippe, Duke of Orleans, who was lucky enough to draw the bean, and thereby became Monarch for the nonce. "My cousin," said Louis XIII., "is King at last!" "I will never accept such title," answered the over-modest Duke; "I acknowledge no other King in France but your Majesty, and will not usurp the name even in jest!" Excellent man! he was at that very moment intriguing to tumble from his throne that very King, loyalty for whom he expressed with so much of unnecessary and enforced ceremony.

The *haricot blanc*, or white kidney bean, deserves to be introduced more generally into our kitchens. There are various methods of dressing them; but the best is to have them softened in the gravy of a leg of mutton; they are then a good substitute for potatoes. They are nearly as good, dressed with oil or butter; and Napoleon was exceedingly fond of them, dressed as a salad. Of course, we allude here to the bean which, in full maturity, is taken from the pod, and eaten in winter. In England we eat the pod itself, (in summer,) split, and served with roast mutton and venison. The mature bean, however, makes an excellent dish.

And *à-propos* to Monarchs, it is to Alexander that we are indebted for the Indian "haricot;" and the vegetable had a fashion in Greece and Rome worthy of its distinguished introducer. But this fashion was not a mere consequence; for grey peas were as universally eaten. The people were so fond of these, that political aspirants bought votes of electors in exchange for them. They formed the principal refreshment of the lower citizens at the circus and the theatre, where, instead of the modern cry of "Oranges, biscuits, porter, and bill of the play!" was to be heard that of "Peas! peas! ram peas! grey peas! and a programme of the beasts and actors!"

Green peas were not known in France until the middle of the sixteenth century. They were grown, but people no more thought of eating them than we do the sweet pea. The gardner Michaux was born, and he it was who first sent green peas to a Christian table.

When Alexander, son of Pyrrhus, wished to keep all the beans that grew in the Thesprotian Marsh for his own eating, the gods dried up the marsh, and beans could never be made to grow there again. So, when King Antigonus put a tax on the healing spring that flowed at Edessa, the waters disappeared; and the people were not, in either case, benefited. What lumbering avengers were those heathen deities!

The cabbage has had a singular destiny,—in one country an object of worship; in another, of contempt. The Egyptians made of it a god; and it was the first dish they touched at their repasts. The Greeks and Romans took it as a remedy for the languor following inebriation. Cato said that in the cabbage was a panacea for the ills of man. Erasistratus recommended it as a specific in paralysis; Hippocrates accounted it a sovereign remedy, boiled with salt, for the colic; and Athenian medical men prescribed it to young nursing-mothers, who wished to see lusty babies lying in their arms. Diphilus preferred the beet to the cabbage, both as food and as medicine,—in the latter case, as a vermifuge. The same physician extols mallows, not for fomentation, but as a good edible vegetable, appeasing hunger and curing the sore-throat at the same time. The asparagus, as we are accustomed to see it, has derogated from its ancient magnificence. The original "grass" was from twelve to twenty feet high; and a dish of them could only have been served to the Brobdignagians. Under the Romans, stems of asparagus were raised of three pounds' weight,—heavy enough to knock down a slave in waiting with. The Greeks ate them of more moderate dimensions, or would have eat them, but that the publishing doctors of their day denounced asparagus as injurious to the sight. But then it was also said, that a slice or two of boiled pumpkin would re-invigorate the sight which had been deteriorated by asparagus. "Do that as quickly as you should asparagus!" is a proverb descended to us from Augustus, and illustrative of the mode in which the vegetable was prepared for the table.

The gourd does not figure at our repasts as commonly as it did in the east of Europe in mythological times, when it was greedily eaten, boiled hot, or preserved in pickle. The readers of Athenæus will remember, how a party of philosophers lost their temper, in a discussion as to whether the gourd was round, square, or oblong,— how a coarse-minded doctor interrupted the discussion by a very incongruous remark,—and how the venerable sage who was in the chair called the rude man to order, and then bade the disputants proceed with their argument.

A still more favourite dish, at Athens, was turnips, from Thebes. Carrots, too, formed a distinguished dish at Greek and Roman tables. Purslain was rather honoured as a cure against poisons, whether in the blood by wounds, or in the stomach from beverage. I have heard it asserted in France, that if you briskly rub a glass with fingers which have been previously rubbed with purslain, or parsley, the glass will certainly break. I have tried the experiment, but only to find that the glass resisted the pretended charm.

Broccoli was the favourite vegetable food of Drusus. He ate greedily thereof; and as his father, Tiberius, was as fond of it as he, the master of the Roman world and his illustrious heir were constantly quarrelling, like two clowns, when a dish of broccoli stood between them. Artichokes grew less rapidly into aristocratic favour; the *dictum* of Galen was against them; and, for a long time, they were only used by drinkers, against head-ache, and by singers to strengthen their voice. Pliny pronounced artichokes excellent food for poor people and donkeys! For nobler stomachs he preferred the cucumber,—the Nemesis of vegetables. But people were at issue touching the merits of the cucumber. Not so, regarding the lettuce, which has been universally honoured. It was the most highly esteemed dish of the beautiful Adonis. It was prescribed as provocative to sleep; and it cured Augustus of the malady which sits so heavily on the soul of Leopold of Belgium,—*hypochondriasis*. Science and rank eulogized the lettuce, and philosophy sanctioned the eulogy in the person of Aristoxenus, who not only grew lettuces as the pride of his garden, but irrigated them with wine, in order to increase their flavour.

But we must not place too much trust in the stories either of sages or apothecaries. These Pagans recommended the seductive, but indigestible, endive, as good against the headache, and young onions and honey as admirable preservers of health, when taken fasting; but this was a prescription for rustic swains and nymphs, —the higher classes, in town or country, would hardly venture on it. And yet the mother of Apollo ate raw leeks, and loved them of gigantic dimensions. For this reason, perhaps, was the leek accounted, not only as salubrious, but as a beautifier. The love for melons was derived, in similar fashion, probably, from Tiberius, who cared for them even more than he did for broccoli. The German Cæsars inherited the taste of their Roman predecessor, carrying it, indeed, to excess; for more than one of them, as may be seen in another page, submitted to die after eating melons, rather than live by renouncing them.

I have spoken of gigantic asparagus: the Jews had radishes that could vie with them, if it be true that a fox and cubs could burrow in the hollow of one, and that it was not uncommon to grow them of a hundred pounds in weight. It must have been such radishes as these that were employed by seditious mobs of old, as weapons, in insurrections. In such case, a rebellious people were always well victualled, and had peculiar facilities, not only to beat their adversaries, but to eat their own arms. The horse-radish is, probably, a descendant of this gigantic ancestor. It had, at one period, a gigantic reputation. Dipped in poison, it rendered the draught innocuous, and, rubbed on the hands, it made an encounter with venomed serpents mere play. In short, it was celebrated as being a cure for every evil in life,—the only exception being, that it destroyed the teeth. There was far more difference of opinion touching garlic, than there was touching the radish. The Egyptians deified it, as they did the leek and the cabbage; the Greeks devoted it to Gehenna,—and to soldiers, sailors, and cocks that were not "game." Medicinally, it was held to be useful in many diseases, if the root used were originally sown when the moon was below the horizon. No one who had eaten of it, however, could presume to enter the Temple of Cybele. Alphonso of Castile was as particular as this goddess; and a Knight of Castile, "detected as being guilty of garlic," suffered banishment from the royal presence during an entire month.

Parsley has fared better, both with gods and men. Hercules and Anacreon crowned themselves with it. It was worn both at joyous banquets and funeral feasts; and not only horses, but those who bestrode them, ate of the herb, in order to find the excitement to daring which otherwise lacked. In contrast with parsley stood the water-cress, a plant honoured and eaten only by the Persians. It was, indeed, medically esteemed as curative of consumption, and, by placing it in the ears, of tooth-ache. But the wits and Plutarch denounced its use in any case; and few cared to affect love for a plant which was popularly declared to have the power of twisting the noses of those who put it into their mouths!

Parsley was as popular in what may be called "classical" times, as the asparagus has invariably been with a particular class in France. This vegetable has ever been, I know not wherefore, a favourite vegetable with the officials of the Gallican Church. One day, Monseigneur Courtois de Quincy, Bishop of Belley, was informed that an asparagus head had just pierced the soil in His Eminence's kitchen-garden, and that it was worth looking at. Cardinal and *convives* rose from table, visited the spot, and were lost in admiration at what they saw. Day by day the Bishop watched the growth of the delicious giant. His mouth watered as he looked at it, and happy was he when the day arrived in which he might with his own hands take it from the ground. When he did so, he found, to his disappointment, that he held a wooden counterfeit, admirably turned and painted by the Canon Rosset, who was famous for his artistic abilities, and also for his practical jokes. The joke on this occasion was taken in good part, and the counterfeit asparagus was admitted to the honour of lying on the Bishop's table.

I have noticed, that asparagus has been suggested as one of the substitutes for coffee. In this case, the seeds are taken from the berries, by drying the latter in an oven, and rubbing them on a sieve. When ground, the seeds make a full-flavoured coffee, not inferior, it is said,—but that is doubtful,—to the best Mocha.

It was the opinion of Pliny, that nature intended asparagus to grow wild, in order that all might eat thereof. That was esteemed the best which grew naturally on the mountain-sides. The famous Ravenna asparagus was cultivated with such perfection, that three of them weighed a pound. Lobster surrounded with asparagus was a favourite dish; and the rapidity with which the latter should be cooked, is illustrated, as I have said, by a proverb: " *Velocius quam asparagi coquuntur!*" There is a story told of an intrusive traveller forcing his company at supper on another wayfarer, before whom were placed an omelette and some asparagus. The intruder had not before seen any "grass," and inquired what it was. "O, it is very well in its way," said the other, " and we will divide both omelette and asparagus ;" and therewith, after carving the first, he cut the bunch in two, and gave the white ends to the importunate visitor. The greatest indignation ever experienced by Carême, was once at hearing that some guests had eaten asparagus with one of his new *entremêts*, and mixed it in their mouths with iced champagne.

There is an opinion current in some parts of England, that they who eat of old parsnips that have been long in the ground invariably go mad; and on this account the root is called "madnip." On some such "insane root," it is said, the Indians, named by Garcilasso, whetted their appetites before they ate their dead parents. Such form of entombment was accounted most dignified and dutiful. If the defunct was lean, the children boiled their parent; but obesity was always honoured by roasting. Fathers and mothers were religiously picked to the very bones, and the bones themselves were then consigned to the earth. This, however, is not an exclusively Indian custom. The Indians only devoured their deceased parents; but I have seen, in Christian England, many a son devouring father and mother, too, during their lives, swallowing their very substance, and *then*, like the Indians, committing their bones to the bosom of a tender mother,—earth.

Perhaps there is nothing, in the vegetable way, more insipid than parsnips; but these are sometimes as mischievous as insipid persons. This is the case, if the above-named tradition be worthy of credit, wherein we are told, that *old* parsnips are called "mad-nips," and that the maids who eat of them invariably become more like Salmacis than the youth she wooed, and are as much given to dancing as though they had been bitten by a tarantula. I fear the "mad-nip" is too much eaten in many of our rural districts, and perhaps by the *acerba virgo* of metropolitan towns and episcopal cities also. But let us look at our ancient friend, the potato.

It has been well said, that the first art in boiling a potato, is to prevent the boiling of the potato. "Upon the heat and flame of the distemper sprinkle cool patience;" for without patience, care, and attention,—extreme vigilance being implied by the latter, a potato will never come out of the pot triumphantly well boiled.

The potato has been found in an indigenous state in Chili, on the mountains near Valparaiso and Mendoza; also near Monte Video, Lima, Quito, in Santa Fé da Bogota, and on the banks of the Orizaba, in Mexico. Cobbett cursed the root as being that of the ruin of Ireland, where it is said to have been first planted by Raleigh, on his estate at Youghal, near Cork. Its introduction into England is described as the effect of accident, in consequence of the wrecking of a vessel on the coast of Lancashire, which had a quantity of this "fruit" on board.

The common potato (*solanum tuberosum*) was probably first brought to Spain from Quito by the Spaniards, in the early part of the sixteenth century. In both of those countries the *tubers* are known by the designation of *papas*. In passing from Spain into Italy, it naturalized itself under the name of "the truffle." In 1598, we hear of its arrival at Vienna, and thence spreading over Europe. It certainly was not known in North America in 1586, the period at which Raleigh's colonists in Virginia are said to have sent it to England; and in the latter country it was not known until long after its introduction, as noticed above, into Ireland. In Gerard's Herbal (1597) the *Batata Virginiana*, as it is called, to distinguish it from the *Batata Edulis*, or "swee potato," is described; and the author recommends the root, no for common food, but as "a delicate dish." The sweet potato was the "delicate dish" at English tables long before the introduction of its honest cousin. We imported it from Spain and the Canaries, and in very considerable quantities. It enjoyed the reputation of possessing power to restore decayed vigour. This reputation has not escaped Shakespeare, who makes Falstaff exultingly remark, in a fit of pleasant excitement, that "it rains potatoes!" The Royal Society of England, in 1663, urgently recommended the extensive cultivation of the root as a resource against threatened famine; but as late as the end of that century, a good hundred years after its first introduction, the writers on gardening continued to treat its merits with a contemptuous indifference; though one of them does "damn with faint praise," by remarking, that "they are much used in Ireland and America as bread, and may be propagated with advantage to poor people." As late as 1719, the potato was not deemed worthy of being named in the "Complete Gardener" of London and Wise, and it was not till the middle of the last century that it became generally used in Britain and North America. The "conservatives of gulosity" of that day continued long to disparagingly describe it as "a root found in the New World, consisting of little knobs, held together by strings: if you boil it well, it *can* be eaten; it *may* become an article of food; it will certainly do for hogs; and though it is rather flatulent and acid in the human stomach, perhaps, if you boil it with dates, it may serve to keep soul and body together, among those who can find nothing better."

Some sixty years since, the Dutch introduced the potato into Bengal. The produce was sold in Calcutta at 5s. a pound. The English tried to raise them, and all their plants grew like Jack's bean-stalk, but lacked its strength. The Hollanders continually cut the swiftly-growing plant, and so compelled it to produce its fruit beneath the ground. The secret was as well worth knowing as that other touching potatoes during frost. The only precaution necessary is, to retain the potato in a perfectly dark place, for some days after the thaw has commenced. In America, where they are sometimes frozen as hard as stones, they rot if thawed in open day; but if thawed in darkness, they do not rot, and lose very little of their natural odour and properties. So, at least, they assert, who profess to have means of best knowing. The potato is said to have been first planted, in England, in the county of Lancashire, which was once as famous for the plant as Lithuania is for beet-root. It is not much more than a century since cabbages reached us from Holland. They were first planted in Dorsetshire, by the Ashleys; and I may add here what I have omitted in speaking of it in earlier times, namely, that the Athenians administered the juice of it in cases of slow parturition. Let me further add, that such terms as "cow-cabbage," "horse-radish," "bull-rush," and the like, do not imply any connexion between the article and the animal. The animal prefix is simply to signify unusual size. The prefix was commonly so applied by the ancients: hence the name of Alexander's charger; and a not less familiar illustration is afforded us in the case of the "horse-leech." Cabbage used to have said of it what Lemery, physician of Louis XIV., more truly said of spinach; namely, that "it stops coughing, allays the sharp humours of the breast, and keeps the body open." Spinach, to be truly enjoyed, should never be eaten without liberal saturation of gravy; and French epicures say, "Do not forget the nutmeg." This vegetable goes excellently with swine's flesh in every shape, but especially ham, the stimulating flavour of which it strongly modifies.

Rice, as an article of food, has something remarkable in it. Its cultivation destroys life; and when the grain is eaten, its value as a supporter of strength is very uncertain. The cultivation of this production, where it does not destroy life, does destroy comfort, and slaves may be compelled, but freemen will not go voluntarily, to raise the "paddy crop." In India, where the people of many districts depend upon it entirely as a chief article of food, famine is often the result, simply because the failure of one crop leaves the unenergetic people without any other present resource.

And now, by way of a concluding word to those who read medicinally, I would say, on the best authority, first, that of the haricot-bean I have nothing to add to what I have already stated. With regard to peas, they are, like many other things, most pleasant and wholesome when young. Old, they are the fathers of gaseous colic; and, when swallowed with the additional tenacity of texture derived from being made into pudding,—why, then the unhappy consumer is a man to be pitied. Potatoes are best baked, or roasted lightly. In the latter case, they are scarcely less nutritious than bread; but the potato must be in full health, and the cooking unexceptionable. There is many a cook who would execute, to a charm, the *fricandeau* invented by Leo X., who has not the remotest idea of cooking a potato. When the Flemings sent us the carrot, in the reign of Elizabeth, it is a pity they could not have deprived it of its fibrine texture, the drawback to be set against its saccharine nutritiveness. As the Romans waxed strong upon the turnip, we may allow that it has some virtues, and that Charles the First's Secretary, Lord Townshend, did good service by re-introducing it to his countrymen. Like the Jerusalem artichoke it requires a strong accompaniment of salt and pepper, to counteract its watery and flatulent influences. As for radishes, he who eats them is tormenting his stomach with bad water, woody fibre, and acrid poison; and if his stomach resents such treatment, why, it most emphatically "serves him right." As for cucumber, in the days of Evelyn, it was looked upon as only one remove from poison, and it had better be eaten and enjoyed with that opinion in memory. It was a pity that what is pleasant is not always what is proper. Thus the cucumber is attractive, but not nutritive; while the onions at whose very name every man stands with his hand to his mouth, like a Persian in the act of *ad-oration*, is exceedingly nourishing and wholesome. But I can never think of it, without remembering the story of the man who, having breakfasted early on bread and onions, entered an inn on a bitterly cold morning, with the remark, that for the last two hours he had had the wind in his teeth. "Had you?" said the unfortunate person who happened to be nearest to him: "then, by Jove, the wind had the worst of it!"

An onion is all very well as an ingredient in a sauce, but to make a meal of it! Well! it is on record that a dinner *has* been made, at which nothing was served but sauces. A dinner of sauces must have been quickly prepared; but, for quick preparation, I know nothing that can vie with a feat accomplished, on the 19th of March of the present year, at the Freemasons' Tavern. The "Round-Catch-and Canon Club" were to dine there at half-past five P. M. An hour previously, the active Secretary, Mr. Francis, Vicar-Choral of St. Paul's, arrived, to see that "all was right." He found all wrong. Through some mistake, no company was expected; and, there being no other dinners ordered for that day, the weary proprietors, and their chief "aids," were enjoying a little relaxation. Not only were the high priestesses of the kitchen "out," but the sacred fires of the altars had followed their example. Great was the horror of the able counter-tenor Secretary; but the difficulty was triumphantly met by the accomplished officers of the establishment; and, at six o'clock precisely, forty-two of us sat down to so perfect a banquet, that the shade of Carême might have contemplated it with a smile of unalloyed satisfaction. This house may boast of this *tour de force* for ever!

SAUCES.

The donor of the sauce dinner, mentioned in the last page, was an eccentric old Major. He invited three persons to partake of this unique repast. The soup consisted of gravy sauce, and oyster and lobster sauce were handed round instead of *filet de sole*. Then came the sirloin in guise of egg sauce, on the ground, I suppose, that an egg is proverbially "full of meat." There was no pheasant, but there was bread sauce, to put his guests in mind of the flavour; and if they had not plum-pudding, they had as much towards it as could be implied by brandy sauce; just as Heyne says, that Munich is the modern Athens in this far,—that if it has not the philosophers, it has the hemlock, and has Alcibiades' dog, as a preparation towards getting Alcibiades. The sauceboats were emptied by the guests. The wine was well resorted to after each boat, and a little brandy settled the viand that was represented by the egg sauce. Half the guests, between excess of lobster sauce and Cognac, were all the worse for the banquet; but that proved rather the weakness of their stomachs than the non-excellence of the feast. It is said that the Major, when alone in the evening, wound up with a rump-steak supper,—a process rather characteristic of the "old soldier;" but I have heard in a provincial town, of large parties to "tea," followed by a snug family party, when the guests were all departed, to a hot supper, with the usual *et cæteras*. But let *us* get back from the supper to the matter of seasonings.

Seasonings may be said to form an important item in the practice and results of cookery. The first, and most useful and natural, is salt. The ancients did not allow, at one time, of its use in sacrifices; but Homer called it "divine," and Plutarch speaks of it as acceptable to the gods. Its value was not known to men until the Phœnicians, Selech and Misor,—so, at least, says an ancient legend,—taught mankind the real worth of this production as a condiment, and thereby gave to meat increased flavour, and to the eaters of it increased health and improved digestions.

The Roman soldiers received their pay in *salarium*, or "salt-money." The Mexican rulers punished rebellious provinces by interdicting the use of salt; and Holland, some years since, cruelly took vengeance on the breakers of the law, by serving them with food, without salt, during the term of their imprisonment. The poor wretches were almost devoured by worms, in consequence of this inhuman proceeding.

Of course, the salt-money of the soldiery was, like the pin-money of a married lady, employed in other ways than those warranted by its appellation. For above three centuries, soldiers served *gratis*, and supported themselves. Then came "salt-money," or *salarium*, in the shape of a couple of *oboli* daily to the foot, and a *drachma* to the cavalry. This was to the common men. The Tribunes were, however, exorbitantly paid, if Juvenal's allusion may be trusted, wherein he says that,—

> ——"*alter enim, quantum in legione Tribuni
> Accipiunt, donat Calvinæ vel Catienæ;*"

or, as it may be translated,

> "Such sums as a full Colonel's coffers swell,
> He flings to Lola, or to Laura Bell!"

But this must have been in very late times, previous to which frugality, modesty, and indifferent pay were ever the Tribune's share of the national virtues and their consequences, lauded by Livy. The first Cæsar doubled the *salarium* of the army, and decreed that it should never be reduced. His successors followed the example of increase. Augustus fixed the salt-money at ten *asses* a day, and by the time of Domitian it was considerably more than double that amount. From that period, the soldiery fed better, and fought worse, than ever. Up to the time of the Empire they had been frugal livers, and were not above preparing the rations of corn allowed them with their own hands: some ground it in hand-mills, others pounded it between stones, and the hastily-baked cakes were eaten contentedly upon the turf, with nothing better to wash them down than pure water, or, at best, *posca*, which was water mixed with vinegar,—and a very wholesome beverage, too, in hot weather.

The Jewish dispensation, unlike that of the early Olympian theology, enforced the use of salt in all sacrificial ceremonies. That of the Dead Sea was abundant; and Galen pronounced it as the most favorable for seasoning, and for promoting digestion. The Greeks learned to call it "divine," and at last consecrated it to their gods. Spilling salt was accounted as unlucky in the days when "young Time counted his birthdays by the sun," as in these modern times when the schoolmaster is abroad,—sometimes too much abroad.

Ancus Martius was the first of the Roman Kings who levied a duty on salt. He was not visited by the gods—as legends say other Kings were who created such imposts—by some dire calamity. The bad example of Ancus Martius has continued over nearly the whole of Europe; and a slave cannot eat salt to his bread without paying tribute to the King.

The word "salt" was often used for life itself. When Dordalus says to Toxilus, in the "*Persa*," "*Eodem mihi pretio sal prœhibetur quæ tibi*,"—"I get my salt at the same price as you do,"—he simply means that his manner of life is as good as that of Toxilus, and that a slave-merchant is as respectable as the very best-fed of slaves themselves. Catullus employs the word to denote beauty; other poets use it to signify virtues of various kinds; and in Terence we find a man without salt to mean a man without sense. Plutarch was not wrong when he styled salt "the condiment of condiments." I do not know that it has ever been used to point a proverb with a contemptuous meaning, except in Greece, where he who had nothing to dine upon was called a "salt-licker." Rome, where it was of such commercial importance, honoured it more by giving to the road along which it was conveyed the **name of the "Salarian Way."**

There were people who never knew its use, as in Epeiros; some who have steadily rejected it, as the Bathurst tribe in Australia. The Peruvians delighted in it, and ate it mixed with hot pepper and bitter herbs, as a sort of "sweetmeat." How sacred it is in Arabia, we all know; and, in illustration of it, I have heard of an Arab burglar accidentally letting his tongue come in contact, as he was plundering a house by night, with a piece of salt. He instantly deemed he had partaken of the owner's hospitality, and he departed without booty. Could Christian thieves be so influenced, we should salt our plate-baskets and cash-boxes nightly!

In Sicily a salt is spoken of that melts only in fire, and hardens in water. At Utica, one of the great salt suppliers of the ancient world, it lay about in such huge mounds, hardened by the sun and moon, that the pickaxe would scarcely penetrate it. In Arabia whole cities were once built of it, the blocks of salt being cemented by water. It is still procured with most difficulty in Abyssinia, where the clouds are supposed to deposit the crystal in sandy plains, of heat so furious, that it is only during one or two hours of the night that the seekers of it dare dash into the locality, and carry off, as hastily as possible, what they seek. It is procured far more pleasantly in those parts of Chili where it is found deposited on the leaves of plants. Off the warmer coasts of South America, and the still hotter shores of Africa, blocks weighing from one to two hundred weight have been picked up. Some writers tell us that lakes are nothing more than salt plains in solution; and others, that salt plains are merely lakes congealed. However this may be, it is known that generally four gallons of water produce one of salt; but there is great difference of result in various localities, some water yielding a sixth, other only a sixteenth. The deep sea-water is the most highly productive. There are various strange ingredients, too, used in different places to make the salt "grain" properly. White of egg, butter, ale, and even blood, are employed to produce the desired result. In its fossil or mineral state it is nowhere seen to such great advantage as in the mines of Williska, in Poland. I have seen those near Salzburg, in southern Austria; but these are mere salt-cellars, compared with the Polish mine, which forms a large subterranean city, has its streets, citizens, and coteries, and is an underground republic, many of the natives of which die without seeing a blade of grass, or a gleam of sunlight, upon the bosom of the upper earth.

Finally, salt is the most natural stimulant for the digestive organs; but it should be remembered that too much of it is *almost* as bad as too little. The lowering of the price of salt, a consequence of the abolition of the duty, was beneficial to the poor, and ruinous to the worm-doctors. It is a singular production. In small quantities it is a stimulating manure; in large quantities it begets sterility. A little of it accelerates putrefaction, while a large quantity prevents it. Farther, it is to be remembered,—and I have mentioned the fact in another page,—that the salt in salted meat is not (whatever it may once have been) the table salt, the use of which is so favourable to digestion. In the meat it undergoes a chymical change, by which it deteriorates itself as well as the object to which it is applied. "Sweet salt" was the name once given to sugar; and in reference to this latter production, it may be safely averred, that its introduction worked a considerable change in society. And it appears to have been early added to that "significant luxury," wheat. In Isaiah xliii. 24 there is an allusion made to it in these words: "Thou hast bought me no sweet cane with money, neither hast thou filled me with the fat of sacrifices." And again, in Jeremiah vi. 20: "To what purpose cometh there to me incense from Sheba, and sweet cane from a far country?" It would seem, however, that though the sweet cane may have been known, its uses were not very speedily appreciated, or, if they were, that they were for a long time forgotten. Thus, as late as the thirteenth century of our era, a writer speaks of a novel sort of salt that has been discovered, the flavour of which was sweet, and, as he suggests, might be found acceptable to sick persons, because of its soothing and cooling properties. "Honey out of the rock," which was the sweetener most early noticed in Scripture, fell into comparative disuse, after sugar had become a necessary of life, after being first a medicine, and then a luxury. The Spaniards received it from the Arabs, and familiarized it in Europe. Its first settlement beyond the Continent was in Madeira, and at length it found a congenial soil in the islands of the Western Indies. God gave the gift, but man has discovered how to abuse it to his own destruction; and, from the sweet food offered by an angel, he has distilled the fire-water, which slays like the pestilence. But to return, for a moment, from the sweets to the salts, and especially to the latter in the form of brine.

The Romans were fond of brine,—water in which bay-salt had been dissolved,—as a seasoning; and after dinner, those who could not guess the riddles that were put to them, were punished, like the refractory gentlemen at the Nightingale Club, by being compelled to swallow a cupfull, without drawing breath. Apicius invented a composition made up of salt, pepper, ginger, thyme, celery, rocket, and anise-seed, with lamoni, wild marjoram, holy thistle, spikenard, parsley, and hyssop, as a specific to be taken, after heavy dinners, against indigestion. They who could digest the remedy need not have been afraid of the dinner.

That universal seasoning of the classical world, the *garum*, was originally a shrimp sauce; but it was subsequently made of the intestines of almost any fish, macerated in water, saturated with salt; and when symptoms of putrefaction began to appear, a little parsley and vinegar were added; and there was the famous *garum*, of which the inventors were so proud,—and particularly of a *garum* which was prepared in Spain. Flesh instead of fish was occasionally used, with no difference in the process of preparation; and it would be difficult to say which was the nastier. But, perhaps, if we could see the witchery of preparing any of our own flavouring sauces, we should be reluctant ever to allow a drop of the polluted mixture to pass our lips. There *is* a bliss in ignorance.

Pythagoras showed better taste in the science of seasonings, when he took to eating nothing but honey wherewith to flavour his bread. Hybla sounds sweet, the very word smells sweet, from its association with honey. Aristæus, who is said to have discovered its use, merited the patent of nobility, whereby he was declared to have descended from the gods; and the placing the honeycomb and its makers under the protection of Mellona, expressly made by men for this purpose, was a proof of the value in which they were held. Theophrastus placed sugar among the honeys,—the honey of reeds,—or the "salt of India," as some strangely called it. The Greek physicians recommended its use, both as food and flavourer. It was at one time as scarce as cinamon,—that precious bark of which the phœnix made its nest, and which the Cæsars monopolized. Cinnamon and cloves were not employed in seasoning until a comparatively modern period. The good people of earlier days preferred verjuice, in certain cases prescribed by Galen. They seemed to have a taste for acids: hence the admiration, both in Greece and Rome, for vinegar and pickles. Vinegar figured in the army statistics of Rome especially; but it once, at least, figured in a still more remarkable way in the statistics of the French army, in the time of Louis XIII., when the Duc de la Meilleraye, Grand Master of the Artillery of France, put down £52,000 as the sum expended by him in cooling cannons. How hot the war must have been, and at what a price the fever must have been maintained, when the merely refrigerating process cost so much!

French epicures maintain that the pig was born to be "ringed," and that his mission was to rout at the foot of the yoke-elm trees, and turn up truffles! Pliny gravely looked upon the truffle as a prodigy sown by the thunder-bolt in autumnal storms. However, this may be, all lovers of good things eat the truffle with a sort of devout ecstasy, in spite of the wide differences of opinion which exist among the faculty of guessers, as to whether the truffle be nutritious or poisonous, fit for food, or monster sire of indigestion. The fact is, that they should be delicately dealt with,

8*

like mushrooms; of which he who eats not of them at all is safe from blaming them for bringing on indigestion—as far as *he* is concerned.

The truffle is thus elaborately, yet not verbosely, described by Archimagirus Soyer: "The truffle is a very remarkable vegetable, which, without stems, roots, or fibres, grows of itself, isolated in the bosom of the earth, absorbing the nutritive juice. Its form is round, more or less regular; its surface is smooth, or tuberculous; the colour, dark brown outside, brown, grey, or white within. Its tissue is formed of articulated filaments, between which are spheric vesicles, and in the interior are placed reproductive bodies, small brown spheres, called '*truffinelles.*' Truffles vegetate to the depth of five or six inches in the high sandy soils of the south-west of France, Piedmont, &c. Their mode of vegetation and reproduction is not known. (?) Dogs are trained to find them, as well as pigs, and boars also, who are very fond of them. They are eaten cooked under the ashes, or in wine and water. They are preserved when prepared in oil, which is soon impregnated with their odour. Poultry is stuffed with them; also geese's livers, pies, cooked pork, besides numerous *ragoûts*. They possess, as it is said, exciting virtues." The latter, we suppose, is a paraphrase for the sentiment of "Falstaff," before cited, "It rains potatoes!" Shell-fish had the same reputation in the olden time. "*Tene marsupium*," says Italius to Olympio, in the *Rudens*:—

> "*Abi atque obsonia propera; sed lepidè volo
> Molliculas escas, ut ipsa mollicula est.*"

As for the mushroom, if it be not in itself deadly, it has been made the vehicle of death. Agrippina poisoned Claudius in one, and Nero, his successor, had a respect for this production ever after. Tiberius, in Pagan, and Clement VII., in Papal, Rome, as well as Charles VI. of France, are also said to have been "approximately" killed by mushrooms. Seneca calls them "voluptuous poison," and of this poison his countrymen ate heartily, and suffered dreadfully.

The mushroom was not rendered harmless by the process of Nicander,—raising them under the shadow of a well-irrigated and richly-manured fig-tree.

One of the most perfect illustrations of "sauce," in its popular sense, with which I am acquainted, is conveyed in the reply once given by a French *Curé* to his Bishop. It is a regulation made by canonical law, that a Priest cannot keep a female servant to manage his household, unless she be of the assigned age of, at least, forty years. It once happened that a Bishop dined with a *Curé*, at whose house the Prelate had arrived in the course of a visitation tour. On that occasion he found that they were waited on at dinner by two quietly pretty female attendants, of some twenty years each. When diocesan and subordinate were once more alone, the former remarked on the uncanonical condition of the household, and asked the *Curé* if he were not aware that, by rule of church, he could maintain but one *menagère*, who must have attained, at least, forty years of age? "I am quite aware of it, *Monseigneur*," said the rubicund *Curé*; "but, as you see, I prefer having my housekeeper in two volumes!"

With respect to the use of spices, it may be safely said, that the less they are used, the better for the stomach. A *soupçon* of them in certain preparations is not to be objected to; but it must be recollected that in most cases, however pleasant they must be to the palate, the apparent vigour which they give to the stomach is at the expense of the liver, and the reaction leaves the former in a worse condition than it was in before.

The world probably never saw a second time such a trade in spices as that which was carried on of old between Canaan and Egypt. The Dutch and Amboyna was a huckstering matter compared with it. Egypt sent Canaan her corn, wine, oil and linen; and Canaan sent, in return, her spicery, balm, myrrh, precious woods, and minerals. The Ishmaelites were the carrying merchants; and, while each class of them had its especial article of commerce, they all dabbled a little in slave-dealing. Thus, the men of the tribe that purchased Joseph dealt in spicery only,—a term including balm and myrrh. The Egyptian demand for this article was enormous. At the period of the sale of Joseph, spicery was most extensively used, not only for the embalming of men, but of sacred animals. In after times, this practice ceased to a great extent, on account of a large failure in the supply.

There is something very characteristic of the "ancient nation" in the transaction of the brethren with respect to Joseph. The general proposal was to slay him; but it was Judah, first of his race, who, with a strong eye to business, exclaimed, " What *profit* to slay our brother, and conceal his blood? Come, let us *sell him* to the Ishmaelites." The opposition to fratricide, on the part of Judah, was not on the principle that it was a crime, but that it brought nothing. But no sooner had he pointed out how they might get rid of the troublesome brother, and put money in their purses to boot, than the profligate kinsmen adopted the project with alacrity, preferring lucrative felony to downright profitless murder. Do I hear you remark, Sir, that it has ever been thus with this rebellious Jewish people? Well, let us not be rash in assertions. Judah was a very mercenary fellow, no doubt; but it was better to sell a live brother into a slavery which gave him the chance of sitting at the table of Pharaoh Phiops, than to murder one for the mere sake of making money by the sale of the body, as was done by a Christian gentleman of the name of Burke.

There are some plants used in seasoning which have been esteemed for other virtues besides lending a fillip to the appetite. Others of these seasoning plants have acquired an evil reputation. Thus orach was said to cause pallor and dropsy. Rocket had a double use: it not only was said to remove freckles but an infusion of it in wine rendered the hide of a scourged convict insensible to the whip. Fennel was, unlike asparagus, held to be good for the sight. Dill, on the other hand, injured the eyes, while it strengthened the stomach. Anise-seed was in great favour with the medical philosophers, who prescribed it to be taken, fasting, in wine; and hyssop wine was a specific for cutaneous eruptions, brought on by drinking wine of a stronger quality. Wild thyme cured the bite of serpents,—if the sufferer could only collect it in time; and pennyroyal was sovereign for indigestion. Rue cured the ear-ache, and nullified poisons; for which latter purpose it was much used by Mithridates. Mint was gaily eaten, with many a joke, because it was said to have been originally a pretty girl, metamorphosed by Proserpine. The Romans, now and then, ate camomile at table, just as old country ladies, when tea was first introduced, and sent to them as a present, used to boil the leaves, and serve them, at dinner, like spinach. Capers, in the olden time, were vulgar berries, and left for democratic digestion. "I once saw growing in Italy," said an Irish traveller, fit to be "own correspondent" to one of the morning papers, "the finest anchovies I ever beheld!" A listener naturally doubted the alleged fact; and the offended Irishman not only called him out, but shattered his knee-cap by a pistol shot. As he was leaping about with intensity of pain, the Irishman's second remarked to his principal, that he had made his adversary cut capers, at any rate. "Capers!" exclaimed the Hibernian, "capers! 'faith, that's it. Sure, Sir," he added, advancing to his antagonist, "you were right; it was not anchovies, but capers, that I saw growing. I beg pardon: don't think any more about it." Let us add, that, if the aristocratic ancients deeply declined capers, they were exceedingly fond of assafœtida, as a seasoning ingredient. Green ginger was also a popular condiment; and it is commonly eaten in Madagascar at this day. I suppose that, in former times, Hull imported this production in large quantities, and that therefore one of her streets is called "the Land of Green Ginger." The Romans gave wormwood wine to the charioteers, perhaps considering that the stomachic beverage would secure them from dizziness.

I have mentioned above that Mithridates patronized rue as a nullifier of poisons. He was in the habit of swallowing poisons, as people in the summer swallow ices; and he was famous for inventing antidotes, to enable him to take them with impunity. One consequence is, that he has gained a sort of immortality in our pharmacopœia; and "Mithridate," in pharmacy, is a compound medicine, in form of an electuary, serving as either a remedy or a preservative against poisons, being also accounted a cordial, opiate, sudorific, and alexipharmic. "Mithridate" is, or rather, I suppose, was, one of the capital medicines in the apothecaries' shops. The preparation of it, according to the direction of the College, is as follows; and I request my readers to peruse it attentively, and to get it by heart, in case of necessity supervening. Here is the facile recipe: "Take of cinnamon, fourteen drachms; of myrrh, eleven drachms; agarich, spikenard, ginger, saffron, seeds of treacle-mustard, frankincense, Chio turpentine, of each ten drachms; camel's hay, costus, Indian leaf, French lavender, long pepper, seeds of hartwort, juice of the rape of cistus, strained storax, opopanax, strained galbanum, balsam of Gilead, or, in its stead, expressed oil of nutmegs, Russian castor, of each an ounce; polymountain, water germander, the fruit of the balsam tree, seeds of the carrot of Crete, bdellium strained, of each seven drachms; Celtic nard, gentian root, leaves of dittany of Crete, red roses, seed of Macedonian parsley, the lesser Cardanum seeds freed from their husks, sweet fennel seeds, gum Arabic, opium strained, of each five drachms; root of the sweet flag, root of wild valerian, anise-seed, sagapenum strained, of each three drachms; spignel, St. John's wort, juice of acacia, the bellies of scinks, of each two drachms and a half; of clarified honey, thrice the weight of all the rest: dissolve the opium first in a little wine, and then mix it with the honey made hot. In the mean-time, melt together, in another vessel, the galbanum, storax, turpentine, and the balsam of Gilead, or the expressed oil of nutmeg," (I have no doubt that one will do quite as well as the other; and this must be highly satisfactory for sufferers to know,) "continually stirring them round, that they may not burn; and, as soon as these are melted, add to them the hot honey, first by spoonful and afterwards more freely. Lastly, when this mixture is nearly cold, add by degrees the rest of the spices reduced to powder,"—*and*, as the French quack used to say of his specific for the toothache, if it does you no harm, it will certainly do you no good. For my own part, I think the remedy worse than the disease; but a gentleman just poisoned may be of another opinion; and I can only say, that if, with prussic acid knocking at his pylorus, he has leisure to wait till the above prescription is made up for him,—till the bellies of scinks an' the camel's hay are procured, and till the ingredients are amalgamated "by degrees,"—he will, *if* he survive the poison, the waiting, and the remedy, have deserved to be called, κατ' ἐξοχὴν, the "patient." But here are the pastry and the fruits; and there are people who are given to believe that pastry and poison are not very wide asunder.

When Murat wished to instigate the Italians to labour, he cut down their olive-trees. The Jews were forbidden to destroy fruit-trees, even in an enemy's country; and it used to be a law in France, and may be so still, that when an individual had received permission to cut down one of his trees, it was on condition of his planting two. The planters of vineyards enjoyed many privileges under the Jewish dispensation, and heathen governments placed both vineyards and orchards under the protection of the most graceful of their deities, and these deities were supposed to have a special affection for particular trees. The Romans were skilled in forcing their fruits, which were produced at the third course, and not, as with the Greeks, at the second.

Minerva is popularly said to have given birth to the olive, which was the emblem of Peace, the latter being naturally born of Wisdom. But the poisoned shafts of Hercules were made of the olive, perhaps to symbolize those armed neutralities which are generally so fatal to powers with whom the neutrals affect to be at peace. The Autocrat of Russia, for instance, has been dealing very largely in olive shafts, tipped with death. But the olive was known to the world before Wisdom, taking flesh, sprang in her bright panoply from the brain of her sire, and was called Minerva. From Judea the olive was taken into Greece; it was not planted within the territory of Rome until a later period; and, finally, in Spain it found a soil as favourable to cultivation as that of Decapolis, on holy ground. The Ancona olives were the most highly esteemed by the Roman patricians, at whose tables they opened and closed the banquet. While the olives were greedily swallowed, the expressed oil was distributed by way of largess to the people. It was declared to possess, if not a vital principle, something that stimulated and maintained vitality. Augustus, who was for ever whiningly hoping that he might die easily, and for ever chanting the prayer, "Euthanasia!" asked Pollio how he might best maintain his health and strength in old age. "You have nothing in the world to do," said Pollio, "but to drink abundance of wine, and lubricate your imperial carcase with plenty of oil!"—a prescription which does not say much for the medical instruction of Pollio. Olive oil was so scarce at one time, in Europe, that in 817 the Council of Aix-la-Chapelle authorized the priests to manufacture anointing oil from bacon. With regard to the fruit itself, it has not even yet undisputed possession of the public approval; and I am very much of the opinion of the farmer who, having taken some at his landlord's table, expressed his indignation on reaching home, that he had been served with gooseberries stewed in——brine.

The palm-tree wine of the Hebrews inspired song, and thence, perhaps, did the palm itself pass into the possession of the mythological Muses. The palm-tree deserved to be a popular tree: its wood furnished man with a house, its branches with fuel; its leaves afforded him garments, and a bed; and from them he could manufacture baskets, wherein to carry the fruit, bread, and cakes which he could make from its dates. I am only astonished that tradition has not made the palm, rather than the beech or the oak, the original tree which first fed, clothed, and sheltered man.

The cherry, compared with the palm, is but as a rustic beauty, compared with Cleopatra. Mithridates and Lucullus share the glory of making men acquainted with its fruit. From Cerasus, in Asia, Lucullus, no doubt, transplanted a cultivated fruit-tree, of a peculiarly fine sort; but the fruit itself was not unknown to the Romans long anterior to the time of Lucullus. It was slow in acquiring an esteem in Italy. The most extraordinary species of cherry with which I am acquainted, is the Australian cherry, which grows with the stone on the outside. But Nature, in Australia, is distinguished for her freaks. There the pears are made of wood, and salt-water fish abound in the fresh-water rivers! The nastiest species I know of, grows in the vicinity of, nd some of them within, the cemetery of Père-la-Chaise, at Paris. They are magnificent to the eye, and are not ill-flavoured; but, at the heart of each there is a maggot, as fat as one of Rubens's Cupids, and, saving a slight bitterness, with as much of the taste of the cherry in him as a citizen of ripe Stilton has of the cheese of which he is so lively a part. There is not a bad story told of an old and poor Spanish Grandee, who used to put on spectacles when he sat down to his modest dinner of bread and cherries, in order that the fruit might gain, apparently, in magnitude. There was philosophy in this pleasant conceit! If the poor nobleman had had a dish of our cherries, from Kent, Berks, or Oxfordshire, he would not have stood in need of his merry delusion.

How grateful to the palate is the Armenian apricot, blushing, in its precocity, like a young nymph; or the Persian peach, for a couple of which the Romans would give a score of pounds! The peach has an evil tradition with it. It is said to have been originally poisonous, but to have lost its deadliness when it was transplanted. Perhaps the peculiarly peachy odour of prussic acid may have contributed to give currency to a very long-lived, but entirely foundationless, tradition,—except, indeed, that poison may be extracted from the kernel; but so may arsenic from a Turkey carpet, and, indeed, from applepips also, as Sir Fitzroy Kelly told the jury, when endeavouring to save from the gallows a man who had murdered his mistress, in order that he might not put in peril his respectability! Perhaps, the plum tree, whether of Africa or Asia, from Egypt or Damascus, has been more fatal to health, if not to life, than any other of the stone-fruits. When Pliny complained of their superabundant propagation in Italy, he probably had in view the usual consequence of a very plentiful plum season.

The apricot was not known in France till the eleventh century, and then they were accounted dear at a farthing each. In the same century cherries used to appear at the royal table in May. To effect this, lime was laid at the roots of the tree, which was irrigated with warm water! Louis XIII. was fond of early fruit, and he had strawberries in March, and figs in June: this is more than the most expert fig-rearers in Sussex ever accomplished! The fig used to be esteemed as only inferior to that compound of luscious savours, the pine,—a fruit which, in the seventeenth century, was religiously patronized by the Jesuits. The same sort of sanction was given in the East to dates, though these were fashionable in Rome, after a basket of them had been sent from Jericho to Augustus. The Tunis dates are the best; but indulgence in them is said to loosen the teeth, and produce scurvy. The Tunisian ladies, however, were as fond of them as the French ladies were of sweet citrons, before oranges were patronized by Louis XIV. The ladies used to carry them about, and occasionally suck them, the operation being considered excellent to produce ruby lips. The citron was hardly less popular than the Reine Claude plum, which received its pretty name from the Queen of Francis I., and daughter of Louis XII. I have noticed the Sussex fig; the white fig of the Channel Islands is also highly prized; and there is a tree at Hampton Court renowned for its fruit, but they who eat had better not too curiously inquire as to where the root of that productive tree penetrates, in order to accomplish its productiveness. In Sicily, they acupuncture the tree, and drop into it a little oil, and this is said to improve the flavour of the fruit. To what I have previously said of the peach, I may add here what the Chinese say of it; namely, that it produces eternity of life, and prevents corruption until the end of the world. This species would be a popular one in England.

Some writers assert that the apple was originally an African; but a negro with a red nose would be an anomaly; and the apple-tree does not look as if it came from the country of the children of the sun. Nevertheless, historians assert that it crossed the Mediterranean, and reached Normandy through Spain and France. The apple has been as productive of similes as of cider; and perhaps the prettiest in that of Jeremy Taylor, who says, in his Sermon on the "Marriage Ring," that the "celibate, like the fly in the heart of an apple, dwells in a perpetual sweetness; but sits alone, and is confined, and dies in singularity:"—a figure of speech, by the way, not highly calculated to frighten a bachelor. But, after all, the sentiment of Jeremy Taylor is preferable to that of Gregory of Nazianzum, who calls a wife "an acquired evil; and, what is worse, one that cannot be put away." However this may be, apples were once productive of matrimony in Wales. When the fruit-dealers there could not find a market, they proclaimed a dance. The revellers paid entrance-money, and received apples in return. These meetings were called "apple lakings;" and the fruit was sauce for many a consequent wedding dinner. The finest used to be kept for accompaniment to the roast goose eaten on St. Crispin's Day. Brides, in remote times, used to carry a love-apple in their bosoms; as fond thereof as the pitman's wife of Northumberland was of the two lambs which she suckled, after their dams had been killed in a storm. This was a more creditable affection than that of Marc Antony's daughter for a lamprey, which she adorned with ear-rings, and which she exhibited at dinner; as Lord Erskine did the leeches which had cured him of some complaint, and which, enclosed in a bottle, he sent round with the wine. He called one "Cline" and the other "Home," from the great surgeons of those names; and noble guests, before filling their glasses, gravely inspected the leeches, and then duly passed on the reptiles and the wine.

This is what a Frenchman would have called a "*triste plaisanterie à l'Anglaise;*" and, by the way, I may remark, that Theophile de Garancières imputes the alleged melancholic nature of Englishmen to the great use which we make of sugar. Our sires used to make one curious use of sugar, undoubtedly; namely, when they put it into the mouth of the dying, in order that their souls might pass away with less bitterness!

There is a German proverb which says, that "it is unadvisable to eat cherries with potentates." In English this might mean, "Do not make too free with your betters." Few royal families, however, have given their inferiors more frequent opportunities to "eat cherries" with them, than that of Prussia. I am reminded of this while upon the subject of pine-apple, a slice of which was once given by Frederick William III. to a lad employed in the gardens at Sans Souci. "Here," said the King, pleasantly, "eat, enjoy, and reflect while thou art eating. Now, what does it taste like?" The boy looked puzzled, as he munched the pine; thought of all the most delightful things that had ever passed over his palate and clung to his memory, and, at last, with a satisfied expression, exclaimed, "I think,—yes, it does,—it tastes like sausage!" The courtiers laughed aloud; and the King, philosophizing on the boy's answer, said, "Well, every one has his own standard of taste, guiding his feelings and judgment, and each one believes himself to be right. One fancies he discovers in the pine-apple the flavour of the melon; another, of the pear; a third, the plum. Yon lad, in his sphere of tastes, finds therein his favourite food—the sausage."

The lad's answer was as much food for mirth at Sans Souci, as was that of the Eton boy who was invited by Queen Adelaide to dine at Windsor Castle, and who was honoured with a seat at Her Majesty's side. The boy was bashful,—the Queen encouraging; and, when the sweets were on the table, she kindly asked him what he would like to take. The Etonian's eyes glanced hurriedly and nervously from dish to dish; pointing to one of which, he, in some agitation, exclaimed, "One of those twopenny tarts!" His young eye had recognised the favourite "*tuck*" he was in the habit of indulging in at *the* shop in Eton, and he asked for it according to the local phrase in fashion. Reverting to the lad who compared pine-apple to German sausage, I may remark, that pine-apple is most to be enjoyed when the weather is of that condition which made Sydney Smith once express a wish, that he could "slip out of his fat, and sit in his bones."

The quince is a native of Cydon, in Crete; and first Greece and then Rome, Gaul, and Spain, learned to love the fruit, and drink a quince wine, which was said to be excellent either as a stomachic or as a counter-poison.

Galen recommended the pear as an astringent, which is more than a modern practitioner will do. St. Francis de Paul introduced one sort into France when he paid a medical visit to Louis XI. The species was named from the saint, "*le bon Chrétien*."

The apple may lay fair claim to antiquity of birth. The fruit has been diversely estimated by divers nations; but the general favour has usually awaited it. In ancient times, both in Greece and Persia, it was the custom for a bridegroom at his nuptial feast to partake of a single apple, and of nothing else. The origin of the custom is said to arise from a decree issued by Solon. It was the sight of an apple that always put Vladislas, King of Poland, into fits. It is the best fruit that can be taken as an accompaniment to wine; and the best sorts for such a purpose are the Ribstone Pippin and the Coster Pearmain. The golden apples stolen by Hercules were lemons; and they are suspected to have been the "Median apples" of Theophrastus. The Romans, at first, employed this Asiatic fruit only as a means for keeping moths out of garments; from this household use it passed into the ancient pharmacopœia, and it took rank among the counter-poisons. Its acknowledged reputation in scurvy and punch, if I may so express myself, was not made until a much later period of civilization. The orange disputes with the lemon the honour of being the "Hesperides apples,"—which is a dispute of a very Hibernian character. China was probably its native place; and the Portuguese oranges are merely descendants of the original "Chinaman." It was not known in France until introduced there by the Constable de Bourbon. In England, an orange, stuck full of cloves, was a fitting New Year's present from a lover,—being typical of warmth and sweetness.

The fig-tree appears to have been, like the vine, very early used as a symbol of peace and plenty. It was a tree of Eden; yet the Athenians claimed it as a native tree, asserting by way of proof, that it had been given them by Ceres,—not reflecting that Ceres *may* have brought it from a region farther east. If it be commonly employed in Scripture as a symbol, so an American poet has taken it, with its scriptural allusions, to illustrate worldly marriages, of which he says, that—

"———— they are like unto
  Jeremiah's figs :
The good are very good indeed ;
The bad, not fit for pigs."

The authorities of Attica were so fond of *their* figs, that they passed a law against the exportation of the fruit. The advocates of free trade in figs broke the law when they could do so with profit; and the men who affected to be on friendly terms with them, in order to betray their proceedings to the Magistrates, were called by a name which is now given to all fawning traitors, they were styled, *sycophants*, or "fig-declarers." Even the philosophers in Greece became greedy in presence of figs; and with figs famished armies have been braced anew for the fight. The *athletæ* ate of them before appearing in the arena; and more than one invasion has been traced to the taste of the invader for figs. Medical men were divided in opinion as to the merits of this fruit. It was considered indigestible; but, to remedy that, almonds were recommended to be eaten with it! The Romans, perhaps, were wiser, who took pepper with them, as we do with melon; and Dr. Madden says that we should never eat figs at all, if we could only spend half an hour in Smyrna, and see them packed. So, as I have before said, a sight of the kitchen, just before dinner, would take away appetite; but as people do not commonly go to Smyrna, or sit with their cooks, why, figs and dinners will continue to be eaten. Modern professors have resembled ancient philosophers in an uncontrollable appetite for figs. Who has not heard of the famous Oxford fig, which, in its progress to luscious maturity, was protected by an inscription appended to it, conveying information to the effect that "this is the Principal's fig!" which a daring Undergraduate one day devoured, and added insult to injury by changing the old placard for one on which was written, "A fig for the Principal!" The felonious fig-stealer must have been more rapid in his sacrilege, than the poet Thomson was in his method of enjoying his own peaches in his garden at Kew. Attired in the loosest and dirtiest of morning-gowns, the author of the "Castle of Indolence" used to watch his peaches ripening in the sun. When he saw one bursting with liquid promise, he was too lazy to take his unwashed hands from his well-worn pockets, and pluck the blushing treasure. No; "Jamie" simply sauntered up to it, contemplated it for a moment with a yawn, and finished his yawn by biting a piece out of the fruit,—leaving the ghastly remains on the branch for wasps and birds to divide between them.

As the Athenian rulers kept their figs, so did the Persian Kings their walnuts,—and more selfishly; for no one but their most sacred Majesties dared eat any; but one would think that even they would find it hard to digest all the walnuts that the country could produce. It is averred, that walnuts entered into the Mithridatic recipe against poison. The modern recipe, called "Mithridate," I have given elsewhere; but that which Pompey is said to have found in the palace of the King whom he had overthrown, was as follows: "Pound, with care, two walnuts, two dried figs, twenty pounds of rue, and *a grain of salt.*" Yes, we should say it must be taken *cum grano.* Howbeit, the royal physician goes on to say, "Swallow this mixture,—precipitate it with a little wine,—and you have nothing to fear from the action of the most active poison for the space of four-and-twenty hours." There would, probably, be less to fear after that time had elapsed than before.

Nuts have not had respectability conferred on them, even by Nero, who was wont to go *incog.* to the upper gallery of the theatre, and take delight in pelting them on the bald head of the Prætor, who sat below. That official knew the offender, and was rewarded for bearing the attack good-humouredly; and thence, perhaps, the proverb which characterizes something falling, at once sudden and pleasant, by the term, "That's nuts!" Of course, nuts were in fashion; not so chestnuts,—these were as much disliked by the Patricians as the filbert and hazel were said, in France, to be hated by the sun. When they were ripening, the inhabitants used to issue forth at sunrise, and endeavour to frighten the luminary out of the firmament, by making a horrid uproar, with pots, pans, and kitchen utensils generally. And this was done under a Christian dispensation. The people were not heathen Chinese, trying to cure an eclipsed planet by attacking the dragon that was supposed to be swallowing it, with a *tintamarre* of caldron, kettle, tongs, and trivet.

The Athenians were great hands at dumplings, consisting of fruit, covered with a light and perfumed paste; and Rhodes, verifying the proverb, that "extremes meet," was as famous for its gingerbread as for its Colossus. The Roman wedding-cake was a simple mixture of sweet wine and flour; and the *savilum* pie, made of flour, cheese, honey, and eggs, was a dish to make all sorts of guests jubilant. It was, in short, the national pie; and if there were a dish that was more popular, it was the *artocreas*, a huge mince-piece, and the imperial pie of Verus, compounded of sow's flank, pheasant, peacock, ham, and wild boar, all hashed together, and covered with crust. If Emperors invented pies, so did philosophers create cakes; and the *libuna* of Cato was a real cheese-cake, that gave as much delight as any of the same author's works in literature. Cheese was a favourite foundation for many of the Roman cakes; but he was a bold man who added chalk, and so invented the *placenta*. Yet the *placenta* was eaten as readily as Charles XII. swallowed raspberry-tarts, Frederick II. Savoy cakes, or Marshal Saxe—who loved pastry, pastrycooks, and pastrycooks' daughters—macaroons.

The Church honoured pastry,—or would so pious a King as St.

Louis have raised the pastrycooks to the dignity of a guild? The Abbey of St. Denis, long before this, stipulated with the tenant-farmers, that they should deliver a certain quantity of flour, to make pastry with; and, in some cases, in France, portions of the rent for land was to be paid in puff pastry. This was at a time when fennel-root tooth-picks used to appear at table, thrust into the preserved fruits, and every one was expected to help himself. Certainly our refined neighbours had some questionable customs. See what L'Etoile says: (1596:) "*Les confitures sèches et les massepains y étaient si peu épargnés que les dames et demoiselles étaient contraintes de s'en décharger sur les pages et laquais, auxquels on les baillait tout entiers.*"

Prince George of Denmark, the consort of Queen Anne, was never suspected of intermeddling with the foreign policy of the kingdom; but he was something renowned for his appetite, and for the bent of it towards pastry. I think it is Archdeacon Coxe, in his "Life of the Duke of Marlborough," who says of this illustrious Prince, that he would leave the battle-field, in the very heat of action, and come into camp, with the hungry inquiry, if it were not yet dinner-time. This was something worse than drawing off the hounds, or unloading the fowling-pieces, because the "Castle bell" was peremptorily ringing to luncheon. Prince George was just the sort of man—fond of good living, and able to entertain others with the same predilection—who was likely to be surrounded by parasites; and the remembrance of this fact suggests that, while the wine is passing round, I may venture to give a sketch of that ancient and remarkable gentleman, "the Parasite." It is better than getting upon controversial subjects, which are productive of anything but unanimity. I remember one of the very pleasantest of "after-dinners" being marred by a guest, who, having slipped into the assertion that the Jews were the earliest of created people, was indiscreet enough to try to maintain what he had asserted, and weak enough to be angry at finding it summarily rejected. Why, Father Abraham himself was but a foreign Heathen, from Ur of the Chaldees; and to claim primeval antiquity for the Jews is only as absurd as if one was to say, that Yankees and mint-juleps were anterior to Alfred's cakes and the Anglo-Saxons.

But many a hasty assertion has been simply the effect of an antagonism between imperfect chymification and the oppressed intellect. Mind and matter have much influence on each other; and, for the guidance of those interested in such questions, I may, while on the subject of dinner, notice, that from Dr. Beaumont's "Table," drawn out to show the mean time of digestion in the stomach (or *chymification*) of various articles of food, we learn that boiled tripe ranks first in amiable facility, being disposed of in about one hour. Venison steak requires some half hour more. Boiled turkey and roast pig are classed together, as requiring two hours and twenty-five minutes for the process of digestion; while roast turkey and hashed meat demand five minutes more. Fricasséed chicken is not more facile of digestion than boiled salt beef, both requiring two hours and three-quarters. Boiled mutton, broiled beefsteak, and soft-boiled eggs take three hours; while roast beef and old strong cheese trouble the stomach for some three hours and a half. Roast duck, and fowls, whether boiled or roasted, are alike slow of digestion: they require four hours as their mean time of chymification, and are only exceeded by boiled cabbage, which requires full half-an-hour more. I borrow these details from an article in the "Journal of Psychological Medicine," for January, 1851, a periodical edited by Dr. Forbes Winslow. I believe I do not err in attributing the article in question ("Mental Dietetics") to the able pen of the accomplished Editor himself, than whom no man has a better right to speak *ex cathedrâ* on the subject in question. It will be seen by the following extract from this article, that diet influences the mind as well as the body. "The nutritive particles of the food," says Dr. Winslow, "being in the form of chyle, mixed with the blood, and supplying it with the elements which enable it to repair the waste of the animal system, it is obvious that the health of both the body and of the mind, must depend on the quality and quantity of the vital stream. According to Lecanu, the proportion of the red globules of the blood may be regarded as a measure of vital energy; for the action of the serum and of the globules on the nervous system is very different. The former scarcely excites it, the latter do so powerfully. Now those causes which tend to increase the mass of blood, tend also to increase the proportion of red globules; whilst those which tend to diminish the mass of blood, tend to diminish the proportion of the globules. The result is obvious. A large quantity of stimulating animal food, without a proper amount of exercise, augments the number of the red globules, and diminishes the aqueous part of the blood. Hence the nervous system becomes oppressed, the brain frequently congested, and the intellectual faculties no longer enjoy their wonted activity. In the mean time, the system endeavours to relieve itself by throwing a counter-stimulus upon certain other organs, the functions of which are morbidly increased. The blood, in such cases, becomes preternaturally thickened, and its coagulum unusually firm. On the other hand, if the system be not supplied with the requisite amount of nutrition, the blood becomes, by the loss of its red corpuscles, impoverished in quality, and, in cases of extreme abstinence, diminished in quantity. In these cases the powers of the mind soon become enfeebled."

But we will pass from these scientific matters, to seek the company of one who, if ignorant of science, was, generally, a great man in the profession of his peculiar art,—the ancient parasite.

THE PARASITE.

——" Pity those whose flanks grow great,
Swell'd by the lard of others' meat."—Herrick.

Para, "near," and *sitos*, "corn," pretty well explain what the Greeks understood by the word "parasite." As the worthless weed among the wheat, so was this classical Skimpole in the field of society. As the weed hung for support to the substance that promised to yield it, so did the parasite cling to the side of those who kept good tables, and lacked wit to enliven them.

The parasite was too delicate a fellow to allow of invidious distinctions. He supped or dined wherever he was invited, and at marriage-feasts waited for no invitation at all. *There* he was in his glory. He was the cracker of jokes, and of the heads of those who did not agree with every word that fell from the lips of the Amphitryon of the hour. He usually, however, got his own skull bruised by the watch, when staggering home through the dark, "full of the god," and without a slave to direct his steps. But it was only with the morning that he became conscious at once of pain from the bruises, and the necessity of providing, at the cost of others, for his own breakfast.

These professional "livers out" were, however, not always unattended. The victims whom they flattered sometimes lent them a slave. Their wardrobe seldom extended beyond two suits, one for the public, and one for wear at home. They looked abroad for dupes, just as our ring-droppers used to do, and for the same purpose. The parasite generally attached himself to the first simple-looking personage he encountered, provided he bore with him proofs of being a man who could afford to live well. *Simplex* usually swallowed with complacency all the three-piled flattery with which the parasite troubled him; and if he were expecting friends to dinner, the gastronome, who wanted one, was probably invited. But there was always an understanding, that, in return for the invitation, he was to maintain, for the diversion of the company, a continual fire of jokes. If he proved but a sorry jester, he was promptly scourged into the street, down which he ran, nothing abashed, to look for hearers whom indifferent jests could move to ready laughter.

The parasite looked upon the fortune and table of others as a property which was properly to be held in common. Monsieur Prudhon really started a parasitical precept, when he tried to establish that what belonged to one man belonged to a great many others besides. But if, as regarded his own share in property that was *not* his own, the parasite was so far a Communist, he was the most charitable of fellows, his earnest prayer being, that none of his patrons might ever fall into such distress as to be unable to give good dinners. The dinner-table was his arena. If he got but one meal a day, he consumed enough thereat to satisfy half-a-dozen appetites; and, as he ate, it was matter of perfect indifference to him whether he was called upon to find wit for the guests, or to be the butt of their own. You might buffet him till he were senseless, provided the blows were afterwards paid for in brimming glasses.

He was always first at a feast; and as he was as common an object at a feast as the sauce itself, so "sauce" was the common name for a parasite. There he was not only wit, butt, and bully, but porter also; and his office was not merely to knock down the drunken, but to carry them out when incapable of performing that office for themselves. The parasites had a dash, too, of the "bravo" in their character, and let themselves out for a dozen other purposes besides dining. The stronger-bodied and the braver-souled let out their strength. "Do you want a wrestler?" says the parasite, in Antiphæus, "here I am, an Antæus. If you want a door forced, I have a head like a ram to do it; and I can scale a wall like Capaneus. Telamon was not stronger than my wrist; and I can wreathe into the ear of beauty like smoke." Some of these Bobadils are even said to have ventured into battle, and to have especially distinguished themselves in the Commissariat department!

Others boasted of their powers of fasting,—always provided good pay assured them of compensating banquets at the end of their service. "I can live on as little as Tithymallus," says one; and the individual in question is said to have supported life on eight lupines a day,—a hint to Poor-Law Commissioners. Another makes a merit of being as thin as Philippides, who, like Hood's friend, was *so* thin, that, when he stood sideways you could not see him! The merits of a third are summed up by him in saying, that he can live on water, like a frog; on vegetables, like a caterpillar; can go without bathing, like Dirtiness herself, if there be such a deity; can live in winter with no roof but the sky, like a bird; can support heat, and sing beneath a noon-day sun, like a grasshopper; do without oil, like the dust; walk barefooted from break of day, like the crane; and keep wide awake all night, like the owl.

Of such a profession the parasite was proud, and even declared that its origin was divine; and that Jupiter Amicalis (Ζεὺς ὁ φίλιος) was its patron saint! As Jove entered where he chose, ate and drank of what most took his fancy, and, after creating an atmosphere of enjoyment, retired without having any thing to pay; just so, it was argued, was it with the parasite. In Attica, parasites were admitted to the commemorative banquets that followed the sacrifices to Hercules; proof enough that they were accounted as being the same kidney as heroes. In later times came degenerate men and manners; and then, instead of honorable men sitting with gods and heroes, the office of parasite was so degraded, that none but the hungry wits exercised it. Flattery to mortals then took the place of praise to gods. The parasite was ready to laud every act of the master of the feast,—

"————— *laudare paratus*
Si bene ructavit, si rectum minxit amicus,"

and to eulogize a great number of other acts besides, as may be found noted by those who are very curious, and not over-nice, in the fragments of Diodorus of Sinope.

The fellows were witty, too, however degraded. When Chorephon had, uninvited, slipped into a vacant position at a wedding-dinner, the gynæconomes, as inspectors of the feast, counting the guests, came upon him at last, and said, "You are the thirty-first: it is against the law; you must withdraw." "I do not dispute the law," said the parasite, "but I object to your manner of counting. Begin the numbering by me, and your conclusions will be undisputable."

The parasite, Philoxenus, happened to be supping with a host who gave his guests nothing but black bread. "This is not a loaf, but a spectre," whispered the professional wit: "if we eat any more of it, we shall soon be in the shades."

There was more wit in Bithys, the parasite of the avaricious King Lysimachus, who one day, at dinner, flung a wooden scorpion at the flatterer. The latter affected great fright, but afterwards remarked, "I will, in my turn, terrify you, O King; be good enough to give me a talent."

Clisophus, another of this strange brotherhood, either fooled or flattered King Philip to the very top of his bent. The King having lost an eye, Clisophus always sat down to dinner in his presence with a bandage over one of his own; and when the Monarch limped, from a wound in the leg, Clisophus went "halting at his side;" and if, by chance, an ill odour affected the royal nostrils, Clisophus wore, all day long, a grimace upon his features, as if he were sick with disgust. However absurd this may appear, the parasites of Louis XIV. flattered him as grossly as the original practitioners did the early and heathen Kings. People shaved their heads and wore periwigs, because the monarch, having little hair of his own, wore long locks cropped from other heads. So, when once at dinner he complained of having lost his teeth, a young flatterer who sat next him swore, with a broad smile which displayed his incisors, that nobody had teeth now-a-days. And again, when the King, on his seventieth birth-day, inquired the age of a person from whom he had received a petition, the reply was, that the person was of everybody's age,—about three-score and ten. Nay, the Court preachers flattered the Sovereign quite as coarsely as the mere courtiers, and would not have received invitations to dinner if they had not done so. "My brethren," said one of these, "all men must die;" and at that very moment he perceived the eye of the King glaring uneasily upon him:—"that is to say, Sire, *almost all* men!" and the complaisant preacher was at the royal table that day. The same parasitical spirit prevailed at the English Court, especially when bolster neckcloths were worn, simply because the King was compelled to wear one, in consequence of a disease in the glands of the neck. But, to translate the sentiment of the French poet,—

> "From royal example slaves have never shrunk:
> When Auguste tippled, Poland soon got drunk.
> When the great Monarch breathed the air of love,
> Hey, presto, pass! Paris was Venus' grove!
> But turn'd a Churchman and devout, alas!
> The courtiers ran and beat their breasts at mass."

It is said by ancient writers that the species of flattery which Clisophus paid Philip, was obligatory on all the guests and officials in the ancient royal Courts of Arabia. There, if the King suffered in any member, every courtier was bound to be in pain in the same limb. This species of flattery was, in fact, a conclusion logically arrived at; for the Arab lawgivers said that it would be absurd in the courtiers to vie with one another for the honour of being buried alive with the King defunct, if they did not suffer with him in all his bodily pains when living.

The Celtic King of the Sotians maintained a body of men who were called the "Eucholimes," or the "Death Volunteers." They amounted to six hundred men; they were lodged, clothed, and tended like the King, with whom they daily sat at meat; but they were also bound to die with their master; and it is alleged that the chance was eagerly incurred, and that no man ever failed, when called upon by the King's decease, to accompany His Majesty on a visit to his royal cousin, Orcus.

But your regular parasite preferred to live and flatter living Monarchs. "See," said Niceas, when he saw Alexander troubled by a fly that stung him, "there is one that will be King over all flies; for he has imbibed the blood of him who is King over all men." The flattery was not more delicate which Chirisophus once paid at dinner to Dionysius the Tyrant. Chirisophus, seeing the King smile at the other end of the table, burst into a roar of laughter. The King asked, "Wherefore?" seeing that the parasite could not have heard the joke. "True," said Chirisophus; "but I saw that Your Majesty had heard something worth laughing at, and I laughed in sympathy." This species of parasite is not uncommon in English houses; but perhaps they do their office more refinedly than Chirisophus.

The flatterers of the younger Dionysius were far more disgusting in their adulation. They were simply absurd, when they pretended to be short-sighted, like him, and to be unable to see a dish, unless they thrust their noses into it. But they were filthy followers when they offered their faces to the King to "void his rheum" upon, and even went to extremes of nastiness at which human nature shudders, but at which Dionysius smiled. And yet Dionysius was hailed by some of them as a god. It was the custom, we are told, in Sicily, for every individual to make sacrifices, in his own house, before the figures of the nymphs, to get devoutly drunk before the altar, and to dance round it as long as the pious devotee could keep upon his legs. It was accounted as an exquisite piece of flattery in Damocles, **the parasite, that he** refused to perform such service before inanimate deities, while **he went** through the whole duty before Dionysius as his god. The Athenians, it will be remembered, were horror-stricken at such impious laudation as this. They fined Demades ten talents for having proposed to award divine honours to Alexander; and Timagoras, whom they sent as Ambassador to the King of Persia, they put to death **for compromising** the Athenian dignity by prostrating himself before that King. And, indeed, let us do justice to Alexander himself. He had more than misgiving touching of his own alleged divinity. He had once—"his custom in the afternoon"—eaten and drunk so enormously, that in the evening he was forced to a necessity which compels very mortal people,—take physic. He made as many contortions, on swallowing it, as a refractory child; and Philarches, his parasite, remarked, with a rascally hypocritical smile, "Ah! what must be the sufferings of mortal man under such medicine, if you, who are a divinity, feel it so much?" The idea of a deity drawing health out of an apothecary's phial was too much even for Alexander, who declined to accept the apotheosis, and called Philarches an ass.

But Philarches was only giving the King a taste of the parasite's professional craft. The noble Nicostratus of Argos quite as impiously flattered the Sovereign of Persia, when, for the sake of currying favour with that majestic barbarian, he every night, in his own house, prepared a solemn supper, richly provided, and offered to the genius of the King, (τῷ δαίμονι τοῦ Βαδιλέως,) for no better reason than that he had learned that such was the custom in Persia. Whether he profited or not by this delicate attention, Theopompus does not inform us.

The Anactes or Princes of the royal family of Salamis maintained two distinct families, in whom, if I understand Athenæus rightly, the office of flatterer (and of spy, I may add) was hereditary. These were the Gerginoi and the Promalangai. The former did the dirty work of circulating among the people, worming themselves into their confidence, getting invited to their tables, and then reporting to the Promalangai all they had heard. The last-named took such portions of the report as were worth communicating to the Anactes, with whom they sat at table, where such a dish of scandal was daily served as would puzzle the social spies of Paris to set before their lord.

But the profession was not accounted vile; and the professors themselves gloried in their vocation. They extolled the easiness of their life, compared, for instance, with that of the painter, or the labourer, or, in fact, with that of any other individual but those of their own guild. "Truly," says one, in a fragment of Antiphanes, "since the most important business of life is to play, laugh, trifle, and drink, I should like to know where you would find a condition more agreeable than ours."

Once, and once only, a faction of parasites contrived to get possession of a kingdom; and the dinners they gave, and the government they maintained, are matters to which description can hardly do justice. The faction in question was headed by, and almost solely consisted of, three men in Erythra, who stood, in regard to Cnopus, the King, as "adorers and flatterers" (πρόσκυνες καὶ κόλακες). They murdered their Sovereign, and, by a *coup-d'-état*, possessed themselves of his authority. Their names were Ortyges, Irus, and Echarus; and they ruled with a triple rod of iron, held in very effeminate fingers. They silenced all opponents by slaying them; and, when no one dared utter a breath against them, they vaunted their universal popularity. They administered a ferociously absurd sort of justice at the gates of Erythra, where they sat decked out in purple and gold. They were sandaled like women, wore ornaments only suitable to females, and sat down to dinner in diadems that dazzled the company.

The guests were once free citizens, who were now compelled to bear the litters of their *parvenu* masters, to cleanse the streets, and then, by way of contrast, to attend the banquet of the Triumvirs, with their wives and daughters. If they objected to drag these latter to the scene of splendid infamy, the objection was only made at the price of death. The unhappy women were nothing the safer from insult by the decease of their natural protectors; and the scenes at the palace were such as only the uncleanest of demons could rejoice in. If the authorities had reason to be grave, the whole city was compelled to affect sorrow; and duly-appointed officers went round, with hard-thonged whips, to scourge a sense of "decent horror" into the countenances of the bewildered inhabitants. Things at last reached such a pitch of extravagant atrocity, that the people took heart of grace, screwed up their courage by Chian wine, and swept their oppressors into Hades;—and, for years afterwards, commemorative banquets celebrated the restoration of the people from the oppression of the parasites.

I would recommend those who would see the parasite in action, to study the comedies of Plautus, wherein he figures as necessarily as the impertinent valet in a Spanish comedy. Plautus calls the parasites *poetæ*, as being given to lying; and it is singular that the Gauls called their poets "parasites," as being fond of good living, and not being always in a condition to procure it. They had their "dull season:" it was when the wealthy were at their villas; at which time the parasites dined upon nothing, in town, with good "Duke Humphrey." When the city was again resorted to by the rich, then the parasite might sometimes be seen purchasing, by order of his patron, the provisions for the evening feast. We find one of these gentry, in Plautus, boasting that he knows a story that will be worth thirty dinners to him. Before the era of printing, the parasite, with his jests and histories, was a sort of living Circulating Library. Saturion (another of Plautus's pictures of the parasite) is at peace with himself, because, as he says, he can provide for his daughter by bequeathing to her his rich collection of jokes and dinner-stories. "They are all sparkling Attic," he says; "and there is not a dull Sicilian anecdote among them."

If the race were, in some sense of the word, "literary," they were not at all in love with science, or the improvements wrought by its application. Witness the bitterness with which Plautus makes one denounce the sun-dial, then of recent introduction. Before that tell-tale appeared, dinners used to be served when people were hungry; but *now* even hungry people wait for the appointed hour. In short, throughout life, they worked but for the sake of the banquet and wine-pot; and even after death, they longed for libations, as appears in the epitaph on the parasite, Sergius of Pola, who is made to say, from the grave,—

> " *Si urbani perhiberi vultis*
> *Arenti meo cineri,*
> *Cantharo piaculum vinarium festinate.*"

> "If you've any regard for this corpse here of mine,
> Be so good as to damp it with hogsheads of wine."

Finally, these diners-out by profession were essentially selfish; and the fire of their attachment blazed up, or died away, according to that in the kitchen of the Amphitryon by whom they were maintained.

A good specimen of the parasite of the last century may be found in the Captain Cormorant of Anstey's "Bath Guide;" but the race is by no means extinct, though the individual be more rarely met with; and, be it said as their due, they execute their office with something more of decency than did their ancient predecessors. Modern flattery, like modern oils, is "double refined." Let us see if we can trace the course of this refinement through the Table Traits of Utopia and the Golden Age.

THE TABLES OF UTOPIA AND THE GOLDEN AGE.

The good Archbishop Fénelon, in his "*Voyage dans l'Ile des Plaisirs*," cites some charming examples of the pleasant way in which people lived in the Utopian Land of Cocagne, which he describes from imagination, and where the laws were characterized by more good sense than distinguishes the legislation of the Utopian authorities of More.

The "*Voyage*" of Fénelon was probably founded on a fragment of Teleclides, who has narrated, in rattling Greek metres, how the citizens of the world lived and banqueted in the golden age of its lusty youth. The poet puts the description into the mouth of Saturn, who says, "I will tell you what sort of life I vouchsafed to men in the early ages of creation. In the first place, peace reigned universally, and was as common as the water you wash your hands with. Fear and disease were entirely unknown; and the earth provided spontaneously for every human want. The rivers then poured cataracts of wine into the valleys; and the cakes disputed with loaves to get into the mouth of man, as he walked abroad, supplicating to be eaten, and giving assurances of excellent flavour and quality. The tables were covered with fish which floated into the kitchens, and courteously put themselves to roast. By the sides of the couches rolled streams of sauces, bearing with them joints of ready-roasted meat; while rivulets full of *ragoûts* were near the guests, who dipped in, and took therefrom, according to their fancy. Every one could eat of what he pleased; and all that he ate was sweet and succulent. There were countless pomegranate-seeds for seasoning; little *pâtés* and *grives*, done to a turn, insinuated themselves into the mouths of the banqueters; and tarts got smashed in trying to force their way into the throat. The children played with sow-paps and other delicacies as they would with toys; and the men were gigantic in height, and obese in figure."

The above is a specimen of the classical idea of that delicious—

> ———————"Land of Cocagne,
> That Elysium of all that is friand and nice,
> Where for hail they have bon-bons, and claret for rain,
> And the skaters, in winter, show off on cream-ice.

It is a theme with which modern poets have been as fond of dealing as Teleclides and others of the tuneful children of song, in the early period when young Time counted his birth-days by the sun. It has been well treated by Béranger, who thus describes, through my imperfect translation, his own impressions of

A JOURNEY TO THE LAND OF COCAGNE.

Ho, friends, every one!
Let us up, and be gone;—
To where care is not known,
   Let us hasten away;
Yes; fired with champagne,
I reel o'er the plain,
And see dear Cocagne
   In its sunny array.

O! land full of glee,—
Here long may I be,
And laugh merrilie
   At Fate's changeable way.
For here—what a treat!—
I may love, drink, and eat,
And—this makes it more sweet—
   There is nothing to pay!

My appetite's great,
And I see the huge gate
Of a tower of state
   At my elbow, handy:
The tower is a pie;—
And tall guards, standing by,
Carry spears ten feet high,
   All in sugar-candy.

Ah! banquet of fun,
It will please ev'ry one:
Look, there is not a gun
   But of sugar is made!
See the paintings, how grand
And the statues, they stand,
All wrought by the hand
   Out of sweet marmalade.

Here the people repair
In gay crowds to the square,
Where the jests of a fair
   With loud merriment shine;
Where the fountains so gay
Not with water do play,
But are sparkling away
   With rich, rosy, old wine!

Here, the baking's begun;
There the baking is done;—
See the folks how they run,
   With beef, mutton, and veal.
And the eaters think fit,
That the man who lacks wit,
Shall be made a "turnspit,"
   And be bound to the wheel.

To the palace I haste,
With two Falstaffs I feast,
(Twenty stone weighs the least,)
   And with them hob and nob.
And here, too, I've found,
Where such good things abound,
Shy Venus quite round,
   And young Cupid a squab.

No sadness of brow,
No pedantic vain show,
No pompous state-bow,
   Can be ever allow'd :—
But with feasting and song
We carry night on,
Drink deep and drink long
   And toast beauty aloud.

Now, good-natured lasses,
To the music of glasses,
As the sweet dessert passes,
   Let's laugh the time by.

Let fools sigh and snuffle,
And merriment muffle,
But you, dears, shall ruffle
   Our pro-priety.
   *   *   *   *   *   *

So, in this joyous way,
With fresh loves ev'ry day,
And with no debts to pay,
   We scamper time o'er ;
While between drinking deep,
And light visions in sleep,
Our young years will creep
   To a hundred or more.

Yes, dear old Cocagne,
It 's with thee,—free from pain,—
But who checks my strain,
   In an accent so shrill ?
For, while singing, I thought,—
But, my friends, we are caught—
'T is the waiter who 's brought
   His confounded long bill.

The fairy land of Cocagne is said to derive its name from the Latin *coquere* "to cook." Duchat says, that its flocks and herds present themselves perfectly cooked, and that the larks descend from the skies ready roasted. For it is there alone—

> "Where so ready all nature its cookery yields,
> *Maccaroni au Parmesan* grows in the fields ;
> Little birds fly about with the true pheasant taint,
> And the geese are all born with a liver complaint."

The Utopian banquets, which are described by More, present an imaginary view of society in another extreme. The learned Chancellor, amid much invented nonsense, pictures the manners of the citizens of Amaurat after the fashion of those of Crete and Lacedæmonia, especially with regard to their common halls for their repasts,—a fashion, by the way, which was partially followed in the club-rooms of Attica. Others of the author's ideas have been realized since he wrote; and, in this respect, his Utopia may be said to have done good service; but there is a woful residue of nonsense, nevertheless, which is neither amusing nor useful.

Sir Thomas describes the citizens of Amaurat as possessing provision markets abundantly supplied with herbs, fruits, bread, fowl, and cattle. The latter were previously slain in extra-mural slaughter-houses, well furnished with running water, for washing away the filth after killing. The butchers were slaves, (for serfdom "was a peculiar institution" of this happy republic,) the free citizens not being permitted to kill animals, lest such pursuit should harden their singularly tender characters. "In every street," we are told by the author, "there are great halls that lie at an equal distance from one another, and are marked by peculiar names. The Syphograuts dwell in those, that are set over thirty families, fifteen lying on one side of it, and as many on the other. In these they do all meet and eat. The stewards of every one of them come to the market-place at an appointed hour, and, according to the number of those that belong to their hall, they carry home provisions. But they take more care of their sick than of any others.....After the steward of the hospitals has taken for them whatever the physician does prescribe for them, at the market-place, then the best things that remain are distributed equally among the halls, in proportion to their numbers; only, in the first place, they serve the Prince, the Chief Priest, the Tranibors, and Ambassadors, and strangers, if there are any, which, indeed, falls out but seldom, and for whom there are houses well-furnished, particularly appointed, when they come among them. At the hours of dinner and supper, the Syphogranty, being called together by sound of trumpet, meets and eats together, except only such as are in the hospitals, or lie sick at home. Yet, after the halls are served, no man is hindered to carry provisions home from the market-place, for they know none does that but for some good reason; for, though any that will may eat at home, yet none does it willingly, since it is both an indecent and foolish thing for any to give themselves the trouble to make ready an ill dinner at home, when there is a much more plentiful one made ready for him so near at hand. All the uneasy and sordid services about these halls are done by their slaves; but the dressing and cooking of their meat, and ordering of their tables, belong only to the women, which goes round all the women of every family by turns. They sit at three or more tables, according to their numbers; the men sit towards the wall, and the women sit on the other side, that if any of them fall suddenly ill, which is ordinary to those expecting to be mothers, she may, without disturbing the rest, rise and go to the nurses' room, who are there with the suckling children, where there is always fire and clean water at hand, and some cradles in which they may lay the young children," &c. But, to return from this public nursery to the public dining-hall, " all the children under five years of age dined with the nurses: the rest of the younger sort of both sexes, till they are fit for marriage, do either serve those that sit at table; or, if they are not strong enough for that, they stand by them in great silence, and eat that which is given them by those that sit at table, nor have they any other formality of dining." The whole formality was bad enough, and that last-mentioned was a Doric custom prevailing in Crete. As to the personal arrangements at these Utopian tables, the infelicitous guests stood much upon their order of precedence: the Syphogrant and his wife, the *gnädige Frau Syphograntinn*, presided at the centre of the cross table, at the upper end of the hall. After the Magistrates and their mates, came the Priests and their ladies,—for More placed the Church below the State, and hinted that celibacy in the Clergy was not to be commended. Below these, groups of the young and gay were placed, between flanking companies of the aged and grave, to spoil their mirth, and improve their manners; and this Spartan custom was occasionally imitated at Athenian feasts, albeit the Athenians looked with something like contempt upon the institutions of old Laconia. The best dishes were placed before the oldest men, and the latter gave of the dainty bits to the young, if these merited such favour by their behaviour; if not, they took their chance of what the older gourmands might leave, were obliged to be content with the plainer fare allotted to them.

During this delectable process, the young could not have offended by their gaiety, nor the old have improved them by conversation, seeing that a reader was appointed, to assist digestion by reading aloud an Essay on Morality. The Romans had the same office performed at some of their meals by learned slaves. More expressly says that the Utopian lecture was so short, that it was neither tedious nor uneasy to those that heard it; and that after it, the elders not only wagged their beards by "pleasant enlargements," but encouraged the young to follow them in the same track. This must have been after the supper, when it was the law of Utopia, not to "run a mile," but to "rest awhile." The dinners were dispatched quickly, because work awaited the diners, while the supper-eaters had nothing to do afterwards but sleep. This must have been all terribly dreary, if it had ever been realized. The only pleasant feature in More's Utopian banquets is, that wherein he says that there was always music at supper, and fruit served up after meat, (which, by the way, was a cruel trial for the digestive powers,) and that as the repast proceeded, "some burn perfumes, and sprinkle about sweet ointments, and sweet waters; and they are wanting in nothing that may cheer up their spirits; for they give themselves a large allowance in that way, and indulge themselves in all such pleasures as are attended with no inconvenience. Thus," he adds, "do they that are in towns eat together; but in the country, where they live at a greater distance, every one eats at home, and no family wants any necessary sort of provision; for it is from them that provisions are sent in to them that live in the towns."

I have noticed above the slave-readers at Roman diners. These were seldom born slaves; indeed, of born slaves, among the Greeks or Romans, the numbers were fewer than might be reasonably imagined. Those who became authors or teachers, were the distinguished and illustrious of their class; and it was they who relieved the tedium of a Roman repast by reading livelier sallies than Essays on Morality, like the Utopians. If their rank in humanity was low, their ability secured for them many privileges which even freedmen did not enjoy. Of this rank of reading slaves was Andronicus, the inventor of dramatic poetry. Plautus, the witty, but coarse, play-writer, miller, and Jack of all trades, was a slave. Terence was also a dramatist, and not only a slave, but a Negro slave. Æsop the fabulist, Phædrus, his imitator, and the Moral philosopher Epictetus, were slaves. The latter, who was as low in condition among bondsmen as he was exalted in his character of teacher of mankind, was the slave of one who had been a slave,—a depth of degradation than which there can be none deeper. But his mission was a great one; for he appears to have been an instrument employed to prepare men's minds for a change from the vices of Paganism to the virtues of Christianity. His writings are as stepping-stones across the dark and rapid stream dividing error from truth. They are admirably calculated to enable men to go forward; not only to induce them to make the first step out of infidelity; but having made it, rather to make a second in advance towards Christ, than go backward again in the direction of the dazzling unintelligibilities of the Capitoline Jove.

From slavery, if we turn our eyes towards mere poverty, the next condition to it, we shall see that the poor men characteristically paid their addresses to poetry;—and they were the "lions" at the dinners and assemblies of Rome. Such was Horace, who, if he were not in want, was of inferior descent, his father having been a slave, and subsequently, on being enfranchised, a tax-gatherer. Virgil was of equally mean descent on the paternal side; but he derived some portion of nobility from his mother. Juvenal, too, was not only poor and a poet,—a condition that could draw upon it only a serf's contempt,—but he was, moreover, an exceedingly angry poet. In equal proportion as he was poor, angry, and satirical in poetry, was Lucian poor, angry, and satirical in prose.

If the dining-out poets were poor, it was much the same with the philosophers. The proudest walks of philosophy were trodden by Demosthenes, the blacksmith. Socrates was the ill-featured, but original-minded, son of a mason and midwife. Epicurus was only rich in a valueless boast of being descended from Ajax; and Isocrates, whose father manufactured the musical ancestry from which are descended the modern families of piano-forte and fiddle, was also one of the immortal race of intellectual giants.....Of other writers we may remark, that Quintus Curtius, whose "Alexander the Great" is the first historical romance that ever was written, and contains the best description of a Babylonian banquet that ever was painted in words, was of an ignoble family. Celsus was, at least, not a Roman citizen, though resident at Rome; and Plutarch was just " respectable," and nothing more;—though to be worthy of respect, as the term implies, is as high rank as a man need sigh for.

But though art and science, though the Nine Sisters who made Parnassus vocal, were thus worshipped by the slave and his cousin the beggar; wealth was by no means a synonymous term for either sloth or incapacity. The opulent Lucretius, who believed nothing; the two Plinies, the soul of one of whom, "with a difference," entered into Horace Walpole, and who wrote about his slave Zozimus, as Walpole does of his favourite servants; the tender and chivalrous Tibullus,—a Latin Sir Philip Sidney: the profligate Sophocles; Æschylus, the bottle-drainer; and the lofty Euripides: all these mounted Pegasus with golden spurs, and gave glorious dinners to guests with whom they could contend in the battle of brains. Some, like Martial, got their mouths filled with the sugar-candy of imperial recompense. Cæsar, the Commentator, was the descendant of the Sabine Kings, and the founder of an empire. In Plato we see the double condition of aristocrat and slave. From the latter condition he was rescued by his noble friends at the cost of three thousand *drachmas;* more fortunate in this than Diogenes, who, being friendless, was left to hug his irons, and teach his master's sons to love virtue and liberty.

And the mention of the name of Plato reminds me of a more

modern philosopher, who did not lack reverence for him,—I mean Bacon,—and Bacon naturally brings me from my digression to the subject of "Table Traits" in imaginary Utopias. This philosopher, in his "New Atlantis," is even more felicitous than More, both in the framing of his fiction, and the extracting from it of a moral. The table laws spoken of in Solomon's house, have more of a jolly aspect than those drawn by Sir Thomas More. For instance, "I will not hold you long with recounting of our brewhouses, bakehouses, and kitchens, where are made divers drinks, breads, and meats, rare and of special effects. Wines we have of grapes, and drinks of other juice, of fruits, of grains, and of roots; and of mixtures with honey, sugar, manna, and fruits dried and decocted; also of the tears and wounding of trees, and of the pulp of canes: and these drinks are of several ages, some to the age at least of forty years. We have drinks also brewed of several herbs or roots, and spices, yea, with several fleshes and wine-meats, whereof some of the drinks are such as they are in effect meat and drink both. So that divers, especially in age, do desire to live with them with little or no meat or bread; and, above all, we strive to have drinks of extreme thin parts, to insinuate into the body, and yet without all biting sharpness, or fretting; insomuch as some of them put upon the back of your hand will, with a little stay, pass through to the palm, and yet taste mild to the mouth. We have also waters which we ripen in that fashion as they become nourishing, so that they are, indeed, excellent drink, and many will use no other. Breads we have of several grains, roots, and kernels, yea, and some of flesh and fish drink, with divers kinds of leavenings and seasonings, so that some do extremely move appetites; some do nourish so as divers do live of them without any other meat, who live very long. So, for meats, we have some of them so beaten and made tender and mortified, yet without all corrupting, as a weak heat of the stomach will turn them into good chylus, as well as a strong heat would meat otherwise prepared. We have some meats, also, and breads and drinks which, taken by some, enable them to fast long after; and some other that will make the very flesh of men's bodies sensibly more hard and tough, and their strength far greater than otherwise it would be."

In this way could philosophy disport itself, and not with much attendant profit, beyond amusement. Before I conclude this section, I may notice a more graceful fiction touching banquets, than any thing to be met with among the philosophers. The inhabitants of the coast of Malabar believe that the double cocoas of the Moluccas, annually thrown on their shore by the waves, and joyfully welcomed by the expecting inhabitants, are the produce of a palm-tree growing in the fathomless recesses of the ocean; and that they arise from among coral-groves endowed with supernatural qualities and attributes. For a detailed account of this supposed phænomenon, and a very pretty illustration of the theory of seeds transported by winds and currents, I refer all curious enquirers to the "Annals of *My* Village," by a Lady. In the mean time, I venture to put into verse, the supposed scene which occurs at the annual cocoa-banquet in Malabar:—

  'Neath the waves of Mincoy grows a magical tree,
   In the sunless retreat of a dark coral-grove,
  Where slumber young sprites,—the gay elves of a sea
   Flinging back the bright blue of its heaven above.
  There they sip the sweet fruit of that palm-tree, and leave
   Of its best and its ripest for maidens who stray,
  And laugh away time with their lovers at eve,
   And sing to those elves of the deep by the way.

  O! to see them at sunset, when down by the shore
   Of their own Malabar in gay clusters they stand,
  Like spirits of light shedding softness all o'er
   The broad sea, and its tribute of fruit, from the land!
  There troops of young girls, in their light-hearted mirth,
   Are laughing at youths who, reclined on the earth,
  Drink the white wine of Kishna;—while some are at play,
   Flinging glances and handsfull of roses, in showers,
  That their lovers can't tell, as they bend 'neath the fray,
   Which are falling the fastest, the glances, or flowers

And then on the sands where these young people meet,
  What hushing of songs and suppressing of glee,
As the waves bring in gently, and waft to their feet,
  The ripe fruit of the palm that lives under the sea!
There, while, half in earnest, fair Malabar's daughters,
Half play, dip their white, sandal'd feet in the waters,
To catch the ripe cocoas, and run back again,
  As the wave washes over their small anklet bells,
There are some, youths and maidens, who, link'd in a chain,
  Like pearls strung, and mixed, here and there, with sea-shells
Dash into the flood for the fruit of the palm,
  Which they strive for, and, winning, bring joyously out;
Then lean on their lovers, all panting and warm
  With laughter and splashing the waters about.

O, who would not like to pass summer away
  Amid scenes such as this? O, who would not love
With Malabar's daughters, at twilight, to play,
  And taste the ripe fruit of that dark coral-grove?"

The Malabar palm was not the only tree of its kind that used to afford holidays and banquetings to the people of the East, that is, according to the poets. The Talipot palm of Ceylon, or, as the natives unmusically call it, "*lanka dwipa*," *was*, in the olden time of pleasant fiction, one of this gifted species. But the banquet it afforded was not of annual occurrence; for the tree never flowers till it is fifty years old, and dies immediately after producing its fruit. The Kings of Candy used to bestow the rich gift of some of its blossoms on the favoured fair one whose head rested on the bosom of the Sovereign at the feast, and who lifted the bowl to his painted lips. It was, however highly esteemed, not such a present as Demetrius Poliocretes made to Lamia, after that accomplished courtezan had erected at Sicyon a portico so superb, that Polemo wrote a book to describe it; and poem and portico became the table-talk of all Greece. The gift of Demetrius was a magnificent purse, containing two hundred and fifty talents, which by the way, he had compelled the reluctant Athenians to contribute; and this he sent to Lamia, saying, that it was merely "for soap." The extravagant lady spent it all in one single, but consuming, feast! How pleasantly, by contrast, shines that courtezan, Leæna, whose wit made guests forget that the feast was frugal; and to whom the Athenians erected a bronze lioness, without a tongue, in honour of the lady who heroically had bitten out her own, that torture might not make her betray the accomplices of her protector Harmodius, in the murder of her tyrant Hipparchus!——

We have not found much of the refinement we looked for in these remote periods and banquets. Let us see what may be discovered in the Table Traits of England in Early Times.

TABLE TRAITS OF ENGLAND IN EARLY TIMES.

When Diodorus Siculus wrote an account of the aboriginal inhabitants of Britain, some fifty years before the Christian era, he described the island as being thickly inhabited, ruled by many Kings and Princes, and all living peaceably together,—though with war-chariots and strong arms, to settle quarrels when they occurred. But if our ancestors lived peaceably among themselves, they can hardly be said to have lived comfortably. Their habitations were of reed, or of wood; and they gathered in the harvest by cutting off the ears of corn. These ears they gathered in subterranean repositories, wherefrom they daily culled the ripest grain; and, rudely dressing the same, had thence their sustenance. Diodorus says that our primitive sires were far removed from the cunning and wickedness of the rest of the world; and other writers contrast them favourably with the Irish, who are said to have fed on human flesh, to have had enormous appetites for such food, and to have been given to the nasty habit of devouring their deceased fathers; but it is not uncommon for others, as well as for Irish sons, to devour, at least, their parents' substance, even at the present day. The food of an Irish child was certainly illustrative of character,—we should rather say that the solemnity of offering the first food to a child was characteristic. Caius Julius Solinus, a writer of the first century, says, that "when a Hibernian mother gives birth to a male child, she puts its first food on the point of her husband's sword, and lightly inserts this foretaste of meat into the mouth of the infant, on its very tip; and, by family vows, desires that it may never die but under arms." In other words, the relations wished that the little stranger might never be in want of a row, when disposed to distinguish the family name!

In the days of Julius Cæsar, our stalwart sires supported their thews and sinews on milk and flesh,—the diet of a pugilist. We see how much progress was made by the time of Constantine,—the Constantine that was crowned in Britain,—" when," says a contemporary writer, " the harvests sufficed alike for the gifts of Ceres and Bacchus, and the pastures were covered with innumerable multitudes of tame flocks, distended with milk, or laden with fleeces."

I very much fear, however, notwithstanding the rather poetical accounts of certain early writers, that our aboriginal ancestry were very little superior to the New Zealanders. They were, perhaps, more uncivilized, and quite as ignorant; and their abstinence from the flesh of hares and poultry, and, in the northern parts of the island, from fish, bespeaks a race who lacked, at once, industry and knowledge. Indeed, it is by no means certain, that we do not wrong the New Zealanders by suggesting their possible inferiority to the Britons, seeing that the latter are very strongly suspected of being guilty of the most revolting cannibalism.

They were clever enough to brew mead and ale; but wine and civilization were brought to them by their enemies, the Romans,—invaders whom, for some reasons, they might have welcomed with a sentiment akin to the line in Béranger:—

" *Vivent nos amis! nos amis, les ennemis!*"

They ate but twice a day. The last meal was the more important one. Their seats were skins, or bundles of hay, flung on the ground. The table was a low stool, around which Cabinet Chiefs sat, and, even in the locality occupied by modern Belgravia, tore their food with teeth and nails, or hacked at it with a wretched knife, as bad as anything of the sort now in common use in Gaul. In short, they committed a thousand solecisms, the very idea of which is sufficient to make the Sybarites of Belgravia very much ashamed of their descent from the savages of Britain.

It was characteristic of the sort of civilization which the Anglo-Saxons brought with them to England, that they introduced the rather vulgar custom of taking four meals a-day. The custom was, however, one solemnly observed by the high-feeding nobility of the Saxons. They ate good solid joints of flesh-meat, boiled, baked, or broiled. It would seem, that, in those days, cooks were not of such an illustrious guild as that which they subsequently formed. A cook among the Anglo-Saxons was little more accounted of than the calf he cut up into collops. The cook, in fact, was a slave; and was as unceremoniously bequeathed by his owner, in the latter's last will and testament, as though the culinary artist had been a mere kitchen utensil. At Saxon tables, both sexes sat together,—a custom refined in itself, refining in its effects, and of such importance, that half-a-dozen nations claim the honour of being the inventors of that excellent custom. In Europe, Turkey alone has obstinately refused to follow this civilizing example; and Turkey is falling to pieces. It may, therefore, be logically proved, that where table rights are not conceded to the ladies, nations slowly perish; and—"serve them right."

It is a mark of Anglo-Saxon delicacy, that table-cloths were features at Anglo-Saxon feasts; but, as the long ends were used in place of napkins, the delicacy would be of a somewhat dirty hue, if the cloth were made to serve at a second feast. There was a rude sort of display upon the board; but the order of service was of a quality that would strike the "Jeameses" of the age of Victoria with inexpressible disgust. The meat was never "dished," and "covers" were as yet unknown. The attendants brought the viands into the dining hall on the spits, knelt to each guest, presented the spit to his consideration; and, the guest having helped himself, the attendant went through the same ceremony with the next guest. Hard drinking followed upon these same ceremonies; and even the monasteries were not exempt from the sins of gluttony and drunkenness. Notwithstanding these bad habits, the Anglo-Saxons were a cleanly people. The warm bath was in general use. Water, for hands and feet, was brought to every stranger on entering a house wherein he was about to tarry and feed; and, it is said that one of the severest penances of the Church was the temporary denial of the bath, and of cutting the hair and nails.

With the Normans came greater grandeur and increased discomfort. They neither knew nor tolerated the use of table-cloths or plain steel forks; but their bill of fare showed more variety and costliness than the Saxons cared for. Their cookery was such an improvement on that of their predecessors in the island, that Norman French, and Norman dishes, flung the Saxon tongue and table into the annihilating position of "vulgarity." The art was so much esteemed, that Monarchs even granted estates, on condition that the holder thereof should, through his cook, prepare a certain dish at stated periods, and set it before the King. It was under the Normans that the boar's head had regal honours paid it; and its progress from the kitchen to the banquet was under escort of a guard, and behind the deafening salutes of puffy-cheeked trumpeters. The crane was then what the goose is now,—highly esteemed; yet labouring under the shadow of a suspicion of being "common." The peacock, on the other hand, was only seen, tail and all, at the tables of the wealthy. Their beverage was of a very bilious character,—spicy and cordialed; namely, hippocras, piment, morat, and mead. The drink of the humbler classes partook of a more choleraic quality. It consisted of cider, perry, and ale. The Norman maxim for good living and plenty of it, was to "rise at five, dine at nine, sup at five, and bed at nine, if you'd live to a hundred all but one." *Dinner* at nine is, however, a contradiction of terms; for *dinner*, as I have said, is the abbreviation of *dixième heure*, or "ten o'clock," the time at which all people sat down to a solid repast in the days of the first Williams.

In the two following centuries, cooks and Kings launched into far greater magnificence than had ever, hitherto, been seen in England. Richard II. entertained ten thousand guests daily at his numerous tables; and the exceedingly fast Earl of Leicester, grandson of the equally slow Henry III., is said to have spent twenty-two thousand pounds of silver in one year, in eating, alone. His thirsty household retainers drank no less than three hundred and seventy-one pipes of wine, in the same space of time. At great banquets, the dishes were reckoned by thousands, and Kings in vain dictated decrees denouncing such dinners; for cooks and *convives* considered them with contempt. As a show of moderation, the old four meals a-day were now reduced to two; but these two were connected by such a savoury chain of intermeats and refections, that the board was spread all day long, and guests were never weary:—

> "Their life like the life of the Germans would be,
> *Du lit à la table; de la table au lit.*"

To have things "brennying like wild-fire," was the characteristic of the cookery of that period. Confectionery of the richest sorts were the lighter materials of meals, which were abundantly irrigated by hippocras, piment, or *claret*, or the simpler and purer wines of France, Spain, Syria, and Greece. Thus might a host say:—

> "Ye shall have rumney and malespine,
> Both ypocrasse and vernage wine;
> Mountresse and wyne of Greke,
> Both algrade and despice eke,
> Antiocho and bastarde,
> Pyment also and garnarde,
> Wyne of Greke and muscadell,
> Both clary, pyment, and Rochelle."

Ricobaldi of Ferrara, writing, about the year 1300, of the Italian social condition in the age of Frederick II., illustrates the former rudeness of the Italian manners, by showing that in those days "a man and his wife ate off the same plate. There were no wooden-handled knives, nor more than one or two drinking-cups in a house. Candles of wax or tallow were unknown; a servant held a torch during supper. The clothes of men were of leather unlined; scarcely any gold or silver was seen on their dress. The common people ate flesh but three times a week, and kept their cold meat for supper. Many did not drink wine in summer. A small stock of corn seemed riches. The portions of women were small; their dress, even after marriage, was simple. The pride of men was to be well provided with arms and horses; that of the nobility to have lofty towers, of which all the cities in

Italy were full. But now, frugality has been changed for sumptuousness; every thing exquisite is sought after in dress,—gold, silver, pearls, silks, and rich furs."

The Household-Book of the Earl of Northumberland admirably illustrates the interior and table life of the greater nobles of the period of Henry VII. In this well-known and well-kept record, the family is described as consisting of one hundred and sixty-six persons, masters and servants; and hospitable reckoning is allowed for more than half a hundred strangers who are expected daily to partake of the Earl's good cheer. The cost for each individual, for board and fuel, is settled at twopence halfpenny daily, about one and sixpence of our present money, if we take into account the relative value of money, and the relative prices of provisions. The Earl allots for his annual expenditure £1178. 17s. 8d. More than two-thirds of this is consumed in meat, drink, and firing; namely, £797. 11s. 2d. The book carefully states the number of pieces which the carver is to cut out of each quarter of beef, mutton, veal, pork, nay, even stock-fish and salmon; and supervising clerks were apppointed to see that this was carried into effect, and to make due entry of the same in their registers. An absent servant's share is to be accounted for, and not to be divided amongst the rest. The absentee, if he be on "my Lord's" business, received 8d. per day, board wages, in winter, and 5d. in summer; with 2d. additional daily for the keep of a horse. A little more than a quarter of wheat, estimated at 5s. 8d. per quarter, is allowed for every month throughout the year; with this, 250 quarters of malt, at 4s. (two hogsheads to the quarter,) and producing about a bottle and a third of intermediate beer to each person, does not say much for the liberality of the Lord, though it may for the temperance of his retainers. One hundred and nine fat beeves are to be bought at All-Hallow's Tide, at 13s. 4d. each; a couple of dozen of lean kine, at 8s. are to be bought at St. Helen's, to be fattened for service between Midsummer and Michaelmas. All the rest of the year, nine weary months, the family was on salted provisions, to aid the digestion of which, the Earl, so chary of his liquor, allows the profuse aid of one hundred and sixty-six gallons of mustard. 647 sheep at 1s. 8d., to be eaten salted between Lammas and Michaelmas; 25 hogs at 2s., 28 calves at 1s. 8d., 40 lambs at 10d. or 1s.,—are other articles which seem to have been reserved rather for the upper table than for the servants, whose chief fare was salted beef, without vegetables, but with mustard *à discretion!* There was great scarcity of linen, and the little there was, except that for the chapel, not often washed. No mention is made of sheets; and though "my Lord's" table had eight "table-cloths" for the year, that of the Knights had but one, and probably went uncovered while the cloth was "at the wash." If the ale was limited, the wine appears to have been more liberally dispensed; and ten tuns and two hogsheads of Gascony wine, at £4. 13s. 4d. per tun, show the bent of the Earl's taste. Ninety-one dozens of candles for the year, and no fires after Lady-Day, except half-fires in the great room and the nursery; twenty-four fires, with a peck of coals daily for each, (for the offices,) and eighty chaldrons of coals, at 4s. 10d., with sixty-four loads of wood, at 1s. a load,—are the provisions made for lighting and firing. It must have been cold work to live in the noble Earl's house in Yorkshire, from Lady-Day till the warm summer came; which advent is sometimes put off till next year. The family rose at six, or before; for Mass was especially ordered at that hour, in order to force the household to rise early. The dinner-hour was ten A.M.; four P.M. was the hour for supper; and at nine the bell rang for bed. I have omitted the breakfast, which took place at seven, after Mass; when my Lord and Lady sat down to a repast of two pieces of salt-fish, and half-a-dozen red herrings, with four fresh ones, or a dish of sprats, and a quart of beer, and the same measure of wine. This was on meagre days. At other seasons, half a chine of mutton, or of boiled beef, graced the board of the delicate Earl and Countess, who sometimes forgot that they had to dine at ten. Capons, at 2d. each, were only on the Lord's table, and plovers, at a penny, (at Christmas,) were deemed too good for any digestion that was not carried on in a "noble" stomach. Game generally is specified, but without intimation as to limit of the board. No doubt the fragments were not rejected at the servants' table; but much certainly went in doles at the gate. My Lord maintained between twenty and thirty horses for his own use. His mounted servants found their own; but their keep was at the noble master's cost. Of mounted servants, not less than three dozen attended their Lord on a journey; and when this journey was for change of residence from one mansion to another, the illustrious Percy carried with him bed and bedding, household furniture, pots, pans, and kitchen utensils generally. The baggage waggon bore these *impedimenta;* and before and behind them went chiefs and serving men, including in the array eleven Priests,—two hundred and twenty-three persons in all,—and only two cooks to look after their material happiness! No notice is taken of plate; but the "hiring of pewter vessels" is mentioned; and with these rough elements did the Earl construct his imperfect social system, so far taking care for his soul as well as his body, inasmuch as that he contributed a groat a year to the shrine of our Lady of Walsingham, and the same magnificent sum to the holy blood at Hales, on the express condition of the interest of the Virgin for the promotion of the future welfare of the Earl in heaven. Such is an outline of a nobleman's household in the good old days of Henry VII.

In the reign of the same King, fish was a scarce article, and for a singular reason; namely, people destroyed them at an unlawful season, for the purpose of feeding their pigs or manuring the ground. The favourite wine at table was Malmsey: it came from Candy; and there was a legal restriction against its costing more than four pounds per butt. In this reign our cooks wrought at fires made with wood imported from Gascony and Languedoc, whence also much wine was brought, but, by law, only in English bottoms. The richest man of this reign was Sir William Stanley, into whose hands fell nearly all the spoil of Bosworth Field; and

10*

therewith he maintained a far more princely house and table than his master.

In Pegge's "*Cury*" there is an account of the rolls of provisions with their prices, in the time of Henry VIII.; and we find that, at the dinner given at the marriage of Gervase Clifton and Mary Nevile, the price of three hogsheads of wine (one white, one red, one claret) was set down at £5. 5s.

The dining-rooms—and, indeed, these were the common living rooms in the greatest houses—were still uncomfortable places. The walls were of stone, partially concealed by tapestry hung upon timber hooks, and taken down whenever the family removed, (leaving bare the stone walls,) lest the damp should rot it. It was a fashion that had lasted for centuries; but it began to disappear when mansions ceased to be fortresses. The tapestry, it may be observed, was suspended on a wooden frame projecting from the wall, between which and the hangings there was a passage wide enough to kill a man, as Hamlet did Polonius, "behind the arras." It was not till the reign of Charles I. that houses were built with under-ground rooms; the pantry, cellars, kitchens, and store-rooms were, previous to this reign, all on the ground-floor; and the officials presiding in each took there, respectively, their solemn post on great days of state-dinners. There were certain days when the contents of these several offices, meat and drink, were bountifully supplied to every applicant. To revert to tapestry: we see the time of its change, in the speech of Falstaff, who wishes his hostess to sell her tapestry, and adopt the cheaper painted canvas which came from Holland.

At this time, and, indeed, long after, our English yeomanry and tradesmen were more anxious to invigorate their bodies by a generous diet, than to dwell in well-furnished houses, or to find comfort in cleanliness and elegance. "These English," said the Spaniards who came over with Philip II., "have their houses made of sticks and dirt; but they fare commonly as well as the King."

Previous to the age of Elizabeth, even the Monarch, well as he might fare, and gloriously as he shone in pageants, was but simply lodged. The furniture of the bed-room of Henry VIII. was one of the very simplest; and the magnificent Wolsey was content with deal for the material of most of the furniture of his palace. But the community generally was, from this period, both boarded and bedded more comfortably and refinedly than before. The hours for meals were eight, noon, and six; but "after-meats," and "after-suppers," filled up the intervals. It was chiefly at the "after-supper" that wine was used. The dinner, however, had become the principal meal of the day. It was abundant; but the jester and harper were no longer tolerated at it, with their lively sauce of mirth and music. It was the fashion to be sad, and ceremonious dinners were celebrated in stately silence, or a dignified *sotto voce*. Each guest took his place according to a properly marshalled order of precedence; and before sitting down to dinner, they washed with rose-water and perfumes, like the parochial boards of half a century ago, who used also to deduct the expenses of both dinners and rose-water from the rates levied for the relief of the poor; this, too, at a time when men who were *not* parish authorities were being hanged for stealing to the amount of a few shillings.

By the reign of Elizabeth, napkins had been added to table-cloths. The wealthy ate the manchet, or fine wheaten bread; the middle classes were content with a bread of a coarser quality called "*chete;*" and the ravelled, brown, or *maslin* bread was consumed by those who could afford to procure no better. There was a passion for strong wines at this time. Of this France sent more than half a hundred different sorts, and thirty-six various kinds were imported from other parts of Europe. About 30,000 tuns were imported yearly, exclusive of what the nobility imported *free of duty*. The compound wines were in great request; and ladies did not disdain to put their lips to distilled liquors, such as *rosa-solis* and *aqua-vitæ*. Ale was brewed stronger than these distillations; and our ancestors drank thereof to an extent that is terrific only to think of. Camden ascribes the prevailing drunkenness to the long wars in the Netherlands, previous to which, we had been held, "of all the northern nations, the most commended for sobriety." The barbarous terms formerly used in drinking matches, are all of Dutch, German, or Danish origin, and this serves to confirm Camden's assertion. The statutes passed to correct the evil were disregarded. James I. was particularly desirous to enforce these statutes; but his chief difficulty lay in the fact, that he was the first to infringe them.

In Elizabeth's reign the "watching candles" of Alfred (to mark the time) were in use in many houses. This is a curious trait in in-door life. We have an "exterior" one, in the fact that the Vicar of Hurley, who served Maidenhead, had an addition of stipend on account of the danger he ran, in crossing the thicket, when he passed to or from the church—and his inn. It was not a delicate period, and if caraways always appeared at desert, every one knew that they were there for the kind purpose of curing expected flatulence in the guests.

In James the First's reign, the fashion of Malmsey had passed away, and the Hungarian red wine (*Ofener*) had taken its place. It came by Breslau to Hamburg, where it was shipped to England. It is a strong wine, and bears some resemblance to port.

In country-houses in the seventeenth century, the Knight or Squire was head of a hoast of retainers, three-fourths of whom consumed the substance of the master on whose estate they were born, without rendering him much other service than drinking his ale, eating his beef, and wearing his livery. Brief family prayers, and heavy family breakfasts, a run with the hounds, and an early dinner, followed by long and heavy drinking, till supper-time, when more feeding and imbibing went on until each man finished his posset, or carried it with him to bed,—such was the ordinary course: but it admitted of exceptions where the master was a man of intellect, and then the country-house was a temple of hospitality rather than of riot; and good sense and ripe wit took the place of the sensuality, obscurity, and ignorance that distinguished the boards where the Squire was simply a "brute."

Of the table traits of this century, the best examples are to be found in Pepys and Evelyn. In the Diary of the former, may be seen what a jolly tavern life could be led by a grave official, and no scandal given. Evelyn takes us into better company. We find him at the Spanish Ambassador's, when his Excellency, by way of dessert, endeavoured to convert him to the Roman Catholic Church. We go with him to the feast where the Envoy from the Emperor of Morocco figured as so civilized a gentleman, while the representative of the Czar of Muscovy comported himself like a rude clown; and we dine with him at Lady Sunderland's, where the noble hostess had engaged for the amusement of the guests, a man who swallowed stones, and who not only performed the feat in the presence of the company, but convinced them there was no cheat, by making the stones rattle in his stomach. But, *nous avons changé tout cela*, and not only changed in taste but improved in manners.

Pepys gives a curious account of a Lord Mayor's dinner in 1663. It was served in the Guildhall, at one o'clock in the day. A bill of fare was placed with every salt-cellar, and at the end of each table was a list of "the persons proper" there to be seated. Here is a mixture of abundance and barbarism. "Many were the tables, but none in the hall, but the Mayor's and the Lords' of the Privy Council, *that had napkins or knives*, which was very strange. I sat at the merchant-strangers' table, where ten good dishes to a mess, with plenty of wine of all sorts; but it was very unpleasing that we had no napkins, nor change of trenchers, and drank out of earthen pitchers and wooden dishes. The dinner, it seems, is made by the Mayor and two Sheriffs for the time being, and the whole is reckoned to come to £700 or £800 at most." Pepys took his spoon and fork with him, as was the custom of those days with guests invited to great entertainments. "Forks" came in with Tom Coryat, in the reign of James I.; but they were not "familiar" till after the Restoration. The "laying of napkins," as it was called, was a profession of itself. Pepys mentions, the *day before* one of his dinner-parties, that he went home, and "there found one laying of my napkins against to-morrow, in figures of all sorts, which is mighty pretty, and, it seems, is his trade, and he gets much money by it." The age of Pepys, we may further notice, was the great "supping age." Pepys himself supped heartily on venison pasty; but his occasional "next-morning" remark was like that of Scrub: "My head aches consumedly!" The dashing Duchess of Cleveland supped off such substantials as roast chine of beef; much more solid fare than that of the Squires in a succeeding reign, who were content, with Sir Roger de Coverley, to wind up the day with "good Cheshire cheese, best mustard, a golden pippin, and a pipe of John Sly's best."

A few years earlier, Laud had leisure to write anxiously to Strafford on the subject of Ulster eels. "Your Ulster eels are the fattest and fairest that ever I saw, and it's a thousand pities there should be any error in their salting, or any thing else about them; for how the carriage should hurt them I do not see, considering that other salted eels are brought as far, and retain their goodness; but the dried fish was exceeding good." There was a good deal of error in the preserving of other things besides eels, if Laud had only known as much.

It may be mentioned as something of a "Table Trait," illustrating the popular appetite in the reign of Charles II., that he sent sea stores to the people encamped in Moorfields; but they were so well provisioned by the liberality of the nation, that they turned up their noses at the King's biscuits, and sent them back, "not having been used to the same." There was some ungrateful impertinence in this; but there was less meanness in it than was shown by the great ladies of Queen Anne's reign, who were curious in old china, and who indulged their passion by "swopping" their old clothes for fragile cups and saucers, instead of giving the former to the poor.

Dryden speaks, in the Preface to his "Love Triumphant," of a remarkable trait of the time of William III. "It is the usual practice," he says, "of our decayed gentry, to look about them for some illustrious family, and then endeavour to fix their young darling, where he may be both well educated and supported.

Shaftesbury reveals to us an illustration of George the First's reign. "In latter days," he says, "it has become the fashion to eat with less ceremony and method. Every one chooses to carve for himself. The learned manner of dissection is out of request; and a certain method of cookery has been introduced, by which the anatomical science of the table is entirely set aside. *Ragoûts* and *fricassées* are the reigning dishes, in which every thing is so dismembered, and thrown out of all order and form, that no part of the mess can properly be divided or distinguished from another." But we have come to a period that demands a chapter to itself; and even with that implied space, we can hardly do justice to the Table Traits of the Last Century.

TABLE TRAITS OF THE LAST CENTURY.

When Mr. Chute intimated to Horace Walpole that his "temperance diet and milk" had rendered him stupid, Walpole protested pleasantly against such an idea. "I have such lamentable proofs," he says, "every day, of the stupefying qualities of beef, ale, and wine, that I have contracted a most religious veneration for your spiritual nouriture. Only imagine that I here, (Houghton,) every day, see men who are mountains of roast beef, and only seem just roughly hewn out into the outlines of human form, like the giant rock at Pratolino! I shudder when I see them brandish their knives, in act to carve, and look on them as savages that devour one another. I should not stare at all more than I do, if yonder Alderman, at the end of the table, was to stick his fork into his jolly neighbour's cheek, and cut a brave slice of brown and fat. Why, I'll swear I see no difference between a country gentleman and a sirloin: whenever the first laughs, or the latter is cut, there run out just the same streams of gravy! Indeed, the sirloin does not ask quite so many questions. I have an aunt here, a family piece of goods, an old remnant of inquisitive hospitality and economy, who to all intents and purposes, is as beefy as her neighbours."

Certainly, I think it may be considered that, in diet and in principles, we have improved upon the fashion of one hundred and ten years ago;—and, perhaps, the improvement in principles is a consequence of that in diet. There was a profound meaning in the point of faith of some old religionists, that the stomach was the seat of the soul. However this may be, the "beefy" men of Walpole's time had, occasionally, strange ideas touching honour. Old Nourse, for instance, challenged Lord Windsor, who refused to fight him, either with swords or pistols, on the plea that Nourse was too aged a man. Thereupon, Nourse, in a fit of vexation and indigestion, went home from the coffee-house and cut his throat! "It was strange, yet very English," says Walpole. Old

Nourse must have had Japanese blood in him. At Jeddo, when a nobleman feels himself slighted, he walks home, takes the sharpest knife he can find, and rips himself open, from the *umbilicus* to the *trachea!*

Quite as certainly, strong diet and weak principles prevailed among our great-grandsires and their dames. Lady Townshend fell in love with the rebel Lord Kilmarnock, from merely seeing him at his trial. She forthwith cast off her old lover, Sir Harry Nisbett, and became "as yellow as a jonquil" for the new object of her versatile affection. She even took a French master, in order that she might forget the language of "the bloody English!" She was not so afflicted, but that she could bear the company of gay George Selwyn to dine with her; and he, believing that her passion was feigned, joked with her, on what was always a favourite topic with himself,—the approaching execution. Lady Townshend forthwith rushed from the table in rage and tears, and Mr. Selwyn finished the bottle with "Mrs. Dorcas, her woman," who begged of him to help her to a sight of the execution! Mrs. Dorcas had a friend who had promised to protect her, and, added she, "I can lie in the Tower the night before!" This is a pretty dining-room interior of the last century. As for George Selwyn, that most celebrated of the diners-out of a hundred years ago, he said the pleasantest thing possible at dessert, after the execution of Lord Lovat. Some ladies asked him how he could be such a barbarian as to see the head cut off. "Nay," said he, "if that was such a crime, I am sure I have made amends; for I went to see it sewed on again!" "George," says Walpole, "never thinks but *à la tête tranchée;* he came to town t' other day to have a tooth drawn, and told the man that he would drop his handkerchief for the signal."

Selwyn kept his powers bright by keeping good company; while Gray the poet was but indifferent society, from living reclusely, added to a natural turn for melancholy, and "a little to much dignity." Young, a greater poet than Gray, was as brilliant in conversation as Selwyn himself, as long as, like Selwyn, he polished his wit by contact with the world. When he dined with Garrick, Quin, and George Anne Bellamy, he was the sprightliest of the four; but when he took to realizing the solitude he had epically praised, Young, too, became a proser. Quin loved good living as much as he did sparkling conversation; and Garrick, the other guest noticed above, has perfectly delineated Quin the epicure in the following epigram, as he subsequently did Quin, the man and brother of men, in his epitaph in Bath Abbey :—

"A plague on Egypt's art! I say;
Embalm the dead, on senseless clay
Rich wines and spices waste!
Like sturgeon, or like brawn, shall I,
Bound in a precious pickle, lie,
Which I shall never taste?

"Let me embalm this flesh of mine
With turtle fat and Bordeaux wine,
And spoil th' Egyptian trade.
Than Humphrey's Duke more happy I;
Embalm'd alive, old Quin shall die,
A mummy, ready made."

A good many female mummies were prepared during the last century after a similar receipt. Witness Walpole's neighbour at Strawberry Hill, "an attorney's wife, and much given to the bottle. By the time she has finished that and daylight, she grows afraid of thieves, and makes her servants fire minute-guns out of the garret windows. The divine Asheton," he proceeds, "will give you an account of the astonishment we were in last night at hearing guns. I began to think that the Duke (of Cumberland) had brought some of his defeats from Flanders."

Young denounces, in his "Satires," both tea and wine, as abused by the fair sex of the last century. In Memmia he paints Lady Betty Germain, in the lines I have quoted under the head of "Tea;" and then, hurling his shafts of satire at that which another poet has described as "cups which cheer, but not inebriate," he adds,—

"Tea! how I tremble at thy fatal stream!
As Lethe, dreadful to the love of fame.
What devastations on thy banks are seen!
What shades of mighty names which once have been!
A hecatomb of characters supplies
Thy painted altar's daily sacrifice.
Hervey, Pearce, Blount, aspersed by thee, decay,
As grains of finest sugars melt away,
And recommend thee more to mortal taste:
Scandal's the sweetener of a female feast."

And then adverting to the ladies who, like Walpole's "attorney's wife," were much given to the bottle, the poet exclaims,—

"But this inhuman triumph shall decline,
And thy revolting Naiads call for wine;
Spirits no longer shall serve under thee,
But reign in thy own cup, exploded Tea!
Citronia's nose declares thy ruin nigh;
And who dares give Citronia's nose the lie?
The ladies long at men of drink exclaim'd,
And what impair'd both health and virtue blamed.
At length, to rescue man, the generous lass
Stole from her consort the pernicious glass
As glorious as the British Queen renown'd,
Who suck'd the poison from her husband's wound."

Manners and morals generally go hand in hand; but those of the ladies satirized by Young were not so bad as those of the French Princesses of a few years before, when they and Duchesses were so addicted to drinking, that no one thought it a vice, since royalty and aristocracy practised it. The Dauphine of Burgundy is indeed praised by her biographers as not drinking to any great excess during the last three years of her life. But this was exceptional. The Duchess of Bourbon and her daughters drank like dragoons; but the latter were unruly in their cups, whereas the old lady carried her liquor discreetly. Henrietta, Madame de Montespan, and the Princess di Monaco, were all addicted, more or less, to tippling. The Duchess de Bourbon and Her Grace of Chartres added smoking to their other boon qualities; and the Dauphin once surprised them with pipes which had been *cullotés* for them by common soldiers of the Swiss Guard! In France, devotion even was a means towards drunkenness. Bungener tells us, in his " *Trois Sermons sous Louis XV.*," that Monsieur Basquiat de la House owned a small estate in Gascony, which produced a wine which no one would buy. Being at Rome, as Secretary of an Embassy, he procured a body from the catacombs, which he christened by the name of a saint venerated in his part of the country. The people received it with great pomp. A *fête* was appointed by the Pope, a fair by the Government, and the wine was sold by hogsheads! It was a wine as thin as the beverage which Mr. Chute lived on when he had the gout, at which time, says Walpole, " he keeps himself very low, and lives upon very thin ink."

There was a good deal of latitude of observation and conversation at the dinner-tables of the last century; and the letter-writer I have just cited affords us ample evidence of the fact. John Stanhope, of the Admiralty, he informs us, " was sitting by an old Mr. Curzon, a nasty wretch, and very covetous; his nose wanted blowing, and continued to want it; at last Mr. Stanhope, with the greatest good breeding, said, 'Indeed, Sir, if you don't wipe your nose, you will lose that drop.'"

A hundred years ago, Walpole remarked that Methodism, drinking, and gambling were all on the increase. Of the first he sneeringly says, " It increases as fast as any religious nonsense did." Of the second he remarks, " Drinking is at the highest wine-mark;" and he speaks of the third as being so violent, that " at the last New-market meeting, in the rapidity of both gaming and drinking, a bank bill was thrown down, and, nobody immediately claiming it, they agreed to give it to a man who was standing by!"

There was a love of good eating, as well as of deep drinking, even among the upper classes of the last century. What a picture of a Duchess is that of her Grace of Queensberry, posting down to Parson's Green, to tell Lady Sophia Thomas "something of mportance;" namely, "Take a couple of beefsteaks, clap them together as if they were for a dumpling, and eat them with pepper and salt: it is the best thing you ever tasted! I could not help coming to tell you this;"—and then she drove back to town. And what a picture of a Magistrate is that of Fielding, seated at supper with a blind man, a Drury-Lane Chloris, and three Irishmen, all eating cold mutton and ham from one dish, on a very dirty cloth, and "his worship" refusing to rise to attend to the administration of Justices' justice! It is but fair, however, to Fielding to add, that he might have had better fare had he been more oppressive touching fees. And, besides, great dignitaries set him but an indifferent example. Gray, speaking of the Duke of Newcastle's installation at Oxford, remarks, that "every one was very gay and very busy in the morning, and very owlish and tipsy at night. I make no exceptions, from the Chancellor to Blewcoat." Lord Pembroke, truly, was temperate enough to live upon vegetables; but the diet did not improve either his temper or his morals. Ladies —and they were not over delicate a century ago—as much dreaded sitting near him at dinner, as their daughters and grand-daughters dreaded to be near the late Duke of Cumberland, who was pretty sure to say something in the course of dinner expressly to embarrass them. The vegetarian Lord Pomfret was so blasphemous at tennis, that the Primate of Ireland, Dr. George Stone, was compelled to leave off playing with him. For Primates handled the rackets then, as Pope and Cardinals do now the cue. Pio Nono and the expertest of the Sacred College play *la poule* at billiards, after dinner, with the view of keeping down the good Pontiff's obesity. This is almost as curious a trait as that of Taafe, the Irishman, who conceiving himself to have been insulted at dinner, and not being then able, as a Roman Catholic, to wear a sword, changed his religion, and ran his adversary through the body. The confusion of ideas which prompted a man to follow a particular faith, in order that he might commit murder, was something like that which influenced the poor woman who, suddenly becoming pious, after hearing a sermon from Rowland Hill, went to a book-stall, and stole a Bible.

I have noticed the love of good eating, and the coarseness connected with it. There was also a coarse economy attendant on it. The Duchess of Devonshire would call out to the Duke, when both were presiding at supper after one of their assemblies, "Good God, Duke! don't cut the ham; nobody will eat any;" and then she would relate the circumstances of her private *ménage* to her neighbour: "When there's only my Lord and I, besides a pudding, we have always a rich dish of roast,"—no very dainty fare for a ducal pair. Indeed, there was much want of daintiness, and of dignity, too, in many of those with whom both might have been looked for as a possession. Lord Coventry chased his Lady round the dinner-table, and scrubbed the paint off her cheeks with a napkin. The Duke and Dutchess of Hamilton were more contemptible in their pomposity than their Graces of Devonshire were in their plainness. At their own house they walked into dinner before their company, sat together at the upper end of their own table, ate together off one plate, and drank to nobody beneath the rank of Earl. It was, indeed, a wonder that they could get any one of any rank to dine with them at all. But, in point of dinners, people are not "nice" even now. Dukes very recently dined with a railway potentate, in hopes of profiting by the condescension; and Duchesses heard, without a smile, that potentate's lady superbly dismiss them with an "*au reservoir!*"—an expression, by the way, which is refined, when compared with that taught by our nobility, a hundred years ago, to the rich Bohemian Countess Chamfelt; namely, "D—n you!" and, "Kiss me!" but it was apologetically said of her, that she never used the former, but upon the miscarriage of the latter. This was at a time when vast assemblies were followed by vast suppers, vast suppers by vast drinking, and when nymphs and swains reached home at dawn with wigs, like Ranger's in the comedy, vastly battered, and not very fit to be seen.

Pope, in the last century, moralized, with effect, on the deaths of the dissolute Buckingham and the avaricious Cutler; and the avarice of Sir John was perhaps more detestable than any extravagance that is satirized by Pope, or witticized by Walpole. But Sir John Cutler was ingenious in his thrift. This rich miser, ordinarily travelled on horseback and alone, in order to avoid expense. On reaching his inn at night, he feigned indisposition, as an excuse for not taking supper. He would simply order the hostler to bring a little straw to his room, to put in his boots. He then had his bed warmed, and got into it, but only to get out of it again as soon as the servant had left the room. Then, with the straw in his boots, and the candle at his bed-side, he kindled a little fire, at which he toasted a herring which he drew from his pocket. This, with a bit of bread which he carried with him, and a little water from the jug, enabled the lord of countless thousands to sup at moderate cost.

Well, this sordidness was less culpable perhaps than slightly overstepping income by giving assemblies and suppers. At the latter there was, at least, wit, and as much of it as was ever to be found at Madame du Deffand's, where, by the way, the people did *not* sup. "Last night, at my Lady Hervey's," says Walpole, "Mrs. Dives was expressing great panic about the French," who were said to be preparing to invade England. "My Lady Rochford, looking down on her fan, said, with great softness, 'I don't know; I don't think the French are a sort of people that women need be afraid of.'" This was more commendable wit than that of Madame du Deffand herself, who, as I have previously remarked, made a whole assembly laugh, at Madame de Marchais', when her old lover was known to be dying, by saying as she entered, "He is gone; and wasn't it lucky? He died at six, or I could not possibly have shown myself here to-night."

Our vain lady-wits, however, too often lacked refinement. "If I drink any more," said Lady Coventry at Lord Hertford's table, "if I drink any more, I shall be 'muckibus.'" "Lord!" said Lady Mary Coke, "what is that?" "O," was the reply, "it is Irish for *sentimental!*" In those days there were no wedding breakfasts: the nuptial banquet was a dinner, and bride and bridegroom saw it out. Walpole congratulates himself that, at the marriage of his niece Maria, "there was neither form nor indecency, both which generally meet on such occasions. They were married," he adds, "at my brother's in Pall Mall, just before dinner, by Mr. Keppel; the company, my brother, his son, Mrs. Keppel and Charlotte, Lady Elizabeth Keppel, Lady Betty Waldegrave, and I. We dined there; the Earl and new Countess got into their post-chaise at eight o'clock, and went to Navestock alone, where they stay till Saturday night." Walpole gives instances enough—and more than enough—where matters did not go off so becomingly. Lords and Ladies were terribly coarse in sentiment and expression; and the women were often worse than the men. "Miss Pett," says the writer whom I have so often quoted, "has dismissed Lord Buckingham: *tant mieux pour lui!* She damns her eyes that she will marry some Captain: *tant mieux pour elle.*" This is a sample of Table Traits in 1760; and it was long before manners and morals improved. The example was not of the best sort even in high places. The mistress of Alfieri dined at Court, as widow of the Pretender; and Madame du Barry was publicly feasted by our potential Lord Mayor.

Some of the women were not only coarse in speech, but furies in act, and often sharpers to boot. Thus, when "Jemmy Lumley," in 1761, had a party of ladies at his house, with whom, after dinner, he played whist, from six at night till noon the next day, he lost two thousand pounds, which, suspecting knavery, he refused to pay. His antagonist, Mrs. Mackenzie, subsequently pounced upon him in the garden of an inn at Hampstead, where he was about to give a dinner to some other ladies. The sturdy "Scotch-woman," as Gray calls her, demanded her money, and, on meeting with a refusal, she "horsewhipped, trampled, bruised," and served him with worse indignities still, as may be seen by the curious, in Gay's Letter to Warton. Lumley's servants only with difficulty rescued their master from the fury, who carried a horsewhip beneath her hoop. The gentlemen do not appear to have been so generous, in their character of lovers, as their French brethren, who ruined themselves for "*les beaux yeux*" of some temporary idol. Miss Ford laughed consumedly at Lord Jersey, for sending her ("an odd first and only present to a beloved mistress") a boar's head, which, she says, "I had often the honour to meet at your Lordship's table before....... and would have eat it, had it been eatable."

The public are pretty familiar with the Household-Book of the Earl of Northumberland; and have learned much therefrom touching the Table Traits of the early period in which it was written. A later Earl did not inherit the spirit of organization which influenced his ancestor. "I was to dine at Northumberland House," says Walpole, in 1765, "and went there a little after hour. There I found the Countess, Lady Betty Mackinsy, Lady Stratford, my Lady Finlater,—who was never out of Scotland before,—a tall lad of fifteen, her son, Lord Drogheda, and Mr. Worseley. At five" (which is conjectured to have been the hour of extreme fashion a century ago) "arrived Mr. Mitchell, who said the Lords had commenced to read the Poor Bill, which would take, at least, two hours, and, perhaps, would debate it afterwards. We concluded dinner would be called for; it not being very precedented for ladies to wait for gentlemen. No such thing! Six o'clock came,—seven o'clock came,—our coaches came! Well! we sent them away; and excuses were, we were engaged. Still, the Countess's heart did not relent, nor uttered a syllable of apology. We wore out the wind and the weather, the opera and the play, Mrs. Cornely's and Almack's, and every topic that would do in a formal circle. We hinted, represented—in vain. The clock struck eight. My lady, at last, said she would go and order dinner; but it was a good half-hour before it appeared. We then sat down to a table of fourteen covers; but, instead of substantials, there was nothing but a profusion of plates, striped red, green, and yellow,—gilt plate, blacks, and uniforms. My Lady Finlater, who never saw those embroidered dinners, nor dined after three, was famished. The first course stayed as long as possible, in hopes of the Lords; so did the second. The dessert at last arrived, and the middle dish was actually set on, when Lord Finlater and Mr. Mackay arrived! Would you believe it?—the dessert was remanded, and the whole first course brought back again! Stay—I have not done! Just as this second first course had done its duty, Lord Northumberland, Lord Strafford, and Mackinsy came in; and the whole began a third time. Then the second course, and the dessert! I thought we should have dropped from our chairs with fatigue and fumes. When the clock struck eleven, we were asked to return to the drawing-room and take tea and coffee; but I said I was engaged to supper, and came home to bed!" This dinner may be contrasted with another given at a later period, by a member of the same house. The nobleman in question was an Earl Percy, who was in Ireland with his regiment,—the Fifth Infantry; and who, after much consideration, consented to give a dinner to the Officers in garrison at Limerick. The gallant, but cautious, Earl ordered the repast at a tavern, specifying that it should be for fifty persons, at eighteen-pence per head. The officers heard of the arrangement, and they ordered the landlord to provide a banquet at a guinea *per* head, promising to pay the difference, in the event of their entertainer declining to do so. When the banquet was served, there was but one astonished and uncomfortable individual at the board; and that was the Earl himself, who beheld a feast for the gods, and heard himself gratefully complimented upon the excellence both of viands and wines. The astonished Earl experienced an easily-understood difficulty in returning thanks when his health was drunk with an enthusiasm that bewildered him; and, on retiring early, he sought out the landlord, in order to have a solution of an enigma that sorely puzzled him. Boniface told the unadorned and unwelcome truth; and the inexperienced young Earl, acknowledging his mistake, discharged the bill with a sigh on himself, and a cheque on his banker.

A host, after all, *may* appear parsimonious without intending to be so. "This wine," said one of this sort to the late Mr. Pocock of Bristol, who had been dining with him, "costs me six shillings a bottle!" "Does it?" asked the guest, with a quaint look of gay reproof, "then pass it round, and let me have another sixpenn'orth!"

But, to return to our Table Traits of the last Century. In 1753, on the 4th of June, there was an installation of Knights of the Garter, at Windsor Castle, followed by a great dinner, and a ball. It would seem as if the public claimed the right of seeing the *spectacle* for which they had to pay; for we read that "the populace attempted several times to force their way into the hall where the Knights were at dinner, against the Guards, on which some were cut and wounded, and the Guards fired several times on them, with powder, to deter them, but without effect, till they had orders to load with ball, which made them desist." This is an ill-worded paragraph from the papers of the day; but it is a graphic illustration of the manners of the period.

These few samples of what society was in the last century, would suffice alone to show that it was sadly out of joint. What caused it? Any one who will take the trouble to go carefully through the columns of the ill-printed newspapers of the early part of the last century, will find that drunkenness, dissoluteness, and the sword hanging on every fool's thigh, ready to do his bidding, were the characteristics of the period. People got drunk at dinners, and then slew one another, or in some other way broke the law. Lord Mohun and Captain Hall dined together before they made their attempt to carry off Mrs. Bracegirdle; and when defeated in their Tarquin-like endeavour, they slaughtered poor Will Montford, the player, in the public streets, for no better reason than that Montford admired the lady, and Hall was jealous of the admirer. But neither copious dining, nor copious drinking, could make a brave man of Mohun. In proof of this, it is only necessary to state that before he fought his butchering duel with the Duke of Hamilton, he spent the previous night feasting and drinking at the Bagnio, which place he left in the morning, with his second, Major-General M'Carty, as the "Post-boy" remarks, "seized with fear and trembling." "The dog Mohun," as Swift styled him, was slain, and so was the Duke; but it is uncertain whether the latter fell by the hand of his adversary, or the sword of that adversary's second. A few years later we read of Fulwood, the lawyer, going to the play after dinner, drawing upon Beau Fielding, running him through, rushing in triumph to another house, meeting another antagonist, and getting slain by him, without any one caring to interfere.

In one of the numbers of the "Daily Post" for 1726, I find it recorded that a bevy of gallants, having joyously dined or supped together, descended from a hackney-coach in Piccadilly, bilked the coachman, beat him to a mummy, and stabbed his horses. Flushed with victory, they rushed into a neighbouring public-house, drew upon the gallants, terrified the ladies, and laughed at the mistress of the establishment, who declared that they would bring down ruin upon a place noted for "its safety and secrecy." The succeeding paragraph in the paper announces to the public that the Bishop of London will preach on the following Sunday in Bow-church, Cheapside, on the necessity for a reformation of manners!

The Clubs, and especially the "Sword Clubs," with their feastings and fightings, were the chief causes that manners were as depraved as they were. After supper, these Clubs took possession of the town, and held their sword against every man, and found every man's sword against them. The "Bold Bucks," and the "Hell-Fires," divided the Metropolis between them. The latter, a comparatively innocent association, found their simple amusement in mutilating watchmen and citizens. The "Bold Bucks" took for their devilish device, "Blind and Bold Love," and, under it, committed atrocities, the very thought of which makes the heart of human nature palpitate with horror and disgust. No man could become a member who did not denounce the claims both of nature and God! They used to assemble every Sunday at a tavern, close to the church of St. Mary-le-Strand. During divine service, they kept a noisy band of horns and drums continually at work: and, after service, they sat down to dinner, the principal dish at which was a "Holy-Ghost pie!" Assuredly the sermon of the metropolitan Prelate was much needed; but, when preached, reformation did but very slowly follow, especially in high places. At the very end of the century we hear of the Prince of Wales dining at the Duke of Queensberry's, at Richmond, with the last mistress of Louis XV.; and nobody appears to have been scandalized. And this was the characteristic of the time: vice was not only general, but it did not very seriously offend the few exceptional individuals. For the first three quarters of the century the epitaph of that time might have been taken from the eulogium passed by a May-Fair preacher in his Funeral Sermon upon Frederick, Prince of Wales: "He had no great parts, but he had great virtues; indeed, they degenerated into vices: he was very generous; but I hear his generosity has ruined a great many people; and then his condescension was such, that he kept very bad company."

I have, elsewhere, spoken of some of the roystering Clubs of the last century; but I cannot refrain from adding two other instances here, as examples of the Table Traits of the same period. The Calves'-Head Club established itself in Suffolk-Street, Charing Cross, on the anniversary of the martyrdom of King Charles, in the year 1735. The gentlemen members had an entertainment of calves' heads, some of which they showed to the mob outside, whom they treated with strong beer. In the evening, they caused a bonfire to be made before the door, and threw into it, with loud huzzas, a calf's head, dressed up in a napkin. They also dipped their napkins in red wine, and waved them from the windows, at the same time drinking toasts publicly. The mob huzzaed, as well as their fellow brutes of the Club; but, at length, to show their superior refinement, they broke the windows; and at length became so mischievous, that the Guards were called in to prevent further outrage.

The above was, no doubt, a demonstration on the part of gentlemen of republican principles. Some few years later, a different instance occurs. The "Monthly Review," May, 1757, mentions, that "seven gentlemen dined at a house of public entertainment in London, and were supposed to have run as great lengths in luxury and expense, if not greater, than the same number of persons were ever known to do before at a private regale. They afterwards played a game of cards, to decide which of them should pay the bill. It amounted to £81. 11s. 6d.; besides a turtle, which was a present to the company." This was certainly a heavy bill. A party of the same number at the Clarendon, and with turtle charged in the bill, would, in our days, find exceeding difficulty in spending more than £5 each. Their grandsires expended more than twice as much for a dinner not half as good.

It is only with the present century that old customs disappeared; and, with regard to some of them, society is all the better for their disappearance. Even plum porridge did not survive the first year of this half-century; when the more solid and staple dynasty of plum-pudding was finally established. Brand relates, that on Christmas-Day, 1801, he dined at the Chaplain's table, at St. James's, "and partook of the first thing served and eaten on that festival, at that table, namely, a tureen full of rich luscious plum-porridge. I do not know," he says, "that the custom is any where else retained." The great innovation, after this, was in the days of the Regent, when oysters were served as a prelude to dinner. This fashion was adopted by the Prince on the recommendation of a gentleman of his household, the elder Mr. Watier, who brought it with him from France, and added an "*experto crede*" to his recommendation. This fashion, however, like others, has passed away; and oysters and drams, as overtures to dinner, are things that have fallen into the domain of history.

There was a custom in these later days, much observed at Christmas time, which deserves a word of notice. I allude to the "Christmas-tree." The custom is one, however novel in England, of very ancient observance elsewhere. Its birth-place is Egypt. The tree there used was the palm; and the ceremony was in full force long before the days of Anthony and Cleopatra. The palm puts forth a fresh shoot every month. Its periodical leaves appear as regularly as those of Mr. Bentley's "Miscellany." In the time of the winter solstice, when parties were given in ancient Misraim, a spray of this tree, with twelve shoots, was suspended, to symbolize the completion of another year. The custom passed into Italy, where the fir-tree was employed for the purposes of celebration; and its pyramidal tips were decorated with burning candles, in honour of Saturn. This festival, the *Saturnalia*, was observed at the winter solstice, from the 17th to the 21st of December, and, during its continuance, Davus was as good a man as Chremes. The *Sigillaria*, days for interchanging presents of figures in wax, like those on the Christmas-tree, followed; and, finally, the *Juvenalia*, when men became "boys with boys," matrons turned children once again, and young and old indulged in the solemn romps with which the festival closed, and which *used* to mark our own old-fashioned festivities at Christmas time. That the Egyptian tree passed into Germany, may be seen in the pyramids which sometimes there are substituted for the tree. But the antique northern mythology has supplied some of the observances. The *Juel Fesi* was the mid-winter "Wheel Feast;" and the wheel represented the circling years which end but to begin again. The yule-log, as we call it, was the wheel-shaped log; in front of which was roasted the great boar,—an animal hateful to the god of the sun, but the flesh of which was religiously eaten by his worshippers. At this festival presents were made, which were concealed in wrappers, and flung in at open windows, emblematical, we are told, of the good, but as yet hidden, things which the opening year had in store.

The Church generally made selection of the heathen festivals for its own holy-days. In the early days, this was done chiefly to enable Christians to be merry without danger to themselves. It would not have been safe for them to eat, drink, and rejoice on days when Pagan Governments put on mourning. They were glad, then, when these were glad, and feasted with them, but holding other celebrations in view. Hence the German tree; only, for the sun which crowned the Roman tree, in honour of Apollo, the Germans place a figure of the Son of God; and, for the Phoebus and his flocks at the foot, they substitute "the Good Shepherd." The waxen figures are also the *sigillaria*, but with more holy impress. The *Saturnalia* have a place at the table joys that attend the exhibition of the tree, in presence of which joy is supposed to wither.

In conclusion, I cannot but notice one other table custom, which is of Teutonic origin. I allude to the Cabinet dinners given by Ministers previous to the opening of Parliament, and at which the Royal Speech is read, before it is declared in the presence of collective wisdom. This, at all events, reminds us of the ancient German custom, mentioned by Tacitus, who tells us, that the Teutonic legislators and warriors consulted twice touching every question of importance: once, by night, and over the bowl; and once, by day, when they were perfectly sober. Of course, I would not insinuate that ministers could possibly indulge too fondly over their cups, like the Senators of the Hercynian forest; and yet Viscount Sidmouth's vice, as Lord Holland tells us, " was wine;" and we have heard even of grave Lord-Stewards so drunk as to pull down the Monarchs they held by the hand, and *should* have supported. The last unfortunate official who so offended, should have craftily qualified his wine with water; and the mention of that subject reminds me of the origin of wine and water, of which I will say a few words, after adding one or two more traits of table manners.

I have spoken, in another page, of the unlucky exclamation touching haddock, which caused the perpetual exile of Poodle Byng from Belvoir. There was, however, no offence meant. How different was the case with that impudent coxcomb, Brummell, who managed to be the copper-Captain of fashion in London, when the true Captains were fighting their country's battles! When Brummell was living almost on the charity of Mr. Marshall, he was one of a dinner party at that gentleman's house, whither he took with him, according to his most impertinent custom, one of his favourite dogs. The " Beau " had, during dinner, helped himself to the wing of a roasted capon stuffed with truffles. He chose to fancy that the wing was tough, and, delicately seizing the end of it with a napkin-covered finger and thumb, he passed it under the table to his dog, with the remark, "Here, *Atout!* try if you can get your teeth through this; for I'll be d——d if I can." Not less ungratefully impudent was this gentleman-beggar on another occasion. A French family had given a dinner entirely on his account. It was perfect in its way. The ortolans came from Toulouse, the salmon was from the waters in the neighbourhood of Rouen, and the company most select. A friend, encountering him the next day, asked how the dinner had gone off. Brummell lifted up his hands, shook his head in a deprecatory manner, and said, "Don't ask me, my good fellow; but, poor man! he did his best."

The two most recent examples of Table Traits of the present century, that I have met with, illustrate the two extremes of society; and as they refer to a period of not above a month ago, they will serve, not inaptly, to close this section of my series. The first example is that afforded by a dinner given at Boston, in Lincolnshire, to twenty aged labourers. At this dinner, one of the gentlemen donors, of the feast, gave "the Ladies," and called on the octogenarian Chairman to return thanks. The old President, however, shook his head, with a mixed melancholy and cunning air, as if he too well knew there was nothing to return thanks for. The venerable "Vice" was then appealed to; but his reply was, that the least said about the subject of the toast would be the soonest mended. At length, a sprightly old man of threescore and ten was requested to respond, he having a gay look about him which seemed warranting gallantry; but he surprised the toast-giver by answering, that "as for t' leddies, he'd nowt to say; for his part, he'd never liked 'em." This unchivalrous sentiment awoke, at last, the spirit of a strip of a lad who was only sixty-five; and he responded to the toast, with a touch of satire, however, in his remarks, that left it uncertain whether he were so much a champion of the fair sex, as the company expected to find in him. The second "Trait" of the customs of this country is presented by the dinner given in February of the present year, by Earl Granville, the guests at which were Lord Aberdeen, the Bishop of Oxford.

11*

and Mr. Bright. There were not such startling contrasts at the reconciliation dinner which brought Wilkes and Johnson together, as at Earl Granville's unique banquet. The host and the Premier represented—the first, smiling courtesy; the second, the most frigid severity of a freezing civility. But the strongest contrast was in the persons of the Bishop and the " Friend :"—Dr. Wilberforce, highest of Churchmen, briefest of Preachers, and twice as much curled as the son of Clinias himself; while Mr. Bright, with every hair as if a plummet depended at the end of it, hating the Church, but not indifferent to *petits patés à la braise*, must have looked like the vinegar of voluntaryism that would *not* mingle with the oil of orthodoxy. To have made this banquet complete, there should have been two more guests,—Dr. Cumming and Dr. Cahill, with appropriate dishes before each :—a plate of sweatbreads in front of the gentle apostle of the Kirk; and a bowl of blood-puddings opposite the surpliced Priest who has gained a gloomy notoriety by the " glorious idea," to which I have referred, of a massacre of English heretic beef-eaters, by the light-dieted holders of Catholic and continental bayonets. But Dr. Cahill, it may be hoped, is something insane, or would he have deliberately recorded, as he did the other day in the " Tablet," that it were much better for Romanists to read immoral works than the English Bible ? His excellent reason is, that " the Church " easily forgives immorality, but has no mercy for heresy. Well, well; we should not like to catch a Confessor of this school sitting next our daughter at dinner, and intimating that Holywell-street literature was better reading than the English version of the Sermon on the Mount.—But let us sweeten our imagination with a little Wine and Water.

WINE AND WATER.

Early age, and the oldest poets, confessed, that wine was the gift of the gods to men. The latter would appear to have abused the gift, if we may believe Philonides the physician, who wrote a treatise "On Perfumes and Garlands" (Περὶ Μύρων καὶ Στεφάνων.) In this treatise he asserts, that, when Bacchus brought the vine from the Red Sea into Greece, men drank to such excess, that they became as beasts, and incapable of performing manly duties. A party of these revellers were once drinking by the sea-shore, when a sudden storm drove them into a cave for shelter. They do not seem, however, to have been inveterate tipplers; for, according to Philonides, they left their cups on the beach. When the shower had passed, they found the wine in them mingled with rain-water; and, very much to their credit, they liked the mixture so well, that they solemnly thanked the "good genius" who had sent it. Hence, when wine was served at Grecian repasts, the guests invoked this good genius; and when the turn came for wine mixed with water, they acknowledged the benevolent inventor by the name of *Jupiter Saviour*. I may take this opportunity to state, that at one period, it was the fashion to attend these drinking entertainments in a pair of "Alcibiades," or boots which had been rendered popular by being first worn by the curled son of Clinias. Thus we see, that in our fashion of conferring on boots the authorities of great names, we are doing nothing original; and that men used to call for their "Alcibiades," as they do now for their "Wellingtons," "Bluchers," or "Alberts."

To revert, for a moment, to the question of wine and water, I would state, that it has been discussed in its separate divisions by German writers, the substance of whose opinions I will venture to give in verse, without desiring, however, to be considered as endorsing every sentiment in full. As French music-books say, it is an "*Air à faire*."

Do you ask what now glows
In this goblet of mine?
 Wine! wine! wine! wine!
To the stream do ye ask,
 Shall my cup-bearer go?
 No! no! no! no!
Let water its own frigid nature retain;
Since water it is, let it water remain!
Let it ripple and run in meandering rills,
And set the wheels going in brook-sided mills.
In the desert, where streams do but scantily run,
If so much they're allowed by the thirsty old sun,
There water *may* be, as it's quaff'd by each man,
Productive of fun to a whole caravan.
   But ask what now glows, &c.

Yes, water, and welcome, in billows may rise,
Till it shiver its feathery crest 'gainst the skies;
Or in dashing cascades it may joyously leap,
Or in silvery lakes lie entranced and asleep;—
Or, e'en better still, in full showers of hope,
Let it gaily descend on some rich vineyard's slope,
That its sides may bear clusters of ripening bliss,
Which, in Autumn, shall melt into nectar like this.
   Like this that now glows, &c.

Let it bear up the vessel that bringeth us o'er
Its freight of glad wine from some happier shore.
Let it run through each land that in ignorance lies:
It the Heathen will do very well to baptize.
Yes, water shall have ev'ry due praise of mine,
Whether salt, like the ocean, or fresh, like the Rhine
Yes, praised to the echo pure water shall be,
But wine, wine alone is the nectar for me!
  For 't is that which now glows
  In this goblet of mine.
   Wine! wine! wine! wine!
  No attendant for me
  To the river need go.
   No! no! no! no!

The various merits and uses of the respective liquids are fairly allowed in the above lines; but I may observe, that wine apologists, generally, are sadly apt to forget, that there are such things as conscience and to-morrow morning. For their edification and use, I indite the following colloquy, to be kept in mind, rather than sung, at all festivities where the " *Aqua Pumpaginis* " is held in abhorrence :

See the wine in the bowl,
 How it sparkles to-night?
Tell us what can compete
 With that red sea of light;
Which breathes forth a perfume
 That deadens all sorrow,
And leaves us blessed now,
  (Conscience *loquitur*.)
" With a headache to-morrow!"

Where are spirits like those
 That we find in the bowl,
Shedding joy round our brows,
 Breathing peace to the soul?
Our tongues feel the magic,
 There our strains, too, we borrow
We 're Apollos to-night,
  (Conscience *loquitur*,)
" To be songless to-morrow!"

O, this rare inspiration!
 How gay are the dreams
Of the thrice triple blest
 Who may quaff of thy streams!
It expels from the heart
 Sulky care, that old horror,
And tells laughter to-night
  (Conscience, ashamed of the rhyme)
" To wake sadness to-morrow!"

Drink deep, though there be
 Thirstless fools, who may preach
Of the sins of the bowl,—
 Do they act as they teach?

.f we're sinners, what then!
　　As we're not friends to sorrow
We'll be glad ones to-night,
　　　(Conscience *loquitur*,)
"To be sad ones to-morrow!"

Ah! that was old Conscience:
　　Him we'll drown in the wine!
Plunge him in! hold him down!
　　Ah! he dies!—now the Nine
May, to write in his praise,
　　From our Helicon borrow.
He 'n done talking to-night;
　　　(Conscience, from the bowl,)
"You shall hear me to-morrow!"

Finally, being on Pegasus, and he ambling along through this chapter of Wine and Water, I will take the opportunity, as connected with my subject, of doing justice to a flower whose "capability," as Mr. Browne used very properly to say, has been overlooked,—I mean the tulip:—

Praise they who will the saucy vine,
With her thousand rings and her curls so fine!
　　　But I fill up,
　　　To the tulip-cup,
All looking as though it were bathed in wine.
　　　Ah, show me the flower,
　　　In vale or bower,
That looks half so well as this bowl of mine!
　O, who this night will fail to fill up.
　Or to sing in praise of the tulip-cup?"

Praise they who will the willow-tree,
With her drooping neck and her tresses free,
　　　That bend to the brink
　　　Of the brook, and drink
Of a liquid that will never do for me!
　　　While tulip-cup
　　　Is for ever held up,
As though she could drink for eternity.

>   And that is the very bowl for me,
>   Who hate the sickly willow-tree!
>
>   The water-lily praise they who will:
>   Of water we know that she loves her fill.
>   But what, pray, is she,
>   To the tulip, that we
>   Have loved for so long, and love so well still?"
>   Ah! who doth not think her
>   A mere water-drinker,
>   That quaffs but such wine she can get from the rill?
>   Then fill up to-night to the tulip tall,
>   Who holds forth her cups, and can drain them all!

See how naturally we drop out of the subject of "Wine and Water," into that of "Wine," to which we now, reverently, yet joyously address ourselves.

THE BIRTH OF THE VINE, AND WHAT HAS COME OF IT.

The birth of the vine was in this wise. On the day of the creation, the trees vied with each other in boasting; and each exulted in the enjoyment of his own existence. "The Lord himself," said the lofty cedar, "planted me, and in me has he united stability and fragrance, strength and durability." "Me," said the shade-spreading palm, "hath the beneficence of Jehovah appointed for a blessing, joining together in me utility and beauty." Then the apple-tree spoke: "As a bridegroom among youths, so am I resplendent among the trees of the woods." "And I," said the myrtle, "stand among the lowly bushes, like a rose among thorns." In this manner boasted they all, the olive and the fig; yea, the pine even, and the fir exulted.

The vine alone, in silence, stooped to the ground. "It seems," said she to herself, "as if everything were denied me,—stem and branch, blossom and fruit; but, such as I am, I will hope and wait. Thus speaking, she sank to the earth, and her branches wept.

But not long did she thus wait and weep; for, behold, cheerful man, the earthly god, drew nigh unto her. He saw a weak plant, the plaything of the breeze, sinking under its own weight, and pining for assistance. Touched with compassionate feeling, he upheld it, and trained the delicate tree over his own bower. More freely now sported the air among its branches. The warmth of the sun penetrated the hard green berries, preparing therein the delicious juice,—a drink for gods and men. Laden with clustering grapes, the vine now bowed herself before her lord, and the latter tasted of her refreshing sweets, and named her his friend—his own grateful favourite. It was now that the proud trees envied her, but many of them lived on in sterility, while she rejoiced, full of gratitude at her slender growth, and patient humility; and therefore it is, that it is given to her to make glad the heart of sorrowing man, to elevate the cast-down spirit, and to cheer the afflicted.

"Despair not," says Herder, who thus tells the old traditionary story of the vine,—"Despair not, O thou that art deserted, but endure patiently. Sweet streams issue from unlikely sources; and the feeble vine affords the most potent draught in the world."

Let us, however, turn from poetical tradition to prosaic reality. The vine is, by birth, a Persian. Its cradle was on the sunny slopes of the hilly regions on the south shores of the Caspian Sea. There, in the Caucasus, and in Cashmere, the wild vine still climbs and clings to the very necks of the most towering trees. Its life-blood in those regions is seldom turned to evil purpose. In Caubul it is taken less in potions than in powder. The Caubulese dry and grind it to dust and eat thereof, finding it a pleasant acid. This is half matter of taste and half matter of medicine, just as over-wearied digestions in Germany drive their wretched owners into vineyards, to abstain from meat, and live for a while, upon raisins. Indeed the vine was never meant entirely for enjoyment. It is one of the most perfect of chymists; and if it offers grapes in clusters, its twigs afford carbonate of potash, serviceable for many purposes, and, among others, for correcting the acidity brought on by too free indulgence in the fruit, or in its expressed liquid.

In the olden days, when the Patriarchs worshipped Heaven in the "cathedral of immensity," Palestine was renowned for the glory of its grapes. There were none other to compare with them upon earth. When the desert-traders were waiting the return of their emissaries, whom they had sent from Kadesh-Barnea to spy the Promised Land, their thirsty impatience was exchanged for delight at beholding their agents re-appear, bearing between them, upon poles, gigantic clusters,—the near fountains whence their dried up souls might draw new life and vigour. The grapes of Palestine are still remarkable for their great size. Clusters are spoken of, each of which exceeds a stone in weight; and vines are mentioned, whose stems measured a foot and a half in diameter, and whose height reached to thirty feet; while their branches afforded a tabernacle of shade, to the extent of thirty feet square. But it could not have been from such a vine that the men from Kadesh-Barnea collected the grapes which they could scarcely carry. The Welbeck grapes which the Duke of Portland sent to the Marquess of Rockingham, were of Syrian origin; and these —on a single bunch, weighing nineteen pounds, and measuring three-and-twenty inches long, with a maximum diameter of nearly twenty inches—were borne upon a pole a distance of twenty miles, by four laborers; two to carry, and two to relieve. So that the conveying grapes in this fashion may have been more on account of their delicacy than of their weight. The Hampton Court vine, too, produces clusters of great weight, and covers a space of not less than 2,200 feet.

The vine has been figuratively employed as an emblem of fruitfulness, of security, and peace; and no doubt can exist of its having been cultivated at a very early period. Noah planted the vine immediately after the Deluge; and, from the first thing planted, sin came again into the world, bringing with it widely-extending consequences. Bread and wine are mentioned in Genesis. Pharaoh's chief butler dreamed of a vine with three branches; and the Israelites (in Numbers) complained that Moses and Aaron had brought them out of Egypt into a dry and barren land, where there were neither figs nor vines. So, in after-years, the companions of Columbus sailed tremblingly with their calm Captain over trackless seas, and murmured at him for bringing them from the olives and vines of Spain, to the very confines of creation, where terror reigned, and death sat enthroned.

Jacopo di Bergamo gives a singular account of the reason which induced Noah to plant the vine. The Patriarch did so, he says, because he saw a goat in Cicily eat some wild grapes, and afterwards fight with such courage, that Noah inferred there must have been virtue in the fruit. He planted a vine, therefore, and wherefore is not told—manured it with the blood of a lion, a lamb, a swine, and a monkey, or ape. But this, perhaps, only signifies that, by drinking wine, men become bold, confiding or meek, filthy or obscene.

It is stated by Theodoret, that Noah himself, after pressing the grapes, became intoxicated through inexperience, as he had been a water-drinker for six centuries! The sin of Lot is supposed to have been committed, not merely under the influences of wine, but of a maddening and drugged draught. The evil power of wine is well illustrated by the story of the Monk, to whom Satan offered a choice of sins,—incest, murder, or drunkenness. The poor Monk chose the last, as the least of the three; and, when he was drunk, he committed the other two.

Commentators pronounce our rendering under the single word "wine," the thirteen distinct Hebrew terms used in the Bible to distinguish between wines of different sorts, ages, and condition, as a defect of great magnitude; and no doubt it is so. The knowledge of mixing wines appears to have been extensively applied by the ancient people; and it is said of the beautiful Helen, that she learned in Egypt the composition of the exhilarating, or rather, stupefying, ingredients which she mixed in the bowl, together with the wine, to raise the spirits of such of her guests as were oppressed with grief. I may notice, too, here, that our word *shrub*, or *syrup*, is an Eastern word. In Turkey, a *shirub-jee* is simply a "wine-seller."

Yes, despite the Prophet, the Turks drink wine more than occasionally, and under various names. Tavernier speaks of a particular preparation of the grape drunk by the Grand Seignior, in company with the ladies of the seraglio; and a similar beverage, it is conjectured, was quaffed by Belshazzar and his concubines out of the holy vessels, and was offered in vain to the more scrupulous Daniel, it was a rich and royal drink, made strong by the addition of drugs; and the object of drinking the potent mixture was the same as that which induced Conrad Scriblerus and the daughter of Gaspar Barthius to live for a whole year on goat's milk and honey. Either mixture was better than that of the Persians, who "fortified" their wines, or syrup of sweet wines, by adding to them the very perilous seasoning of *nux vomica*. But none of these were so curious as the "wine-cakes" eaten by Mr. Buckingham: these were, I suppose, made of wine preserves.

But pure wine may be eaten, or rather, be rendered harder than any of our common food. Thus we hear of Russian troops being compelled, in very hard winters, to cut out their rations of wine from the cask with a hatchet.

I think it is the renowned Dissenter, Toplady, who remarks, that the only sarcastic passage in Scripture is to be found in the cutting speech of Elisha to the Priests of Baal: "Is not Baal a god, seeing that he eateth much meat?" There is, however, another ironical passage, in reference to wine. "Give *Shechar* unto him who is ready to perish," is the satirical speech of Lemuel's mother, who warns her royal son against the deceitful influences of intoxicating beverages, representing them as especially destructive to those who are charged with the government of nations; and then ironically points to the man who foolishly concludes, that in the sweet or strong drink he may bury all memory of the cares and anxieties brought upon him by his own profligacy.

There is, however, a difference of opinion touching the spirit in which the last words quoted from Scripture are used. The Rabbins interpret the passage as a command to administer wine to the individual about to suffer death. Thus wine mingled with myrrh was offered to One of whom the Gospel records, that He refused what His enemies presented.

The custom of offering doomed criminals a last earthly draught of refreshment is undoubtedly one of considerable antiquity. The right of offering wine to criminals on their passage to the scaffold was often a privilege granted to religious communities. In Paris, the privilege was held by the convent of Filles-Dieu, the Nuns of which kept wine prepared for those who were condemned to suffer on the gibbet of Montfaucon. The gloomy procession halted before the gate of the monastery, the criminal descended from the cart, and the Nuns, headed by the Lady Abbess, received him on the steps with as much, perhaps more heartfelt ceremony than if he had been a King. The poor wretch was led to a crucifix near the church door, the feet whereof he humbly kissed. He then received, from the hands of the Superior, three pieces of bread, (to remind him of the Trinity,) and *one* glass of wine (emblem of Unity). The procession then resumed its dread way to the scaffold.

Elie Berthet tells us of a poor wretch, who, on being offered the usual refreshment, quietly swallowed the wine, and coolly put the bread in his pocket. When again in the cart, his observant Confessor asked him his reason for the act. "I suppose, Father," answered the moribund, "that the good sisters furnished me with the bread that it may serve me in paradise; on earth, at all events, it can no longer be of use to me." "Be of good cheer," said another Confessor, who was encouraging a criminal on the *Grève;* "be of good cheer. To night you will sup in paradise." "*Tenez, mon Père,*" answered the poor fellow; "*allez-y-vous à ma place; car, pour moi, je n'ai pas faim.*" This incident had been made good use of by the "ballad" writers both of England and France.

"Bowl-yard," St. Giles's-in-the-Fields, preserves in its name the memory of a similar custom in England. This yard, or alley, adjacent to the church, is a portion of the site of the old Hospital for Lepers, the garden of which was a place of execution. Lord Cobham, under Henry V., and Babington and his accomplices, for conspiring against Elizabeth, were executed here. Stow tells us that, "at this hospital, the prisoners conveyed from the city of London toward Tyburn, there to be executed for treason, felonies, or other trespasses, were presented with a great *bowl* of ale, thereof to drink at their *pleasure,* (?) as to be their last refreshment in this life." In later days, the criminals were sometimes supplied by their friends from the public-houses on the line of road. In one case, a convict happily tarried drinking for a longer space of time than usual. The rope was just round his neck, when the arrival of a reprieve saved him. Had he drunk a glass less, he would have been hanged a moment sooner; and society would thus have been deprived of his valuable services. He was a luckier man than the saddler in Ireland, who, on his way to the gibbet, refused the ale and wine offered him on the road, who was accordingly very rapidly dispatched, and for whom a reprieve arrived a minute too late for him to profit by it. Hence the proverb, applied by those who press reluctant people to drink, "Ah, now go away wid you. Ye 're like the obs'inate saddler, who was hanged for refusing his liquor." It certainly was not a custom with Irish convicts to decline the "thrink," before trial or after. "The night before Larry was stretch'd," is a slang lyric, graphically illustrative of the grace with which Irish criminals took leave of life. The most singular thing, however, connected with the popular lay question, is, that it was written by a Clergyman. But, at the time of its production, such authorship excited no surprise in the literary public. The "cloth" was still of the quality of that in which Fielding's Newgate Chaplain walked; and he, it will be remembered, was a pious gentleman, who candidly avowed that he was the rather given to indulge in punch, as that was a liquor nowhere spoken against in Scripture!

But it was not English or Irish Chaplains, of the olden time, who stood by themselves in their respect for good liquor. If that reverend and rubicund gentleman, Walter de Mapes, wrote the best Latin drinking-song that Bacchanalian inspiration ever produced, so did a German Prelate preach the best sermon on the same text. I allude to the Bishop of Triers, or Trèves. Here is an odour, caught by the way, of the full bottle of counsel which he poured out to his hearers:—

"Brethren, to whom the high privilege of repentance and penance has been conceded, you feel the sin of abusing the gifts of Providence. But, *abusum non tollit usum*. It is written, 'Wine maketh glad the heart of man.' It follows, then, that to use wine moderately is our duty. Now there is, doubtless, none of my male hearers who cannot drink his four bottles without affecting his brain. Let him, however,—if by the fifth or sixth bottle he no longer knoweth his own wife,—if he beat and kick his children, and look on his dearest friend as an enemy,—refrain from an excess displeasing to God and man, and which renders him contemptible in the eyes of his fellows. But whoever, after drinking his ten or twelve bottles, retains his senses sufficiently to support his tottering neighbour, or manage his household affairs, or execute the commands of his temporal and spiritual superiors, let him take his share quietly, and be thankful for his talent. Still, let him be cautious how he exceed this; for man is weak, and his powers limited. It is but seldom that our kind Creator extends to any one the grace to be able to drink safely sixteen bottles, of which privilege he hath held me, the meanest of his servants, worthy. And since no one can say of me that I ever broke out in causeless rage, or failed to recognise my household friends or relations, or neglected the performance of my spiritual duties, I may, with thankfulness and a good conscience, use the gift which hath been intrusted to me. And you, my pious hearers, each take modestly your allotted portion; and, to avoid all excess, follow the precept of St. Peter,—'Try all, and stick by the best!'"

The sermon is not a bad illustration of what was, and remains, historical fact. The first Archbishop of Mayence was the Englishman Boniface; and most of his successors might have been characterized by his name. They were more powerful than the Emperors, and more stately than Moguls. The Canons of the Cathedral, supported by its enormous revenues, lived a jovial life. The Pope, indeed, reproved them for their worldly and luxurious habits; but they uproariously returned for answer, "We have no more wine than is needed for the Mass; and not enough to turn our mills with!"

Good living, as it was erroneously called, was certainly, at one time, an universal observance in Germany, when the sole wish of man was, that he might have short sermons and long puddings. When this wish prevailed, every dining-room had its *faulbett*, or sot's couch, in one corner, for the accommodation of the first couple of guests who might chance to be too drunk to be removed. Indeed, in German village-inns, the most drunken guests were, in former days, by far the best off; for, while they had the beds allotted them, as standing in most need of the same, the guests of every degree, whether rich or poor, the perfectly sober—wherever such phenomena were to be found—and those not so intoxicated but they could stagger out of the room, all lodged with the cows among the straw.

Probably, no country on the earth presented such scenes, arising from excessive drinking, as were witnessed in Saxony and Bohemia, a few generations back. These scenes were so commonly attended by murder, or followed by death, that it was said to be better for a man to fall among the thickest of his enemies fighting, than among his friends when drinking. There were deadly brawls in taverns, deadly drunken feuds in the family circle, and not less deadly contentions in the streets. When the city-gates were closed at night, the crowds of drunkards, issuing to their homes in the suburbs, were met by as dense and drunken a crowd, returning from their revels in the country. And then came the insulting motion, the provoking word, the hard blow, and the harder stab. Then fell the wounded and the dead; then rose the shrieks of women and of children, and, loud above them, the imprecations and blasphemies born in the wine-sodden brains of men. Suddenly, a shot or two is fired from the walls, right into the heaving mass below. And then ensue the flying of the people, and the venting of impotent rage from the rash and resolute. But, gradually, the two opposing streams glide through each other, the gates are at length closed; and, by the light of the moon, on the almost deserted esplanade, may be observed, stretched on the ground, some half-dozen human forms. Some of these are dead, some are still drunken and helpless, and both equally uncared for.

This is no overdrawn picture of an ancient German Period. It is on record that once, on the banks of the Bohemian Sazawa, a party of husbandmen met for the purpose of drinking twelve casks of wine. There were ten of them who addressed themselves to this feat; but one of the ten attempting to retire from the contest before any of his fellows, the remaining nine seized, bound him, and roasted him alive on a spit. The murderers were subsequently carried to the palace for judgment; but the Duke's funeral was taking place as they entered the hall, and the Princes who administered justice were all so intoxicated, that they looked upon the matter in the light of a joke that might be compensated for by a slight fine.

There was a joyous revelry at that time in every direction. A father would not receive a man for a son-in-law who could not drink; and in Universities the conferring of a degree was always followed by a carouse, the length of which was fixed, by College rules, as not to exceed eight hours' duration. Yet, during this generally dissolute period, a strange custom was prevalent at the tables of Nuremberg. In all well-regulated households, there used to hang a little bell beneath the dining-table; and this bell was struck by the master of the family, if he were sober enough, whenever any one uttered an unseemly phrase.

Even so, in public, a voice of indignation was sometimes raised against the profligacy of the period. The voice to the people at large was as the bell to the guests at Nuremberg. Its effects who can tell? It may have induced Luther to be content with dignified Virgil rather than with unclean Plautus; it may have driven the Monk Schwartz from the refectory to the alembic; and it may have called Gutemberg from the brutalities of the camp to the wonders of the printing-press. In the two latter cases the consequences bear a very tipsy appearance; for it was a soldier who invented printing, and a Monk who first manufactured gunpowder!

Let us not hasten to condemn our fellows of the olden time and distant land. Manners as fearfully outraging prevailed but very recently among young Englishmen. M. de Warenne, a French officer in our Indian army, describes the manners and customs there prevalent as any thing but edifying. In his "*Inde-Anglaise*" he describes himself, on one occasion, as being disinclined for

12

study, and consequently joining a party of his comrades who were at the moment occupied in an unreserved enjoyment of the pleasures of the table. They were from fifteen to twenty in number, married and single, but all young, full of hope, good prospects, and gaiety. Deep were the libations made by this riotous company, seated at a festive board in the open air, looked down upon by a brilliant moon, and gently fanned by the evening breeze.

"While the attendant servant," says the author, "poured out, with Indian profusion, fresh supplies of tea, coffee, beer, punch, and grog, a dense vapour rose from our cigars, and joyous shouts rang from every lip at the conclusion of songs, bacchanalian and anacreontic. Toasts succeeded each other rapidly, alternately exciting the laughter or approbation of the carousers. One of them caused in me, at the time, a singular impression. A young, wild brained fellow, in pouring out a bumper, called on us to fill our glasses, in order to sanction the strange wish of a rash ambition,—'A bloody war, and a sickly season!'"

The blasphemous sentiment, as M. de Warenne rightly terms it, was drunk with enthusiasm; and the gay and thoughtless drinkers had yet the cup to their lips, when one of them was stricken with the cholera, the presence of which in camp was hardly known;— the next day the funeral salute was fired over his grave. The author adds, that the music played on returning from the funeral was joyously and daily hummed by the daily diminishing survivors. He says that there was a mockery in the waltzes they continued to dance; for death was also daily decreasing their orchestra. The stricken, we are told, felt themselves relieved from further anxiety, recovered their temporarily shaken self-possession, and died with indifference. The strong who lived are described as, for the most part, diverting their thoughts, outraging decency, and defying God, by composing or chanting songs whose inspiration certainly savours of hell. Here is a specimen of one of these devil's canticles, roared over wine, to frighten away the cholera:—

I.

We meet 'neath the sounding rafter,
  And the walls around are bare;
As they shout back our peals of laughter,
  It seems as the dead were there.
Then stand to your glasses!—steady!
  We drink 'fore our comrades' eyes;
One cup to the dead already:
  Hurrah for the next that dies!

II.

Not here are the goblets glowing,
  Not here is the vintage sweet;
'T is cold as our hearts are growing,
  And dark as the doom we meet.
But stand to your glasses!—steady
  And soon shall our pulses rise;
One cup to the dead already;
  Hurrah for the next that dies!

III.

There's many a hand that's shaking.
  And many a cheek that's sunk;
But soon, though our hearts are breaking,
  They'll burn with the wine we've drunk.
Then stand to your glasses!—steady!
  'T is here the revival lies;
Quaff a cup to the dead already;
  Hurrah for the next that dies!

IV.

Time was, when we laugh'd at others,
  We thought we were wiser then:
Ha! ha! let them think of their mothers,
  Who hope to see them again.
No! stand to your glasses!—steady!
  The thoughtless is here the wise;
One cup to the dead already;
  Hurrah for the next that dies!

V.

"Not a sigh for the lot that darkles,
    Not a tear for the friends that sink;
We'll fall 'mid the wine-cup's sparkles,
    As mute as the wine we drink.
Come! stand to your glasses!—steady!
    'T is this that the respite buys;
One cup to the dead already;
    Hurrah for the next that dies!

VI.

"Who dreads to the dust returning?
    Who shrinks from the sable shore,
Where the high and haughty yearning
    Of the soul can sting no more?
No! stand to your glasses!—steady!
    This world is a world of lies!
One cup to the dead already;
    Hurrah for the next that dies!

VII.

"Cut off from the land that bore us,
    Betray'd by the land we find,
When the brightest are gone before us,
    And the dullest are most behind,
Stand! stand! to your glasses!—steady!
    'T is all we have left to prize!
One cup to the dead already!
    Hurrah for the next that dies!"

After this, the most rigid examiner of public morals in all countries need not exclusively frown on the old Germans, nor on their profane canticle, the burthen of which is:—

"*Gaudeamus, igitur, juvenes dum sumus*
Post jucundam juventutem,
Post molestam senectutem,
Nos habebit, nos habebit, nos habebit tumulus!"

There is, however, more reason, and healthy sentiment, and pure principle, in such lines as the following,—extracted from Walter Savage Landor's "Last Fruit off an Old Tree,"—than in reams of such fiery invocations to quaff deeply as those cited above. Hear the old man:—

" The chrysolites and rubies Bacchus brings,
    To crown the feast where swells the broad-vein'd brow,
Where maidens blush at what the minstrel sings,
    They who have courted, may court now.

" Bring me a cool alcove, the grape uncrush'd,
    The peach of pulpy cheek and down mature ;
Where ev'ry voice, but bird's or child's, is hush;.
    And ev'ry thought, like the brook nigh, runs pure."

There was a Persian sage, whose philosophy was of a different complexion from that of the eloquent moralist of "the old garden near Bath." "In what can I best assist thee?" demanded the Minister, Nizam-al-Mulk, as he warmly greeted his friend Omar Keyoomee. "Place me," said Omar, enamoured of poetry and ease, "where my life may pass without care or annoyance, and where wine, in abundance, may inspire my muse." A pension was accordingly assigned him in the fertile district of Nishapour, where Omar lived and died. His tomb still exists, and Mr. J. B. Fraser, in his "Persia," informs us that he heard Omar's story told over his grave by a brother rhymester, and a most congenial spirit. The system of Omar was explained by himself, in something after this fashion:—

    I ask not for much : let the miser seek wealth ;
      Let the proud sigh for titles and fame :
    All the riches I ask are a fair share of health.
      And the hope of a true poet's name.
    Let the flatterer talk of his worth to the Shah.—
      Of his greatness, too, all the day long ;—
    I envy them not, for I love better far
      To pay my poor tribute in song.

    A kaftan of honour! a gem from the King
      To be gain'd in the field or divan ?

Ah! rather around me the bright mantle fling
   Of the poets of gay Laristan.
Let the gems be for those of the glittering crowd
   Who would die, the Shah Inshah to please;
But *I'm* not ambitious, I never was proud,
   I sigh but for sherbet and ease,

Do I wish for command in dark history's page,
   Do I long in fond record to shine?
Yes, let me have sway, till the last sigh of age,
   Over cohorts of old Shiraz wine.
And as for renown, it may be very well,
   But Keyoomee the honour will wave;
Contented if some brother rhymester will tell
   Keyoomee's glad life, o'er his grave.

THE MAKING AND MARRING OF WINE.

It used to be said of the old learned and liquor-loving Germans, that they did not care what Latin they spoke, so long as it *was* Latin; nor what sort of wine they drank, so long as it *was* wine. I have read somewhere of a feudal German Baron becoming intoxicated upon pious principles. He was seated, with his wife at his side, at the centre of his own table, presiding at a banquet. He had drunk till he had scarcely power left to carry the goblet up to his ever-thirsty lips. The Frau Baroninn had repeatedly remonstrated, in whispers, with her lord; who replied, that he must needs drink when toasts were given, or his want of faith would be marked by his guests. He was about to raise a full goblet to his beard, when his lady, overturning, as if by accident, the cluster of lights which illuminated the board, begged of her consort to fling his wine away upon the floor; adding, "It is dark; nobody will see you." "Nay," said the orthodox Baron, solemnly, "God sees me!" and therewith he finished his draught, and was soon after conveyed to his couch, under such benison as the Chaplain could give, who congratulated his master upon the flavour of his wine, and the strength of his principles!

In no country in the world has more wine been drunk than in Germany; and no where has adulteration thereof been practiced so systematically. "*Vaticana bibis, bibis venenum,*" says Martial, in the sixth book of his Epigrams. For "*Vaticana,*" read "*Germanica;*" and the line had, at one time, as fitting an application. The method pursued appears to have been of classical derivation; and the Germans, like the Romans, adulterated their wine with lead. It has been a matter of vexation to Teutonic scholars, that they have never been able to discover the name of the ingenious person who first realized the deadly idea of employing lead in the adulteration of wine. All that they can say of him is, that he was very wicked, but decidedly clever.

The Roman wine-merchants treated the matter in a business-like way. Lead arrested the acetous fermentation of wine, did not alter its colour, and did improve its taste. This was all that was desirable, as regarded *them* as merchants. If the beverage gave death, by slow or speedy means, to those who drank, that was an affair which concerned the imbibers, their medical men, and their families. They were ignorant and godless Heathens, of course, who committed this crime; and as nothing like it has ever been known as a characteristic of some of the professors of a better dispensation,—why, our righteous indignation may be intense. One excuse, indeed, may be offered for the old Romans. "At lovers' perjuries," as they were told, "Jove himself condescended to laugh;" and, if so, they might feel canonically certain, that Mercury would not call them to account, but rather applaud their proficiency in cheating. But Galen was more just than the gods of either the Greek or Roman mythology, and sternly denounces the tricks at which the son of Maia would have smiled.

The same ancients were accustomed to boil new wine in metal vessels; and, when the quantity had been reduced by the process, to add sea-water and bad wine, and send the mixture to market as something that would make the very eyes of Bacchus twinkle with delight. A process not less distasteful, if less deadly, was that of boiling lime and plaster of Paris in inferior wine. The former was supposed to add an intoxicating quality to the mixture, which must have been as detestable as "Masdeu." To this day, certain wines of the Mediterranean are subjected to a similar process; and, perhaps, if lime be judiciously used, the results may not be very injurious. It corrects acidity; but too much of it would enable the drinker to find out, as Falstaff did, that there was "lime in the sack." We are wise in our generation, in employing carbonate of soda for this purpose, rather than lime, slaked or unslaked; and we also do well to reject gypsum,—a compound of sulphuric acid and lime, and which is seldom procurable in a sufficiently pure state to authorize its being employed. The rejection of plaster of Paris, for the purpose of improving wine, is, however, more general than universal. After all, it is not worse than calcined shells, and is innocuous when compared with the use of sugar of lead.

The Roman law was not levelled against the adulteration of wine; it no more controlled the sale or manufacture, than, in Thevenot's days, the Tunisian government interfered with the sale of wine at Tunis, which was left to slaves, who did with it as they liked, for their own profit, and the destruction of infidel stomachs. It was otherwise in Germany, where Diets were assembled to discuss what was, in truth, no unimportant matter; the members of which began to think, that if wine was worth having, it was worth providing for its purity. For centuries Governments made laws, but bad wine was drunk in spite of them.

Beckmann gives it as his opinion, that wines cannot be poisoned by gypsum; but *that* is more readily said than proved. The ancients clarified their wine with it; but they did so at the expense of a portion of the spirituous part. Old ordinances against the adulteration of wine, in Brussels, by vitriol, quicksilver, and *lapis calaminaris*,—and in France, by lead and litharge, —may still be read as curiosities, but they have no present application.

A German Monk, named Martin Bayr, is damned to everlasting fame, as the first who adulterated wines within the territory of the Kaiser. Pickheimer, the friend of Albert Durer, is particularly inveterate against Bayr and his followers in evil. The indignation of the lover of pure wine is carried to an incredible extent. He narrates, in a rapt fury, the consequences of drinking injurious wines; beginning with an assurance, that adulterated wine keeps the married childless, and adding, by a sort of bathos, that it causes certain inward pains, "than which none can be more excruciating." He mentions many ingredients employed, and adverts to some, "the names of which I should be ashamed to mention;" and then he calls for vengeance on the offenders, both in this world and the next. "You hang the counterfeiters of the public coin," says he; "do not these miscreants, whose misdeeds have caused indignant Nature to check the growth of our grapes, deserve something worse? Cast their accursed beverage, I say, into the sewers, and themselves into the flames: and so may Martin and his disciples perish in this world, and inherit everlasting damnation in the next!"

Adulteration, however, still went on, until the penalty of death, and confiscation of property, was levelled against the employment of sulphur and bismuth,—used by the most noble wine-makers to sweeten their spoiled and sour commodity. Offenders, however, again grew bold. The tribunals treated them leniently. First, fines were levied; then came confiscation of property, imprisonment, and hard labour; next, banishment: and none of these meeting the evil, the Judges at length cut off the head of an incorrigible criminal, Ehrni of Erlingen; and, for a while, terrified the whole brotherhood of wine-spoilers into a temporary observance of honesty.

The next struggle which occurred in Germany, was between those who applied tests to detect the presence of metals, and those who invented processes to defy them. It was a scientific struggle between two species of assassins,—those who swiftly killed by brewing poisonous wine, and the physicians who racked their brains to invent detective tests, and save their patients for a slower process of extinction. This was very rudely said by rude people, who looked upon themselves as the victims sought for by the two contending parties,—the distillers on one side, and the doctors on the other.

The use of milk by the Greeks was, probably, not for adulterating, but for refining, their wines. Isinglass is at present generally employed for the last-mentioned purpose.

As it is the tendency of the world to improve, so the not inconsiderable world of adulterators in England has profited, like philosophers, by the discoveries of those who have preceded them. A mixture of strong port, rectified spirit, Cognac brandy, and rough cider, can be concocted into what is called "fine old crusted port." It costs the maker about sixteen shillings a gallon, and is sold retail at five shillings a bottle. Sloe-juice is another ingredient, and poisonous tinctures give it a seductive hue. Powder of catechu does for it what hair-powder does for the individual,—gives a crust of antiquity to secure for it the veneration of the ignorant. A decoction of Brazil wood, and a little alum, will impart to the corks the requisite air of corresponding age; and these the credulous gaze at and believe.

"Madeira, neat as imported," is the definition of a beverage cleverly manufactured much nearer Fenchurch-street than Funchal. Home-made Madeira is a compound of bad port, Vidonia, that African nastiness called "Cape," sugar-candy, and bitter almonds; and the Vidonia, which is an ingredient in itself, often adulterated with cider and rum; and a little carbonate of soda, "to contumace the appetite's acidities." The lowest and cruellest insult to human tastes and stomachs is, perhaps, the adulteration of Cape. It is bad enough in itself; but Cape, with something worse in it, is only fit for the thirsty hounds of Pluto. Gooseberry, passed off as Champagne, is an impostor, and even with strawberries in it, to give it an aristocratic pinkness, it is still a deception; but, compared with Cape, even in its best condition, gooseberry *may* be imbibed without very much disgust.

A *fracas* between the waiters and their employers at the last Lord-Mayor's dinner, betrayed another pleasant process regarding wine. The attendants in question declared that, after many hours' toil, they had not had a glass even out of a *dovered* bottle. They were as much surprised when the Magistrate asked the meaning of "*dovering*," as the sailor was, when he stood before a Lord High Chancellor ignorant of the signification of "'baft the binnacle." A complaisant Ganymede enlightened the darkened mind of the metropolitan Cadi: "*Dovering*," said he, "is the collecting of three-quarter emptied decanters from the dinner-table, and re-decantering the same, serving it up as freshly uncorked." Dover has the bad reputation of being the locality where this process was first invented.

One of the most ingenious—perhaps we should say, one of the

most scientific—tricks that we have heard of, in connexion with wine-doctoring, proves that the modern chymical brewers of superior beverages, which seem what they are not, are vastly superior to the mere experimentalists of former days. In the royal cellars of Carlton House, there was enshrined, if we may so speak, a small quantity of wine which, like the gems worn by the Irish lady, was both "rich and rare." It was only produced by George IV. when he had around him his most select and wittiest friends. The precious deposit gradually diminished; year by year, as in the case of the famous shagreen skin of the French novelist Balzac, it grew less, until, at last, a couple of dozen bottles only were left, gleaming at the bottom of their bins like gems in a mine, and full of liquid promise to those who needed the especial comfort which it was their duty to impart. These, however, were left so long unasked for, that the gentlemen of the King's suite who had the control of the grape department, deemed them forgotten, and at their own mirthful table drank them all but two, with infinite delight to themselves, and to the better health of their master. They soon found, however, that there was garlic in the flowers," as the Turkish proverb has it; and their embarrassment was not small, when the King, giving his orders for a choice dinner on a certain night, intimated his desire that a good supply of his favourite wine should grace the board. In Courts, "to hear is to obey;" and the officials who had drunk the wine, at once resorted to an eminent firm, well-skilled to give advice in such delicate wine-cases. The physician asked but for a sample bottle, and to be told the exact hour at which the favourite draught would be asked for. This was complied with, and in due time a proper amount of the counterfeit wine was forwarded to Carlton House, and there broached and drunk with such encomiums, that the officers who were in the secret had some difficulty in maintaining an official gravity of countenance. The brewer of the new wine was certainly a first-rate artist; and if he ever achieved knighthood and a coat-of-arms, I would give him a "Bruin" for his crest, and, "The drink! the drink! dear

Hamlet!" for his device. This anecdote, I may farther notice, has often been told, and nearly as often been discredited; but I am assured by an officer of the household, who speaks "*avec connaissance de fait*," that it is substantially true.

One of the merits of the wine above mentioned consisted in its great age. There has, indeed, always been a sort of mania for wine that bears the load of years. But this rage is pronounced by Cyrus Redding to be one of the most ridiculous errors of modern epicurism. The "bee's wing," the "thick crust on the bottle," the "loss of strength," and so on,—all these are declared by the best judges to be nothing more than forbidding manifestations of decomposition, and the disappearance of the very best qualities of the wine. Many years ago, I made a "note" on this subject, but am now unable to recollect from what work, nor can I say whether the following remarks on the qualities of wine were made by the author of an original work, or by a reviewer commenting thereon. Such as they are, however, they are not without value.

"The age of maturity," says the writer, "for exportation from Oporto, is said to be the second year after the vintage; probably sometimes not quite so long. Our wine-merchants keep it in wood from two to six years longer, according to its original strength, &c. Surely this must be long enough to do all that can be done by keeping it. What crude wine it must be to require even this time to ameliorate it! the necessity for which must arise either from some error in the original manufacture, or a false taste, which does not relish it till time has changed its original characteristics.

"Port, like all other wines, ripens in a shorter, or longer, time, according to its lightness, or its strength, the quality of the grapes, according to the fermentation they have undergone, and the portion of brandy that has been added to it. Also one cellar will forward wine much sooner than another. Sound good port is generally in perfection when it has been from three to five years in the wood, and from one to three in bottle.

"Ordinary port is a very uncleansed fretful wine; and we have been assured by wine-merchants of good taste, accurate observation, and extensive experience, that the *best* port is rather impoverished than improved by being kept in bottle longer than two years; that is, supposing it to have been previously from two to four years in the cask in this country; observing that all that the outrageous advocates for *vin passé* really know about it is that sherry is *yellow*, and port is *black ;* and that if they drink (more than) enough of either of them, according to the colours, it will make them drunk.

"White wines, especially sherry and Madeira, being more perfectly fermented and thoroughly fined before they are bottled, if kept in a cellar of uniform temperature, are not so rapidly deteriorated by age.

"The temperature of a good cellar is nearly the same throughout the year. Double doors help to preserve this. It must be dry, and be kept as clean as possible.

"The art of preserving wines is to prevent them from fretting, which is done by keeping them in the same degree of heat and careful working, in a cellar where they will not be agitated by the motion of carriages passing. If persons wish to preserve the fine flavour of their wines, they ought on no account to permit any bacon, cheese, onions, potatoes, or cider, in the wine-cellars; for if there be any disagreeable stench in the cellar, the wine will indubitably imbibe it; consequently, instead of being fragrant, and charming to the nose and palate, it will be extremely disagreeable.

"It must be well-known that almost all our home-made wines, for public sale, are made, and suffered to cool, in leaden vats. Nothing can be more injurious or detrimental to health. Every chymist is aware that any vegetable acid that comes in contact with lead, and is suffered to remain only a few hours, produces what we call 'sugar of lead,'—a most deadly poison. How many there are that complain that cider will not agree with them! and several who cannot take even a wine-glass full without vomiting almost immediately. They know not the reason; and thus many are prevented from taking a most delightful beverage in warm weather; while others are labouring under its baneful influence. Often do we see servants run for vinegar in a pewter or publican's pot; and the answer we receive when correcting them for the same is,—they have often done the same without any serious consequence. May be so; but if vinegar, or any other vegetable acid, as before said, be suffered to remain in such vessels only a short time, the health and constitution must suffer from the acid so taken; and we will venture to say that almost all paralytic affections are caused by persons, predisposed to such attacks, drinking water impregnated with lead. For if there be any carbonic acid in the water, which there most assuredly is in every kind, a carbonate is thus formed, just as injurious as the acetate (sugar of lead); and where shall we find a cistern in London that is not made of this pernicious, yet highly useful, material?"

The consideration of these subjects, when drinking home-made wines, (if, indeed, there *be* people bold enough to venture on such an experiment,) or the other beverages mentioned above, might serve the purpose of the custom observed among the ancient Egyptians. It was one less barbarous than singular. A skeleton of beautiful workmanship, in ivory, and enclosed in a small coffin, was carried round at a feast, by a slave, who, holding it up to each guest, remarked, "After death you will resemble this figure; drink, then, and be happy!" It must have encouraged the mirth "consumedly." But there was a grave wisdom in the custom, notwithstanding.

IMPERIAL DRINKERS AND INCIDENTS IN GERMANY.

The stories of the gigantic drinkers of antiquity are startling; but I think they may be accounted for. Natural philosophers inform us, that objects seen through a mist are magnified to the senses; and so it is with the feats which we are asked to contemplate through the mist of ages: they are probably not so astounding as they appear. One may say of each story, so venerable and enlarged by age, as the good Dominican did to the congregation whom he had affected to tears by the warmth of one of his legendary sermons. "Do not cry so, my brethren," said the Preacher; "for, after all, perhaps it's not true."

It must be allowed, however, that the stories of wine-bibbers of later times than those when the son of Aristides gained his living by singing ballads in the streets of Athens, or the heir of Cicero drank draughts longer than his sire's orations, lack nothing whatever of the marvellous. And this reminds me of an incident, *quod alibi narravi*, and which I will narrate here, by way of illustration of this portion of my subject.

AN INCIDENT OF TRAVEL.

It is now some twelve years ago that I was, in company with two Norwegians, in Prague, loitering beneath the tower of that sacred edifice dedicated to the fearful dancer, St. Vitus. The tower was the same which the drunken Emperor Wenceslaus had caused to be shortened, by some thirty or forty feet, because he took it into his head that it would one day fall, and crush him as he lay on his uneasy couch in the Hradschin. I remarked to my companions, that the empire, in its palmy days, had often been wellnigh lost through the mad caprices of tippling Kaisers.

"There was not a Kaiser of them all," said Löwenskiold, "who permanently injured either himself or his country by his devotion to drinking."

"What!" said I; "not even Maximilian?"

"Not even Maximilian," remarked Knudtzen. "The people, indeed, were occasionally a trifle startled at seeing their ruler proceed, either to the camp or council, with as much white wine in him as might serve the universe for sauces. They slightly objected on hearing that he walked rosy and reeling to confession; and they were not edified at understanding that his private Almoner stirred up his punch with a silver crucifix. They even remonstrated with Maximilian when he had been once within an ace of destroying Ulm in a drunken frolic. And what was his reply? He kept the deputation of remonstrants the whole night in his palace, and invited the citizens to assemble, at day-break, on whatever spots commanded a view of the towers of the cathedral. The Emperor and the Committee of Moderates finished two hundred and ten bottles of Rhine wine while they waited for sunrise. This, among a temperate party of one score and one, was a tolerable allowance for each individual. At dawn, all Ulm was up, and every eye directed to the cathedral. The towers had scarcely flung back the first rays from heaven, when a joyous procession issued from the imperial residence. The whole party, the Emperor excepted, were as drunk as Æschylus. With difficulty did they follow their Lord, who, at the very top of his speed, and carrying a heavy waggon-wheel on his shoulder, ran to the cathedral, ascended the stairs leading to the summit of one of the towers and appeared on the rampart, before his straggling followers had reached the low-arched door beneath. With a light bound, he sprang on one of the highest parts of the castellated portion, where there was scarcely footing for him. In that position, however, he poised the wheel aloft with his right hand, let it gently descend on to the foot which he extended above the heads of the multitude, and, holding it there for a moment or two, ended by hurling it into the air, and catching it again, ere it fell on the astounded and admiring crowd below.

"'There, you calves!' cried the Emperor, as he gazed tranquilly down on the sea of heads below; 'do you dare complain that Niedersteiner touches your master's nerves?'

"'Never again!' exclaimed the delighted mass. 'What can we do to testify our affection for Your Majesty?'

"'Toss those gentlemen into a tub of Selzer-water,' said Maximilian, 'and send me half-a-dozen of Hochheimer, and half-a-dozen blood-puddings, for breakfast.'"

I could *almost* believe this tradition; for I had seen a nearly similar feat once performed by a woman on a projecting mass of rock in the Ahr Thal. The rock is, doubtless, well known to all who have ascended that lovely Rhine-valley, at eve, to eat *Forellen*, and drink Wallportzheimer. They who do so, generally return the next morning with an inclination for nothing but the cooling mineral waters to be had at Hippingen.

"Besides," said Knudtzen, "*à-propos* to cathedrals, sober principles have done them more injury than jolly Emperors. Do you forget that Caroline Bonaparte razed a cathedral in Italy to the ground?"

"I remember hearing of the deed as connected with a church," said I; "but I have forgotten the reason alleged for it."

"It was a very sufficient reason for a Bonaparte. Her Highness lived next door to the church; and she had it destroyed, because the noise of the organ kept her awake, and the smell of the incense made her head ache."

"Royal minds," I remarked, "cannot condescend to the weaknesses of common people. According to our 'Philosophical Transactions,' the pigeons at Pisa were as destructive as Caroline Bonaparte. Pigeons, for many ages, built under the roof of the great church there. Their dung spontaneously took fire at last; and the church was consumed. But to return to the old, defunct King of Saxony. He was afflicted with a super-delicate attack of virtue; and, during the prevalence of the disorder, he issued a decree for the expulsion, from his picture-gallery, of all those master-pieces, the merit of which lay in the glory of their flesh-colouring. He had grown as modest as the Monk who declared that he had never seen any portion of his body save his face and hands. He is worthy of going down to posterity arm in arm with that old Polish King, who was a cleaner, but not a less delicate, man than the Monk, and who boasted to his Confessor that his purity of mind was so excessive, that he had never touched his own skin with an ungloved hand. In short, the old King of Saxony admirably illustrated the saying of Dean Swift, that 'a nice man was a man of nasty ideas.' He had not been a sparer of the wine-flask. Indeed, he had rather sinned that way; and, in expiation thereof, he undertook to perform a pilgrimage to the Holy Sepulchre on foot. A fever of expectation shook Dresden, all the China in it, and the whole line of road, at the idea of again beholding a Christian King turning to the neglected shrine. The expectation was not altogether fulfilled; but the Monarch, nevertheless, performed the pilgrimage."

"We never heard of it," exclaimed the travellers, looking at each other with some manifestation of surprise.

"That is to say," I resumed, "that his Majesty performed it after a fashion. He inquired the distance from his own country-house at Pilnitz, to the Armenian Convent at the Holy City; and, in spite of his education, he was nothing less than astonished, to find that it was something more serious than a promenade to Töplitz. I do not know if he had a vision of boiling his peas, as an English pilgrim did, of whom I could tell you something; but he certainly experienced some unpleasant sensations at the idea that, the way being so long, he might chance to find himself without peas to boil. He wept at the reflection that he might not only be a devout, but a hungry, King, while one half of Dresden were solacing their appetites on the terrace of Bruhl, and the other, at the Baths of Link, or at the Bastei. He thought of the dangers; but he *would* be devout. The attendant pains were great; but the resulting pleasures were not to be denied. In short, he would *not* go to Jerusalem; but he *would* perform the pilgrimage. Accordingly, the exact distance having been ascertained, he started from his room, and walked the entire number of leagues by pacing up and down a long gallery, deducting from the distance the amount of water passage, which was but fair. If admiration had been great at the commencement, surprising fun was excited during the performance. Every evening the citizens of Dresden knew how far their religious Ruler had proceeded on his way, or how far he would have proceeded, if he had but set out. *Now*, he was breakfasting, in imagination at Breslau; sleeping (in fancy) at Olmutz; and passing, by a pleasant fiction, through Buda. During two days that his Majesty suffered from a real bilious attack, the result, perhaps, of a Barmecidal repast at Essek on the Drave, the King rested at Belgrade, while confined to his bed in Dresden. But his zeal soon reinvigorated his liver; and, as he glided to and fro by his palace windows, the mystified multitude below learned that the Monarch was lodging in the house of the Saxon Legation at Istamboul. The pilgrim-traveller suffered a little from the heat (of the room) as he descended from the western coast of Asia Minor; but the inconveniencies of the route were things beneath the thoughts of him who—whether at Bursa, Smyrna, or any other locality on his way—could ring his bell in the Desert, and order Champagne out of his own cellar. The King was puzzled one mid-day, (he had by calculation just reached Beyrout,) his progress being checked by the unexpected arrival of a portion of the imperial family from Vienna. Visitors of such condition must be attended to; nevertheless, his pilgrimage must be continued; and he, like the clever and facetious palmer that he was, did both. He attended his guests with much politeness, during their stay of two days; and he put down the time thus spent, as consumed in a sea voyage from Beyrout to Acre. The moment they left, the royal pilgrim went ashore again, and happily accomplished the remaining distance to Jerusalem, through Nassara and Nablous, without any other hindrance or obstruction than his going one night to see a French *vaudeville*, while supposed to be enjoying his well-earned repose at Rama or Muddin. And thus was accomplished that royal pilgrimage that was never performed. The King reached Jerusalem without going there; and the people saw *him* return who had never departed."

"Well," said Harold Knudtzen, "the Kings of Saxony are no longer such simpletons. The present Monarch loves, indeed, good wine, 'craftily qualified;' but he also, like Uzziah, King of Judah, loves husbandry. Josephine herself had not half so frantic a passion for flowers as he; and not for flowers alone in their beauty,— not for botany, either, merely for amusement's sake, but for phytology and pharmacy, as connected with it."

"He lisped Linnæus," said Löwenskiold, "before he could speak plainly."

"And by reputation, he knew Tournefort better than he did Knecht Rupert," added Harold.

"He himself told us, when we met him in Dalmatia," continued the latter, "that he could spell *Dodecandria* and *Trigynia* before he could read Grimm's Story Book; and that he knew the meanings of *monopetalous* and *campaniform* before he was acquainted with the languages from which the terms were derived. I never saw a man so eager in pursuit of *apetalous amentaceous* flowers; and as for *carryophylous*"——

"Leave off your abominable phrases!" said I, "and begin by telling me how you two very modest fellows introduced yourselves to the acquaintance of the Sovereign of Saxony."

"The introduction was effected through a very light-hearted and intelligent fellow-botanizer, whom we met on our way from Zara up to the mountains. We had all three lost our way while endeavoring to find an *infundibuliform*"——

"Nay," interrupted I, "I care not what you found, if you choose to tell it in pentameters."

"Well," resumed Knudtzen, "we were in a wild part of the country,—weary, hungry, cold, and in the dark. Wanderers could not be in a worse plight. We were as *flûté* as Junc's columns, near the church of St. Helia; and the skeleton doing duty there for that of St. Simeon of Judæa, the pride and palladium of the people of Zara, looked in far better condition, and in, especially, better raiment, than could be boasted of by us humble pedestrians. We had walked many leagues, when we reached a sorry inn kept by a Gipsy, where we hoped to find rest and refreshment, but were permitted to enjoy neither. Our swarthy host stood in his door-way, like Horatius Cocles at the head of the bridge. Beds he did not even profess to find for travellers. He had not slept for years, and was none the worse, he said, for the privation. Leopold asked for wine.

" 'We have three sorts of wine,' said the Gipsy, 'which travellers like yourselves once tasted and paid for. I have the very wines which the seven Schwaben asked for in the Goldenes Kreutz at Ueberlingen.'

" 'What! old Sauerampfer?' cried Löwenskiold.

" 'The same,' said our singular host. 'It is not quite so sour as vinegar, but it will pierce the marrow of your bones like a sword; and it will so twist your mouth, that you shall never get it straight again.'

" 'We will try something better than this acid water,' said I: 'we will'——

" 'Try the Dreimännerswein? I am sorry there are only women in the house!'

" 'What, in the name of all your saints in Zara, have your women to do with the refreshment we need?'

" 'Do! nothing in the world! that is precisely it! You will want three men each of you. For Dreimännerswein is three times as rough and ten times as sour as vinegar; and he who drinks it must be held fast by two men, while a third pours the liquid down his throat!'

" 'And what of the third of these Olympic beverages?' said I.

" 'It is called *Rachenputzer*, and has peculiar qualities too. He who lies down to sleep with a flask of it in his body, must be aroused every half-hour, and turned over. Otherwise a pint of Rachenputzer would eat a hole right through his side!'

"The Gipsy laughed aloud as he uttered these words. We

ourselves laughed in despite of our vexation; and, somewhat startlingly, a fourth voice took up the cachinnatory affection, and laughed even louder than the original three. As the new-comer stood in the light of the door-way, the landlord touched his cap, withdrew hastily into the passage, and slammed the door in our faces, leaving us in Cimmerian darkness, summer trousers, and a drizzling rain. The matter was no longer risible, and we were beginning to be seriously annoyed, when the mysterious stranger, whom we could but indistinctly see, invited us to accompany him we knew not whither, and hospitably to partake of we knew not what. We accepted the invitation most gratefully; and after a full half-hour's walk, we found ourselves on the skirt of a wood. In less than half that time, we subsequently reached a neat little house within the wood itself; and I do not think ten minutes had elapsed, ere we had made such toilette as travellers may, and, with some doubt as to the reality of the circumstance, detected ourselves in the act of eating vermicelli soup, and wondering how it had reached us.

"Before our repast was entirely dispatched, our host, in whom we saw a young, well-made, and exceedingly amiable personage, informed us that he was on a botanizing expedition for the benefit of an establishment in Northern Germany; that he had been two months settled in the house in which we then were, and that he had already given temporary shelter to three plant explorers, who had resorted, in their need, to the house of Djewitzki, the Gipsy, and who had found to their sorrow, that it had nothing of the quality of an inn about it, except the sign.

"We talked of flowers that night," continued Knudtzen, "as though they were the foremost as well as the fairest things in all the world. But we were sciolists in the science, and, contrasted with us, our host was a sage. He knew that agrimony was under Jupiter, and angelica under the Sun in Leo; that milfoil was under the influence of Venus, and that garden basil was a herb of Mars. If every new idea be worth the knowing, why, we gained knowledge by the information, that all the dodders are under

Saturn. We heard, for the first time, the virtues of the plant enchusa."

"But," interrupted Löwenskiold, "we were enabled to remind our host of what Dioscorides says about it,—that if any who have newly eaten of it do spit in the mouth of a serpent, the reptile instantly dies."

"True," said Knudtzen, "we have not been at Upsal for nothing."

"We may all aid each other by turns," I remarked to my two friends, as we arrived, after descending from the cathedral, on the old bridge over the Moldau. A large herd of cattle was crossing it at the time; and some of the foremost black oxen of this herd had bunches of *amara dulcis* (or "woody nightshade") hung round their necks; a common custom in Germany, as I told the young travellers, and employed as a remedy against dizziness in the head.

"Of the owner or the ox?" said Harold, with a laugh.

"Of him who wears it," I rejoined, "But I want to see the entry of your King of Saxony," I continued, "and not to listen to the description, uses, and property of herbs, plants, and flowers; maiden-hair, moon-wort, and *ornithogalum spicatum*."

"So much the worse!" answered Knudtzen, "or Leopold and I had told you what we learned from our entertainer of celandine; and what he told us, from Pliny, of the anemone: how he recommended us, should we ever visit Naples, never to retire to rest without strewing about our bed-chamber some chopped leaves of arse-smart, a herb most murderous to the numerous light troops cantoned in Neapolitan sleeping-rooms; how balm was good for the bite of scorpions; how Pliny recommends end-weed for the quinsy;—and a thousand other matters touching leaves, herbs, trees, flowers, roots, and barks. But I *will* tell you that our Amphitryon was light as well as learned, and loved fun as he did flowers. He would discourse upon *ballets* as well as battles; knew all about logarithms and the new opera; told anecdotes; remembered sermons; and, finally, lighted us to bed, with a Latin quotation, and a brass candlestick. By daybreak we were all out in the vicinity of the house, looking for rare plants, with as much avidity as though they equalled diamonds in value. We returned together to a breakfast exactly adapted to our tastes and capacities; after which, our knapsacks were once more on our shoulders, and, having made due acknowledgment for the hospitality received, we begged to be permitted to know the name of our entertainer.

"'You might call me,' said he, 'the Dalmatian botanist, if I particularly cared about maintaining my *incognito*. But I hope we shall meet again; and, if you ever visit Dresden, come to me, and you shall have better fare than I have been able to afford you here. Ask for the King of Saxony,' he added, observing our inquiring looks; 'and in the mean time write your names on these tablets, and you shall find that in Dresden I have not forgotten the night in Dalmatia.'"

"And did you and the good Frederick Augustus ever meet again?"

"Twice," said Harold. "We saw one another for a moment, a month afterwards, in Zara. He was accompanying the Emperor of Austria, followed by a brilliant staff, to a review, and he gave us a smile of recognition as he passed."

"The second time we met him," added Leopold, "was in the gardens of the Nymphenburg, near Munich. He was alone amusing himself with feeding the beavers. We spent a very agreeable hour with him in exploring that pleasant retreat of the Kings of Bavaria; and, on parting, he repeated his wish that we might meet again in Dresden,—a circumstance not very unlikely, as we are now on our way to the Sächsische Schweitz."

A FEW ODD GLASSES OF WINE.

The anc'ent people who loved the juice of the grape, kept in grateful remembrance the names of the first planters of vines. Bacchus came from India, through Egypt, into Europe; and he and his joyous company made vineyards bloom amid many a desert. But the introduction of the vine was not opposed. The Chinese accepted gratefully the rosy gift from Œnopia; and the branch was hailed on its passage through Greece, Sicily, and Italy. But in Greece the vines were destroyed wherever the order of Lycurgus had force; and it was in Athens that, under King Cranaus, men first diluted the potent draught with water. The gods visited Greece with an inundation in consequence; but the Sicilians, nothing daunted, adopted the temperance that was not sanctioned in Olympus. Domitian did for the vines carried into Gaul, from Tuscany, what Lycurgus did for those of Lacedæmonia; but Probus restored them to the thirsty Gauls. Numa had taught his people to train the vine which Janus had given them; and, by placing the statue of Minerva by the side of that of Bacchus, he taught them a lesson which Domitian could not comprehend. *He did not know how to be merry and wise.*

It was long before the Egyptians acknowledged, by grateful use, the excellence of the vine. The Scythians, some of the Persians, and the Cappadocians would not drink the delusive draught upon any account; but then these were barbarians. The Cappadocians especially not only refused wine, but liberty. When the latter was offered them by the Romans, the reply of the water-drinkers was, "that they would neither accept liberty nor tolerate it!" It is to be remarked, however, that all these people tardily attained to a better taste, like the great Hippocrates himself, who, after touching on the advisability of mixing wine with water, finally decides, like the enthusiastic Athenians, that it is much better to take the beverage neat. He thinks that, when grief is at the heart, pure wine is a specific; and no doubt Ariadne thought so too, or she would not have turned to Bacchus after Theseus had abandoned her to a short-lived inconsolability. Rome long honoured Bacchus even as Ariadne did; and he who stole a bunch of grapes from a vineyard incurred the penalty of death. Italy was, indeed, proud of her vines and their produce. Of the two hundred varieties of wine then known in the world, only fourscore were declared to be "excellent;" and of these fourscore, nearly thirty were said to be natives of Italy. The Chian wines, however, maintained for ages a marked pre-eminence. It was a vase filled with wine of Chios that the poet Ion gave to every Athenian who was present at the representation of a tragedy, for which the poet was publicly crowned. "*Pauper es, ut solent poetæ*," was therefore, evidently, a line that could not be universally applied to the poets of Greece.

They loved old wine, too, did those old people. Wine, as old as the years to which ravens are reported to attain,—a century, or even two,—was served up at Rome. It was in consistency something like the clotted cream of Devonshire. But there was wine of a more solid consistency than this. I have elsewhere spoken of wine chopped in pieces by an axe, before it could be used. This was because of an accident which had happened to the wine; but the Romans had various preparations which were served up in lumps; and we hear of wines being kept in the chimney like modern bacon, and presented to the guests "as hard as salt." The ancients are also reported to have been able to change red wine into white, by means of white of egg and bean-flour, shaken together with the red wine in a flagon. It would require much shaking before a degenerate modern could effect the mutation in question. But if Cato could imitate the best Chian by means of his own gooseberries, the other feat may hardly be disputed. It is certain that the ancients could boldly swallow some questionable mixtures. Thus they drank their wine with sea-water, in order to stimulate and whip up energies exhausted by being overdriven the night before. Myrtle wine, on the other hand, was copiously drunk at dawn by those who could not sleep, but who could afford to remain in bed, and try to court Nature's soft nurse.

There were Roman ladies who were not born before nerves were in fashion. These had their especial drinks, sovereign in their effects, to calm a nervous system too sorely excited. The most efficacious of these was the "*Adynamon*," or "powerless wine;" that is, powerless to intoxicate, but excellent as an invigorator. It consisted simply of a mixture of water and white-wort; and when Julia or Lalage had tremblingly sipped thereof, her nerves were so braced, that she could stand by and look on while Geta was flogged for an hour.

On the point of secret drinking, the early Romans were quite as particular and more merciless regarding their wives. When Micennius detected his wife in the act of "sucking the monkey," that is, feloniously imbibing his wine through a straw at the bung-hole, he then and there slew her. Complaint was made by her friends to Romulus; but that chief and sole magistrate confined himself to the remark, that she had been justly served. The wine-casks at home were for years afterwards accounted sacred by the wives in the absence of their lords. It would appear, too, by this incident, that wine was commonly produced long before Numa introduced the improvement of training the vine. There *were* ladies who were rendered more cautious, but not less bold, by the judgment pronounced by Romulus. We hear of one caught in the fact by some members of her own family, who were so disgusted with her immorality, that to preserve the respectability of their house, they starved her to death. As years wore on, Judges grew more good-natured, and only deprived tippling married women of all right in their marriage portions. The Empire could hardly have been inaugurated, before thirsty ladies adopted a custom that had been denied them under the Commonwealth. Livia, the consort of Augustus, was eighty-two when she died; and it was her boast that wine alone had made her an octogenarian. What wine she drank is not stated. She may have had a head that could bear old Falernian undiluted; but that was not the case with many of her sex. The Roman ladies' wine was, generally speaking, little more than a sweet *tisane*, distilled from asparagus or marjoram; from parsley, mint, rue, wild thyme, or pennyroyal. These were sipped at breakfast-time; and the hour and the ingredient would seem rather to point to Æsculapius than to Bacchus. They were, in fact, medicinal drinks. The strong wines were drunk at other hours, and these more innocent draughts were swallowed in the morning, with reflections as bitter as the beverage. Wormwood wine, too, was a favourite morning stimulant with intoxication; and it cannot be denied, that if modern guests were condemned to a "pint of salt water" with their wine, the hilarity after dinner would not be of a very joyous aspect. Some of the "sea-wines" of the Greeks, however, owed their name and reputation chiefly to being immersed, in casks, in the ocean. Our Madeira may thus be called a "sea-wine," when it has been to the East Indies and back for the benefit of its health.

"Chambertin" was the favourite wine of Napoleon. The "*vinum dulce*" obtained after drying the grapes in the sun, during three days, and crushing them beneath the feet, in the hottest hours of the fourth day, was the drink for which Commodus had a predilection. It was after draughts of this beverage that he used to fight in the Circus as the "Roman Hercules," as proud of his performance as Mr. Ducrow, when he used to ride round it in the same character. Commodus, too, like the great equestrian, was an artist in his way; but he ruined the managers by the exorbitant salaries which he wrung from them, whenever he condescended to appear in the arena!

For the games of the Circus, and for bread after the sport was over, the Romans have been reproachfully pointed at as alone caring. Considering the plight into which they had been plunged by their Rulers and Priests, they seem to me to have been wise in their sentiment. One circumstance is clear,—that they might dip their pennyworth of bread into a deep cup of "sack" at the same price. Wine cost but sixpence a gallon,—a sufficient quantity for half-a-dozen gentlemen just returned from the Circus; or for half-a-dozen ladies, who had learned to break through the total-abstinence principle of the women of the Republic. There was much wine to be had for a trifling outlay of money. In Greece, it was cheaper still. In Athens, wine was dear at fourpence per gallon; and ordinarily, Davus, out on a holiday, might get drunk upon four quarts of it, at a halfpenny per quart; but Chremes would nearly flay him alive, if he caught him before he was sober.

I may add, that this was the price of wine, that is, of French wine, in England, under John. A tun of Rochelle wine cost twenty shillings, and it was retailed at fourpence per gallon. But taking the value of money into consideration, this was rather a high price.

When Probus restored the vine to the Gauls, he sent cuttings of the precious plant into Britain; and many localities in the south part of the island produced a very respectable beverage, of which the parent stock had no reason to be ashamed. "As sure as God is in Gloucestershire!" was a common phrase when that picturesque county was covered with monasteries; and many of the monastic gardens were famous for their grapes and the liquor distilled from them. The little village of Durweston, near Blandford, in Dorsetshire, was once as remarkable for its peculiar grape and its product, as that restricted Rhenish locality, whose grapes produce the Lieb Frauenmilch. Of the respective merits of the English grapes, I will say nothing. The merits of French wines have, however, occupied the attention of rival medical colleges, whose professors have shed much ink, and cracked whole legions of bottles, in order to discuss, rather than settle, the divers deserts of Burgundy and Champagne. The question is yet an undecided one, as is also that respecting the devotion of the Gauls to the grapes. Arnaud de Villeneuve praises the mediæval people of France, who intoxicated themselves monthly upon hygienic principles. While other writers assert, that "in the middle ages, and in the sixteenth century, intoxication was severely punished in France." I am the more inclined to believe in the latter assertion, as the laws against drinking and drinkers, from Charlemagne to Francis I., have often been cited; and they are marked by a severity—which Rabelais did not care for, a button!

Our own wine-trade with France began after the Norman Conquest, and was very considerable when our English Kings were proprietors of the French wine districts. About the middle of the sixteenth century, the *maximum* price of wine was fixed twelve-pence per gallon; but at this time no one was allowed to have in his house a measure that would contain above ten gallons, unless, indeed, he were of noble birth, or could expend a hundred marks annually.

Of all French wines, that of Burgundy is the most difficult of carriage. Some Burgundies cannot bear it at all; others are transported in bottles covered with a cottony paper, or bedded in salt. Pure Burgundy exhilarates without intoxicating; and there is not a liver complaint in a hogshead of it. It is the alcoholic wines that massacre the *jecur*.

The Burgundy vineyards were originally in connexion with the Burgundian monasteries, and there were no better *vignerons* than the monks. The modern quality of the wine is inferior to its ancient reputation, simply because modern proprietors are not artistical monks, but mere money-makers. Napoleon adhered to the wine as long as he could; but at St. Helena he took to Bordeaux,—Chambertin would have lost its best qualities in the voyage thither.

The Emperor was, perhaps, the best judge of his favourite Chambertin that France ever could boast of, except, probably, in the case of the good Lindsay, of Balcarras, Bishop of Kildare. This Prelate long resided at Tours, and was an excellent connoisseur in wine, though he modestly used to say, "*If* I know any thing, it is the management of turnip crops and mangel-wurzel." It is no disparagement of the episcopal bench to say, that many of its members could not justifiably make a similar boast. Lord

Brougham, I believe, used to say, that "if *he* knew any thing, it was, that claret should always be drunk after game." There is an imperial authority in favour of Champagne. When the Emperor Wenceslaus visited France in the fourteenth century, to negociate with Charles VI., it was impossible ever to get him sober to a conference. "It was no matter," he said; "they might decide as they liked, and he would drink as *he* liked; and thus both parties would be on an equality." There is something curious in the caprices of Champagne; particularly of the *vin mousseux*, or effervescing wine. In the same cellar, the same wine, all similarly placed, will *mousser* in some bottles, and not in others. It will even, poured from the same bottle, *mousser* in some glasses into which it is poured, while in others it will fall as heavily placid as oil. In warm weather, however, a great Champagne cellar is a very lively place; so lively, that it is unsafe to walk through the serried hosts of bottles, without a wire mask over the face.

There are one or two sorts of French wine which are considered to be improved by letting a small portion of the stalk be trodden in with the grape. But, probably, in the selection of the grape, there is no where such care taken, as in the matter of imperial Tokay. The grapes are selected with the greatest care; sometimes a second selection is made from the first selected lot. No grape is chosen that it is not perfectly sound. The resulting wine is of a highly delicious flavour; but I need not add, that the general public know but very little about it. To them is vouchsafed the brewage from the damaged grape, or the distillation of the refuse of the first grape. The product is an acid one, resembling moderately good Rhine wine; but it is *not* Tokay.

"Old Wortley Montague" was a great drinker of Tokay. He lived to the patriarchal age of eighty-three. Gray, writing of him, says, that it was not mere avarice, and its companion, abstinence, that kept him alive so long. He imported his own wine from Hungary, in greater quantity than he could use, and he sold the overplus,—drinking himself a half-pint every day,—for any price he chose to set upon it. It was a fashionable wine with the drinkers of the last century. Walpole records its being offered at a supper given by Miss Chudleigh to the Duke of Kingston, her then "protector." "At supper she offered him Tokay, and told him she believed he would find it good." The entertainment was splendid, and untidy. "The supper was in two rooms, and very fine; and on all the sideboards, and *even on the chairs*, were pyramids and troughs of strawberries and cherries; you would have thought she was kept by Vertumnus!"

Our ancient acquaintance, "mustard," was originally raised to the character of "wine," in common with some other of the seeds used at ancient tables. Our warm friend mustard was the *mustum ardens*, or "hot wine." It was held as good for persons of bilious temperament, and as being more beneficial in summer than in winter. Coriander was used in the same season. It was mixed with vinegar, and poured over meat to preserve its freshness. There are some men who faint at the smell of linseed. A bread made therefrom was once, however, readily eaten by various European and Asiatic people. Cakes made of it were placed before the altars of gods,—men making willing sacrifice of what they accounted as of small value. Similar sacrifices are made daily even now; only they are not in the form of aniseed cakes.

It is said of the Arabs, that they manufactured an intoxicating wine from linseed. This beverage was worthy of being served with that strange dish at dessert,—fried hempseed,—a dish that would have been appropriate enough at a highwayman's last supper, the night before he rode to Tyburn.

It used to be said of old, that wine was a sympathetic liquor; and this is alluded to by more than one writer. Sir Kenelm Digby in his "Dissertation on the Cure of Wounds," makes a singular remark with respect to wine. "The wine-merchants observe every where, (where there is wine,) that during the season the wines are in the flower, the wines in the cellar make a kind of fermentation, and percolate forth a little white lee (which I think they call 'the mother of the wine') upon the surface of the wine, which continues in a kind of disorder till the flower of the vines be fallen;

and then this agitation being ceased, all the wine returns to the same state as it was in before."

It was a custom with the ancients to swallow, to the health of their mistresses, as many cups or glasses as there were letters in her name. To this custom Martial refers:—

> "*Nævia sex cyathis, septem Justina bibatur,*
> *Quinque Lycas, Lyde quatuor, Ida tribus:*
> *Omnis ab infuso numeretur amica Falerno.*"

It became us, as a more mechanical people, to drink upon pegs rather than letters; the peg-tankards were said to be the invention of King Edgar. The two-gallon measure had eight pegs; and the half pint, from peg to peg, was deemed a fitting draught for an honest man; but as the statute, or custom, did not define how often the toper might be permitted to indulge in this measure, people of thirsty propensities got rather more inebriated than they had dared to be previously. As the half-pint was roughly set down as the *maximum* of their draught, it was a point of honour with them never to drink less,—and to drink to that extent as often as opportunity offered. The Council of London (Archbishop Anselm's "Canons," A.D. 1102) expressly warned the Clergy against the perils of peg-drinking; but the same Council looked upon perukes as being quite as perilous as these pegged half-pints, and denounced wigs with as much intensity as tankards,—and to about as much purpose. Karloman understood the Ecclesiastics better; at least, if traditionary history be worthy of any respect.

Among the legends of the Rhine connected with my present subject of wine, there is one which is worth mentioning. The great Karloman, who loved good liquor, bequeathed to the brotherhood of Monks at Rheinfield a marvellous and covetable butt of wine, which had not only the merit of being of first-rate quality, but which never decreased, though it was continually running at the spigot! This wine was for the use of the brethren; but the good Emperor also left a sum of money which he desired should be spent in treating visitors to the monastery with good Rhenish wine. When a weary traveller claimed the hospitality of the Monks, he was immediately conducted to an inner apartment. Here he was invested with the collar of Karloman, and gravely informed that, it being necessary that he should be baptized, he had only to say whether he preferred that the ceremony should be performed with wine or with water. If, like an honest fellow, he selected wine, he was gently constrained to swallow three bumpers of Muscatel. He was then crowned with a parcel-gilt coronet, and so became installed one of the jolly Knaves of St. Goar. There were some privileges attached to this dignity; among others, was the right to fish on the summit of the Lurley Berg, where there is no water; and of hunting on the sand-banks of the Rhine, where there is not safe footing for a sparrow. The poor temperate wight, on the other hand, who preferred the modest medium of water for the ceremony of his baptism, was proclaimed a blind heathen, and was immediately drenched to the skin, from outpouring buckets of water that were showered upon him in all directions. Such was the solemnity of the Hänsel, as instituted by Karloman. This Emperor's affection for the Rhine and its vicinity was as strong as that of an old gastronomic English Bishop for his native island. The episcopal attachment is exemplified in the story of the Prelate's last moments, when his faithful servant John endeavoured to encourage him. "Be comforted, my Lord," said John: "your Lordship is going to a better place." "Ah, John!" said the Bishop, "there is no place like old England!"

There was a practice among the Romans with regard to wine, which should win the respect of all our Inns of Court. All law business was suspended during vintage time. "*Sanè*," says Minucius Felix, "*et ad vindemiam feriæ judiciorum curam relaxaverunt;*" and this was no poor holiday: it was the Long Vacation of the Roman Bar, extending, as the Rev. Hubert Ashton Holden remarks, in his admirable edition of the "*Octavius*," from August

22nd to October 15th. And here let me remark, parenthetically, how much preferable it would be to make a school-book of the "*Octavius*" of Minucius Felix, so rich in early Christian information, and so pure in its Latinity, rather than pursue the old course of letting boys read Ovid and similar authors. The Abbé Gaume, in his "*Ver Rongeur*," traces all the evils by which society is afflicted, to the study of erotic Latin and Greek authors. The Abbé rushes from one extreme into its opposite, and wishes to confine our sons to the mawkish Latinity of the Lives of the Saints, and the Pastorals (so unlike the Eclogues) of Bishops. The works of Minucius Felix just occupies the safe medium of the two remote points,—erotic Heathenism, and Monkish mendacity, told with much violation of grammar. It is a book that ought to be on the list of works to be studied in every locality devoted to the education of "ingenious youth."

It is hardly necessary to write of the effects of wine on bodily economy. They are too familiarly known. There is an old adage that—

"He who goes to bed, and goes to bed sober,
    Falls as the leaves do, and dies in October;
But he who goes to bed, and goes to bed mellow,
    Lives as he ought to do, and dies a good fellow."

This is poor poetry, worse sentiment, and deadly counsel. Half the evils that torture men arise from intemperance; and, next to excess in alcohol, immoderation in wine is the most fatal practice to which humanity can bind itself slave. An Arab says of his horse, that the horse's belly is the measure of its corn. Men are too apt to allow a similar metage with respect to themselves in the matter of wine. It were safer to remember that we cannot drink too little, and that we soon may be drinking too much. Panard very justly says,—

"Se piquer d'être grand buveur,
    Est un abus qui je déplore.
Fuyons ce titre peu flatteur ;
    C'est un honneur qui déshonore.

> *Quand on boit trop, on s'assoupit,*
> *Et l'on tombe en délire :*
> *Buvons pour avoir de l'esprit,*
> *Et non pour le détruire."*

As good[1] advice, more eloquently delivered, is given by our own Herbert, a poet next to Shakespeare for felicity of expression. Our reverend minstrel and monitor says,—

> " Drink not the third glass, which thou canst not tame
>   When once it is within thee, but before
> May'st rule it as thou list ; and pour the shame,
>   Which it would pour on thee, upon the floor,
> It is most just to throw that on the ground,
> Which would throw *me* there, if I keep the round."

And again :—

> " If reason move not, gallants, quit the room ;
>   (All in a shipwreck shift their several way ;)
> Let not a common ruin thee entomb ;
>   Be not a beast in courtesy, but stay,
> Stay at the third cup, or forego the place :
> Wine, above all things, does God's stamp deface."

This is admirable counsel, logic, and theology. The people who at least stood in need of such a triad of excellent aids to good living were the Egyptians, at that particular period of their career when they confined themselves to drinking

> "Beer small as comfort, dead as charity."

And this may naturally lead us to look in, for a moment, on both the ancient and the modern Egyptians, when seated at table. But, previous to doing so, there is a little philological matter I would fain settle, as far as so indifferent an authority may presume to do so, and which may interest, not merely wine-bibbers, but etymologists, and zealous correspondents to "Notes and Queries." It may be very briefly discussed.

I have noticed, in another page, the fact that nearly all our old-fashioned drinking phrases are but corruptions of foreign terms. A "carouse," for instance, is derived from "*gar aus*," "altogether empty," sufficiently indicative of what a reveller was to do with his full glass. There is one—a rather vulgar term—of the origin of which, however, I have never heard any account. But I think I may have discovered it in a little German poem, by Pfarrius, called "*Der Trunk aus dem Stiefel*," and which, thus roughly done into English, may serve to show

THE ORIGIN OF "BOOSEY."

In the Rheingraf's hall were of Knights a score,
And they drained their goblets o'er and o'er,
And the torches they flung a lurid glow
On the Knights who were drinking there below.

"Ho, ho!" said the Rheingraf, "Sir Knights, I find,
Our courier has left a boot behind;
He who can empty it off at a breath,—
The Hufflesheim village is his till death."

Then laughing, he filled the boot to the rim,
Till the bright red wine flowed over the brim;
And said, as he mark'd their sparkling eyes,—
"Good luck to you, Knights—you know the prize!"

Then Johann von Sponheim sat silent by,
But pushed his neighbour to rise and try;
And Meinhart, his neighbour, could nothing do
But scowl at the boot, and sit silent too.

Old Florsheim, he nervously stroked his beard;
And Kunz von Stromberg spoke never a word;
And even the giant Chaplain stared
At the monster boot, as though he were scared.

Then Boos von Waldeck did loudly call,—
"Here, hand me that thimble!" and "Health to all!"
And then, in one breath, to the very last drain,
He drank, and fell back on his seat again,

And said, "O, Sir Rheingraf, it were my mind,
Had the fellow his other boot left behind,
To empty that, too, at a breath; and take
For my prize Norheim village, near the lake."

Then loud laughed they all at Waldeck's good jest,—
Of all landless tipplers, till then, the best;
But the Rheingraf, he kept his knightly word,—
And Boos of the Boot was Hufflesheim's lord!

If therein be not the origin of "boosey," why, let the lexicographers look to it. But my readers will have had enough of these uncouth names. I have now to introduce them to hosts with names equally unmusical; but, luckily, we have now to do more with acts than appellations, and therewith pass we to golden Egypt, and her well-spread boards. I will only first add another word respecting spirits, as a beverage. All authorities are agreed, that reason has no more deadly foe than alcohol. The effects of the latter are well described by Dr. Winslow, whom we have previously quoted in the matter of mental dietetics,—a gentleman who might, with justice, have given a plump denial to the remark of Macbeth, had it been addressed to Dr. Winslow, when the royal patient uncivilly told his medical adviser, "Thou canst not minister to a mind diseased." Dr. Winslow says: "The alcoholic elements introduced into the blood, and brought into immediate contact with the tissues of different organs, will derange the functions which they are severally destined to perform; and the amount and character of the mischief so produced will correspond with, and be modified by, the peculiarities of their individual organic structure. With these facts before us, when we consider the delicate structure of the brain, as revealed to us by the progress of microscopic anatomy, we must be prepared for the physical and mental derangement which must arise, either from the alcohol, itself, or its elements, being brought into direct contact with the vesicular neurine or granular matter entering into the composition of its white and grey substance. According to our most recent physiological views, the vesicular matter is the source of nervous power, and associated, as the material instrument of the mind, with all its manifestations, whether in the simple exercise of perception, or the more complicated operations of the thinking principle. We are then to conceive the simple or organic structure dedicated to this high function brought into contact with irritating and noxious elements. The result must obviously be a disturbance in the manifestations of the mind proportioned to the organic derangements so produced; and without, therefore, taking a materialistic view of the changes which take place, the obliteration of some, and the derangement of other of the intellectual faculties, are hereby satisfactorily accounted for. It is certain, that when the circulation in the grey matter of the convolutions is retarded by congestion, or accelerated by unwonted stimulation, there is a corresponding state of stupor or mental activity, amounting even to delirium, produced; and, indeed, it has been suggested, by some of our most eminent physiologists, that every idea of the mind is associated with a corresponding change in some part, or parts, of the vesicular surface." And if they who sit, "amid bumpers brightening," could only hold this truth in sober memory, there would be less imbibed at night, and more sunshine in their souls on the morrow. And now let us pass to the cradle of wisdom, the ancient Misraim, where, despite the national boast, folly was, perhaps, as much deified as in any locality upon earth.

Yes, let us now to ancient Egypt, where, as good old Herbert so finely expresses it,—

> "Men did sow
> Gardens of gods, which every year did grow
> Fresh and fine deities. They were at great cost
> Who for a god clearly a sallet lost!
> O, what a thing is man devoid of grace,
> Adoring garlic with a humble face!
> Begging his food of that which he may eat,
> Starving the while he worshippeth his meat!
> Who makes a root a god, how low is he,
> If God and man be served infinitely!
> What wretchedness can give him any room,
> Whose house is foul, while he adores his broom?"

THE TABLE OF THE ANCIENT AND MODERN EGYPTIANS.

If neither the grave of the Pharaohs nor physiology will, nor Dr. Hincke nor Chevalier Bunsen can, reveal to us the secret of the origin of the Egyptians, we, at all events, know that they were majestically-minded with respect to the table. The science of living was well understood by them; and the science of killing was splendidly rewarded; seeing that the soldiery, besides liberal pay, allowance of land, and exemption from tribute, received daily five pounds of bread, two of meat, and a quart of wine. With such rations they ought not to have been beaten by the Persians, when the latter had so degenerated, that their almost sole national boast was, that they could drink deeper than any other men, without seeming half so drunk. The Egyptians, too, were tolerably stout hands, and heads to boot, at the wine-pot; and there were few among even their Kings who, like the King of Castile, would have choked of thirst, because the grand butler was not by to hand the cup.

The pulse and fruits of Egypt, the fish of the Nile, the corn waving in its fields, which needed neither sun nor rain to exhibit productiveness,—all these were the envy, and partly the support, of surrounding nations. The corn was especially prized; and a reported threat of St. Athanasius to obstruct the importation of Egyptian corn into Constantinople, threw the Emperor Constantine into a fit of mingled fright, fever, and fury.

An Egyptian Squire commonly possessed a hundred or two cows and oxen, three hundred rams, four times that number of goats, and five times that number of swine, for the supply of his own little household. The apartments in the mansions of these gentlemen were beautifully painted, and were furnished with tables, chairs, and couches which have supplied models for the upholstery of modern times. They were lovers of music, and willingly suspended conversation at their feasts, in order to listen to the "concord of sweet sounds."

Cleopatra was but a febrile creature; but she sat down with good appetite, and love in her eyes, to the banquet given by Antony, at which fifteen whole boars smoked upon the board. But Cleopatra, frail and fragile, like many thin people, ate heartily; and when she herself treated Cæsar, it was with such a banquet that slaves died to procure it, and the guests who were present, wondered at the rarities of which they partook. There was every thing there that gastronomy could think of, except mutton,—an exception in favour of the divine Ammon with the ram-like head. I believe that even roast-beef and plum-pudding were not lacking; for these delicacies were popular in Thebes, as was broiled and salted goose, with good brown stout, strong barley-wine, to cheer the spirits and assist digestion.

Excessively proud, too, were the old Egyptians of their culinary ability. When the Egyptians, under their King, attacked Ochus, Sovereign of Persia, the former were thoroughly beaten, and their Monarch was captured. Ochus treated him as courteously as the Black Prince did John of France, and invited him to his own table, at the simplicity of which the Egyptian laughed outright. "Prince," said the uncourteous captive, "if you would really like to know how happy Kings should feed, just let my cooks—if you have caught the rascals, as you have me—prepare you a true Egyptian supper." Ochus consented, enjoyed himself amazingly at the banquet, and, then, turning to his Egyptian prisoner, punished him by saying, "Why, what a sorry fool art thou, whose ambition has lost thee such repasts, and reduced thee to henceforth envy, as thou wilt, the moderate meals that suffice us honest Persians!" The implied threat was worse than the sentiment.

The dinner-table of the Egyptians was sometimes covered with a linen cloth imitating palm-leaves, sometimes left uncovered. Plates and knives, but not forks, were in common use. In place of the latter were short-handled spoons of gold, silver, ivory, tortoise-shell, or alabaster. The dining-table was circular: ornamented rolls of wheaten bread were placed before each guest; and supplies of the same were heaped in gay-looking baskets on the side-board, where also were kept the wine, the water, ewer, and napkins, which slaves, fair or swarthy, Greek or Negro, were ready to present at the bidding of the guests.

Previous to sitting down to the repast, the company put a spur to their appetite, and a cordial to their stomach, in the shape of pungent vegetables or strong *liqueurs*. Glasses for beer, decanters and goblets for wine, appear among the ancient pictorial illustrations of Egyptian table-furniture. It would seem, too, from the position of those at table, that they rose from their chairs to challenge each other to drink, to propose toasts or healths, or to inflict speeches upon the vexed ears of compulsory listeners.

In these "counterfeit presentments" of Egyptian life may be seen the entire science of epicureanism, and its practical application put into action. The poultry-yard, the slaughter-houses, the markets and the kitchen, are so graphically depicted, that we see at once, that the art of making life comfortable was one most profoundly respected by the ancient and mysterious people. The selecting, purchasing, and killing are vividly portrayed. The cooking is carried in a large bronze caldron, on a tripod, over a fire, which is stirred by an under-cook, with a poker that may have been bought any day at Kippon and Burton's. The butcher is there, too, in order decently to dissect the fowls; and our ancient friend carries before him the identical steel for sharpening his knife, which may be seen any day hanging from the waists of the butchers of London. There is a pastrycook, also, in one of these "civil monuments of Egypt," who is carrying a tray of tartlets on his head; and to the tray is suspended the inscription signifying "one thousand," which probably means, that this "Birch, Pyramid-place, Cairo," drives such a trade, that he makes and sells a thousand tarts or a thousand varieties of them daily.

A dinner *fresco*, in a tomb at Thebes, shows us an entertainment given by a naval officer to some of his professional brethren.

This *fresco* is described as being in compartments, and, perhaps, the most curious is that in which "you see on one side the arrival of an aristocratic guest, in his chariot, attended by a train of running footmen, one of whom hastens forward to announce his arrival by a knock at the door, sufficient to satisfy the critical ear, and rouse the somnolent obesity, of the sleepiest and fattest hall-porter in Grosvenor-square. The other compartment presents you with a *coup-d'œil* of the poultry-yard, shambles, pantry, and kitchen; and is completed by a side view of a novel incident. A grey-headed mendicant, attended by his faithful dog, and who might pass for Ulysses at his palace-gate, is receiving, from the hands of a deformed, but charitable, menial, a bull's head, and a draught of that beer, for the invention of which we are beholden to the Thebans."

The story of Mycerinus, the Egyptian King, is grandly told by Mr. Arnold, in his popular volume of poems; and, succinctly, by Herodotus. An incident of the story connects it with our subject. Mycerinus was persecuted by the Gods for rendering Egypt happy, instead of oppressing it, like his predecessors, and as the oracles had declared it should be oppressed for many years to come. In punishment for such impious piety, as his offence may be called, poor Mycerinus was told by the oracle at Buto, that he should live only six years longer. "When Mycerinus heard this, seeing that his sentence was now pronounced against him, he ordered a great number of lamps to be made, and having lighted them, whenever night came on, he drank and enjoyed himself, never ceasing night or day, roaming about the marshes and groves, wherever he could hear of places most suited for pleasure; and he had recourse to this artifice for the purpose of convicting the oracle of falsehood, that by turning the nights into days, he might live twelve years intead of six." Poor fool! He probably succeeded in his object, but after a sorry fashion. It may be good poetry to say that—

> "The best of all our ways
> To lengthen all our days
> Is to take a few hours from night, my dear;"

but it is bad in principle, and universally unsuccessful in practice. A recent describer of his travels in Egypt has said, that nothing is so easy as to show that the Egyptians gave jovial banquets within the sepulchral hall of tombs. I think that nothing would be so difficult as to prove this. The nearest approach to it would be the case of the skeleton that was carried about at Egyptian banquets, the bearer, at the same time, warning the guests that, eat, drink, and laugh as they might, to *that* "complexion they must come" at last. The assertion, however, was probably made, in part, to excuse a barbarous festival, at which the writer was present, in the tombs Eilythyias. The *locale* was one of the huge halls, whose colossal columns serve to support the huger mountain that is above. The dinner, we are told, was laid out between the columns, with strings of small lamps suspended in festoons over head.

The civilized and Christian ladies and gentlemen who were the guests at this feast, broke up the coffins of the pagan and barbarian Kings and Queens, in order to procure wood to boil their vegetables! They laughed, joked, and sang joyous songs, and wondered what the buried majesty of Misraim would say, could it burst its cerements, and see northern men of unknown tongues drinking Champagne at its august feet. And if, for a moment, a reflecting guest contrasted the savage revelry with the ensigns hung out by the King of Terrors to intimate his irresistible dominion over the company,—why, reflection was soon banished by the appearance of the Awalim and Ghawazi girls, whom strong coffee and more potent brandy had primed for their lascivious dancing. "O Father Abraham! what these Christians are!"

These tombs are full of instruction to those who can read them. They show us that the chief butler and cook—the "keeper of the drinks," and the Prince (*sar*) of his cooks—were probably Princes of the blood of Pharaoh. In all pictorial representations of banquets, it is the eldest son who hands the viands to his father, the eldest daughter to the mother. The bill of fare of the trimestrial banquet of the dead, held in the noble hall of the tom's of Nahrai at Benihassan, is still extant. It is as long as that of a score of Lord Mayors'; and hundreds of men were fed from what remained. All the retainers of Nahrai, who was a Prince in Egypt a full century before the time of Joseph, were buried in the vaults beneath the hall; and every one who could claim kindred with them had a right to partake of the feast. The manner of service appears to have been after this fashion:— The youngest children of the house received the viands from the cooks, and those children passed them on to the elder, until they reached the first-born, who placed the dish at the feet of his sire, by whom a portion was cut off, which the daughters, according to their age, transferred from one to the other till it reached the separate table of their mother. All remained standing, at these festival-dinners, until the two seniors of the house had finished the first dishes of the repast. Portions from these were then served to the children, when the whole party sat down together; the children eating of the remains of the first dish, while "the governor" and his lady partook of the integral second; and so on, through a long service. On the wall of a tomb at Ghizeh,— that of Eimei, one of the Princes of the Saphis,—the bill of fare directs ninety-eight dishes to be placed, at once, on the table, at the fortnightly banquets which glad survivors held in honour of the departed, who appear to me always to enjoy an immense advantage over those whom they leave behind them.

But now let us look in upon the modern Egyptian. If he be the master of a house, while he is at ablutions and prayers, his wife is making his coffee; and it is to be hoped that she is allowed the privilege alluded to in the Augustinian sentiment, *orat qui laborat.* The cup of coffee and pipe, taken early, generally suffice the Egyptian till noon, at which hour comes the actual breakfast, usually consisting of bread, butter, eggs, cheese, clotted cream, or curdled milk, with, perhaps, a thin pastry, saturated with butter, folded like a pancake, and sprinkled with sugar. A dish of horse-beans (terrific dish!) sometimes adorns the table. They have been slowly simmering through a whole night in an earthen vessel, buried up to the neck in the hot ashes of an oven; and the sauce for this indigestible dish is linseed oil or butter, and, perhaps, a little lime-juice. Those to whom butter is difficult of procuring, or to whom good dinners are rarities, often make a meal, and are content, upon dry bread dipped in a mixture of salt, pepper, wild marjoram, with various other herbs, pungent seeds, and a quantity of chick-peas. The bread is dipped into this *ragoût*, and so eaten.

The supper is the principal meal in Egypt. The cooking is especially for this repast; and what remains is appropriated for the next day's dinner, despite the apophthegm of Boileau, that—

"*Un diner rechauffé ne vaut jamais rien.*"

It is only an amiable *paterfamilias* that dines with his wives and children; and, in truth, where the wife appears in the plural number, the husband can hardly expect a quiet meal. The washing before eating is almost of universal observation. The table is a round tray placed low, so that the squatters on the ground may conveniently eat thereat. Bread and limes are placed on the tray. The bread is round, as among the ancient Egyptians, and often serves as plate. The spoons, too, are of the materials I have named in speaking of the older nation. The dishes are of tinned copper or china; and several are put upon the table at one time. Among the Turks, only *one* dish appears at a time. Twelve persons, with one knee on the ground and the other (the right) raised, may sit round a tray three feet in diameter. Each guest tucks up his right sleeve, and prepares for his work, after imitating the master of the house in uttering a low *Bismillan*, "In the name of God." The host sets the second example of commencing to eat; and the guests again follow the good precedent. Knives and forks are not used; spoons only for food like soups and rice. The thumb and two forefingers are the instruments otherwise employed; and they are employed delicately enough. Generally, a piece of bread is taken, doubled together, and dipped into the dish, so as to enclose the morsel of meat which the guest designs for himself, or, if it be a savoury bit, and *he* be courteous, intended for presentation to his neighbour. The food is suited to such practices. It consists of stewed meats, with vegetables of endless variety, or of small morsels of mutton or lamb, roasted on skewers: clarified butter compensates for want of fat in the meat. A fowl is summarily torn asunder by two hands, either of the same person, or the right hands of two guests. Dexterous fellows, like our first-rate carvers, will "joint" a fowl with one hand. The Arabs do not use the left hand at all at table, because it is used for unclean purposes. The disjointing is easily done; and even a whole lamb, stuffed with pistachio nuts, may be pulled to pieces much more easily than we divide a chicken. Watermelons, sliced, set to cool, and watched, lest serpents should approach, and poison the dish by their breath, generally form, when in season, a part of an Egyptian meal,—a meal which usually closes with a dish of boiled rice, mixed with butter, salt, and pepper; but occasionally this dish is followed by a bowl of water, with raisins that have been boiled in it, and sugar added, with a little rose-water, to give it an odour of refinement. A bottle of six-year-old port is preferable.

As soon as each person has satisfied his appetite, he ceases, murmurs, "Praise be to God!" drinks his sweetened water, rises, and goes his way. They who drink wine, do it in private, or with confidential friends, call it "rum" to save their orthodoxy; and if a visitor call while this process is going on, the ready servant informs him that his master is abroad or in the harem. Sweet drinks and sherbets, approved by the Law and *the* Prophet, are in common use, and pipes and prayer end "the well-spent day."

Egyptian women have some little fancies connected with the table that may be mentioned. In order to achieve that proportion of obesity which constitutes the beautiful, they eat mashed beetles, and they chew frankincense and laudanum, to perfume the breath. The Egyptian peasantry live upon the very sparest of diets, not often being able to procure even rice. They, like the Bedouins, are, however, remarkable for strength and health; but an Egyptian or Bedouin diet would not produce the same results in an English climate.

It will have been observed, that in Egypt each man says his own "grace," before and after meat, for himself. The same custom prevails in Servia. At table, instead of one person asking for a blessing on the food, each individual expresses, *in his own words*, (an improvement on the Egyptian plan,) his gratitude to the Supreme Being. In drinking, the toast or sentiment of the Servian is, "To the glory of God!" and a very excellent sentiment, only the Servian is apt to get very drunk over it. The Servian qualification for a chairman at a convivial party is, that he should be able to deliver an extempore prayer; and a very good qualification, provided it be not a mere formality, and that the spirit of prayer be the strongest spirit there. The combination, however, of Collects and conviviality reminds me of some strange parties at old-fashioned houses in our provincial towns, where comic songs are followed by discussions on the Millennium, and seed-cake and ginger wine season both.

I have spoken more of the achievements of Egyptian cookery, than of the quality of the cooks. The fact is, that it is far more easy to speak decidedly of the former, than of the latter. Mr. St. John describes the Arab cooks in Egypt as being great gastronomers, and serving up "their dishes in a style which could not have displeased Elagabalus himself!" Mr. Lane equally lauds their excellence, and the delicacy of the manner of eating. Herr Werne, on the other hand,—and he is a man of wide experience in this matter,—speaks very differently both of Turkish eating and Arab cooking in Egypt. Werne, indeed, speaks of the remote district of Bellad Sudam, rather than of Cairo and Alexandria; but his observations have an extensive application, nevertheless. He is disgusted with the general want of cleanliness; and he remarks, that "the cooks are dirtier in themselves, and more filthy in their dress, than any other class of people." The dirty Arab cook is in a dirty kitchen, a dirty pipe ever in his mouth, and with the dirtiest of hands manipulating savoury preparations for the mouths of his masters. He knows little more than how to boil or roast meat, boil beans, and prepare vegetable dishes. Even the female slaves of the harem, who act as cooks to their lords, are remarkable for uncleanliness. "All the meat to be used for the dinner is sodden together in one huge caldron, and separated for arrangement in various dishes, all of which partake of general flavour, having been cooked together, and there is but scant nourishment in any of them." The vegetables are described by him as being wretchedly cooked, and saturated with bad butter, or the water in which they have been boiled. The dishes are not larger than our plates; the plates, when such are used by the guests, about the size of our saucers: but "each guest at once plunges his hand into any or every dish that pleases him, and gropes about till he gets hold of the best bits, pulls them out, and swallows them. Very often a bite is only taken from the piece thus seized on, and the rest returned to the dish; but, in spite of the clean treatment it has undergone, it is again soon seized hold of by another, and, perchance, again similarly handled, till all is finally bolted. The Turks eat incredibly rapidly, as they bolt everything, and keep cramming into the mouth more, ere the former mouthful has been swallowed; while a smacking of lips, and licking of sauce-dripping fingers, succeed, and proclaim their pleasure in the meal. Bread is generally to be found on the table, but neither salt, oil, vinegar, nor pepper; although, when they dine with Europeans, they show no dislike to highly-seasoned dishes or strong drinks. Although these dishes are numerous, they contain but little. If there are many courses, or more dishes than the table will hold at one time, the entertainer is ever busied making signs to the attendants which are to be removed; and not seldom the guest finds, that the very dish he was about to help himself from is carried off from under his very nose. The Pasha used often to amuse himself by playing tricks on his guests, by ordering off, with the utmost rapidity, those dishes he saw their longing eyes fixed on, ere their outstretched hands could convey any portion of their into their watering mouths. At first, in spite of the *pilau*, we never were quick enough to get sufficient to eat, not having been brought up to bolt our food; and that the Turks are so quickly satisfied, and by so little, is wholly owing to this bolting of their food, is undeniable; and this also produces the repeated eructations they so loudly and joyfully give vent to, as proving their high health and vigour."

The Turks and Arabs of Egypt "chaw," carrying their quid between the front teeth and upper lip. The blacks of Gesira mix tobacco and nitron, dissolving the latter in an infusion of the former. This they call "bucca;" and they take a mouthful of it at a time, which they keep rinsing over their teeth and gums, for, perhaps, a quarter of an hour, before they eject it. They have "bucca" parties, as we have tea parties; and *then* is the circle in the very highest state of enjoyment,—imbibing, gurgling, gargling, and ejecting,—and not a word uttered, except at the close, when the guests return thanks to their host "for this very delightful evening!"

Egypt was the locality wherein the saints of old especially shone with respect to their table arrangements, or their contempt for them; and these gentlemen fairly claim a due share of notice at our hands. So, now "for the desert!"

THE DIET OF SAINTS.

Fasting, under certain circumstances, at certain seasons, and for certain ends, is undoubtedly sanctified by apostolical recommendation. The earlier fathers, however, say little on the subject. Clement of Alexandria mentions weekly fasts at Easter; and Tertullian, in an article especially recommending the observation, bitterly bewails that it has fallen into a general disuse. The Church of Alexandria also ordained a fast on Wednesdays and Fridays; on Wednesday, because on that day Christ was betrayed; on Friday, because on that day he was crucified. In Alexandria too arose the saying, that the aspen-tree shook because it was the tree from which the wood for the cross was taken. The fasting generally consisted in abstaining from food until three o'clock in the afternoon, but a religious liberty was allowed, connected with its observance, until the sixth century, when a Council of Orleans decreed excommunication against all who did not fast according to the laws of the Church. Nor did the authorities stop at this penalty; for in later times the unlucky wight detected in relieving hunger by eating prohibited meats, was punished by having all his teeth drawn—the offending members were summarily extracted. The prohibited food in Lent was flesh, eggs, cheese, and wine; subsequently flesh alone was prohibited; and this tenderness of orthodoxy so disgusted the Greek Church, that it lost its temper, flew off into schism, and forgot charity in maintaining that the use of meat in Lent was damnable.

The Xerophagia, or "dry eatings," were the days on which nothing was eaten but bread and salt. This was in very early times. Innovators added pulse, herbs, and fruits—no unpleasant fare in hot countries. The Montanists made this fast obligatory, and were very much censured in consequence. The Essenes, who, whether as Jews or Jewish Christians in Alexandria, were singularly strict observers of the Sabbath, carrying their strictness to a point which my readers may find in Jortin, if they are curious thereupon, observed also this fast very rigidly, and on the stated days ate nothing with their bread but salt and hyssop.

Most of the saints recorded on the canon roll of Rome, appear to have maintained very indifferent tables, and to have considerably marred thereby their strength and efficiency. Saint Fulgentius abstained from everything savoury, and even drank no wine, says his biographer; which looks as if the good men *did* take some for their stomach's sake; and indeed Fulgentius himself took a little negus when he was indisposed to plain water; and "small blame to him" for so harmless a proceeding. St. Eugenius never broke his fast till sunset; and when a bunch of grapes was sent to a sick monk of the desert, he forwarded it to a second, and a second to a third, and so on to a twentieth, until his health-inspiring offering, made for man by God, was withered and nasty. These monks did not pray like Pope:—

> "The blessing thy free bounty gives
> Let me not cast away,
> For God is paid when man receives,—
> To enjoy is to obey."

But this is a sentiment in the opposite extreme, or might be easily carried in that direction. Palladius says of one of these desert monks, St. Macarius, that for years together he lived only on raw herbs and pulse; that during three consecutive years he existed on four or five ounces of bread daily; and that he consumed but one small measure of oil in a twelvemonth—a substitute for the gallons of sack with which profaner men washed down their modicum of bread. St. Macarius, however, surpassed himself in Lent; and an alderman might be excused for fainting at the idea of a human being passing forty days and nights in a standing position, with no more substantial support than a few raw cabbage-leaves on a Sunday! St. Genevieve was hardly inferior in austerity, and only ate twice in the week, on Sundays and Thursdays, and then only beans and bread. When she grew old and infirm, and she was prematurely both, she indulged in a little fish and milk. Simeon Stylites surpassed both in culpable austerity. He spent an entire Lent without allowing anything to pass his lips; and at other seasons this slow suicidal saint never ate but on Sundays. His chief occupation upon the pillar, which looks much more like a column of pride than a monument of humility, was in praying and bowing. An admiring monk, who must have had as little of active usefulness to employ his time with as poor Simeon, exultingly records, that he did not eat once during the day, but that he made one thousand two hundred and forty-four bows of adoration in that time. Oh, Simeon! well for thee, poor fellow-mortal, if those reverences be not accounted rather as homage to thyself than to Him to whom homage is due.

It is extremely difficult for the human mind to realize the idea of a Bishop of London never breaking his fast till the evening, and then being satisfied with a solitary egg, an inch of bread, and a cup of milk and water; such, however, is said to have been the daily fare of St. Cedd, a predecessor of Dr. Bloomfield in the metropolitan diocese. "How unlike *my* Beverly?" St. Severinus, an Austrian Prelate, had a more indifferent table than St. Cedd, especially in Lent, when he ate but once a-week. St. William of Bourges never tasted meat after he was ordained. St. Theodosius, the Cenobiarch, was more frugal still, and bread often lacked, we are told, even for the holy offices of the Church. This would seem to intimate, however, that the officers of the Church may have eaten it. Be this as it may, when bread was needed for the sacrament, a string of mules miraculously appeared in the desert, bearing the necessary provision. "Necessary provision," may be well said, for if the Cenobites consumed little themselves, they presided at tables where occasionally sat a hundred hungry guests who must have much needed a dinner, seeing that they crossed the desert to obtain it.

Some of the most self-denying saints, like St. Felix of Nola, if they declined wine in its liquid form, took it in pills,—swallowing grapes. St. Paul, the first hermit, lived on the fruit of a tree which produced a fresh supply daily, the bread to temper which was brought every morning by a raven. The diet was sufficiently invigorating to give strength to the modest man to bite off his own tongue, and spit it in the face of a lady who tried to tempt him, as the Irish nymph tempted the uncourteous St. Kevin of Glendalough. He was, in abstinence, only second to St. Isidore who, when hungry, burst into tears, not because God had mercifully provided him wherewith to satisfy lawful appetite, but because sinful man that he was, he dared to eat at all!

I have spoken of the abstinence of a Bishop of London; there was a Bishop of Worcester, Wulstan, who is worthy of being mentioned with him. Wulstan was rather fond of savoury viands, but he was one day during mass so distracted by the smell of meat roasting in a kitchen, which must have been very close to his church, that he made a vow to abstain from meat for ever. But I do not know, if he kept his vow. St. Euthymius was a more rational man, for he taught his monks that to satisfy hunger was no crime, but that to abuse appetite and God's gifts too, *was* an offence. St. Macedonius, the Syrian, did not discover this truth until he had so impaired his powers by long fasts, that it was impossible to restore them—as he tried to do on a diet of dry bread. And yet he was so prematurely gifted, that his own birth is said to have been the result of his own prayers!

The table kept by St. Publius for his monks was not of a liberal character. He allowed them nothing but pulse and herbs, coarse bread and water. Nothing else! He prohibited wine, milk, cheese, grapes, and even vinegar—which every sour brother might have distilled from his own ichor. From Easter to Whitsuntide was accounted a holiday time, and during that festive period the brotherhood were allowed to grow hilarious, if they could, upon a gill of oil a-piece. St. Paula, "the widow," subjected her nuns to the same lively fare, and she moreover fiercely denounced all ideas of personal neatness and cleanliness, as an uncleanness of the mind. She accounted herself wise in so doing, but her nuns might fairly have put to her the question asked by Mizen, in the

Fair Quaker of Deal:—"Do'st thou think that nastiness gives thee a title to knowledge?"

St. John Chrysostom was as severe as Paula, and it would not have cost Olympias much to defray, as she insisted upon doing, the expenses of his table. The table which the saint kept for guests was, however, hospitably and delicately laden—and perhaps this was an inconsistency in a man who censured what he also encouraged.

They who have made a saint of Charlemagne, aver that he broke his fast but once a day, and that after sunset. I cannot believe this of a man who dealt so largely in the eggs laid by his hens, and in vegetables raised in his garden. Nor do I believe that St. Sulpicius Severus would have written so capital a biography of St. Martin, had he lived, as it is said, on herbs, boiled with a little vinegar for seasoning. Surely, we have heard of the "kitchen" of gentlemen like Sulpicius, and if his condensed Scripture History be as dry as the bread he ate during the task, his letters to Claudia seem to have been written on more generous food. Not that he was immoderate. He kept one cook, a very "plain cook" indeed, as Sulpicius describes him, when he despatched the boy to Bishop Paulinus with a letter which commences with a startling bit of episcopal history, namely, that "*all* the cooks in the kitchen of Paulinus had left him without warning, because the prelate was getting too careless about good living." Some commentators say, that the letter was a joke; but the reply to it is extant, and therein it may be seen how Paulinus did not look upon it as a joke.

Southey, in his "St. Romuald," mirthful as the story is, has not exceeded the truth, or rather has not departed from the narrative told by the good man's biographers:—

> "Then, Sir, to see how he would mortify
> The flesh! If any one had dainty fare,
> Good man, he would come there;
> And look at all the delicate things, and cry,
> O Belly! Belly!

You would be gourmandizing now, I know;
   But it shall not be so!—
Home, to your bread and water. Home, I tell ye."

And thus says Alban Butler of him:—"He never would admit of the least thing to give a savour to the herbs or meal-gruel on which he supported himself. If anything was brought him better dressed, he, for the greater self-denial, applied it to his nostrils, and said, 'Oh Gluttony, Gluttony! thou shalt never taste this! Perpetual war is declared against thee!' St. William of Maleval was of the same opinion when he cried because he ate his dry bread with a relish, and found that what he called "sensuality" was not inseparable from the coarsest food. St. Benedict of Anian, on the other hand, did not decline the use of a little wine, when it was given him; while St. Martinianus, again, lived upon biscuits and water, brought to him twice a-year—and very nasty fare it must have been towards the end of each six-months. It must have been worse than that of St. Peter Damian, who prided himself on never drinking water fresh, and thought there was virtue in having it four-and-twenty hours old. St. Tarasius must have maintained a more decent table, for it is said of him that he used to take the dishes from it and give of them to the poor; and honour be to his name, because of his good sense and his charity! Our venerable acquaintance of the principality, St. David, was not half so wise, however well-intentioned; but St. Charles, Earl of Flanders, followed the better course, and not only lived moderately well, but acted better, by daily distributing seven hundred loaves to the poor. The Welsh saints, generally, kept as austere a table as St. David. There was, for instance, the cacophonous Winwaloe of Winwaloe, who kept his monks at starving point all the week, recalling them to life on Sundays by microscopic rations of hard cheese and shell-fish. His own fare was barley-bread strewn with ashes, and when Lent arrived, the quantity of ashes was doubled, in honour of the season! St. Thomas Aquinas was so abstracted that he never knew, at dinner, what he was eating, nor could remember, after it, if he had dined, which was likely enough. St. Frances, Widow, foundress of the Collations, was in more full possession of her wits; as, indeed, the lady saints were, generally. She had her little fancies indeed, which were "only charming Fanny's way," and her beverage at eve was dirty water, out of a human skull; but she had no mercy for lazy devotees, and invariably told sighing wives that they had active duties to perform, and that they had better keep out of monasteries, at least till they were widows. She was a good, humble woman; and, as a commentator says of the abstinence of St. Euphrasia, without humility these facts would be but facts of devils!

Another gleam of good sense shines upon us from the person of St. Benedict. He drank wine, and so did his monks of Vicovara, who liked his wine better than either the toast or sentiment with which he passed it round to them, and who tried to get rid of him by poisoning his glass; but the saint, full of inspired suspicion, made over it the sign of the cross, and away went the flask into fifty fragments. The taste of the good saint was known after he left Vicovara, and a pious soul once sent him a couple of bottles of wine by a faithless messenger, who delivered but one. "Mind what you are about," said St. Benedict, "when you draw the other cork for yourself." The knave was not abashed, but when he did secretly open the other bottle for the solace of his own thirsty throat, he found nothing therein but a lively serpent, which glided from him after casting at him a reproachful look!

If St. Benedict was right in the ordering of his table, why St. John of Egypt was wrong, for he never drank anything but stagnant water, nor ate anything cooked by fire; even his bread he complacently swallowed before it was baked;—and what his liver was like, it would puzzle any but a physician even to conjecture.

There was infinitely more sense in the table kept by an abbot of the compound Christian and Pagan title and name of St. Plato. He never ate anything but what had been raised or procured by the labour of his own hands; he was consequently never in debt with respect to his household expenses, and if all men so far followed the example of St. Plato, who was a better practical philosopher than his heathen namesake, what a happy world we should make of it! There would be fewer Christmas bills, and many more joyous dinners, not only at Christmas, but all the year round!

St. Plato deserves our respect; he would not live on alms. He was more useful in his generation than the men who, like St. Aphraates, were content to exist on the eleemosynary contributions of the faithful, or than those who, like Zozimus and his followers, wandered through the desert, trusting to chance and calling it providence. What, compared with our friend Plato, was that of St. Droun, the so-called patron of shepherds, who during forty years taught them nothing, and lived on the barley-bread which they brought him in return for his instruction.

I have given one or two instances of the spare tables kept by a few of our ancient bishops; I may here add to them the name of Elphege, some time Bishop of Winchester, and subsequently Archbishop of Canterbury. The smell of roast meat was never known in his palace on any but "extraordinary occasions." This, however, is a very indefinite term, and the table of this primate may have been one to make a cardinal give unctuous thanks for rich mercies, five days out of the seven. There was certainly gastronomic work to do in some of the ancient godly households, or St. James of Sclavonia would not have passed so many years in one, as he did, in the capacity of cook, "improving" the occasion, by drawing ideas of hell from his own fires, which were for ever roasting savoury joints, like those which strike the visitors with awe and appetite in the kitchens at Maynooth.

If in some houses there were busy kitchens, in others there were soft couches, whereon digestion might progress. Thus Adalbert, Bishop of Prague, was a Saint and Martyr; and it is said, that he had a most comfortable bed in his dormitory, but that he never slept upon it! Then, what was the bed for? It is added, that he fasted in private with great severity,—but it is no more "of faith" to believe this, than it is that he slept every night on the floor, under, and not upon, his own excellent feather-bed; for what says the old refrain?—

> "A notre coucher
> Un lit, des draps blancs,
> Une ——
> digue daine, bon !
> Voila la vie que ces moines font !"

But he may have been a profane fellow who wrote these rude rhymes; and we will no more implicitly trust him, than we will the prose historians of the doings and dealings of the saintly men.

It is not an unusual thing to find wine-bibbers mentioned among the members of holy communities; where wine was generally supposed to be a luxury never employed but for the service of the altar,—and perhaps of the sick. The venerable Bede tells a story of a "brother," whom he had known, and whom he wishes to God he had never known, and who was given to worship the spigot. Bede does not give his name, but certifies that the too jolly friar lived ignobly in a noble monastery, where he was often reproved for his acts of drunkenness, and only tolerated because of his gifts,—not spiritual, but as a carpenter. He was a terrible tippler, but a hard workman to boot, and would, at any time, rather labour all day and all night at his bench than join the brethren in chapel. Indeed, when he did go, his thoughts were running on something else. He was like the profane Yorkshire farmer, who praised the institution of the Sabbath because it not only brought roast beef with it as a sacred observance, but it authorized him to attend in his pew at church, where, said he, "I puts up my legs and thinks o' nothing!" Bede's carpenter was characteristically punished for his bibbing; and the story was made much of, by way of monition to others. It was to this effect:—" He, falling sick, and being reduced to extremity, called the brethren, and with much lamentation, and like one dammed, began to tell them that he saw hell open, and Satan at the bottom thereof, and also Caiaphas, with the others that slew our Lord, by um delivered up to avenging flames. 'In whose neighbourhood,' said he, 'I see a place of eternal perdition prepared for me, miserable wretch that I am!' The brothers, hearing these words, began seriously to exhort him that he should repent even then, while he was in the flesh. He answered in despair,—'I have no time now to change my course of life, when I have myself seen my judgment passed.' When he had uttered these words, he died, without having received the saving *viaticum;* and his body was buried in the remotest part of the monastery; nor did any one dare to say masses, sing psalms, or even to pray for him." Which seems a very hard case; for if any one needed such service it was he; and the Church's ability to extricate him could not be denied, when she was duly pre-paid for the service.

Curiously enough, St. Monica, the mother of St. Augustin, ranks among the wine-bibbers. Her pious parents left their children to be brought up by a servant-maid, who had more zeal than discretion, and who would allow none of the children to drink, were they ever so thirsty, except at meal-times, and then only a drop or two of water. "If you cannot restrain your desire to drink now," she would say, "what will it be when you have wine at command?" Now, the effect of this speech was exactly like that of the confessor to the hostler, when he asked the latter, if he never greased the horses' teeth in order to prevent them eating their corn. It gave the young Monica a new idea. She was accustomed to draw the wine for her father's table, and she henceforth began to drink a portion each time that she went to the cellar with her pitcher. And I do not know that Mr. Millais, or any other of the pre-Raphaelite gentlemen, could have a better subject for a picture, than that representing the scene when the horrified nurse-maid beheld her young charge indulging in her cups in the parental wine-vault. The lecture she received worked her conversion, we are told; and she married, and became the mother of St. Augustin, who so far followed the maternal example that, in his earlier years, when, with his eyes upon heaven, his heart was with the good things of the earth, his commonest prayer used to be, "Lord, make me religious, *but not just yet.*"

The nurse-maid of Monica deserved to have been the wife,—and perhaps she was,—of St. Theodotus, the vintner of Ancyra. He was a teetotaller who kept a tavern, and who passed the livelong day in leaning over his counter and begging his customers not to drink! Well, men have been canonized for less useful service to their kind; and Theodotus was more worthily employed in keeping drunkards from his wine-casks, than St. Pius V. was when, every day before dinner, by way of mocking his appetite, he resorted to the public hospitals, and kissed the ulcers of the patients! Nay, biographers tell us that an English Protestant gentleman was *suddenly converted* to Romanism, by observing the condescension and affection with which Pius kissed the ulcers on the feet of some poor men! The pope, if he and the convert dined together after this nasty ceremony, might have confessed that he had been sore put to it for an argument that should carry conviction to an English gentleman in search of a religion.

Let us contrast this pope in his pride with a cardinal in his fall. "When Wolsey," says Mr. Hunter the antiquary, "was dismissed by his tyrannical master to his northern diocese, he passed many weeks at Scrooby. It is a pleasing picture which his faithful servant, Cavendish, gives of him at this period of his life:— 'Ministering many deeds of charity, and attending on Sundays at some parish church in the neighbourhood; hearing or saying mass himself, and causing some one of his chaplains to preach to the people; and that done, he would dine in some honest house of that town, where should be distributed to the poor a great alms, as well of meat and drink, as of money to supply the want of sufficient meat, if the number of the poor did so exceed of necessity." Wolsey was no saint certainly, but he was as honest a man as Pius, and a wiser when he fed the poor rather than kiss their ulcers.

But there is no accounting for taste; the Russian Boniface

used to roll himself among thorns and nettles, in order to get an appetite, or to punish himself for indulging over much. St. Germanus, on the other hand, commenced every repast by putting ashes into his mouth; the modern custom of beginning with oysters certainly is better both for taste and stomach. St. Walthen took wine, but then he put spiders in it. St. Dominic, too, was singular in his diet, and he sometimes spent his half hour before dinner in one of the most curious positions that gentlemen could possibly fix upon. The Abbot of St. Vincent's one day desired his company at dinner, but at the usual hour the saint was in church, and had forgotten the invitation. In the meantime, the turkey and chine were spoiling, and the hungry abbot despatched a monk in quest of the loiterer; the messenger hurried to the church, where, to his very considerable astonishment, he beheld St. Dominic "ravished and in ecstasy," whatever that may mean, "raised several cubits above the ground, and without motion." The Saint, on being told that dinner was ready, graciously smiled at the intelligence, and gently descended to the ground.

St. Laurence would have joked at this, as he did at his own grilling. After he had lain for some time extended on his gridiron, he calmly said to the executioner, "Will you have the kindness to turn me, as I am quite done on the under side." The executioner, a trifle astonished, did as he was required, and soon after, the Saint, again speaking, said, "I shall be obliged if you'll take me up, as I am now fit for eating." This story reminds me of the remark made by an Irishman, when first told that St. Patrick had crossed the ocean on a millstone:—"I can't contradict it! He was a lucky fellow!"

We are told of St. Bernard, who used to walk before dinner on the banks of the Lake of Lausanne, that on hearing two of his monks speak of the beauty of the lake, he declared that no such lake existed, or he had been too much absorbed to have noticed it. So the Trappists used to glory in not knowing where or how they dined, or recollecting anything about it! All this shows less wisdom at table than was exhibited by the royal St. Louis, who, when a certain friar began to discuss doctrinal subjects with the pullets, stopped him with the remark that "all things had their time, and joking was good sauce with chickens!"

St. Laurence Justinian, the first patriarch of Venice, was far less indulgent than the royal saint of France. He was so little so, that when his thirsty monks asked for a little wine, declaring that their throats felt as dry as the high road in summer, he used quite as drily to remark, that if they could not bear parched throats now, what would they do in the fires of purgatory? St. John the Dwarf, Anchoret of Scete, cared as little for wine as St. Laurence, but he was fond of fruit, and he obtained a supply from a strange source. An old hermit bade him plant his walking-staff in the ground, and he not only did so, but watered it regularly for three years, when it bore pippins, sweeter than those that grew at Ribstone up to the time of the death of the late baronet. Before this miraculously-bearing stick, the little man used to read prayers as devoutly as Sir Hollyoak Goodrick, the present Ribstone baronet, does to the villagers in his own parish church, and for the same reason each had much to be thankful for. It must be confessed that John the Dwarf had more taste than his namesake of Cupertino, who not only ate nothing but vegetables, but ate no vegetables that any other human being could be induced to swallow. It was such garbage as only pigs would condescend to. *Arcades ambo*—nasty creatures both.

St. Francis of Assisium exhibited something more of true humility at his table, with a touch of the false metal notwithstanding. He ate nothing dressed by fire, unless he were very ill, and even then he covered it with ashes, or dipped it in cold water. His common daily food was dry bread strewn with ashes; but this founder of the Friars' Minors had the good sense not to condemn his followers to the rigorous diet he observed himself; and "Brother Ass," as he familiarly called that self, was in his opinion worthy of no better fare.

There was a founder of another community who exhibited more singularity than St. Francis, who, despite some mistakes, was a man of whom none other dare speak but with respect,—St. Ammon, founder of the hermitages of Nitria. At the age of twenty-two this young Egyptian noble married a fair girl of Memphis; and instead of a nuptial banquet, he treated his bride to a reading of a particularly edifying chapter from St. Paul, after which he withdrew to solitary meditation. During eighteen long years he occupied himself in training balsam-trees all day, after which he returned home to a supper of fruit and herbs; then came that terrible reiteration of advice from St. Paul, followed by a separate solitary comment on the part of this exemplary pair. At the end of the time above specified, he retired altogether from domestic life, and settled alone on Mount Nitria, and his biographers naïvely remark, this was "with his wife's consent." This saint was of such a "complexion" of virtue, that one day, on accidentally catching sight of an uncovered portion of his body, he was so shocked that he fainted away. If he had only read "Erasmus Wilson, on the Skin," he would have learned to look oftener at his own, and would have been a cleaner man, a better husband, a more grateful feeder, and an improved Christian.

But St. Bruno, the founder of the Carthusians, probably exceeded all other originators of communities in the "fierceness," so to speak, of his dietetic laws; he never spared himself nor his disciples. A Carthusian is never permitted to eat meat under any pretence whatever. In addition to this they fast eight months in the year, and I suppose they starve in Lent, for during that season they are forbidden to eat what is called "white meats," that is, eggs, milk, butter, and cheese. Dry bread with water is their Lenten fare; and a peculiar law connected with them is, that they can never change into another order, because they would thereby profit a little in the way of better living; but a brother of any other order may become a Carthusian, as thereby he increases his mortifications and diminishes his diet. Of course from these remarks the Carthusians of the "Charterhouse" are excepted. If the thin spirit of St. Bruno ever scents the juicy viands that adorn the well-spread table *there*, it probably melts into thin air by the very force of disgust or ghastly envy.

The table kept by St. Bridget, when she married Ulpho, prince of Nericia, in Sweden, was a very modest one for so princely a pair, but what was spared thereby was given to the poor. Bridget and Ulpho, she sweet sixteen, he two years more, read every evening the soothing chapter from St. Paul, which formed the favourite study of St. Ammon and his wife; but, as it would appear, with indifferent success. "They enrolled themselves," say their various biographers, "in the Third Order of St. Francis, and lived in their own house as if it had been a regular and austere monastery." The biographers immediately add without comment,—"They afterwards had eight children: four boys and four girls;" and as the same paragraph goes on to state that "all these children were favoured with the blessings of divine grace," it may be fairly concluded that a domestic observation of a monastic regularity and austerity, is a course that will purchase blessings and olive-branches.

The case of St. Gomer and his wife, the Lady Gwinmary, may perhaps be cited as an exception. But this Gwinmary was an exacting lady at all times, and when St. Gomer betook himself from her to live in the desert on bitterness and biscuits, he fared as sumptuously and lived far more quietly than he had done at home. He was one of the most placid of saints, and it is a positive libel upon him for the French Admiralty to have given his name to one of the most thundering steamers in the service. Its broadsides far more nearly resemble the tongue of Gwinmary than the tones of Gomer.

In charming contrast with this truculent Gwinmary do we meet and greet the gentle St. Elizabeth of Hungary. The record of her good deeds would fill a volume, but out of them I have only to select a table trait—to register which is also to eulogize it. I do not allude to her habitual temperance, to her dry bread and thimble-full of wine, when she sat at meat with kings and queens, her equals in birth; nor to her small feasts with her two maids, in the absence of her consort, Louis the Landgrave; but I allude—

and lister., O ye Benedicts, with grateful rapture—to the fact "that the kitchen she kept out of her own private purse, not to be the least charge to her husband." If celibate priests, who can hardly be supposed capable of appreciating such a fact, canonized so rare a lady, all married men who love banquets but dislike the butchers' bills, will cry "Well done!" and recommend their wives to read the instructive life of Eliabeth of Hungary.

Who would expect to hear good of a Borgia?—St. Francis Borgia was virtuous enough to save his family name from entire infamy. Of no other man or woman of his house could it be said that they gave up suppers, in order to have more time for prayers. It was not for Alexander VI., the papal glory of his house and the shame of mankind, that would have been content with one meal a-day, and that meal—a mess of leeks, or some pulse, with a piece of bread, and a cup of water. At the same time, Francis Borgia kept a table becoming a man of his rank, for the gratification of his guests of high degree. There, while they ate their venison, and quaffed their *lachrymæ Christi*, he nibbled his leeks, and sipped his water, "and conversed facetiously with them, though at table his discourse generally turned on piety." It was very like a Borgia to make piety facetious, but if fun in holiness be of the ingredients necessary to the making of a saint, Sidney Smith has as good a right as Borgia to be on the roll of the *beati*. Our reverend "joker of jokes," indeed, would not have smiled at the cook who put wormwood instead of mint into his broth; and I doubt if Peter Plimley ever thought of doing what Francis Borgia did,—namely, chewing his pills, and swallowing physic slowly, as works of meritorious mortification, bearing compound interest to the profit of the practitioner. St. Wilfrid, who taught the half-starved South Saxons to catch the fish that swarm at their feet, and thereby live, seems to me to have performed a far more meritorious work than if he had passed his life in gnawing leeks or masticating pills. Our native saint, a good man at table, was often better employed than St. Theresa, who is so eulogized because when serving at table, or carrying the dinner from the kitchen, "she was often seen suddenly absorbed in God, with the utensils or instruments of her business in her hands." The hungry and expectant monks might have quoted against the rapt maid, the assertion of the royal sage, that there is a time to eat, as well as to fast and pray. But St. Theresa, with all her good qualities, was as obstinate as the Polish saint Hedwiga, who not only abstained from meat till abstinence had nearly proved suicidal, but who refused to save her life by eating any, until the Pope's legate had issued a very peremptory precept to that effect. St. Peter of Alcantara lost all taste by his nearly total-abstinence principle, and when some one gave him warm water with vinegar in it, he thought it was his usual dinner of bean broth! That actively good saint, Charles Borromeo, was only wisely moderate. "His austerities were discreet," is the phrase of one of his biographers; and his abstemiousness made his health rather than marred it. This was so well known, that they who dieted themselves in order to recover or preserve health, were said to have adopted the remedy of Doctor Borromeo. St. Francis Xavier had something of the discretion of Charles Borromeo,—and of the modesty too, for he dressed his own dinners, even when he was apostolic legate; and that St. Clement of Alexandria belonged to the same class of sagely temperate men, is proved by his maintaining that a little wine taken at evening, after the labours of the day, was good for the body, and cheering for the spirits. So the sainted Archbishop of York had no repugnance to a slice of roast goose, for, as he truly remarked, so good a thing was not designed especially for sinners. And this recalls to my mind a comment, similar in spirit, made by St. Thomas à Becket. A monk once saw him eating a wing of a pheasant with much relish, and the pharisaical fellow thereon affected to be scandalized, saying that he thought Thomas was more of a mortified man. "Thou art but a ninny," said the Archbishop; "knowest thou not that a man may be a glutton upon horse-beans; while another may enjoy with refinement even the wing of a pheasant, and have nature's aid to digest what Heaven's bounty gave?"

This was good sense in the Archbishop, who perhaps had been reading Epicurus, before he sat down to his repast. However this may be, it is certain that the philosopher in question says something very like what Becket said to the friar. "Is man," he asks, " made to disdain the gifts of nature? Is he placed on earth only to gather bitter fruits? For whom then are the flowers that the gods strew at the feet of mortals?...We please Providence when we yield to the divers inclinations which Providence suggests; our duties have reference to His laws; and our innocent desires are born of His inspirations."

There are few things more common in the Lives of the Saints, than to find them, after spare banquets of their own, working penal miracles at the banquets of others. St. Eloy was gifted with terrible power in this way, and endless are the stories of revellers turned to stone by the might of his magic right arm. Other saints had equal power in turning the tables upon those who slighted them; and I will take this opportunity of narrating one instance, and I will set my muse in slippers to detail what occurred at

THE BRIDAL AND BANQUET OF FERQUES.

Near the marble quarries of Ferques, adjacent to Landrecthun le Nord, in the Boulonnais, may be seen a circular range of stones bearing a close resemblance in their shape, though little in their magnitude, to those at Stonehenge; as also to the Devil's Needles, near Boroughbridge, and to the solitary block on the common at Harrogate. Learned people recognise the stones at Ferques by the appellation of the *Mallus*, a Druidical name for an altar; but the traditionary folks, wiser in their generation, acknowledge no other title for these remains of antiquity than *Neuches*, an old provincial word, the corruption, I suppose, of *Noces*, and signifying a bridal, including the banquet which followed it. According to them, the stones at Ferques stand there as a testimony of divine vengeance, inflicted on a fiddler and other individual belongings to a wedding party who refused to kneel before the Host, as it was being borne along by a priest to a dying brother. Rabelais says, that a well-disposed and sensible man believes all that he is told; ("Un homme de bien, un homme de bon sens, croit toujours ce qu'on lui dit, et ce qu'il trouve par écrit;") and *argal*, as the logical grave-digger in *Hamlet* has it, this story of a bridal and banquet will be allowed to pass without question.

    Though around the bleak district there is not a grove
    That can boast of a shade, e'en in summer, for love,
    Nor a walk by the side of a murmuring stream,
    Where somnambulist lovers may talk as they dream;
    Nor a valley retir'd, nor sweet mossy dell,
    Where young hearts that are aching, their anguish may tell;
    Nor a wood where a maiden deserted may sigh,
    Or where youths, stripp'd of hope, may with decency die;—
    Though all it can boast be a desolate heath,
    Where 't would puzzle young Cupid to find him a wreath,—
    Yet e'en here the Idalian has furnish'd full work
    For the hearts of the youths and the maidens of Ferques.

    Of these there were two in the good days of old,
    When the hard iron heel of the baron so bold
    Ground those to the dust whom the mere chance of birth
    Had deprived of the licence to lord it on earth.
    The maid was as light and as shy as the fawn,
    Her eyes dark as night, and her brow like the dawn;
    And her lips, twice as rich and as red as the rose,
    Were more warm than the sky at a summer eve's close;
    While a music fell from them made only to bless;
    And her shape—nay! her shape I must leave you to guess.
    'T would require the power pictorial of Burke,
    To record how sublime was this beauty of Ferques.

    The swain was in manhood's first op'ning bloom,
    In doublet, slash'd hose, martial bonnet, and plume;
    And he look'd, as he walk'd 'neath the moon's silver light,
    Half hero, half mortal;—half *bourgeois*, half knight.

THE DIET OF SAINTS.

If upward he gazed into heaven's soft skies,
He saw nothing there half so soft as her eyes;
Or, at least, the young lover thus gallantly swore,
As he ran the long roll of his soft nonsense o'er,
And mincingly walk'd by the damosel's side,
The latter all fondness, the former all pride;—
With one arm round the maiden, one hand on his dirk,
Irresistibly fine look'd this gallant of Ferques.

These walkings, these gazings, the terrible sighing,
With death, or at least earnest threat'nings of dying;
These sinkings of spirit, these meltings away,
With the watchings by night and the dreamings by day,
What could such a mixture combustible bring,
But a state of incendiarism, like Swing?
When hearts are the haystack, and Love holds the torch,
'T is odds but the hay-stack will soon get a scorch.
And what else could arise from those meetings at eve,
From those flaming assertions which maidens believe,
And those vows warmly breath'd "'twixt the gloam and the murk,"*
But a bridal and banquet to gladden all Ferques?

Love's eddying current, I say it in sooth,
Ran for this young couple remarkably smooth;
For the fathers paternally look'd on each child,
While the mothers maternally wept as they smiled;
Fraternally too a whole bevy of brothers
Look'd on the alliance as fondly as mothers;
And, if the young bride had possess'd but a sister,
These lines would have told how she tenderly kiss'd her.
Suffice it to say, that there never was seen,
In valley, dale, hamlet on moorland or green,
An assembly so joyous as met at the kirk,
To view and to envy the lovers of Ferques.

For, the youthful, the aged, the ugly, the fair,
The idle, the busy, grave and gay, all were there.
Maids with prayers on their lips, for the weal of the bride,
Some who long'd for looks, some for *him* by her side,

---

* " 'Twixt the gloaming and the murk,
    When the kye comes hame."—HOGG.

And, though last, yet most certain, by no means the least,
Stood his Rev'rence, who having been bid to the feast,
Look'd as jocund and joyous, and beaming with smiles,
As the fair Cytherean, when weaving her wiles.*
For where is the priest, be he Pagan, Hindoo,
Yellow Bonze from Japan, olive sage from Loo Choo,
A Franciscan Friar, an opium-drench'd Turk,
But loves a fair feast like this banquet at Ferques?

'Twould be tedious to tell, when the service was done,
How that of the gallants was warmly begun,
How, like the old suitors in Livy's old story,
By 'Cupiditate' (his words) 'et Amore,'†
The hearts of the damsels they ruthlessly task'd,
And finally gain'd twice as much as they ask'd.
Ah, sigh not to think that in Love's stricken field,
The maidens of Ferques were so ready to yield;
For Livy declares that no maid can withstand
The wooer who comes with such arms in his hand,
They're pleasant to talk of, but 'neath them doth lurk
A peril not felt less at Rome than at Ferques.

The banquet was sped, and the floor being clear'd,
Terpsichore's summons distinctly was heard,
In the tuning Cremona that squeak'd forth its call,
Inviting all those light of foot to the ball.
Lovely dance! of thy charms how correct was the notion
Of her who the Poetry, called thee, of Motion!‡
When Beauty her features in smiles deigns to grace,
What are those same smiles but the dance of the face?
And when Dancing and Modesty happily meet,
What is Dancing just then but the smiles of the feet?§
I'd defy e'en a hermit the summons to shirk,
Ask'd a measure to tread by the beauties of Ferques.

* Φιλομμειδὴς 'Αφροδίτη.   Iliad, iii. 414.

† After "Cupiditate et Amore," Livy ungallantly adds, quæ maxime ad muliebre ingentum efficaces preces sunt."

‡ Lady Morgan, I think, calls dancing, "the Poetry of Motion."

§ "Qu'est-ce que la danse? la sourire des jambes. Qu'est-ce que la sourire? la danse du visage."—*Bibliophile Jacob.*

When moonlight has risen to silver the scene,
The party adjourn'd from the ball to the green,
And their laughter was shaking the stars in the sky,
When by chance, on the heels of their mirth, there pass'd by
A Franciscan from Boulogne, Franciscanly shod,*
Who ask'd them to kneel at the sight of their God,
Whose presence mysterious he fully reveal'd.
But the fiddler, he swore, he'd be hang'd if he kneel'd,
And affirm'd—most irreverent charge 'gainst a monk—
That the barefooted priest was decidedly drunk.
And the party applauded each quip and each quirk
That fell from this vile Paganini of Ferques.

But, oh, wonder! those ribalds their scoffs had scarce utter'd,
When, at a low prayer by the Cordelier mutter'd,
Their laughter was heard to change into a moan,
As the priest transform'd each to a figure of stone.
There motionless still do the revellers stand,
Misshapen, as turn'd from their sculptor's rough hand;
Save one, who when moonlight pours down from above,
May be seen from the spot vainly trying to move.
Some affirm 'tis the bridegroom aroused from his trance,
Some declare 'tis the bride gliding forth to the dance.
But 'tis only the fiddler endeavouring to jerk
His bow arm o'er the once magic fiddle of Ferques.

---

* The theatre at Boulogne stands on the site of the old convent garden belonging to the Cordeliers, the sea formerly flowed close to the spot. When Henry VIII. took Boulogne, he converted the convent into a marine arsenal.

THE SUPPORT OF SAINTS OF LATER DAYS.

It may be seen from our last chapter, that the bill of fare of those who dined in the desert was neither very long nor very varied. It was otherwise with the better-fed, but perhaps not better-taught gentlemen of the church of later days. Thus, for instance, the Curé of Brequier kept a very different table from that of the lean Amphitryons of the desert. Brillat Savarin once called on the holy man just as he had dismissed the soup and beef from the table. These were replaced by a leg of mutton *à la royale,* a fat capon, and a splendid salad. The hour was scarcely noon, and the curé had sat down to this saint's fare alone. He was not selfish, however, and he invited his guest to "break bread" with him, but the guest, a prince of "gastronomers" in his way, declined, and the curé, like Coriolanus, did it all alone! He finished the "gigot" to the ivory, the capon to the bones, and the salad to the polished bottom of the bowl. A colossal cheese was then placed before him, in which he made a breach of ninety degrees, and having washed down all with a bottle of wine, he, like the Irishman, thanked God "for that snack," and betook himself to digestion and repose. "Le pauvre homme!"

The nuns were in no ways behind the priests. Madame d'Arestrel, lady Abbess of the nuns of the Visitation of Belley, (*faustum nomen!*) once told a secret to a visitor who feared she was going to expound a chapter from the Prophets. "If you want a foretaste of Paradise in the guise of good chocolate," said she, "be sure to make it over-night, in an earthenware coffee-pot. Its standing still for a night concentrates it, and gives it a velvety taste, which is divine! And Heaven cannot be angry with us for this little luxury, for is not Heaven, too, divine?" How wide the distance between St. Paula, widow, and Madame d'Arestrel, of the convent of Visitation! I may add, that if the Visitandines made good chocolate, the monks of the Feuillants, in Paris, were renowned for their ratafie. But they too have superior authority for good living. A dainty dish in Italy is commonly called a mouthful for a cardinal."—*un boccone di cardinali.*

The canons took the tone from the cardinals. When the French canon Rollet became ill through excessive drinking, his doctor interdicted all strong beverages, and was not a little wroth, on his next visit, at finding the dignitary in bed indeed, but at his bed-side a little table, neatly laid out with bottles and glasses. The canon met the threatened storm by gently remarking:— "Doctor, when you forbade me drinking wine, you did not wish to deprive me of the pleasure of looking at the bottle!" It was such canons who were the best customers of the nuns who distilled liqueurs, and of the Ursulines who manufactured the daintiest drops flavoured by the daintiest essences! But in the Archbishop of Paris himself, M. de Belley, the clergy of France had example to which they might appeal as authority for indulging in good cheer. The archiepiscopal face was wreathed in smiles at the sight of a good dinner. The prelate lived to be a veteran among gastronomers, and was, in other respects, not an unworthy archbishop.

But M. de Belley was at least a gentleman in his gastronomic propensities. He was not, like a Russo-Greek "Papa," a brandy-bibber. The Russo-Greek priests sanctify drinking, in the minds of the people by their evil example. Monsieur Léverson Le Duc, a French Diplomatist in Russia, tells us that he knows of one parish in Muscovy where the people lock up their pastor every Saturday night, in order that he may not be too muzzy for mass on the Sunday. They occasionally find him very drunk, nevertheless, when they have forgotten previously to examine beneath his robe, under which the sinning sot sometimes smuggles his quart of Cognac! Sir George Simpson crossed the Pacific in a Russian vessel. The chaplain had been sent in her to sea, because he was always too drunk to officiate on land. He was kept sober expressly for the hour of service on Sundays, but at other times, he appears to have realized the verse in the old song of Dibdin's, wherein it is said that

"'T other day as our chaplain was preaching,
  Behind him I curiously slunk;
And while he our duty was teaching,
  As how we should never get drunk,
I show'd him the stuff, and he twigg'd it,
  And it soon set his Rev'rence agog.
    And he swigg'd, and Nick swigg'd,
    And Ben swigg'd, and Dick swigg'd,
    And we all of us swigg'd it,—
And we swore there was nothing like grog."

These examples, however, must be understood as occurring mostly, if not exclusively, among the lower classes of the clergy. There was a time when "the Vicar and Moses" illustrated the sad doings of a similar class among ourselves.

The Greek clergy in the South of Europe present us with something no less curious of aspect. The hall-kitchen of the Greek Patriarch, at Constantinople, is crowded with inferior clergy, who take their meals there, and his All-Holiness himself is served with pipes and sweetmeats by nothing less than gentlemen in Deacon's orders. Fancy our Lord Primate ringing his bell for cheroots for two! and having them brought in on a silver tray by the Curate of St. Margaret's!

The Greek usages however are classical. The stranger who dines with the Patriarch has, previous to falling to, water poured over his hands as he holds them over a basin with a perforated cover, and the napkins for drying them are as delicate as rose-leaves. The guest reclines on a low couch, in ancient fashion, and his repast is placed on a low stool at his side. The same custom exists in the convents, but meat is seldom to be found there by a guest who arrives unexpectedly. The monks themselves never eat it at all. During half the year they have but one meal a-day, and that consists of vegetables and bread. On the other days of the year they are permitted the more liberal, but sufficiently eremitic fare of cheese, eggs, fish, wine, and milk; but even on these gala days they are never allowed more than two meals. Poor fellows! the majority of them pass their remarkably well-spent time, when not at table, in tilling the ground or teaching wonderful feats to very accomplished tom-cats!

A Greek monk's idea of an Englishman is that he is a plum-pudding eater. And no wonder, since the English are almost the exclusive purchasers of the currant-grapes which are cultivated all along the northern shores of the Peloponnesus, from Patra to Corinth. As the Chinese think that we take their tea that we may live, so the Greek monks conclude that we *must* buy their currants, or die! At the convent of Vestizza, the good fathers trouble their heads about nothing but the produce and price of their great staple crop. If you ask how many brethren there are in the convent, they will answer, "Three hundred; and what was the price of currants in England when you left?" Inquire if their books be in good order, and they will reply in the negative, adding an assurance that they do their utmost to produce the best currants in the country. And they will give you permission to see their church, if you will only promise to recommend their dwarf grapes to the English merchants who are catering for plum-pudding eaters at home. The grounds of other convents in the peninsula are famous for their nuts, in the exportation of which the brethren drive no inconsiderable trade.

These worthy people are said to be a trifle more enlightened and a degree less slothful than they were some thirty years ago. There was ample room and verge enough for improvement; for at the period mentioned, the Greek priests resisted the introduction of the potato into the kitchen-garden, for the very satisfactory reason that the *pomme de terre* was the very identical apple with which Satan beguiled Eve out of Paradise! Yes, these modern and orthodox saints very generally held that the devil tempted Eve with an "ash-leaf kidney!"

If we cross over to Abyssinia, we shall find that the priests and orthodox people there keep as poor tables, at least on feast days, as the Greeks. Above eight months in the year are assigned by the Abyssinian Christians to abstinence! On these occasions an Abyssinian neither eats nor drinks till long after noon. On festival days, however, they make up for their moderation by unrestrained excess. Mr. Mansfield Perkyns, a traveller who had given us the most recent account of life in Abyssinia, tells us that, in honour of the festival of the Elevation of the Cross, he gave an early breakfast to some dozen guests, who were engaged to half-a-dozen other parties in the course of the same joyous day, and that these guests whetted their appetite for later meals by consuming at breakfast a fine fat cow, two large sheep, and endless gallons of mead! On these occasions the mead is pretty prolific of murder. The guests get dreadfully drunk in honour of the day, exactly as many highly civilized Christian people in happy England do on the yearly recurrence of "merry Christmas." Indeed, a feast of the Elevation of the Cross without plenty of quarrelling and bloodshed would be as dull as Donnybrook fair now is without a row. But the Abyssinian Christian is as clever in establishing a *casus belli* as a Donnybrook Romanist. If the latter sees the fair is likely to end without a fight, he simply takes off his hat, draws a white line round it with chalk, and declaring that he will break the head of the first man who denies that such white line is silver lace, he has speedily abundance of active work before him. So a pious Abyssinian at an "Elevation" banquet, if he finds things dull, merely remarks to his dearest friend and next neighbour, "You are a good sort of man, but you are not so handsome as I am!" and thereupon out fly the knives of the parties and their respective friends, which they proceed to clean by plunging them into each other's ribs!

The people are brought up on a food likely to encourage such pugnacious propensities. Mr. Perkyns, speaking of the slaughtering of oxen for the kitchen, says:—" Almost before the death-struggle is over, persons are ready to flay the carcase, and pieces of the raw meat are cut off, and served up before this operation is completed. In fact, as each part presents itself, it is cut off and eaten while yet warm and quivering. In this state it is considered and justly so, to be very superior in taste to what it is when cold. Raw meat, if kept a little time, gets tough; whereas, if eaten fresh and warm, it is far tenderer than the most tender joint that has been hung a week in England. The taste is perhaps, in imagination, rather disagreeable at first, but far otherwise when one gets accustomed to it; and I can readily believe that raw meat would be preferred to cooked meat, by a man who from childhood had been accustomed to it." Such fare, I may observe, may not be out of place at the table of a patriarch who lives in such a climate as that of Abyssinia, but we suspect that it would as much astonish a dinner party at an episcopal palace in England, as Mr. Perkyns himself would do were he to sit down to that dinner in his ordinary Abyssinian fashion of—a bald head covered with butter!

I have spoken in another chapter of a Brahmin who stuffed himself with sweetmeats until he was nearly suffocated, and who exclaimed, on being recommended to swallow a little water, that if he had room for water he would have swallowed more sweetmeats! It is but justice, however, to these saintly gentlemen to confess that they *can* fast when there is anything to be gained by it. Among the Mahrattas, when a fast man attempts to cheat his creditors, a Brahmin is hired to sit the *dhurna*, and this is the process—a process, by the way, which Monsieur Dimanche tried on Don Juan, but unsuccessfully. The Brahmin goes to the house or tent of the debtor, sometimes attended by numerous followers, and he announces the *dhurna*, by which the debtor must not eat until he has discharged his liabilities. The clerical bailiff sits at his side and is bound to fast also, until the matter is arranged. He who holds out longest wins the day, and if the debtor be famished he will pay rather than die outright, for eat he dare not until his creditor be satisfied; besides if he were to starve the Brahmin to death, the crime would be so heinous, that the debtor himself had better have departed to the world of shadows. It ensues that sitting *dhurna* is more successful in certain districts than it would be in Belgravia, even though the Archbishop of Canterbury himself were to take his seat in the middle of the square, with a declaration that he would neither move nor eat until every inhabitant in the parish had paid his Christmas bills. Poor man! he would have to sit as long as *infelix Theseus*.

The saints of our puritan days were great favourers of public fasts; but these fasts were less numerous after they had consolidated their power, than before. "In the beginning of the wars," says Foulis, in his "History of the wicked Plots of the pretended Saints," "a public monthly fast was appointed for the last Wednesday of every month, but no sooner had they got the king upon the scaffold, and the nation fully secured to the Rump interest, but they thought it needless to abuse and gall the people with a multitude of prayers and sermons, and so, by a particular act of their worships (April 23, 1649), nulled the proclamation for the observation of the former; all which verifieth the old verses:—

"'The devil was sick, the devil a monk would be.
The devil was well, the devil a monk was he.'"

George Fox, the father of the Quakers, remarks in his Journal, of the Puritans and their fasts:—"Both in the time of the Long Parliament, and of the Protector, so called, and of the Committee of Safety, when they proclaimed fasts, they were commonly like Jezebels, and there was some mischief to be done." Taylor, the Water-poet, compares their fasts to hidden feasts. "They were like the holy maid," he says, "that enjoined herself to abstain four days from any meat whatsoever; and being locked close up in a room, she had nothing but her two books to feed upon; but the two books were two painted boxes, made in the form of great Bibles, with clasps and bosses, the inside not having one word of God in them; but the one was filled with sweetmeats, the other with wine; upon which this devout votary did fast with zealous meditation, eating up the contents of one book, and drinking as contentedly the other." Dr. South, in his Sermons, is equally severe. He observes that "their fasts usually lasted from seven in the morning till seven at night; the pulpit was always the emptiest thing in the church; and there never was such a fast kept by them, but their hearers had cause to begin a thanksgiving as soon as they had done." Butler, in his Hudibras, hints that the work of fasting was to be accounted to the faster, righteousness:—

> "For 't is not now who 's stout and bold,
> But who bears hunger best and cold.
> And he 's approved the most deserving,
> Who longest can hold out at starving."

The fasting of the civilians, however, was made to turn to the benefit of the military gentlemen; and, in March, 1644, an ordinance was passed for the contribution of one meal a week towards the charge of the army. There was by far a more considerable liberality of spirit among some of the clergy of the time of Louis XIV. than in the Puritan authorities, inasmuch as they permitted others to follow clerical example rather than precept. The celebrated preacher, Father Feuillot, for instance, stood by while "Monsieur" was enjoying an uncanonical collation in the middle of Lent. His Highness held up a *macaron*, and remarked, "This is not breaking fast, is it?" "Nay," said Feuillot, "you may eat a calf, if you will only act like a Christian." I am afraid that we had not improved at home, in the last century. On one of the fasts of that period, Walpole comments after his usual gay fashion. "Between the French and the earthquakes," he says, in 1756, "you have no notion how good we are grown; nobody makes a suit of clothes now but of sackcloth, turned up with ashes. The fast was kept so devoutly, that Dick Edgecumbe, finding a very lean hazard at White's, said with a sigh, 'Lord! how the times are degenerated! Formerly, a fast would have brought everybody hither; now it keeps everybody away!' A few nights before, two men were walking up the Strand, one said to t' other, 'Look how red the sky is! Well, thank God, there is to be no masquerade!'"

An ex-Capuchin has revealed some of the mysteries of the house of which he was lately a member, and by this it would appear that the Friars of the nineteenth century are as little for slender diet as the fine gentlemen of the eighteenth. "These

Capuchins," he says, "of squalid appearance, clothed in serge, with shaven heads and bare feet, presenting the very type of humility and self-renunciation, enjoy the luxuries of life with a prodigality unknown to you. The poor friars have, with one exception, no enjoyment of the things of this world, their only worldly comfort is good cheer. The friars have three carnivals in the year, of two or three weeks' duration each. These are the only periods at which they can recruit their wasted strength, to enable them to resist the mortifications of the rest of the year. During these few weeks they have seven courses served at dinner, all substantial and choice dishes, the most dainty morsels that can be provided. At supper they have five courses. By that hour, in spite of their plentiful dinner, they have regained their appetites; and their digestion is again most active. These courses are as substantial as those of the dinner, and are despatched with equal facility by these men of iron frame and tranquil conscience. . . . *Lent* is arrived! Well, you must fast, you must mortify the flesh, but you must not die of inanition. A good table is necessary, or you will suffer too much from contrast with the past few weeks. You need double the supply that the secular orders do when they fast, for your digestion is twice as active as theirs. Supper is now a sadly scanty meal; it consists simply of fish, bread, wine, and fruit. A miserable dish! not miserable as to quantity or quality, but because it is the solitary dish during the forty days of Lent, always excepting bread and wine *ad libitum*. Fortunately, the Friars are wise and provident; the slender supper is foreseen and provided against at dinner, which consists of four dishes. The bottle of good wine is valuable now, or they would be overcome with weakness." Such is the testimony of a living witness, who pledges his reputation for the truth of his depositions.

I do not know that there is much that is exaggerated in this, for from Mr. Saurin, we hear that, in France, well-to-do priests mortify the flesh on maigre days by very pretty eating. The bill of fare of those saintly men has been known to include soup *au coulis d'écrevisse,* salmon-trout, an omelette *au Thon,* that would have called a dead *gastronome* to life; a salad, the very smell of which seemed to give eternal youth; Semonal cheese, fruit, confectionary, a light wine, and a cup of coffee. By such self-denial is heaven gained by modern saints, in orders; having fair fortunes, and looks with the same characteristic.

The Dominicans of Italy are in no degree behind their brethren in France. The late "prior and visitor of the order," who recently published his dealings with the Inquisition, thus describes his ancient brethren. "They do nothing," he says, "which they are bound to do by their rules, if these are opposed to their inclinations. They profess never to eat meat in the refectory, or room for their common meals; but there is another room near it, which they call by another name, where they eat meat constantly. On Good Friday, they are commanded by their rules to eat bread and drink water. At the dinner hour they all go together into the refectory, to eat bread and drink water, but having done so for the sake of appearance, they go one after another into another room where a good dinner is prepared for them all. I do not blame them for enjoying it; but I blame them for feigning an abstinence which none of them intend to keep." These Dominicans, honest fellows! are more hungry than the gods of the old regime of whom it is said,—

> "The Gods require the thighs
> Of beeves for sacrifice;
> Which roasted, we the steam
> Must sacrifice to them,
> Who, though they do not eat,
> Yet love the smell of meat."

But our poor friend the monk has witnesses in his favour, as well as opposed to him. Some men call him a living mummy swathed in faith. Another says he is "a moral gladiator who wrestles with his passions, and either stifles them or is devoured by them." A third describes him picturesquely as a sea-worthy vessel moored in a stagnant dock; and a fourth dismisses him contemptuously as a coward who won't fight. Even allowing him to be all these, it does not follow that he is to be deprived of his dinner. If *he* pays homage with his body to the saints, he has earned what is called the mind's daily homage to the body. Dinner should be the peculiar privilege of the monk, for it is as *he* is, in some sense, "the open friend of poverty, the secret foe of riches;" and if dinner be "the breakfast of the poor and the supper of the rich," it is doubly due to the monk, who can claim it by either title. And it must not be supposed that they do not know how to enjoy pleasure like sensible men. The Abbé of St. Sulpice, a Bernardine monastery in the south of France, once invited a party of merry and musical gentlemen from the neighbouring town to come up to the monastery, and give the monks a treat of good music on the *fête* day of their patron saint. A joyous company ascended at early dawn to the monastery; the most remarkable incident connected with which is, that it is seated at the edge of a pine forest, from which a hurricane swept down, in one night, thirty-seven thousand trees. The visitors were received by the cellarer, the abbé not being yet risen, who conducted them to the refectory, where they found awaiting them a paté as big as a church; flanked on the north by a quarter of cold veal; on the south, by a monster ham; on the east by a monumental pile of butter; and on the west by a bushel of artichokes *à la poivrade*. All the necessary adjuncts were at hand; and among others, a party of lay brethren ready to wait upon the visitors, and very much astonished to find themselves out of bed at so early an hour. An array of a hundred bottles of wine bespoke the fathers' idea of good cheer; and the cellarer, having bidden them fall-to and welcome, deplored his inability to join them, not having yet said mass,—and he then took his leave to go and sing "matins."

The breakfast was done ample justice to; after which the visitors retired to take a short repose, subsequently repairing to the church, where they performed a musical service with the usual zeal and energy of amateurs, and received modestly the showers of thanks that descended upon them in return.

Monks and musicians then sat down to a dinner,—ample, admirably cooked, excellently served, and thoroughly enjoyed. The abundance that marked it may be judged of by the fact, that at the second course there were not less than fifteen dishes of roasted meats. The dessert would have made the eyes of a queen sparkle; the liqueurs were choice, and the coffee redolent of Araby the Blest. The enjoyment was long and perfect; and by the end of the repast, there was not a man or monk present who was not in charity with all the world. The "pious, glorious, and immortal memory" of St. Bernard was not forgotten among the toasts.

And then came vespers and more amateur music,—probably more vigorously performed than in the morning. And after vespers there was a division of pleasures: some took to quiet games at cards, some chose a ramble in the wood, and a few looked in again upon their friend the cellarer. As night came on, all again drew together, but the discreet abbot retired, willing to allow the brethren full liberty on a festival which only came "once a year." And to do the brothers justice, they began to make a night of it as soon as the superior had disappeared. Jokes and laughter and winged words flew about like wild-fire, and the exercise got thereby sharpened the general appetite for supper,—a repast which was discussed with a vivacity as if the guest had been fasting up to that very hour. Wit and wine, and wisdom and folly, were all mingled together; and the oldest of the fathers present, with a flush on the cheek and a light in the eye, joined *chorus* in table songs that were *not* sung to the tune of *Nunc dimittis*. It was when the fun was flying most fast and furious, that a voice exclaimed, "Brother cellarer, where is your official dish?" "True!" answered that reverend individual; "I am not a cellarer for nothing;"—and therewith he disappeared, but speedily returned accompanied by three servitors, bearing piles of buttered toast and bowls of what worldly men would have called "punch." If the fun had waxed fast before, it grew fiery now, and fervour for the patron saint glowed at the very fiercest heat that punch could give it. In the midst of it all, the hour of midnight was solemnly tolled out by the convent bell, and the revellers, reverend and laic, swang merrily to bed, satisfied with the day well spent in honour of St. Bernard.

I have now spoken of the Dominicans, Capuchins, and Bernardins. The Franciscans are a not less lively fraternity. When the author of Eöthen was at the Franciscan Monastery in Damascus, he asked one of the monks to tell what places were best worth seeing, in reference to their association with St. Paul. "There is nothing in all Damascus," said the good man, "half so well worth seeing as our cellars;" and forthwith he invited the stranger to "go and admire the long range of liquid treasures that he and his brethren had laid up for themselves upon earth." And, adds the author, "these I soon found were not as the treasures of the miser, that lie in unprofitable disuse; for day by day, and hour by hour, the golden juice ascended from the dark recesses of the cellar to the uppermost brains of the friars, dear old fellows! In the midst of that solemn land, their Christian laughter rang loud and merrily. Their eyes kept flashing with joyous bonfires, and their heavy woollen petticoats could no more weigh down the springiness of their paces, than the filmy gauze of a *danseuse* can cloy her bounding step."

Richard the First, as worthless a human being as ever lived, bankrupt in every virtue save that of brute courage, in making a legacy of his vices, said he would bequeath gluttony to the priests. It was rather a compliment than otherwise, for the inference was, that they lacked what they were willing to surrender, when he could no longer enjoy it. St. Augustin settled this vexed question as to what was "good living," when he said, that "the great fast was abstinence from vice." And in the true spirit of St. Augustin's prose, rings the **rich rhyme in Herrick's Noble Numbers.** "Is this," he says,

> "Is this a fast to keep
>   The larder leane
>   And cleane
> From fat of veales and sheep?
>
> "Is it to quit the dish
>   Of flesh, yet still
>   To fill
> The platter high with fish?
>
> "Is it to faste an houre?
>   Or ragged to go,
>   Or show
> A downcast look, and soure?
>
> "No; 'tis a fast, to dole
>   Thy sheaf of wheat,
>   And meat,
> Unto the hungry soule.
>
> "It is to fast from strife,
>   From old debate,
>   And hate;
> To circumcise thy life.
>
> "To show a heart grief-rent,
>   To starve thy sin,
>   Not bin:
> And that's to keep thy Lent."

This is better philosophy than that given on a similar subject by Montesquieu, who only recommends moderation on the ground that it lengthens the term of enjoyment. "I call moderation," says Pythagoras, "all that does not engender pain;" and by the maxim of the Hellenized Hindoo, Buddha Ghooros, the saints both of the desert and the dining-room may, perhaps, in their several ways be condemned.

In treating of the diet of more modern saints than those of the days of martyrdom, I might have noticed the fact, that in not very remote times, the parsonage-house at Langdale, in Westmoreland, was licensed as an ale-house, the living being too poor to allow the incumbent to make anything like one upon it for himself. The ale-cask became to the priest, what the fruit of the amrite tree was to the Tibetians—the spring of life. This Westmoreland ale was accounted a great strengthener, but so have many less likely things. But enough of the "saints," good men and true the majority of them, earning their right to enjoy the rich blessings of God, by fairer means, perhaps, than many of their censurers. I know no set of men so well to contrast with the saints, as the "Cæsars," and we have yet time before supper to attend that august company to table.

THE CÆSARS AT TABLE.

It s a well-ascertained truth, that the Cæsars at table by no means generally conducted themselves as though they were under the influence of a Roman Chesterfield, as regarded their behaviour; or a Roman Abernethy, as regarded their moderation. Perhaps the great Julius was as much of a gentleman in both the above respects as any of his imperial successors; and even he could reform the calendar with far more eae than he could reform himself.

When he was commanding in the Roman provinces, beyond the Italian frontier, he kept two distinct tables. At one sat his inferior officers and the Greeks who were in his service. The latter do not appear to have epresse d any discontent at not ranking with their Roman comrades. At the other table sat none but Romans of high state, with such native guests of quality as Cæsar chose to invite to meet them. He would watch his servants as sharply as he did the enemy; and on one occasion, having observed that his baker had put down to his guests a coarser bread than that which he had served to Cæsar, he sent the knave to prison, there to learn better manners.

Cæsar was as sober as Sir Charles Napier, who used to sign himself "Governor of Scinde, because I was always a sober man." Cato said of Julius, that he was the only sober man who had ever attempted to subvert a government: "a cutting sarcasm on all preceding patriots." As for sauces, the Duke of Wellington did not inspire Francatelli with more despair upon that head, than Cæsar did *his* cook. It was immaterial to him whether he had sauce to his meat, or not; and as to the quality, he never concerned himself about it. He ate, thankfully perhaps, but thoughtlessly, certainly. His politeness was sometimes ridiculously excessive, as when he ate up the ointment which had been served up instead of sauce, at a table where he was a guest, and where he was courteously resolved to find everything excellent. But although the great Julius was, according to Cato, the only man who came sober to the subversion of his country, he had some unsoberly habits about him. Thus, when invited to a feast, he used to whet his appetite by taking an emetic. This is attested by Cicero, who says, in his letters to Atticus, (lib. xiii. p. 52,) "Unctus est; accubuit; ἐμετικήν agebat. Itaque edit et bibit ἀδεῶς et jucunde." Suetonius agrees with Cato, that Cæsar was moderate with regard to wine :—" Vini parcissimum ne quidem inimici negaverunt."

It is singular that a man who cared so little as he was reported to have done for his stomach, should have cared so much about the outside of his head. He could eat pomatum, and yet be ashamed of the baldness which a proper application of the unguent might perhaps have cured.

Augustus Cæsar, who visited prisoners, like Howard, and cut off heads like an Algerine Dey, was moderate in his cups, and endeavoured to make the people so. When the latter once complained that wine was not only dear, but scarce, he gravely proclaimed that his son-in-law Agrippa had been looking to the aqueducts, and there was no fear of any one dying of thirst.

There were seasons, however, when he could be more than imperially extravagant. Witness the little supper he gave to chosen guests, all of whom attended in the attire of gods and goddesses; and at which feast he presided in the character of Apollo. The wits of the day, who were not invited, denounced this supper as an orgy at which decent people would not have been present, even if asked. Such stupendous iniquity was said there to have been enacted, that the real gods who had at first looked laughingly down from Olympus, withdrew one by one behind their respective clouds. Even Jove himself, who sat gazing longest, at length hurried away from the sight of men, who were greater beasts than the privileged gods!

Like some of the extravagant and unclean banquets at Versailles, this entertainment was given when there was a famine in the city. On the following day, the people exclaimed in the streets, "It is the gods who have devoured the food." The less fearful than these raised an altar to Augustus Phœbus, and there paid mock worship to the Emperor, under the title of Apollo the Tormentor.

It was not every one that deemed himself entitled, that could find access to the table of Cæsar Augustus. He was extremely nice with regard to his associates, but he was not so nice with respect to keeping his guests waiting for his company. It was the maxim of Sir Joshua Reynolds, that it was far less courteous on principle to allow hungry guests to be kept from table out of respect to one man, than it was to go to dinner without him. So also Augustus thought that the many should not be made to wait for one; and, accordingly, he frequently did not appear at table till the repast was half over; and sometimes departed even then, after tasting of from three to half-a-dozen dishes, before it was concluded.

He was dignified and condescending, enjoyed the jokes of those who were bold enough to make them, and encouraged the reserved to be bold and jocund too. When jests lacked from either of those parties, the master of the Roman world then laughed, as he sipped his moderate draught, at the quips and cranks of the hired jesters, whose office it was to be cheerful when the guests grew dull.

It has come down to us that he was a lover of brown bread, small fish, green cheese and green figs. He was so far intemperate that he would never let his appetite tarry till meal-time. He ate when he was hungry, and perhaps he was right. And yet it was but an unedifying sight to see him passing in his chariot through the public streets, returning the greetings of the people with one hand full of bread, the other full of dates, and his almost sacred mouth full of both. He was, in fact, wayward in his attentions to his appetite, and would occasionally fast till sunset if the caprice took him. As to what is said of him that he sometimes rose from the most sumptuous banquets, leaving the viands untouched,— this was perhaps because the edge of his appetite had been altogether destroyed by brown bread and indigestible fruit.

In the day-time he quenched his thirst by eating of bread dipped in water, by drinking water itself, or by taking a slice of cucumber, lettuce, or unripe apple. His moderation in drinking, when he *did* take up the goblet at the evening repast, is much spoken of, but as we hear more of the quantity than of the strength of what he drank, it is difficult to decide upon this point. Suetonius admiringly records that " he never exceeded a quart for his share, or if he did, he was sure to throw it up again." This is but equivocal praise after all. He was a very great man, no doubt, but, demi-god as he almost was, he spelt after the " cacological" fashion of Lord Duberly; and he was more afraid of lying awake in the dark than any little baron or squire in the nurseries of Belgravia and the adjacent squares.

Tiberius, like his predecessor, treated his soldiers occasionally like schoolboys, and when they displeased him, he used to put them on a regimen of barley. Tiberius himself was not a profuse eater; he was rather moderate than otherwise, and when gastronomic extravagancy had reached a high pitch in Rome, he used to dine in public, like the kings of France, but, unlike them, upon cold meat, as a reproof to the luxury of the times. He was not, however, at all moderate in his cups, and the Roman wits, who, like those of Paris, used to make merry epigrams on the worst of their woes, punningly transformed his names of Tiberius Claudius Nero, into *Biberius Caldius Mero.* He had a reverence too for great draughts, and he once raised a common fellow to the office of quæstor, simply because he could drink off a measure of three pints of wine without drawing breath. Most of the Cæsars must have been very unsatisfactory people to dine with, but none more so than Tiberius, who loved discussion, but if he found himself worsted in it, he invariably ordered his opponent to retire—and commit suicide. A hot bath and a vein or two opened soon disposed of an inconvenient adversary. He used to puzzle his guests with all sorts of strange questions, such as would puzzle even the editor of *Notes and Queries* to answer. One of these interrogatory puzzles was "the name of the song chanted by the Syrens." He would not speak the fashionable Greek at table, but conversed in Latin; and his favourite feat at dessert was to run his forefinger through a hard green apple.

Caligula must have been a most unpleasant person to dine with. He entertained himself and his guests with the sight of men tortured on the rack, and he got up little private executions on those occasions to enliven the scene. We read of her Majesty's private concerts, and how "Mrs. Anderson" presided at the piano. But the Romans only heard of their Emperor's killing fun to frighten his guests with, and how his Divinity's private headsman, Niger Barbatus, performed, as usual, with his well-known dexterity. His frolics were really of a frightful character. It was after a banquet, when the capital jest of slaying had failed to make him as merry as usual, that he rushed to the sacrificial altar, attired in the dress of a victim-killer, that is, with a linen apron for his sole costume. He seized the mallet as though he were about to slay the appointed victim, but he turned suddenly round on the resident official and butchered him instead. And thereat, all who had witnessed the frolicsome deed of their master declared that "'Fore Jove, 't was a more capital joke than the last!" His answer to the Consuls who ventured to ask the cause of a sudden burst of laughter in which he indulged at a crowded feast is well known; "I laugh to think," said the amiable creature, "that with one wave of my hand I can sweep all your stupid heads off!" His method of loving was equally characteristic. He would fling his terrible arm round the fair neck he professed to admire, and express his delight that he could cut it off when he pleased. There was the brilliant Cesonia; "I cannot tell," said her imperial lover at a feast, "why it is that I am so fond of that girl. I'll have her put on the rack for a quarter of an hour, that she may be compelled to tell me the reason." Blue Beard was the mildest of Quaker gentlemen compared with this Caligula. A lady might as well have been wooed by a boa constrictor.

Claudius Cæsar has hardly had justice done him, as regards his general character, but as my office is only to show how he looked at table, I must be satisfied with making the remark, and pass on to Cæsar at meat. He was no hero, undoubtedly, for he contemplated suicide, for no better reason than having a pain in his stomach after a repast. In this, however, he did not show less courage than Zeno, the father of the Stoics, who having bruised his finger by a fall, went home and hung himself.

He was largely hospitable, and sometimes entertained six hundred guests at a time. He liked on these occasions to see his own children and those of the nobility seated, according to the ancient fashion, at the lower end of the table. It is to be hoped that they were out of ear-shot of what was being said at the upper end. The jokes were sometimes pleasant enough in their way. Thus a Roman nobleman having carried home with him a gold plate from the imperial table, was gently reminded of this theft when, on the next occasion of dining with Claudius, he saw a reproachfully vulgar earthenware platter put down before him.

He was a man of infinite capacity, was the divine Claudius,— that is, in gastronomic matters. He was ever ready to devour, and always did so greedily. He has been known to have suddenly jumped down from his seat in the forum, allured by the smell of roast meat issuing from the priest's table, in the adjacent temple of Mars. And he would sit down with the reverend gentleman, without waiting for an invitation. It must have surely made the common-place spectators of the feat broadly smile, just as if the twelve judges in Westminster Hall were to leap from their benches, and racing across the churchyard, pour into the first house in the cloisters where the dinner bell was ringing loudest, and the prandial odour was most savoury.

He ate like Baal, and drank like the beast in Fortunatus. He did both to repletion; but his attendants would then tickle his throat with a feather, and so, by exonerating his stomach, enable the imperial animal to eat and drink again. He contemplated making a decree for the benefit of guests at table, which was of a Rabelaisian indelicacy, and which probably never presented itself to the minds of any other men but Claudius and the Curé of Meudon.

Caligula had more affection for his horse than for anything human. He fed him on gilded oats, and the animal was not a more beastly consul than many who were appointed to that high office. The emperor's dinner parties must have presented a strange aspect, when the obsequious senators stood, napkin in hand, to wait upon the guests. Fancy the peers of all the politics, and the commons of every shade of opinion, all ranged behind the dinner-table at Windsor Castle, in the professional uniform of dingy white waistcoats and napless black coats, with their thumbs duly doubled up in napkins, and all offering anxious service, and "dindon à la daube" to our Sovereign Lady and her guests,—fancy this, I say, and you will have the very remotest idea possible of what the sight was like when the senators changed the plates of Cæsar. The personages and their qualities are all different, but the strangeness of one spectacle could only be matched by that of the other.

Nero (who found sport in sitting in an upper gallery at the theatre, and flinging down nuts upon the bald head of the prætor below) was a very common-place individual at table, but he assembled guests about him who were ever ready to consume his good things and applaud his good sayings. Galba, his successor, was at once gouty and gluttonous. He commenced eating at early dawn, and darkness came over him still with appetite unsatiated. He was as mean, however, as he was voracious. He did once so far whip up his liberal spirit as to compel himself to give a dinner-party; but when he read the bill of fare, he fairly burst into tears at the idea of the extravagance and the expense. And yet the most costly dish he could reprovingly point to, when his steward challenged him, was a dish of boiled peas; but perhaps they were out of season, and Galba knew he should be asked for them at least a guinea a quart! *He* would never have been guilty of the prodigality of the Emperor Otho, who daily wasted more bread and milk in making cosmetic poultices to lay on his face than would have served to keep body and soul together in half-a dozen families. The father of Vitellius more gallantly, when he wished to look well at the centre of his table, was wont to besmear himself with a mixture made up of honey and his mistress's saliva. He of course deemed it impossible to say which was the sweeter of the two ingredients. This was even worse than Galba, who was, however, essentially greedy; the latter emperor could not eat with pleasure unless he had more before him than he could digest. When his stomach cried, "Hold, enough!" he used it as the Somersetshire lad did *his*. "Ah!" exclaimed the lad of Wincanton, to certain monitions,—" ye may ake, but, 'vor I ha' done, I'll make ye ake worser." Galba, when no longer able to eat, lay and gazed at what he hoped to attack more successfully after digestion had been accomplished.

Otho is remembered as being the complaisant gentleman who, when Nero had determined to murder his mother, gave an exquisite little supper to both parties by way of a pleasant preliminary. But Otho could at least behave with outward decency, and of this Vitellius was incapable. If he walked through the market-place, he snatched the meat roasting at the cooks' stalls, and greedily devoured it. He was not more reverent even in the temple; where, taking advantage of his vicinity to the altar, he would sweep the latter of the barley that was on it, consecrated to the god, and swallow the same, like the sacrilegious heathen that he was. When about to fly from the enemies who had overturned his throne, he selected only his cook and his butler to be the companions of his flight, and he took the former dear associate with him, in his own covered chair.

The chief table trait which I can call to mind as connected with Vespasian is, that once a month he went without dinner for a day. Such an observance, he said, saved at once his health and his purse. He had so much the less to pay to his purveyor; and in consequence of the fast, less also perhaps than if he had feasted, to his physician. Both the sons of Vespasian, Titus and Domitian, were modest at the banquet. The former had ceased to be a free liver before he put on the imperial mantle; and as for Domitian, he could wash down his Malian apple with a draught of water, and then address himself to sleep, as though he were a virtuous anchorite, and not the most thirsty drinker of human blood that ever disgraced his race.

The five succeeding emperors,—Nerva, Trajan, Hadrian, and the two Antonines,—Antoninus Pius, and Marcus Aurelius,—governed the world during the eighty years which are said, but questionably, I think, to have been the happiest years of the human race. There is little on record as to how these potentates disported themselves at table. Trajan, indeed, is known to have been a fearful drinker; but he loved a quiet, unceremonious dinner, at the house of a friend of modest degree—for there he tippled and talked to his heart's content, and willingly forgot that he was Cæsar. Hadrian is remembered as the first Roman emperor who wore a beard. He had warts on his throat, and he did not like that these should be seen by his guests at table. He once gave an entertainment which cost upwards of two millions sterling, (when Verus was made Cæsar,) and he was sorry for it through the remainder of his life. Many a man of far humbler degree has committed the same kind of extravagance, and experienced the same enduring repentance. Antoninus kept the table of a country gentleman; and Marcus Aurelius dined alone, while Commodus, his son, played at his knee. The board of that son resembled that of Vitellius, and he fell from it one day, full of drugged wine administered to him by a concubine, and was strangled as he lay beneath the table, drunk, and deserving of his fate.

The modest Pertinax was less happy as emperor than when, as a simple official, he had charge of the provisions of Rome. Didius Julianus was deep in the luxuries of the table, and not nearly so deep in wisdom, when he made a bid for the diadem, a few uneasy dinners in the palace, and death. Septimius Severus, cared less for the splendour of his table than the consolidation of his power, but his banquets were choice things, nevertheless.

His sons, Caracalla and Geta, exemplified their fraternal unanimity by keeping different tables. They never sat down together at the same board; and there were two factions in the court, something like that of George the Second, at St. James's, and the son whom he hated, Frederick, Prince of Wales, in Leicester Square. Macrinus was a coarse feeder, and in everything he presented a remarkable contrast with his successor Heliogabalus.

Heliogabalus lay on couches stuffed with hare's down, or partridge feathers. Ælius Verus reclined on couches of lily and rose-leaves. The first-named monster had his funny moments; and sometimes he would invite a certain number of bald men, or of gouty men, or grey-headed men, and he was particularly amused at a company of fat men, so crowded together that they could find room only to perspire. "One of his favourite diversions consisted in filling a leathern table-couch with air instead of wool; and while the guests were engaged in drinking, a tap, concealed under the carpet, was opened, unknown to them,—the couch sank, and the drinkers rolled pell-mell under the sigma, to the great delight of the beardless emperor." He was the first Roman emperor who wore garments of pure, unmixed silk. He cared little for poets or philosophers; but he gave liberal premiums to the inventors of new sauces, provided these pleased his palate. If he disliked them, the inventor was condemned to eat of nothing else, until he had discovered a new condiment to win the imperial sanction. Heliogabalus and George I. had this in common, that they both liked fish a trifle stale. Thus, it is known that George never cared for oysters till their shells began spontaneously to gape; and the Oriental master of the Roman empire, who made a barber præfect of the provisions, would never eat sea-fish except at a great distance from the sea, when they acquired the taint he loved. His delight then was to distribute vast quantities of the rarest sorts, brought at an immense expense, to the peasants of the inland country. The table of his successor, Alexander Severus, was that of a gentleman. Its master was the first Roman emperor to whom that title can be incontestably given; and he loved to have around him accomplished guests of of all varieties of opinion; and this is much more than can be said for that huge and hungry Goth, Maximin. The Gordians brought back some of the elegances of social life, which the uncleanness and severity of Maximin had banished; but at both the private and public, the humble and the imperial, tables of Rome, there must have been small ceremony and permanent fear during the brief and troubled reigns of the foolish men who purchased the right of dining in an imperial mantle by being speedily enveloped in a bloody shroud. Gallienus, alone, shines out upon the list as the very prince of cooks; and if Carême had possessed half the enthusiasm which he so warmly affected, he would have named his son and heir after this imperial inventor of *ragoûts*,—who was also the accelerator of the ruin of Rome. All the temperance of the Gothic Claudius could not restore the remnant of ancient moderation, which had been destroyed by that imperial maker of stews, the ever hungry and cruel Gallienus. Aurelian failed, like Claudius, but the emperor Tacitus was more successful, and the descendant of the great historian, even during *his* short reign, roused the nobles to a sense of dignity, and honoured science by inviting its disciples to his well-ordered table.

A subsequent emperor, Carus, was perhaps one of the most frugal, by habit and inclination, that ever wore the imperial sword upon his thigh. Carus was at once moderate and mirthful. He was seated on the grass, supping on dry bread and grey peas, when the Persian ambassadors came to him suing for peace. "The matter just stands thus, gentlemen," said the emperor, opening his mouth widely, at the same time, to insert a shovel-like spoonful of peas; "if your master does not acknowledge the superiority of Rome, I will render Persia,"—and here he took off the cap which he wore to conceal his entire baldness,—"I will render Persia as destitute of trees as my head is of hair." Having said which, he resumed swallowing his peas, and left the delegates to digest his remark.

We are accustomed to consider Diocletian dining at Salona, on the cabbages he had reared there, as an emperor in reduced circumstances; but the truth is, that the palace, gardens, and table of the ex-emperor were all of a splendid character, and if his table was adorned by the cabbages he had tended to a prize perfection, he was far too wise an epicure to confine himself to that dish alone.

The great Constantine appears under a double aspect, and the least favourable one is offered to us in his maturer years, when he surrendered himself more unreservedly than before to a good living, for which he had peculiar facilities at Byzantium, took to wearing false hair, and became altogether a ridiculous old dandy and *bon vivant;* the ridicule of whom, by his clever and unscrupulous nephew, Julian, I am not at all surprised at; for what is so eagerly seized upon by affectionate nephews as the foibles of their indulgent uncles? Julian was possessed just of that scampish sort of nepotism which leads the modest young relative to eat an uncle's dinners and deride the donor. Julian's own table would have gained the contempt of an editor of the *Almanach des Gourmands.* Its frugality was frigidly parsimonious in its character. The philosophic emperor was a vegetarian, and even of vegetables he ate sparingly, but swiftly, leaping up, as it were, from dining thereon, to hurry to his books or the public business, which he quitted reluctantly when the hour of supper summoned him even to that more frugal meal than the dinner, which he despatched with a celerity not at all admired by those who dined with him. Nothing disgusted him so much as a gross feeder, and probably nothing ever so greatly surprised him as when, on taking possession of Constantinople, he found one thousand cooks waiting to prepare the imperial dinner! A thousand cooks for the man who could dine on a boiled turnip! The Constantines had been accustomed to dine upon birds from the most distant climates, fish from the most remote seas; to have a desert of fruits out of their natural seasons, and to drink foreign wines cooled in the summer snows of the lofty hills. All this was as useless to a man who needed but a crust and an apple to calm his appetite, as were the golden basins and jewelled combs to an emperor like Julian, who seldom washed even his face, and who not only never cleaned his hair, but *felt* the lively luxury of leaving it undisturbed. Julian in this respect was like Anthony Pasquin, who was said to have died of a cold caught by washing his face. There was a famous Irish member of Parliament, who, unlike Julian, was a glutton at dinner, but who was remarkable for his religious abstinence from all ablution. His son was one day standing in the bow-window of White's, when the sire was passing down the opposite side of the street. I believe it was the noble lord who, when Mr. Gunter in the hunting-field remarked that his horse was too "hot" to ride comfortably, suggested to the equestrian pastry-cook that he should *ice* him.—I believe it was the same noble lord who, on the first occasion alluded to above, said to "Jack T———," "Jack! what *does* make your father's hands so dirty?" "Well!" said the old Colonel's affectionate son, "I believe it arises from a bad habit he has of putting them up to his face!" And so of Julian we may say, that if his hands were innocent of water, his famous beard was dirtier than his hands, and that it was not pleasant to lie near the emperor at dinner, unless guardedly ensconced to the leeward of his sacred and dirty person.

If Gratian, who was the first Roman emperor who refused the pontifical robe, had lived but as became the master of an imperial household, his sacrifice would have had more merit; but the emperors of these times had curious ideas as to duties. Thus the second Valentinian delighted in giving splendid dinners, but at these entertainments he always, himself, fasted;—a most discouraging course for the guests,—but he thought there was merit in the work. But Theodosius was at least as good a man, and we know that *he* enjoyed the sensual and social pleasures of the table without excess; and the same taste was shown by that emperor Maximus, who is said to have espoused Helena, the daughter of a wealthy Caernarvonshire lord, and to have renewed the popularity of boiled leeks in Rome; and this was a better taste than that of Honorius, who took to feeding poultry and eating them, while

Stilicho ruled the empire, and the eunuchs lived on the very fat of the land. It was decidedly better too than the taste which led Valentinian the third, after dining with Petronius Maximus and winning his money, to carry off his wife; a Tarquinian insult, which he paid for, however, with his life. Avitus could indulge in such freaks, however, with impunity; and he not only seduced Roman matrons, but invited their husbands to dinner, where the slaves smiled at the imperial raillery directed against them while the courses were changing! His successor, Majorianus, was a man of another stamp, and I would fain believe the pleasant anecdote which says of him that he went to Carthage in the disguise of his own ambassador, and dined with Genseric the king, who was especially chafed when he afterwards discovered that he had entertained, without knowing it, the Emperor of the Romans. Anthemius, if he be famous for little else, is at least famous for the superb wedding-dinner with which he celebrated the nuptials of his daughter with Count Ricimer, a wicked son-in-law who devoured the dinners of his "beau-père," and robbed him of his estate;—no uncommon course for sons-in-law to take. The count placed on the uneasy and vacant throne the epicurean Glycerius, who, having murdered Julius Nepos after a banquet, was made Archbishop of Milan, as one of the recompenses of the act. And then the empire fell into the delicate hands of the weak and beautiful Augustulus, who could not find wherewith in the treasury to maintain a decent table, and who was glad to accept clemency and an annuity from Odoacer, whereby he was enabled, upon six thousand pieces of gold annually, to keep such state in the Castle of Lucullus in Campania, that the surrounding gentry visited him in shoals, and ate his dinners by way of proof that they looked upon him as a man of the highest respectability.

And this was the end of the "twelve vultures," seen by Romulus, foreshadowing the "twelve centuries," more or less, that were to mark the duration of the dominion which he founded; a dominion commenced by a hungry adventurer, and which crumbled to nothing in the hand of that Augustulus, who was but too rejoiced to take in exchange for it, the bed, board, and six thousand a-year with which he set up as a hospitable country gentleman, in his rustic villa, on the slopes of Campania.

As for the Cæsars of the Eastern Empire, they were rather Oriental despots than either Greek or Roman monarchs, just as the Byzantines were ever more Asiatics than Europeans. The sovereigns, for the most part, ate at golden tables, and were served like gods. Some of them, like Romanus, were respectable cooks, and more than one was discussing the merits of a new sauce or dish, when the Saracens were knocking at the frontier gates of the empire. This sort of merry humour indulged in by others may be judged of by a single trait of Michael the Drunkard. This amiable sovereign started up, one day, from table, ere the imperial dinner was well over, and assuming an episcopal dress, he descended into the streets followed by his courtiers. The latter bore the vinegar and mustard that had been on the Monarch's side-board, and mixing the condiments together, they stopped all passers-by, compelled them to kneel, and with horrible profanity and mock psalmody, administered the Sacrament with the above-named horribly compounded elements. Such was one of the Eastern Cæsars at and after dinner, and the easy Byzantines were not much scandalized thereat. Indeed, they troubled themselves very little about the affairs of government, or the doings of the governors; and it would never have entered the head of a Byzantine subject to say of his son what the American citizen once remarked, touching his heir, to Mrs. Trollope, namely, that he would much sooner that his son got drunk three times a-week than that he should refrain from meddling with the politics of his times.

From the palaces of the Cæsars, let us now pass into the mansions of miscellaneous majesties, and see how the first gentlemen of their respective days comported themselves "at meat." Yes, at meat; for "la viande du Roi" was the consecrated phrase, and guards presented arms, and courtiers bowed low, as the king's "meat" was solemnly carried to the royal table, or borne to the bedside, where it remained under the name of an *en cas*, "in case" the august appetite should be lively before morning.

THEIR MAJESTIES AT MEAT.

There was an old custom at Pisa, the origin of which may be traced to the anti-judaical days of persecution. On a certain day in the year, I believe, Good Friday or Easter Sunday, every Jew discovered in the streets, was hunted down by the populace. When the game was caught he was weighed, and compelled to ransom himself by paying his own weight of sweetmeats. It was an advantage, then, at Pisa for a Jew to be of a Cassius cast. It was different in other days, and climes, with regard to kings. Nations used to weigh their monarchs yearly, and if the register showed an increase of dignified obesity, great was the popular rejoicing thereat. If, on the other hand, the too, too solid flesh of the potentate had yielded to irresistible influences, and the father of his people exhibited a falling away in his material greatness, the body of loyal subjects went into mourning and tears, and deplored the evil days on which they had fallen, when monarchs could not be kept up to the old monarchical standard of corpulency. Kings who cared for the affections of their people were, accordingly, disinterestedly solicitous to support their corporeal requirements; for to be fat was to be virtuous, and he was really the greatest of monarchs who required the greatest circumference of belt. You must understand, however, that if kings encouraged their own increase, it was disloyal in the people to imitate them. The monarchs of old, in this respect, were like our Henry VIII., who never stinted his own appetite, but who imprisoned the Earl of Surrey in Windsor Castle, for daring to touch a lamb chop on a Friday.

The most gigantic of royal feeders placed on the record of ancient history, was Thys, king of Paphlagonia, at whose table "the entire animal" was served by hundreds. When he fell into the power of Persia he exhibited more appetite than grief, and banqueted in such a style that the courtiers spoke of it wonderingly to their king Artaxerxes. He replied significantly, "Thys is making the most of the shortness of life."

The kings of Persia were but sorry hosts to dine with. Their table was in a little recess divided from the outward hall by a low curtain. The king sat alone in his alcove, and could behold, without being seen, the guests in the outer hall. The latter were of the highest rank; mere younger brothers, civilians, and undignified people of that sort, sat at meat in the galleries. It was only on two or three high days that the king sat at the same table with his subjects. The royalty of old Persia had once a reputation for temperance, but to be "royally drunk" was no uncommon characteristic of his majesty and the princes of the blood. He generally made drinking parties of a dozen favourites. These sat on the ground, while the king lay on a gold couch, and the conclave drank like dragoons, and got infinitely more tipsy.

In the banquets of state there were a few singularities. Horses and ostriches appear in the bill of fare, among a hundred other delicacies; but no guest did more than just taste what was placed before him; and what he did not eat, he carried home with him. A dainty bit from the king's table was a present meet for lover to make to his lady; and a wooer who brought a rump steak of horse-flesh in his hand, straight from the regal banquet, was scarcely a man to be refused anything.

There was something of grandeur in the banquets of Cleopatra, when Anthony dined with her. The service was in gold, and she made a present of it to her visitor. On the following day there was a new service, and it was again presented to "the favoured guest." Antony himself exhibited infinitely less taste at Athens. He erected in the public theatre a scene representing the grotto of Bacchus, dressed himself like the god, and, with a party of followers as worthless as himself, sat down at day-break, in presence of an admiring and crowded "house," and got dreadfully drunk before breakfast time. And this knave aspired to rule in Rome!

Alexander, and, as may be seen in another page, Augustus, was given to this sort of theological masquerading. The first-named accepted banquets from his great officers; and these exhibited their taste by having all the fruit on the table covered thickly with gold, which, when the fruit itself was presented to the guests, was torn off and flung on the ground, for the benefit of the servants. The father of Alexander had shown in his time a better example of economy. He had but one gold cup, and to prevent that from being stolen, he placed it every night under his pillow, and went to sleep upon it. The mad Antiochus, of Syria, was of another kidney, for whenever he heard of a drinking bout in his own city, he used to order his chariot, and taking with him a measure of wine and a goblet, he would rush down to the place and take a seat uninvited. He was such indifferent company, however, that the guests could not be prevailed upon to tarry, and even the offer of his golden goblet was unable to bribe a man to sit and get drunk with a witless king.

But the most extraordinary meal I have ever heard of was that made by Cambes, king of Lydia. He was a great eater, a great drinker, and of insatiable voracity. It is told of him that he one night cut up his wife and devoured her, and that he awoke the next morning, with one of her hands sticking in his mouth. But I have little doubt that something of an allegory lies under this royal story. Cambes probably had had an argument with this consort,—a lady of the sort spoken of by Dr. Young as one who

> Shakes the curtain with her good advice.

His logic "cut up" her assertions, and thereon he addressed himself to sleep; but he no sooner awoke in the morning than her hand was upon his mouth, to prevent his speaking while she reiterated her follies of the previous night. Poor Cambes! he cut his throat in order to escape from a too loquacious consort, of whom he is accused of being the murderer by the libelling Xanthus.

I may add to the record of these exemplary persons, the name of Dionysius of Heraclea, who, through good living, fell into such a condition of obesity and somnolency that he could only be made conscious by running fine gold needles into his flesh. What a droll thing it must have been for his morning visitors who found the huge mass fast asleep at table! Shaking hands with him, or any other equivalent ceremony, would have been useless. They accordingly took a gold needle from his girdle and tenderly run it into his fat. When it reached a vital point, the uneasy monarch snorted and opened one eye; and this being taken as an acknowledgment of their presence, he straightway went to sleep again. Ptolemy, the seventh king of Egypt, was in nearly as deplorable a condition, and Magas of Cyrene was perhaps even worse. The Ephori, it will be remembered, had a horror of the Lacedæmonians getting fat, and to prevent this undesirable consummation, the youth were obliged to present themselves undraped to the magistrates. Woe to the offenders with prominent stomachs, for they had them punched till the owners hardly knew whether they stood on their head or their heels, and could not digest a dinner for a month afterwards.

They were beaten almost as badly as the unlucky official who went, in Parthia, by the name of the king's friend. It was the duty of this minister to seat himself on the ground at the foot of the lofty couch on which the king lay, and from which the sovereign flung refuse bits to his "friend." If the latter ate too voraciously, his meat was snatched from him, and he was beaten with rods till he had hardly strength left to thank his majesty for the entertainment. Of course, if he ate too slowly, he was subject to similar castigation. The moral, perhaps, is, that "fast" or "slow," it is safer not to be "friends" with the king—of the Parthians.

But let us turn from the ancient records of how the monarchs of old deported themselves at their solemn boards, and contemplate a few brief table traits in connexion with the sovereigns of more modern times.

Clovis was a Christian king, but his behaviour at dinner was not always so exemplary as might have been desired. But the Chesterfields of his time were not exacting, and they probably thought Clovis a gentleman when, on Bishop (St. Gerome) taking leave of him after dinner, the monarch pulled out a hair and placed it in the bishop's palm; the civil ceremony was imitated by the courtiers, and the prelate left the rude palace with more hairs on his hand than he had on his head.

But dismissing the idea of running regularly through the "Tables of the Sovereigns of Europe," and elsewhere, I will simply relate such incidents as are exemplary of royal table life, without pausing to be very nice with regard to chronological order. Thus it occurs to me that Russia, in modern times, exhibits as much barbarism as the court of Clovis, where Christianity and civilization were, as yet, hardly known.

When Peter the Great and his consort dined together, they were waited on by a page and the empress's favourite chambermaid. Even at larger dinners, he bore uneasily the presence and service of what he called listening lacqueys. His taste was not an imperial one. He loved, and most frequently ordered, for his own especial enjoyment, a soup with four cabbages in it; gruel; pig, with sour cream for sauce; cold roast meat, with pickled cucumbers or salad; lemons and lampreys; salt meat, ham, and Limburg cheese. Previously to addressing himself to the "consummation" of this supply, he took a glass of aniseed water. At his repast he quaffed quass, a sort of beer, which would have disgusted an Egyptian; and he finished with Hungarian or French wine. All this was the repast of a man who seemed, like the nation of which he was the head, in a transition state, between barbarism and civilization; beginning dinner with cabbage water, and closing the banquet with goblets of Burgundy.

Peter and his consort had stranger tastes than these. This illustrious pair once arrived at Stuthof, in Germany, where they claimed not only the hospitality of the table, but a refuge for the night. The owner of the country house at which they sought to be guests was a Herr Schoppenhauer, who readily agreed to give up to them a small bed-room, the selection of which had been made by the emperor himself. It was a room without stove or fire-place, had a brick floor, the walls were bare; and the season being a rigorous winter, a difficulty arose as to warming this chamber. The host soon solved the difficulty. Several casks of brandy were emptied on the floor, the furniture being first removed, and the spirit was then set fire to. The czar screamed with delight as he saw the sea of flames, and smelt the odor of the Cognac. The fire was no sooner extinguished than the bed was replaced, and Peter and Catherine straightway betook themselves to their repose, and not only slept profoundly all night in this gloomy bower, amid the fumes and steam of burnt brandy, but rose in the morning thoroughly refreshed and delighted with their couch, and the delicate vapours which had curtained their repose.

The emperor was pleased, because when an emergency had presented itself, provision to meet it was there at hand. Napoleon loved to be so served at his tables when in the field. He was irregular in the hours of his repasts, and he ate rapidly and not over delicately. The absolute will which he applied to most things, was exercised also in matters appertaining to the appetite. As soon as a sensation of hunger was experienced, it must be appeased; and his table service was so arranged that, in any place and at any hour, he had but to give expression to his will, and the slaves of his word promptly set before him roast fowls, cutlets, and smoking coffee. He dined of mutton before risking the battle of Leipsic; and it is said that he lost the day because he was suffering from indigestion, that he was unable to arrange with sufficient coolness, the mental calculations which he was accustomed to make as helps to victory.

As Napoleon, the genius of war, was served in the field, Louis XV., the incarnation of selfishness and vice, was served in his mistress's bower. That bower, built at Choisy for Pompadour, cost millions; but it was one of the wonders of the world. For the royal entertainments, there were invented those little tables, called "servants" or "waiters;" they were mechanical contrivances, that immortalized the artist Loriot. At Choisy, every guest had one of these tables to himself. No servant stood by to listen, rather than to lend aid. Whatever the guest desired to have, he had but to write his wish on paper, and touch a spring, when the table sunk through the flooring at his feet, and speedily re-appeared, laden with fruits, with pastry, or with wine, according to the order given. Nothing had been seen like this enchantment in France before; and nothing like it, it is hoped, will ever be seen there or elsewhere again. The guests thought themselves little gods, and were not a jot more reasonable than Augustus and his companions, who sat down to dinner attired as deities. When kings ape the majesty of gods, it is time for the people to shake the majesty of kings.

Perhaps Louis XV. never looked so little like a king as when he dined or supped in public,—a peculiar manifestation of his kingly character. The Parisians and their wives used to hurry down to Versailles on a Sunday, to behold the feeding of the beast which it cost them so much to keep. On these occasions he always had boiled eggs before him. He was uncommonly dexterous in decapitating the shell by a single blow from his fork; and this feat he performed weekly at his own table, for the sake of the admiration which it excited in the Cockney beholders. But an egg broken by the king, or Damiens broken alive upon the wheel, and torn asunder by wild horses,—each was a sight gazed upon, even by the youthful fair, with a sort of admiration for the executioner!

The glory of the epicureanism of Louis XV. was his "magic table," and the select worthless people especially invited to dine with him thereat. In 1780 the Countess of Oberkirch saw this table, even then a relic and wreck of the past. She and a gay party of great people, who yet hoped that God had created the world only for the comfort of those whom he had honored by allowing them to be born "noble," paid a visit "to the apartments of the late king" in the Tuileries. There, among other things, she saw the celebrated magic table, the springs of which, she says, "had become rusty from disuse." The good lady, who had not the slightest intention in the world to be satirical, thus describes the wondrous article, at the making of which Pompadour had presided:—"It was placed in the centre of a room, where none were allowed to enter but the invited guests of Louis XV. It would accommodate thirty persons. In the centre was a cylinder of gilt copper, which could be pressed down by springs, and would return with its top, which was surrounded by a band, covered with dishes. Around were placed four dumb waiters, on which would be found everything that was necessary." In 1789 the Countess says,—"This table no longer exists, having been long since destroyed, with everything that could recall the last sad years of a monarch, who would have been good if he had not been perverted by evil counsels."

After all, the gastronomic greatness of Louis XV. was small compared with that of his predecessor, Louis XIV. The "state" of the latter was, in all things, more "cumbersome." To be helpless was to be dignified; and to do nothing for himself, and to think of nothing *but* himself, was the sole life-business of this very illustrious king. A dozen men dressed him; there was one for every limb that had to be covered. Poor wretch! His breakfast was as lumbering a matter as his *toilette;* and he tasted nothing till it had passed through the hands of half-a-dozen dukes. It took even three noblemen, ending with a prince of the blood, to present him a napkin with which to wipe his lips, before he addressed himself to the more serious business of the day.

Louis XIV. could not be properly got to the dinner-table, entertained there, and removed, without a still more fussy world of ceremony, and that of a very Chinese or Ko Tou character. The ushers solemnly summoned the guard when the cloth was to be laid, and a detachment of men under arms were at once spectators and guardians at the dressing of the table. They stood by, exceedingly edified, no doubt, while the appointed officers touched the royal napkin, spoon, plate, knife, fork, and tooth-picks, with a piece of bread, which they subsequently swallowed. This was the "trial" against poisoning. The dishes in the kitchen were tried in the same way, and were then carried to the table escorted by a file of men with drawn swords. As the dishes were placed on the table, the loyal officials bowed as though some saintly relics were on the platter!

If there was ceremony at the coming in of the meat, how much more was there at the coming in of him who was about to eat it! Unhappy wretch! what splendid misery enveloped his mutton-chop! He was looked upon as very august, but decidedly helpless. Did he wish to wipe his fingers; three dukes and a prince only could present him with a *damp* napkin; but a dry one might be offered him at dinner, without insult, by a simple valet. Philosophical distinction! Changing his plate required as much attendant ceremony as would go to the whole crowning of a modern constitutional king; and when he asked for drink, there was thunder in heaven, or something like it. The cup-bearer solemnly shouted the king's desire to the buffet; and the buffeteers presented goblets and flasks to the cup-bearer, who carried them to the thirsty but necessarily patient monarch; and, when he finally received the draught into his extended throat, all loyal men present seemed the better for the sight.

But Louis XIV. was so well-used to this, and much more ceremony than I have space to detail, that it interfered in nowise with the comfortable indulgence of his appetite. He was a very gifted eater. The rough old Duchess of Orleans declares in her Memoirs, that she "often saw him eat four platesfull of different soups, a whole pheasant, a partridge, a platefull of salad, mutton hashed with garlick, two good-sized slices of ham, a dish of pastry, and afterwards fruit and sweetmeats!" At the end of such a repast as this, this "most Christian" king (very much so, indeed!) must have been in something of the condition of the young gentleman who went out to dine, and who, after taking enough for three boys of his size, and being invited to take more, answered that he thought he could, if they would allow him to stand!

The Duchess of Orleans, however, is by no means astonished at the Baal-like ability of the king. Of her own performances in that way she says, "I am not good at lying in bed; as soon as I awake, I must get up. I seldom breakfast, and then only on bread and butter. I take neither chocolate, nor coffee, nor tea, not being able to endure those foreign drugs. I am German in all my habits, and like nothing in eating or drinking which is not conformable to our old customs. I eat no soup but such as I can take with milk, wine, or beer. I cannot bear broth; whenever I eat anything of which it forms a part, I fall sick instantly, my body swells, and I am tormented with colics. When I take broth alone, I am compelled to vomit even to blood, and nothing can restore the tone of my stomach but—*ham and sausages!*" Poor lady! she reminds me of the converted cannibal Carib, who was once sick, and who being asked by a missionary what he could eat, answered sentimentally, that he thought he could pick a bone or two of a very delicate hand of a young child!

At a later period even than that of the Duchess of Orleans above-mentioned, the German taste could hardly be said to have improved. For instances of this, I need only refer to the Memoirs of the Margravine of Baireuth. This lady was the daughter of that Frederic William of Prussia, whose portrait is graphically drawn also by his own son, and with additional light and shade by Voltaire. The Princess Frederica subsequently married the Prince of Baireuth—a *mésalliance* which did not displease her easy parents;—they were not as proudly vexed at it as Isaac and Rachel were at the marriage of their son Esau with the daughter of Beeri the Hittite, which certainly sounds as if Esau's father-in-law had been a pugilistic publican;—the Princess Frederica, I say, paints a portrait of her father in very broad style. He used to compel her and his other children to come to his room every morning at nine o'clock, whence they were never allowed to depart till nine in the evening, "pour quelque raison que ce fût." The time was spent by the affectionate sovereign in swearing at them, and he added injury to insult by half-famishing them. He begrudged them even a wretched soup made of bare bones and salt. Occasionally, they were kept fasting the whole day; or, if he graciously allowed them a meal at his own table, the royal beast would spit into the dishes from which he had helped himself, in order to prevent their touching them. At other times he forced them to swallow compositions of the most disgusting description—" ce qui nous obligeait quelquefois de rendre, en sa présence, tout ce que nous avions dans le corps!" He would then throw the plates at their heads; and, as his children rushed by him to escape his fury, the paternal brute, whom it is too much flattery to himself, and too much injustice to the brute creation so to name, would strike fiercely at them with his crutch, and was eminently disappointed when he failed to crack their little, hard, royal, but very dirty skulls. It is known that this madman would have slain his own son, " the rascal Fritz," as he, " the great Frederic," as the world afterwards was used to call him; and little doubt can exist that the great Frederic owed most of his great vices, and none of his great qualities, to the education which he received at the knees of his infamous sire.

The history of the German courts abounds in traits connected with the table, but I am compelled to go little beyond the announcement of such a fact. One or two more, however, I may be permitted to notice before finally leaving this section of my multifaced subject.

Ernest the " Iron " was, perhaps, the least luxurious of his race. He married Cymburga of Poland, the lady who brought into the Austrian family the thick lips, which to this day form a characteristic feature in the imperial physiognomy. Cymburga cracked her nuts with her fingers; and when she trained her fruit trees, she hammered the nails into the wall with her clenched knuckles! Their table was at once copious and simple. Their son Frederic had less strength both of body and judgment. At near fourscore years of age he suffered amputation of the leg, in order to get rid of a cancerous affection. He was " doing well " after the operation, when he resolved upon dining on melons. He was told that such a diet would be fatal to him, as it had already been to one Austrian archduke of his house. Frederic reflected that he would probably die at all events, and that he had already reigned longer than any emperor since the days of Augustus, namely, fifty-three years. "I *will* have melons," said he, "betide what may!" He ate unsparingly, and death followed close upon the banquet.

Frederic would neither drink wine himself, nor allow his consort to do so, although physicians declared that, without it, she was not likely to achieve the honours of maternity. She did abstain, and despite what the oracular doctors had asserted, she became the mother of Maximilian, a prince who drank wine enough to compensate for the abstinence of both his parents. His second wife, Bianca of Milan, whom Maximilian the "Moneyless" married for her dowry, was, like the lady in Young's Satires, by no means afraid to call things by their very broadest names; and she died of an indigestion, brought on by eating too voraciously of snails! They were of the large and lively sort, still reared for the market in the field-preserves near Ulm. If my readers should feel sick at the thought, let them remember their juvenile days, and "periwinkles," and be gentle in their strictures. Leopold the "Angel," the second son of the Emperor Ferdinand, surpassed even his father in abstinence. He reared the most odoriferous of plants, but inflicted on himself the mortification of never going near enough to scent them; and, poor man! he thought that thereby he was adding a step to a ladder of good works, by which he hoped to scale heaven!

The grandson of Ferdinand, **Joseph I.**, was a somewhat free liver, and his intemperate diet was against him when he caught the small-pox. But the medical men were fiercer foes than his way of life; for when the eruption was at its worst, they hermetically closed his apartment, kept up a blazing fire in it, gave him strong drinks, swathed him in twenty yards of English scarlet broadcloth, and then published, on his dying, that his majesty's decease was contrary to all the rules of art. His brother and successor, Charles, did for himself what the doctors did for Joseph.

In 1740 he had the gout, and *would* go out hunting in the wet. He was subsequently seized with what would now be called incipient cholera, and he *would* eat—not melons, like some of his obstinate and imperial predecessors, but that delicate dish for an invalid, mushrooms stewed in oil! He ate voraciously, and the next day symptoms ensued which, he was informed, heralded death. Charles, like Louis Philippe, would not believe his own medical advisers; and there was some reason in this, for they stood at his bed-side, disputing as to whether mushrooms were a digestible diet or the contrary. The emperor dismissed them from his presence, ordered his favourite mushrooms, ate the forbidden "fruit" with intense gastronomic delight, and died in peace.

The table of the great Frederic of Prussia was regulated by himself. There were always from nine to a dozen dishes, and these were brought in one at a time. The king carved the solitary dish, and helped the company. One singular circumstance connected with this table was, that each dish was cooked by a different cook who had a kitchen to himself! There was much consequent expense, with little magnificence. Frederic ate and drank, too, like a boon companion. His last work, before retiring to bed, was to receive from his chief cook the bill of fare for the next day; the price of each dish, and of its separate ingredients, was marked in the margin. The monarch looked it cautiously through, generally made out an improved edition, cursed all the cooks as common thieves, and then flung down the money for the next day's expenses.

The late King of Prussia was a sensible man with respect to his table arrangements. On gala days, and when it concerned the honour of Prussia that the royal hospitality should assume an appearance of splendour, his table was as glittering and gastronomic as goldsmiths and cooks could make it. But in the routine of private and unofficial life, it was simply that of an opulent merchant, something, perhaps, like that of Sir Balaam after he had grown rich. Even then he partook only of the least savoury dishes, and it was seldom, indeed, that he exceeded a third glass of wine. His example enforced moderation, but it did not mar enjoyment, for he loved every man around him to be merry and wise.

His own wisdom he manifested by a characteristic trait in 1809. The royal family had returned to Berlin for the first time since the war had broken out in 1806. The court marshal, deeming that the piping times of peace were going to endure for ever, waited on Frederic William, and asked what amount of champagne he should order for the royal cellars. "None," replied the king; "I will drink neither champagne nor any other wine, until all my subjects—even the very poorest—can afford to drink beer again." The incident was made public, and the king's poor neighbours were especially delighted. Many of them testified their gratitude by sending from their gardens or little farms various articles for his table. The king ate thereof with pleasure, and did *not* forget the givers.

I have spoken of his moderation, but here is an additional trait from his table worth mentioning. When he came to the crown, the grand marshal proposed a more extended list of viands for the royal table. "Marshal," said the king in reply, "I do not feel that my stomach has become more capacious since I became king. We will let well alone, and dine to-day even as we have done heretofore."

In another page I have spoken of Bishop Eylert supping with the king. Such a guest was not an unfrequent one at the royal dining-table. On one occasion the bishop had preached before the court in the morning from Luke xiv. 8—11: "When thou art bidden of any man to a wedding, sit not down in the highest room, lest a more honourable man than thou be bidden of him; and he that bade thee and him come and say unto thee, Give this man place, and thou begin with shame to take the lower room," &c. &c.

The bishop profited by the opportunity to expatiate on the virtues of diffidence and humility, insisting on their observance as necessary for the preservation of our happiness. Now, many dignified officials were present at the banquet in question, and the bishop who had entered the saloon last, (which does not say much for the courtesy of those who preceded him,) meekly took his place at the lower end of the table. There the king's scrutinizing eye fell upon him; and "Eylert," said Frederic William, "I see you are self-applying the text from which you preached to us to-day. But, if I remember rightly, it is also written, 'Friend, go higher.' Come, then, take this chair that is near to me!" and the simple but highly embarrassed prelate walked blushingly to the station appointed him, and all in his vicinity began to recognise a man whom the king himself delighted to honour.

This anecdote reminds me, albeit it be "rue with a difference," of one told of the second of the seven Dukes of Guise, Duke Francis. This celebrated individual was, during one part of his bloody career, engaged in the service of the Pope, to fight the battles of the latter against the King of Naples. He was not successful, and his holiness showered down upon him mordant epigrams and invitations to dinner. He had accepted one of the latter, and repaired to the sacro-regal board, after a day in the course of which he had been engaged serving as acolyte in the Papal chapel, and holding up the trains of very obese cardinals. In the banqueting-hall of the descendant of the poor fisherman, he meekly took the lowest seat. He had scarcely done so, than a French lieutenant endeavoured to thrust in below him. "How now, friend!" said the haughty enough Guise; "why pushest thou so rudely to come where there is no room for thee?" "Marry!" said the soldier, "for this reason that it might not be said that the representative of a king of France had taken the last place at a priest's table!" It was a bold piece of table-talk to so powerful a man as Guise, who recovered, and added to his reputation when he subsequently regained, Calais from the English. Previously to this last feat, when the occupation of Calais formed the subject of conversation at social boards, there arose the proverbial expression applied to the bravest of untried men, and honourable to the reputation of our own ancestors,—"*He* is not the sort of man to drive the English out of France!" The proverb died out of French society from the day when Guise drove old Lord Wentworth out of Calais, and cheated his duchess out of the silks which he found therein, and in which he attired the courtesans whom he invited to his ducal but *not* dignified table.

It may fairly be asserted that kings may wear as graceful an aspect as guests at others' tables, as they do when enacting the host at their own. The Prince Regent, dining off the mutton which he had helped to cook at Colonel Hanger's, is indeed no very edifying spectacle. I will introduce my readers to a royal guest of what Hamlet would call "another kidney."

When the Prussian general Koeckeritz had completed his fiftieth year of service in 1809, he was residing in modest apartments, becoming his celibate condition, near the Neustadt Gate at Potsdam. On the dawn of the day of his martial jubilee, he was harmoniously greeted by the bands of the garrison; but the hautboys did not discourse such sweet music as was conveyed to him in a letter from the king, full of expressions of gratitude for services rendered by him during a long half-century to the crown. At a grand review held in honour of the day, the king embraced him in presence of the army, giving in his person the accolade to every other faithful soldier who had served as long; and when this had been done, Frederic William not only declared he would escort the old warrior to his plainly furnished lodgings, but requested to be invited to the *déjeuner à la fourchette*, which he assumed must then be wanting. Koeckeritz had the pride of Caleb Balderstone, and he turned pale at the idea of exposing his domestic economy to the eyes of a king and court. He grew eloquent in excuses, protested that he was unworthy of the honour designed for him, and piteously muttered an apologetical phrase about "old bachelors." "Then why are you a bachelor?" asked the monarch: "I have often counselled you to marry, and this very day you shall be punished for your disobedience." "Well," said the general, with a sigh, denoting the resignation of despair, "if it must be so, I trust your majesty will allow me a few hours in order to make fitting preparation." The spirit that possessed Caleb Balderstone suggested this petition. "Not five minutes!" exclaimed the sovereign; "you surely have a crust of bread and a glass of wine to give to us who are your comrades, and we desire no more! Come along, gentlemen!"

Of course, no further resistance was to be thought of, and the gay and brilliant escort led the grave Koeckeritz along, looking very much like a criminal who was about to be hanged with riotous solemnity at his own gates.

But, when he reached those gates, his surprise was extreme. The threshold was covered with flowers, the little hall was lined with the royal servants in their state suits, and the space in front of the house was partly occupied by a score of "trumpets," who no sooner perceived the approach of the hero of the day than they received him, as our theatrical orchestras do stage kings, with a "flourish." It is hardly necessary to add, that when the old general conducted his guests within, he found there such a banquet as Aladdin furnished his widowed mother with by means of the lamp. Everything was there, whether in or out of season; and the rare-looking flasks promised pleasure less equivocal than that held out by a Calais Boniface upon his cards, whereon his English visitors were told, that "the wine shall leave you nothing to hope for!"

"Oh! oh!" exclaimed the king, "here is bachelor's fare with a vengeance! Let us be seated, and show that our appetites can appreciate what our comrade Koeckeritz has provided for them." Monarch and servant, honouring and honoured, sat side by side; and so gay and so prolonged was the festival, that the king surprised all those who knew how strictly he lived by rule, by ordering the dinner at the palace to be retarded for a couple of hours. At that banquet he entertained the veteran, affecting to do so in return for the hospitality displayed by the latter in the morning. The scene was not without its moving incidents, for the king had contrived another surprise whereby to gratify his old friend and servant. As the monarch led him by the hand to the dining-room, there stood before him three of the surviving friends of his youth who had fought with him in the Seven Years' War, and whom he had not seen for years. The king had got them together, not without difficulty; the general joy that ensued was as unalloyed as humanity could make it, and never did monarch sit at meat with more right to feel pleased, than Frederic William on this day of Koeckeritz's jubilee. It was a day that Henri IV. of France would have delighted in. That king is said never to have dined better than one evening previous to the battle of Ivry, when he was sojourning in a country house under the name of a French officer. There were no provisions there, but the solitary lady who was the chatelaine intimated that there was a retired tradesman who lived near, who was the possessor of a fine turkey, and who would contribute it towards a dinner, if he were only invited to partake of it. "Is he a jolly companion?" asked the supposed officer. The reply being affirmatively, the citizen and turkey were invited together, and two merrier guests never sat down with a lady to cut up a bird and crush a bottle. Henri was in the most radiant of humours; and it was when he was at his brightest, that the *bourgeois* avowed that he had known him from the beginning, and that after dining with a king of France, he trusted that the monarch would not object to grant him letters of nobility. Henri laughed, which was as good as consenting, and asked what arms his countship would assume? "I will emblazon the turkey that founded my good fortune," answered the aspirant for nobility. "Ventre Saint-Gris!" exclaimed the king, laughing more immoderately, "then you shall be a gentleman, and bear your turkey 'en pal' on a shield!" The happy citizen purchased a territorial manor near Alençon, and le Comte Morel d'Inde was not a *conte pour rire*.

The Russian Empress Catherine used to affect the good fellowship that was natural to the first of the Bourbon kings of France. When she dined with the highly honoured officers of the regiment of which she was colonel, she used to hand to each a glass of spirits before the banquet commenced. At her own table the number of guests was usually select, generally under a dozen. The lord of the bedchamber sat opposite to her, her own seat being at the centre of one of the sides, carved one of the dishes, and presented it to her. She took once of what was so offered, but afterways dispensed with such service. In her days, many of the Russian nobility kept open tables. Any one who had been duly introduced, and knew not where to dine, had only to call at a house where he was known, and to leave word that he intended to dine there in the afternoon. He was sure to be welcomed. At the present time, the Russians are more civilized and less hospitable.

Jermann describes the imperial kitchen at St. Petersburg as good, delicate, and "meagre,"—the latter being a consequence of the continual eating that is going on, and the necessity which follows of providing what is light of digestion. The imperial household tables in the days of Paul were divided into "stations," an arrangement which took its rise from a singular incident. The late empress, like our own Queen Adelaide, was given to inspect the "domestic accounts," and she was puzzled by finding among them "a bottle of rum" daily charged to the Naslednik, or heir apparent! Her imperial Majesty turned over the old "expenses" of the household, to discover at what period her son had commenced this reprobate course of daily rum-drinking; and found, if not to her horror, at least to the increase of her perplexity, that it dated from the very day of his birth. The "bottle of rum" began with the baby, accompanied the boy, and continued to be charged to the man. He was charged as drinking upwards of thirty dozen of fine old Jamaica yearly! The imperial mother was anxious to discover if any other of the Czarovitch babies had exhibited the same alcoholic precocity; and it appears that they were all alike; daily, for upwards of a century back, they stood credited in the household books for that terrible "bottle of rum." The empress continued her researches with the zeal of an antiquary, and her labours were not unrewarded. She at last reached the original entry. Like all succeeding ones, it was to the effect of "a bottle of rum for the Naslednik;" but a sort of editorial note on the margin of the same page intimated the wherefore: "On account of violent toothache, a teaspoonful with sugar to be given, by order of the physician of the imperial court." The teaspoonful for one day had been charged as a bottle, and the entry once made, it was kept on the books to the profit of the unrighteous steward, until discovery checked the fraud,—a fraud, more gigantically amusing than that of the illiterate coachman, who set down in his harness-room book, "Two penn'orth of whipcord, 6*d*." The empress showed the venerable delinquency to her husband, Paul; and *he*, calculating what the temporary toothache of the imperial baby Alexander had cost him, was affrighted at the outlay, and declared that he would revolutionise the kitchen department, and put himself out to board. The threat was not idly made, and it was soon seriously realized. A gastronomic contractor was found who farmed the whole palace, and did his spiriting admirably. He divided the imperial household into "stations." The first was the monarch's especial table, for the supply of which he charged the emperor and empress fifty roubles each daily; the table of the archdukes and archduchesses was supplied at half that price; the guests of that table, of whatever rank, were served at the same cost. The ladies and gentlemen of the household had a "station," which was exceedingly well provisioned at twenty roubles each. The graduated sliding scale continued to descend in proportion to the *status* of the feeders. The upper servants had superior stomachs, which were accounted of as being implacable at less than fifteen roubles each. Servants in livery, with finer lace but coarser digestions, dieted daily at five roubles each; and the grooms and scullions were taken altogether at three roubles a-head. "A wonderful change," says Jermann, "ensued in the whole winter palace. The emperor declared he had never dined so well before. The court, tempted by the more numerous courses, sat far longer at table. The maids of honour got fresh bloom upon their cheeks, and the chamberlains and equerries rounder faces; and most flourishing of all was the state of the household expenses, although these diminished by one-half. In short, every one, save cook and butler, was content; and all this was the result of 'a bottle of rum,' from which the Emperor Alexander, when heir to the crown, had been ordered by the physician to take a spoonful for the toothache."

Herr Jermann, who was manager of the imperial company of German actors in St. Petersburg, frequently dined at the table of the "second station," or officials' table. There were six dishes and a capital desert. He describes the "drinkables" as consisting of one bottle of red and one of white wine, two bottles of beer, one of kislitschi and quass *ad libitum*. The dinner he speaks lightly of, as inferior on the point of cookery to that of the best restaurants in the capital. The wine was a light Burgundy; the beer heavy and Russian. The kislitschi must have been a powerful crusher of the appetite, it being a sour-sweet drink, prepared from honey, water, lemon-juice, and a decoction of herbs. Quass is a plain, cheap beverage, the better sort of which is extracted from malt, while an inferior sort is an extract of bread-crusts. It is the national drink of the lower orders. A stranger finds it at first detestable; but he not only soon becomes reconciled to it, but generally prefers it to any other beverage, especially in the brief scorching summer of St. Petersburg, when the cooling properties of quass are its great recommendation.

To talk of the fierceness of a Russian summer seems paradoxical, but it is simple truth; and probably the court of Naples itself, throughout its long season of heat, does not consume so much ice as their imperial Muscovite majesties do in the course of their slow-to-come, quick-to-go, and sharp-while-it-lasts summer. Nay, the whole capital eats ice at this season. Ice is thought such a "necessary" of life, that the first question in taking a house is, probably, touching the quality and capability of the ice-cellar, wherein they pack away as much of the Neva as they can in solid blocks. They eat it and drink it, surround their larders with it, and mix it with the water, beer, quass—in short, with whatever they drink. Nay, more, when there is a superabundance of the material, they place it on their stoves to cool their apartments. So tremendous is the dust and heat of a Russian summer, that, for inconvenience, it is only the opposite extreme of annoyance to that experienced in the wintry visitations of frost. The ice-tubs of the popular vendors in the streets are enveloped and covered with wet cloths, to protect them from the heat of the sun. I need not say that this is *not* the season at which a visitor should resort to the capital. St. Petersburg in January, and Naples in July, are the respective times and places to be observed by those who can bear the consequences.

I do not know what may be the case with regard to the fruit eaten at the imperial table; but, generally speaking, fruit is never eaten by a Russian until it has been blest by the priest. Jermann, alluding to this custom, praises it on sanitary grounds, for, he says, the fruit has no chance of earning a benediction unless it be ripe; but if it then be taken to church, the blessing is granted with much attendant solemnity.

I do not believe that the czars were ever accustomed to dine in such state as the kaisers. The old emperors of Germany, on state occasions, were waited on at dinner by the two happy feudatory princes of the empire. On one of these occasions, we are told that old General Dalzell, the terrible enemy of Scottish Covenanters, was invited to dine with the kaiser, and the prince-waiter nearest to him in attendance was no less a personage than the Prince of Modena, head of the house of Este. Some years afterwards, the Duke of York (James II.) invited Dalzell to dine with himself and Mary of Modena. That proud lady, however, made some show of reluctance to sit down *en famille* with the old general; but the latter lowered her pride by telling her, that he was not unacquainted with the greatness of the princes of Modena, and that the last time he had sat at table with the Emperor of Germany, a prince of that house was standing in attendance behind the Emperor's chair.

There were other good points about Dalzell's character; in proof of which may be cited his dining with Dundas, an old Covenanting Scotch laird, who would *not* forego his long prayers before dinner, and who especially prayed that Dalzell and his royal master might have their hard hearts softened towards the Covenanting children of the Lord. When the prayer was ended, and dinner about to begin, Dalzell complimented his host on his courage in fearing man less than God. The anecdote reminds me of one in connexion with a dinner given by a gentleman of one of our "Protestant denominations," in honour of the presence of a new minister and his bride. Prayer preceded the repast, and it was given by the host, who, introducing therein the welcomed strangers, said, "We thank thee, O Lord, that thou hast conducted hither in safety thy servants, our new minister and his wife. It is thou, O Lord, who preservest both man and beast!" This was more like a kick than a compliment; but it only called up a smile on the pretty features of the minister's lady.

Let us now cross the Atlantic, with Cortez and his companions, and contemplate Montezuma in his household and at his table. Barbarian as the Spanish invaders accounted him to be, he was superior in many respects to most of his royal contemporaries in Europe. He was not less magnificent than Solomon, and he was far more cleanly than Louis XIV.

On the terraced roof of his palace, thirty knights could tilt at each other, without complaining of want of space. His armouries were filled with weapons almost as destructive as any to be found in the arsenals of civilized Christian kings. His granaries were furnished with provisions paid by tributaries; three hundred servants tended the beautiful birds of his aviaries; his menageries were the wonder and terror of beholders; and his dwarfs were more hideous, and his ladies more dazzling, than potentate had ever before looked upon with contempt or admiration. His palace within and without was a marvel of Aztec art. It was surrounded by gardens, glad with fountains and gay flowers. One thousand ladies shared the retirement of this splendid locality, with a master more glittering than anything by which he was environed,—who changed his apparel four times daily, never putting on again a garment he had once worn, and who, eating off and drinking from gold, (except on state occasions, when his table was covered with services of Cholulan porcelain,) never used a second time the vessels which had once ministered to the indulgence of his appetite.

It is said eulogistically of his cooks, that they had thirty different ways of preparing meat,—a poor boast, perhaps, compared with that of the Parisian *chefs*, who have six hundred and eighty five ways to dress eggs! Three hundred dishes were daily placed before the monarch; and such as were required to be kept hot at table were in heated earthenware stands made for the purpose. And it is even asserted, that this autocrat occasionally killed time before dinner by watching the cooking of his viands, a practice in which, according to Peter Pindar, that honest old English king used to indulge, who dined off boiled mutton at two, and to whom the funniest sight in the world was the clown in a pantomime swallowing carrots.

The ordinary dishes of Montezuma consisted of very dainty fare; namely, domestic fowls, geese, partridges, quails, venison, Indian hogs, pigeons, hares, rabbits, and other productions of his country, including—it is alleged by some and denied by others— some very choice dairy-fed baby, when this choice article happened to be in season! In cold weather enormous torches, that flung forth not only light but warmth and aromatic odours, lent additional splendour to the scene; and to temper at once the glare and the heat, screens with deliciously droll devices upon them, framed in gold, were placed before the brilliant flame.

The sovereign sat, like his links, also protected by a screen. He was not as barbarous as the most Christian kings of France, who fed in public; nor was he personally tended like them by awkward Ganymedes of a middle age. Four Hebes stood by the low throne and table of their master, and these poured water on his hands, and offered him the napkin, white as driven snow, or as the cloth on which the four hundred dishes stood waiting his attention. Women as fair presented him with bread; but even these fair ministers retired a few steps, when his sacred majesty addressed himself to the common process of eating. Then a number of ancient but sprightly nobles took their place. With these Montezuma conversed; and, when he was particularly pleased with a sage observation or a sprightly remark, a plate of pudding bestowed by the royal hand made one individual happy, and all his fellows bitterly jealous. The pudding, or whatever the dish might be, was eaten in silent reverence; and while an Aztec emperor was at meat, no one in the palace dared, at peril of his life, speak above his breath. Montezuma is described as being but a moderate eater, but fond of fruits, and indulging, with constraint upon his appetite, in certain drinks which were of a stimulating quality, such as are found in countries where civilization and luxury are at their highest.

"One thing I forgot, and no wonder," says Bernal Diaz, "to mention in its place, and that is, during the time Montezuma was at dinner, two very beautiful women were busily employed making small cakes, with eggs and other things mixed therein. These were delicately white, and when made, they presented them to him on plates covered with napkins. Also, another kind of bread was brought to him on long leaves, and plates of cakes resembling wafers. After he had dined, they presented to him three little canes, highly ornamented, containing liquid amber, mixed with a herb they call tobacco; and when he had sufficiently viewed and heard the singers, dancers, and buffoons, he took a little of the smoke of one of those canes, and then laid himself down to sleep. The meal of the monarch ended, all his guards and attendants sat down to dinner, and, as near as I could judge, about a thousand plates of those eatables that I have mentioned, were laid before them, with vessels of foaming chocolate, and fruit in immense quantities. For his women and various inferior servants, his establishment was of a prodigious expense, and we were astonished, amid such a profusion, at the vast regularity that prevailed."

What a contrast with the meal of this splendid barbarian is

that of princes of the same complexion, but of different race, the Arab! We may fittingly include among sovereigns those Arab princes whose word, if it be not heeded far, is promptly obeyed within the little circle of their rule. Skins on the ground serve for tablecloths; the dishes are, in their contents, only the reflection of each other, and in the centre of the array whole lambs or sheep lie boiled or roasted. The chief and his followers dine in successive relays of company. Sometimes the skin is spread before the door of the tent, whether in a street or in the plain, and the passers-by, even to the beggars, invited with a "Bismillah," In God's name, fall to; and having eaten, exclaim, "Hamdallilah!" God be praised! and go their way.

Not less may we include, in the roll of Majesty at Meat, those Pilgrim Fathers who were the pioneers of civilization and liberty in America. Scant indeed was the table of that "sovereign people," until they found security to sow seed, and reap the harvest in something like peace. The first meal which they enjoyed, after long months of labour, disease, and famine, was when they had constructed the little fort at Plymouth, behind which they might eat in safety and thankfulness. "The captain," says Mr. Bartlett, in his "Pilgrim Fathers," "had brought with him 'a very fat goose,' and those on shore had 'a fat crane, and a mallard,' and a dried neat's tongue.' This fare was, no doubt, washed down with good English beer and strong waters; and thus, notwithstanding the gloom that hung over them, the day passed cheerfully and sociably away." Such was the first official dinner of the "majesty of the people" beyond the Atlantic.

And having got to the "majesty of the people," I am reminded of a "popular majesty," the citizen king, Louis Philippe. He was a monarch economically minded, and kept the most modest yet not worst furnished of tables. His family often sate down before he arrived, detained as he often was by state affairs. When all rose as he quietly entered the dining room, his stereotyped phrase was, "Que personne ne se derange pour moi," and therewith ensued as little ceremony as when "William Smith" and his household sate down to an uncrowned dinner at the little inn at Newhaven.

They who are curious to see how admirably Louis Philippe was constituted for making a poor-law commissioner, or a parochial relieving overseer, should peruse the graphic biography of the king written by Alexander Dumas. Therein is a list, made out by the monarch, of what he thought was sufficient for the table of the princes and princesses; and Louis of Orleans condescends to name the number of plates of soup, or cups of coffee, that he deemed sufficient for the requirement and support of the younger branches of his house. It shows that the soul of a crafty "gargottier" was in the body of the citizen king. But we have not yet contemplated the appearance and behaviour of our own sovereigns at table, out of respect for whom we now allot a chapter, but a brief one, to themselves.

ENGLISH KINGS AT THEIR TABLES.

The utilitarians of history have declared that half our treasured incidents of story are myths. Rufus was not slain by Sir Walter Tyrrell; Richard III. was a marvellously proper man; and the young princess was not smothered in the Tower. They have laid their hands on our legends, as Augustus did on the nose of the dead Alexander, and with the same effect,—under the touch it crumbled into dust. The infidels refuse even to have faith in that table trait of Alfred, which showed him making cakes, or rather marring them, in the neat-herd's cottage. Mr. Wilkie may have prettily painted the incident, but its existence, anywhere but on canvass and in the poet's brain, they ruthlessly deny. I do not know but they are right.

We march into the bowels of more trustworthy ground, when we pass the frontier of the Roman period. William the Norman we know had a huge appetite for venison; and the Saxon chronicler says, that he loved the "high deer" as if he had been their father, which is but an equivocal compliment to his paternal affection. His table indulgences cost the life of hundreds, and the ruin of tens of hundreds. It brought on corpulency; his corpulency begot a poor joke in Philip of France; and of this joke was born such wrath in the soul of William, that he carried fire and sword into that kingdom, and was cut short in his career, ere he had accomplished the full measure of his revenge.

Rufus was as fat as his father, and as majestic both in his oaths and his appetites. To every passion he yielded himself a slave; and he feasted, like so many who would affect to be disgusted at his dishonesty, without troubling himself as to who "suffered." He never paid a creditor whom he could cheat; and again, like many of the same class, he was most affable at table; his drinking companions were on an equality with him; and in such fellowship, over gross food and huge goblets mantling to the brim, he cut unclean jokes on his own unclean deeds, at which his servile and drunken hearers roared consumedly, and swore he was a god. There was some grandeur in his ideas, however, for he built Westminster Hall, as a vestibule to a palace wherein he intended to hold high revel, such as the world had never seen; and a vestibule it has now become, but to a palace wherein sits a different sort of dignity to that dreamed of by the low-statured, fat, fierce, and huge feeding Rufus.

All the Norman kings were fearful objects at which to fling jokes; and the appetite of Henry I. was ruined, and his sanguinary ire aroused, by a derisive passage in a poem by Luke de Barré. The king made the table shake as he declared that he would let wretched versifiers know what they were to expect if they offended the King of England; and Barré suffered the loss of his eyes. Henry ate and drank none the less joyously for the deed. But *Beauclerc* was a more refined *gastronome* than his brothers, as befitted his name; and though in many respects his court was horribly licentious, yet when he went from one demesne to another, to consume its revenues upon the spot, the feasting there seems to have been attended by as much moderation as merriment.

Stephen had more to do with fighting than feasting, and with keeping castles rather than cooks; but he knew how to gain allies by the fine science of giving dinners, and there was no more courteous host than he. While the king and the barons kept high mirth, however, the people were in the lowest misery. While the king gave political feasts, his subjects were perishing of starvation by thousands.

His successor, the Second Henry, was but a poor patron of cooks, as was to be expected of a monarch who had continually to defend himself against the rebellions, not only of subjects, but of his own children. Of the latter, the only one who loved him was his natural son Geoffrey. It is no wonder that this melancholy king was the first to do away with the old custom of having a coronation dinner thrice every year, on assembling the States at the three great festivals. He was ever in the midst of affrays; and once he fell among a body of monks, who checked their turbulence to complain to the king; their complaint being that their abbot, the Bishop of Winchester, had cut off three dishes from their table. "How many has he left you?" said the king. "Good heavens!" said the monks, "he has only left us ten." "Ten!" said the monarch; "I am content with but three; and I hope your bishop will reduce you to a level with your king." They, of course, were highly disgusted at the remark.

Richard Cœur de Lion, that copper monarch, was too busy with mischief to have leisure for much banquetting; but he loved one thing, and that was venison, the poor stealers of which he punished by the most horrible mutilations. In his reign, an ox and a horse cost four shillings each; a sow was to be bought for a shilling; a sheep, with fine wool, for tenpence, and with coarse wool, for sixpence; so that, taking into account the difference in the valuation of money, people who *had* the money to purchase with could procure mutton and pork at a rate about a dozen times cheaper than the same articles can be procured at now. The sovereign did not trouble himself about paying anybody; and when he gave a banquet, the very last thing he thought of was whether it were ever paid for or not.

Richard had no virtue but courage; and John resembled his worthless brother in everything *but* courage. He had the same love for venison; and a joke at dinner upon a fat haunch, which he said had come from a noble beast that had never heard mass, was looked upon by the clerical gentlemen present as a reflection upon their corpulency. They never forgot it; and it was, perhaps, partly a consequence of their retentive memory, that the monks of Swineshead poisoned the dish of which the king partook on the occasion of almost his last dinner. He certainly never *enjoyed* another.

Henry III. was the first of our kings whose reign exceeded half-a-century in duration. He was a moderate man, loved plain fare, and cared more for masses than merriment. He was an easy, indolent monarch, with troubles enough to have fired him to activity; but he would have given half his realm for the privilege of daily dining in peace and quietness, a boon seldom vouchsafed to him. His subjects must have dined as ill as himself, if we may judge by the extraordinary variation of the prices of articles of consumption during his reign. Thus the price of wheat, for instance, varied from one shilling to a pound a quarter. The royal statute upon ale rather displeased all citizens of this period, for by it the price was fixed at a halfpenny per gallon in cities, while in the country the same quantity might be sold for a farthing. A gallon of ale for a halfpenny ought, however, to have satisfied the most thirsty of drinkers.

The frugal Edward I. very little patronised either eating or drinking, beyond what nature required. He was a very moderate wine-drinker, but he exceedingly offended those who were otherwise, by imposing a duty of two shillings a tun on all wine imported, over and above the old existing duty. The unlucky Edward II. was to the first Edward, what Louis XVI. was to Louis XIV., the scape-goat for the crimes of a predecessor and tyrant too powerful to be resisted. The banqueting-room of this Edward, however, was, as is often the case with such princes, oftener used than the council-room, and the favourites feasted with their weak lord until rebellion marred the festivity. There never was a merrier reign (despite public calamity) closed by so terrible a murder as that of his king, whose last dinner would have almost disgusted a dog.

Edward III. was a gorgeous patronizer of the culinary art; the cooks and his guests adored him; and Windsor Castle, which he built as a fortress and a pleasaunce, is a monument of his power and his taste. But his love for good cheer was imitated by his subjects to their ruin; and king and parliament interfered to remedy by penalty, what might have been obviated by good example. Servants were prohibited from eating flesh, meat, or fish, above once a-day. By another law, it was ordained that no one should be allowed, either for dinner or supper, above three dishes for each course, and not above two courses; and it is likewise expressly declared that *soused* meat is to count as one of these dishes. And of these laws I will only observe, that if they were obeyed, servants and citizens of the days of Edward III. were a very different class of people from what they are at present.

When it is stated of Richard II. that two thousand cooks and three hundred servitors were employed in the royal kitchen, we think we become acquainted with the gastronomic tastes of that unhappy king. But as he was one of those whose virtues were his own, and his vices were of others' making, so this Sardanapalian array of cooks was kept up by those who ruled from behind the throne, and finally left the king to starve, despite his counting cooks by thousands. His chief *cuisinier* is known only by the initials C. S. S., under which he wrote a culinary work in English, "On the Forme of Cury." In this work, he speaks of poor Richard, his royal master, as the "best and royallest viander of all Christian kynges."

Henry IV. kept a princely but not a profuse table. He was the first king in England whose statutes may be said to have acted as a check on the freedom of after-dinner conversation upon religious matters; for in his reign took place the first execution in England, on account of opinions connected with matters of faith. The household expenses of this monarch are set down at something less than £20,000 per annum of the money of the time; and this sum, moderate enough, appears to have been fairly applied to the purposes for which it was intended. A porpoise was a fashionable dish in the time of Henry V., who first had it at the royal table, and thus sanctioned its use at tables of lower degree. Loyal folks in those days copied the example set them by their sovereign, as they did in the later days of George III. boiled mutton and caper sauce, when country gentlemen "dined like the king, sir, at two o'clock." But Henry V. was oppressed with debts, and, like many men in similar positions, his banquets were all the more splendid, and his prodigality was equal to his liabilities. So extravagant a monarch bequeathed but a poor inheritance to Henry VI., who was occasionally as hard put to it for a dinner as ever the Second

Charles was. When Edward IV. jumped into poor Henry's seat, he found a host of angry persons who disputed his power, and these he took care to conciliate by the most powerful, nay irresistible means that were ever applied to the solution of a difficulty, or the removal of an obstruction. He simply invited them to dinner; and, certainly, up to that time England had never seen a king who gave dinners on so extravagantly profuse a scale. They were marked, however, by something of a barbaric splendour; and the monarch, gay and glittering as he was, dazzling in dress, and overwhelmingly exuberant of spirits, was more like William de la Marck than any more knightly host. In short, Edward was but a coarse beast at table. "In homine tam corpulento," says the Croyland chronicler, "tantis sodalitiis, vanitatibus, crapulis, luxuriis et cupiditatibus dedito,"—a sort of testimonial to character which neither monarch nor man could be justified in being proud of. The young Edward V. is the "petit Dauphin" of English history, but with a less cruel destiny, for he was at least not starved to death, amid dirt, darkness, and terror, but mercifully, if roughly, murdered, and so saved from the long and yet unexpiated assassination of the innocent and helpless Louis XVII. His murderer sought to make people forget the heinousness of his crime, by the double splendour of his coronation dinners. The ceremony and the festival took place, not only in London, but in York; and Richard hoped he had feasted both the northern and southern provinces into sentiments of loyalty. A curious incident preceded the first dinner,—the anointing of himself and consort at the coronation. There is nothing singular in the fact, but there *is* in the manner of it. Richard and his queen stripped themselves to the waist, in order that the unction might be more liberally poured over them,—and in Richard's own case perhaps for another reason, that the great nobles who were present might see that they were not about to sit down to dinner with a sovereign who was as deformed in body as his enemies declared him to be.

Almost all young readers of history take their first permanent idea of Henry VII. from that gallant Richmond, in Shakespeare's Tragedy, who comes in like an avenging angel, at the beginning of the fifth act, and has it all his own generous way, until he sticks "the bloody and devouring bear," and sends a note to Elizabeth to come and be married. This Elizabeth, by the way, was the good mother of Henry VIII., and she was the only woman for whom that capricious prince ever felt a spark of pure affection. His love and respect for *her* were permanent, and the fact merits to be recorded. But to return to Henry VII., and to conduct him to the dinner-table, where alone we have present business with him; I do not know that I can find a better "trait" touching himself and his times, than one connected with his royal visit to York.

He was received in the city with more than ordinary ceremony, and loudly-expressed delight at the sight of his "sweet-favoured" face; "some casting out of obles and wafers, and some casting out of comfits in great quantities, as it had been hailstones, for joy and rejoicing of the king's coming." But I must pass over the outward show — how Augustans, Franciscans, Carmelites, and Dominicans met him at Micklegate, and how these, with priors, and friars, and canons of hospitals, and priests, and knights, and noble, and gentle, and simple, accompanied the Monarch to the Minster, and thence to the archbishop's palace, where Henry resided during his stay in the northern capital. The grandest banquet given to him during his sojourn, was in this palace, on the eve of the festival of St. George: the great hall was divided into a centre and two aisles. In each division there were two tables, half-a-dozen in all. The king sat at the centre table arrayed in all the pomp and glory of a king;—George and garter, crown, and England's sceptre. One individual only was esteemed worthy of being seated at the same table, namely, the Archbishop of York, who was quite as powerful a man, in his way, as Henry Tudor himself. Knights carved the joints, and earls waited upon prince and prelate. Lord Scrope, of Bolton, *because* he was a Knight of the Garter, served the king with water; another member of chivalry, handed the cup, and the sovereign's meat was especially carved for him by a Welsh cousin, Sir David Owen. The distribution of the other tables exhibited a judicious mixture of priest and layman. At the first table in the centre of the hall, (the cross-table at the top being occupied by the king and the archbishop) sat two secular dignitaries, the Lords Chancellor and Privy Seal, and with them, the Abbots of St. Mary and Fountains, with the archbishop's suffragans, other prelates and the royal chaplains; thus the chief members of the clergy were seated in greatest numbers near the king. The second table was entirely occupied by lay nobility, earls, barons, knights and esquires of the king's body. Of the two tables in the right aisle, the city clergy and the Minster choir occupied one to themselves. At the upper end of the table were several knights of the garter, all sitting on one side, "and beneath them a void space, and then other honest persons filled that table." We are glad to fall on the term "*other* honest," or we might have been tempted to believe that a distinction was made between honesty and nobility. The tables in the left aisle were occupied, one by the municipal guests, the second by the judges, " and beneath them *other* honest persons," again. At the rear of the king's table a stage was erected, on which stood the royal officer of arms, who cried his "largesse" three times, in the usual manner, and doubtless with something of the stentorian powers made familiar to us by the late Mr. Toole, and the present loud and lively Mr. Harker. "The surnape," we are told, "was drawn by Sir John Turberville, the knight-marshal; and after the dinner there was a voide, when the king and his nobles put off their robes of state, except such as were knights of the garter, who rode to even-song, attired in the habit of their order;" and a very fitting close to a feast,—and a good example is held forth therein to all who rise from a festival without any more thought of being thankful for it, than is implied by trying to find out the reflection of their noses in the mahogany.

The following table story, cited by Southey, furnishes another illustration of social, and, indeed, of political, life about this time:—

"Henry (then Richmond), on his march from Milford, lodged one night with this friend David Llwyd, at Matha'farn. David had the reputation of seeing into the future, and Richmond, whether in superstition or compliment, privately inquired of him, what would be the issue of his adventure. Such a question, he was told, was too important to be immediately answered, but in the morning a reply should be made. The wife of David saw that her husband was unusually grave during the evening; and having learnt the cause, she said, 'How can you have any difficulty about your answer? Tell him he will succeed gloriously. If he does, you will receive honours and rewards. But if it fail, depend upon it, he will never come here to reproach you.'" Hence, it is said, a Welsh proverb, "A wife's advice without asking it."

Henry VIII. loved to take a quiet dinner, occasionally, with his chancellor, at Chelsea; and there he would walk in the garden, with his arm round that neck which he afterwards flung beneath the axe of the executioner. He was given to indulgences of all sorts, and with respect to those of the palate, he was well served by his incomparable clerk of the kitchen, honest and clever William Thynne, who was not a *mere* clerk of the kitchen, but a gentleman and scholar to boot; loving poetry though he was no poet, and editing Chaucer with as much zeal as that with which he regulated the accounts of his kitchen clerkship. Henry ate not wisely, but too well; and this huge feeding brought him at last to such a size that he could not be moved but by aid of "a machine." In other words, I suppose, he could not walk, and was compelled to submit to locomotion in a chair. Among the sovereigns who assembled at the Congress of Vienna, and who were as strangely there together as the half-dozen kings whom Candide met at the *table d'hôte* in Venice, was that monster of a man, the King of Wurtemburg. This mountain of flesh dined daily at the imperial table, where a semi-circular piece was cut out of the mahogany, in order that the stomach of the monarch might rest comfortably against the table, when engaged in its appropriate work. He did not lack wit for abounding in fatness, and to him, I believe, is properly attributed the neat saying, when he saw Lord Castlereagh in simple civilian's dress, without a star, amid the gold lace, gems, jewels, ties, tags, and glittering uniforms around him. The king asked who he was, and on being informed, he remarked: "Ma foi! il est *bien distingué!*" He could not have paid the same compliment to the noble Stewart's wife, if it be true, as was reported, that at one of the state dinners, or state balls, she appeared with her husband's jewelled garter, worn as a *bandeau*, and "Honi soit qui mal y pense" burning in diamonds upon her forehead.

May it not have been the unpleasant effects of Henry's gastronomic indulgences that made of him a dabbler in medicine? Many of his prescriptions in his own handwriting are still extant, and some of them are in the British Museum. He invented a plaister, and was the concocter of more than one original ointment for the cure of indigestion. He also prepared " a plaister for the Lady Ann of Cleves, to mollify and lessen certain swellings proceeding from cold, and to dissipate the boils on the stomach." His majesty in some of his after-dinner ruminations professed also to have discovered a remedy for the plague; the prescription for which he sent to the lord mayor. He was very tender of the health of Wolsey, when the cardinal little regarded his own. His majesty, on one occasion, counsels his minister, if he would soon be relieved from "the sweating," to take light suppers, and to drink wine very moderately, and to use a certain kind of pill. I do not know if Henry's cookery and kitchen at all smelt of unorthodoxy before the Reformation, but it is a fact that, when Cardinal Campeggio came over here on the business of the divorce of Henry and Catherine, he was especially charged by the Pope to look into the state of cookery in England generally, and in the royal palace in particular.

The royal table of Elizabeth was a solemnity indeed. But it

was all a majestically stupendous sham. The attendants thrice bent their knee as they approached to offer her the different dishes; and when these ceremonies had been gone through, the queen rose and retired to a private room, where the meats were placed before her, and she was left to dine as comfortably as the citizens and their wives of Eastcheap and Aldersgate.

Among the numerous new year's gifts made to Elizabeth, and by which she contrived to maintain a splendid wardrobe, gifts of good things for her table were not wanting. One of her physicians presented her with a box of foreign sweetmeats; another doctor with a pot of green ginger; while her apothecaries gave her boxes of lozenges, ginger-candy, and other conserves. "Mrs. Morgan gave a box of cherries and one of apricots." The queen's master-cock and her serjeant of the pastry presented her with various confectionery and preserves.

Elizabeth and her "maids" both dined and breakfasted upon very solid principles and materials. Beef and beer were consumed at breakfast,—"a repast for a ploughman!" it may be said. Alas! ploughmen are content, or seem so, to strengthen their sinews as they best may of a morning with poor bread and worse tea. Elizabeth made a truly royal bird of the goose,—a distinction which her sister Mary failed to give to the cygnet, the stork, and the crane. These no more suited the national taste than the Crimean delicacy, a Russian oyster, and which all Englishmen who have tasted thereof pronounce to be a poisonous dab of rancid putty. Yet Russian princes are fond thereof, and Russian sovereigns order them for especial favourites;—just as the Prince Regent, whenever Lord Eldon was to dine at Carlton-house, always commanded the chancellor's favourite dish to be placed near him,—liver and bacon.

The household expenditure of James I. amounted to £100,000 sterling yearly; double the sum required for the same purpose by Elizabeth; and if "cock a leekie" and "haggis" were dishes to which his national taste gave fashion, the more foreign delicacies of snails and legs of frogs, dressed in a variety of ways, were readily eaten by the very daintiest of feeders. The taste of the purveyors was, however, something clumsy. What would now be said if a *chef* sent up to table four huge pigs, belted and harnessed with ropes of sausages, and all tied together to a monstrous bag-pudding?

The court of James I. was uncleanly enough, but it was made worse by the example of the Danish king and his courtiers, on a royal visit to the Stuart. "The Danish custom of drinking healths was scrupulously observed, and in a company of even twenty or thirty, every person's health was required to be drunk in rotation; sometimes a lady or an absent patron was toasted on the knees, and, as a proof of love or loyalty, the pledger's blood was even mingled with the wine." It is well known that the ladies of the court, as well as the gentlemen, got, "beastly drunk," in honour of the visit of the King of Denmark to his sister, the consort of James I.

James, whose taste in gastronomy was not a very delicate one, used to say that if he were ever called upon to provide a dinner for the devil, his bill of fare should consist of "a pig, a poll of ling and mustard, and a pipe of tobacco for digestion."

There was more temperance under Charles I., and increased moderation under the Commonwealth, when Cromwell's table was remarkable for its simplicity. The civic feasts of those days were also distinguished by their decorous sobriety; and it is, perhaps, worth noticing that the "show" followed, and did not precede the dinner.

Charles I. was served with a world of old-fashioned ceremony, not unlike that which ought to have made Louis XIV. very uncomfortable. The fact, however, is, that both monarchs were pleased with the cumbrous solemnities of state. And nothing affected our English king more in his fallen fortunes than the rude service which he received at the hands of the Puritan Servitors of whose masters he was the captive. When he was in durance at Windsor, his meat was brought to him uncovered, and carried without any observance of respectful form, by the common soldiers. No trial or "say" of the meats was made; no cup presented on the knee.

This absence of ceremony wounded Charles to the very quick. It chafed him more than greater sorrows did subsequently. It was, he observed, the refusal to him of a service which was paid, according to ancient custom, to many of his subjects; and rather than submit to the humiliation, he chose to diminish the number of dishes, and to take his meals in strict privacy.

There are few kings who had such variety of experience in matters of the table as Charles II. The first spoonful of medicine that was offered him he resisted with a determined aversion which never left him for that sort of *pabulum*. His table was but simple enough during the latter years of his father, but it was worse after the fatal day of Worcester. He was glad then, at White Lady's, to eat " bread and cheese, such as we could get, it being just beginning to be day ;" and " bread, cheese, small beer, and nothing else," sufficed him in the oak. Bread, butter, ale and sack, he swallowed in country inns, and seemed rather to look on the masquerade and the meals as a joke.

When he was lying hid in Spring Coppice, the goodwife Yates brought to his most sacred majesty " a mess of milk, some butter, and eggs,"—better fare than the parched peas which were found, in after days, in the pocket of the fugitive Monmouth. The women provided for him as tenderly in his hour of hunger and trial, as their ebony sisters did for Mungo Park in his African solitude. When Charles arrived at the house at Boscobel, he " ate bread and cheese heartily," and (as an extraordinary,) William Penderell's wife made his majesty a posset of fine milk and small beer, and got ready some warm water to wash his feet, not only extremely dirty, but much galled with travel." The king, in return, called the lady " my dame Joan," and the condescension quickened her hospitality; for shortly after, she " provided some chickens for his majesty's supper, a dainty he had not lately been acquainted with. But the king and his followers not only longed for more substantial fare, but were not very scrupulous as to the means of obtaining it. Colonel Carlis, for instance, went into the sheepcot of a farmer residing near Boscobel, and like an impudent as well as a hungry thief " he chose one of the best sheep, sticks him with his dagger, then sends William for the mutton, who brings him home on his back." The next morning was a Sunday morning, and Charles, having muttered his prayers, went eagerly to the parlour to look after the stolen mutton. It was hardly cold, but Will Penderell "brought a leg of it into the parlour; his majesty called for a knife and a trencher, and cut some of it into collops, and pricked them with the knife-point, then called for a frying-pan and butter and fried the collops himself, of which he ate heartily. Colonel Carlis, the while, being but under-cook (and that, honour enough too), made the fire, and turned the collops in the pan. When the colonel," adds the faithful Blount, who records this table trait, "afterwards attended his majesty in France, his majesty, calling to remembrance this passage among others, was pleased merely to propose it, as a problematical question, whether himself or the colonel were the master cook at Boscobel, and the supremacy was of right adjudged to his majesty." Circumstances which made of the royal adventurer a king were the spoiling of an excellent cook. When he was secretly sojourning at Trent, his meat was, for the most part, to prevent the danger of discovery, dressed in his own chamber; "the cookery whereof served him for some divertisement of the time." The king better understood cookery as a science than the machinery of it. When he stood in the kitchen of Mr. Tombs's house at Longmarston, disguised as "Will Jackson," the busy cook-maid bade him wind up the jack. "Will Jackson" was obedient and attempted it, but hit not the right way, which made the maid in some passion ask, "What countryman are you, that you know not how to wind up a jack?" Will Jackson answered very satisfactorily, "I am a poor tenant's son of Colonel Lane, in Staffordshire. We seldom have roast meat, but when we have, we don't make use of a jack;" which in some measure assuaged the maid's indignation. Never had the sacredness of majesty been in such peril since the period when Alfred marred instead of made the cakes of the neatherd's angry wife. But Charles escaped to his rather hungry exile in France:—and see, how sweet are the uses of adversity! When this charming prince was restored to the throne, he brought with him two gifts of which the nation had heard little for some years;—one was the Church Liturgy, and the other, "God d—n ye,"—a fashionable phrase which has tumbled from the court to the alley.

It can hardly be said that Charles, when king, fulfilled the requirement which Lord Chesterfield subsequently laid down, when he insisted that a man should be gentlemanlike even in his vices. When William of Orange came to England as the suitor of the king's niece, the Princess Mary, Charles took an unclean delight in making the Dutchman drunk. Evelyn says:—"One night, at a supper given by the Duke of Buckingham, the king made him (William) drink very hard; the heavy Dutchman was naturally averse to it, but being once entered, was the most frolicsome of the company; and now the mind took him to break the windows of the chambers of the maids of honour; and he had got into their apartments had they not been timely rescued. His mistress, I suppose," adds Evelyn, and it is a strange comment for so sensible a man, "did not like him the worse for such a notable indication of his vigour." The monarch who made his *paulo-post* successor drunk had little difficulty to bring the lord mayor of London into the same condition; and the city potentate and his "cousin the king" had that terrible "other bottle" together, in which men's reason ordinarily makes shipwreck, with their dignity. But his majesty, of blessed memory, was a trifle devout after his drink, and on the "next morning" he heard anthems in his chapel, and by way of devotion, would lean over his own pew and play with the curls of Lady Castlemaine, who occupied the next seat to that of "our most religious and gracious king." When he was pouring the public money into the lap of that precious lady, he was leaving his own servants unpaid; and, on one occasion, when these could not obtain their salaries, they carried off their royal master's linen, and left him without a clean shirt or a tablecloth!

The priests with whom Louis XIV. and Louis XV. used to

transact their religion were wont to excuse all the conjugal infidelities of those anointed reprobates by remarking that they ever treated their consorts with the very greatest politeness. The poets of Charles's days went further, and extolled his marital affection. Waller, for instance, congratulates the poor queen, that if she were ill, Charles was by to tend and weep over her:—

> "But, that which may relieve our care
> Is, that you have a help so near
> For all the evil you can prove;
> The kindness of your Royal Love.
> He that was never known to mourn
> So many kingdoms from his torn,
> His tears reserved for you; more dear
> More prized, than all those kingdoms were!
> For when no healing art prevail'd,
> When cordials and elixirs fail'd,
> On your pale cheek he dropt the shower,
> Revived you like a dying flower."

The illness referred to was a spotted fever; and here is Pepys' plain prose on the subject:—" 20th October, 1663. This evening, at my lord's lodgings, Mrs. Sarah, talking with my wife and I, how the queen do, and how the king tends her, being so ill. She tells us that the queen's sickness is the spotted fever; that she was as full of the spots as a leopard, which is very strange that it should be no more known; but perhaps it is not so; and that the king do seem to take it much to heart, for that he had wept before her; but for all that he hath not missed one night since she was sick, of supping with my lady Castlemaine; which I believe is true; for she says that her husband hath dressed the suppers every night; and I confess I saw him myself coming through the street, dressing up a great supper to-night, which Sarah also says is for the king and her, which is a very strange thing." Oh, depth of royal grief, that required light suppers and light ladies for its solace!

The *Spectator* has preserved for us a pleasant story illustrative both of royal and citizen good-fellowship, in the reign of Charles II., and in the person of the king and that of his jolly lord mayor, Sir Robert Viner. The merry monarch had been dining with the chief magistrate and the municipality, at Guildhall, where he had not drunk so deeply himself but he was aware that the jollity of his entertainers was beginning to render them rather oblivious of the respect due to their royal guest. He accordingly with a curt farewell, slipped away down to his coach, which was awaiting him in Guildhall-yard. But the lord mayor forthwith pursued the runaway, and overtaking him in the yard, seized him by the skirts of his coat, and swore roundly that he should not go till they "had drank t' other bottle!" "The airy monarch," says the narrator in the *Spectator*, "looked kindly at him over his shoulder, and with a smile and graceful air (for I saw him at the time, and do now), repeated this line of the old song:—

"'And the man that is drunk is as great as a king!'

and immediately turned back, and complied with his landlord." This anecdote, however, though it be given on the authority of an alleged eye-witness, is probably overcoloured with regard to the conduct of his worship the mayor. Mr. Peter Cunningham quotes (in his history of Nell Gwyn) from Henry Sidney's Diary, a letter addressed to Sidney by his sister the Countess Dowager of Sutherland, and which refers to the incident of the visit of Charles to Guildhall. The letter in question was written five years after the mayoralty of Sir Robert Viner. "The king had supped with the lord mayor, and the aldermen on the occasion had drunk the king's health, over and over, upon their knees, wishing every one hanged and damned that would not serve him with their lives and fortunes. But this was not all. As his guards were drunk or said to be so, they would not trust his majesty with so insecure an escort, but attended him themselves to Whitehall, and, as the lady-writer observes, 'all went merry out of the king's cellar.' So much was this accessibility of manner in the king acceptable to his people, that the mayor and his brethren waited next day at Whitehall, to return thanks to the king and duke for the honour they had done them, and the mayor confirmed by this reception, was changed from an ill to a well-affected subject."

But as this merry mourner lived, so may he almost be said to have died. It will be remembered with what disgust Evelyn records the scene at Whitehall, a week before the king's decease: —"I can never forget," he says, "the inexpressible luxury and profaneness, gaming and all dissoluteness, and as it were total neglectfulness of God, it being Sunday evening, which this day sennight I was witness of, the king sitting and toying with his concubines, Portsmouth, Cleveland, Mazarine, &c.; a French boy singing love-songs in that glorious gallery; whilst about twenty of the great courtiers and other dissolute persons were at basset, round a large table, a bank of at least two thousand pounds in gold before them, upon which two gentlemen who were with me made reflections in astonishment. Six days after, all was in the dust."

There was more meanness, but not more decency, under James II., but his queen more deeply resented, and that in public, at dinner, the insults levelled at her. When Mrs. Sedly, in 1686, was created Countess of Dorchester, the day on which the nomination passed the Great Seal, and indeed on a subsequent occasion, the queen showed how she was touched by the honours paid to a brazen concubine. "The queen," says Evelyn, "took it very grievously, so as for two dinners, standing near her, I observed she hardly ate one morsel, nor spake one word to the king, or to any about her; though at other times she used to be extremely pleasant, full of discourse and good-humour." Such is one of the table traits of the time of James II.

There is little to be said of William III., save that he kept a well-regulated table, and was excessively angry if he detected any faults in the service. He is described as being kind, cordial, open, even convivial and jocose. He would sit at table many hours, and would bear his full share in festive conversation. Burnet, I think, somewhere intimates, but I cannot recollect the precise words, that he was something more than moderately given to Hollands. As much, indeed, has been said of Queen Anne. But Anne *was* inclined to indulge in good living, and her doctor, Lister, had as many gastronomic propensities as herself. Lister entered into the minutiæ of the kitchen with the exactness of an apothecary weighing poison. On the subject of larks, he says, for the benefit of the queen, and all who love such dainty food, that if twelve larks do not weigh twelve ounces, they are scarcely eatable; they are just tolerable if they reach that weight; but that if they weigh thirteen ounces, they are fat and excellent! On such table matters did royal physicians write, when Anne was queen.

The table of George, Prince Regent, was splendidly served. The court language was French, as though the days of the Normans were come again. But the son of George III., whether as prince or as king, and despite his character of being the first gentleman in Europe, was *not* naturally refined. He loved to have around him men like Humboldt, who, when his guest, amused him with stories as broad as they were long. He himself would tell similar stories, even in the presence of his mother and sisters, and in spite of a sharp "Fie, George!" and an indignant working of her fan on the part of Queen Charlotte. When king, the female society which he assembled at the Pavilion was very décolleté indeed, both as regarded person and principles, and the appearance of these brilliant looking and light dressed individuals in the daytime gave to Brighton an aspect that put Rowland Hill into fits. There were joyous evenings then at Virginia Water, on "tea and marrow bones," and there was everything there but refinement. Refinement, indeed, was not the characteristic of any one prince of the house. The Duke of Cumberland revelled in coarse jests, and was delighted when they embarrassed the modesty that could not even comprehend them. The Duke of Cambridge was perhaps the least offensive of the family. He was the professional diner out of the house; and in his day very few public dinners took place without having the advantage of his presence as president.

He was, on such occasions, punctuality itself, and could not tolerate being kept waiting. In such cases, he sometimes wiled away the time by trying over music with the musical gentlemen whose harmony was to relieve the toasts and tedium of the evening, but his impatience sometimes got the better of his politeness and of his reverence for serious things, and we shall not soon forget the effect he produced at a "religious public dinner," by exclaiming aloud, " Where is the chaplain? d—n him! Why doesn't he say grace?" Before passing to the next reign, we may take notice of a fact that is not generally known, but which nevertheless cannot be disputed. The coronation banquet of George IV. was one of the most splendid upon record. But there was a world of "leather and prunella" about it, in spite of its reputed splendour. Thus, for instance, the king's table was one gorgeous display of gold plate, but the plates and dishes at all the other tables, one only, I believe, excepted, were composed of nothing more costly than good, honest pewter. The metal was indeed so splendidly burnished that to the eye no silver highly polished could have been more dazzling; but the truth remains that the peerage that day dined off pewter. But the occasion gave value to the material, and the dishes, in their character of relics of the glory of the last coronation banquet in Westminster Hall, are as highly prized, and as reverently preserved, as though they were composed of materials less strange to Potosi than tin, antimony, and a trifle of copper.

Court life, in the reign of William IV., was but of a very sombre aspect. The good old king used to indulge in giving toasts after dinner, and he made long and somewhat prosy speeches. Of the latter he was particularly fond, and he made the then young Prince George of Cambridge his pupil, by giving the health of his father, the Duke, and inducing the son to rise and return thanks for the honour conferred. It was no bad discipline for one who intended to become a public man. The young prince became a very fair speaker under the old king's instructions. William detested politics, and he invariably fell asleep during the dessert.

It would have violated etiquette to have awoke him; and the queen and her ladies never thought of rising until the royal eyelids began again to give symptoms of returning wakefulness. He was fond of talking, over the wine, of military details, and was proud of two achievements connected therewith; first, that he had made Colonel Needham shave off his cherished whiskers, according to the new regulations; and that he had succeeded in having all the Waterloo medals worn with the king's head outwards. He frequently fell asleep during these conversations; and then the guests quietly passed the wine from one to the other, and, as they drank off their glasses, bowed to or smiled at the sleeping sovereign the while. In the evening, there generally was music, during which the Queen Adelaide was as generally engaged in worsted work. The king usually honoured some one with an invitation to sit by his side on the sofa. He then fell asleep again, and the unlucky, honoured individual, did not dare leave his "coign of 'vantage" until the king awoke and gave the signal. William was a very moderate joker, and he loved a joke from others. It is reported that, when heir presumptive, he once said to a Secretary of the Admiralty who was at the same dinner table, "C——, when I am king, you shall not be Admiralty Secretary! Eh, what do you say to that?" "All that I have to say to that, in such a case, is," said C——, "God save the king!" I have heard it further said, that William never laughed so loudly as when he was told of a certain *parvenu* lady, who, dining at Sir John Copley's, ventured to express her surprise that there was "no *pilfered* water on the table."

The dining-tables of deceased monarchs belong to history; and, consequently, the limit of this imperfect record is to be found here. One further illustration, however, of "household" matters may here be not inaptly introduced. A few months ago a gentleman, who had been in his early years the personal friend of the Duke of Kent, was desirous of sending from Sicily a testimonial of his respect to the late Duke's daughter, our sovereign lady the Queen. His grateful remembrance took the shape of some very rare and choice Sicilian wine, the proper transmission of which was entrusted to the good offices of a friend of the donor. This honorary agent proceeded to the proper office for instructions, and there he was somewhat surprised at being informed that, as soon as the duty had been paid upon the wine, the latter would be forwarded to the "household." At this strange intimation, the friendly agent wrote to his principal for fresh instructions, and the principal, who had not the slightest intention of showing his respect for the memory of a sire by presenting wine to the "household" of that sire's royal daughter, at once directed the luscious tribute to be divided among friends who had households of their own, and who could appreciate the present. The rule, with regard to offerings like these, was not in former times so ungraciously severe. When Mrs. Coutts used to send her pleasant tributary haunches of venison to the Pavilion, she was not informed that the "household" would condescend to dine upon the venison: on the contrary, a graceful autograph note from the royal recipient not only made cheerful acknowledgment of the gift, but also gave hearty promise that it would be thoroughly enjoyed. There is more independence, perhaps, in the present system, which discourages all tributes, whatever may be their nature; but there is something very ungracious in the method of its application.

Enough, however, of this matter, or we shall have little time to discuss, even briefly, two other subjects, touching which I would say something, before we are finally called to "supper." The first of these comes under the head of "Strange Banquets."

STRANGE BANQUETS.

UNDER this title I was half inclined to include the records of the achievement of those gastronomic heroes, whose spirit was something like that of the boy's who ate with two spoons, and cried because he could not swallow faster. But, from Milo and his entire bull for dinner, down to Dando and his peck of oysters for supper, there is a sameness of very gross detail, and perhaps not very great truth in all. The rustic who was victor at an eating match, "by a pig and an apple pie," was on a level with the ancient kings, who were wont to boast that they could carry more beneath their belts with impunity than any other men. So the ardour of the two villages contemplating their respective champions—gluttons employed for the honour of their several birth-places—and the exultation of one party at finding its favourite a-head "by two turkeys and a pound of sausages," gave proof of as much dignity of humanity as was given in *their* case by those nations of old who weighed their kings annually, and had a general illumination when they found their monarchs growing fatter.

These illustrations of table manners, if indeed they deserve to be so called, we leave to the perusal of those whose devotion is of that cast that they would have reckoned Baal as a god, for no other reason than the sufficient one given of old, namely, that he ate much meat. In more modern times, we have had defunct kings who have been supposed capable of consuming as much as Baal himself, or any of his lively followers; for an illustration of which fact we must pass over, for a short time, to the once kingdom of France.

The last banquet prepared by the culinary officers of Francis I. for that royal personage, was one at which my readers would not have cared to sit in fellowship with the king, nor was it one which that monarch himself could be said to have perfectly enjoyed.

He made, indeed, no remark or complaint, but *that* was for the natural reason that he was dead when he presided at it! How this came to pass I will proceed to relate.

On the first day of March, 1546, Francis I. died in the Chateau de Rambouillet. The whole of the following day his body was in the hands of the surgeon-embalmers, who vainly exercised their office to render that sweet when dead which had by no means been so when living. During six weeks the corpse was deposited at the neighbouring Abbey of Haute-Bruyère. It was then transported to the house of the Archbishop of Paris at St. Cloud, where there was a duplicate "lying in state." The dead king, extended on a couch of richly embroidered crimson satin, was surrounded by a thickly-wedged mass of priests, who, night and day, offered up prayers for the repose of his soul. In the adjacent chamber was the "counterfeit presentment," or effigy of the monarch, made "after nature," reclining on a bed of the most gorgeous description, on and about which was displayed all that could lend additional solemn glory to the scene. The waxen effigy, with hands joined, was decked in a crimson silk shirt, covered by a light blue tunic powdered with *fleurs de lis.* The royal mantle, of a deep violet, lay across the feet; and near it were the orders, chains, and other "bravery" worn by Francis in his lifetime. On the head was a violet velvet scull-cap, and above that the crown. The legs were thrust into boots of cloth of gold, with crimson satin soles—but then they were not made for walking in. In the room, and particularly near the bed, there was a blaze of gold and jewellery, such as dazzled the sight only to look at it. The upper portion of the bed was fashioned like a tent. Sentinels guarded it from without, and priests kept watch with much prayer within. They were of all grades, from cardinals and princes of the Church down to bare-footed friars, who would have been more thankful for a scarlet hat than for a pair of the newest sandals. These were the guests at a banquet where the king was the highly honoured host.

We are told by old Pierre de Chastel, Bishop of Macon, that

the ordinary etiquette of service was rigorously maintained every day, during eleven days, as if the king had been living and laughing in the midst of them. The royal dinner-table was laid out at the side of the bed; a cardinal blessed the viands; and a gentleman of various quarterings presented to the unconscious image a full ewer, wherewith to wash the hands which, folded as they were, seemed like those of the father of Miss Kilmansegg, to be already washing themselves with invisible soap in imperceptible water!

A second gentleman offered to the representative of the defunct king a vase mantling with wine; and a third wiped his lips and fingers, as if either could have been soiled by *not* coming in contact with the cates and the goblet! These functions, and others that may very well be passed over, were performed amid a most death-like silence, and by the fitful light of funereal torches— the only dinner lamps in use, while the dead king was engaged in *not* dining. And such were the clever funeral banquets presided over by the waxen similitude of a defunct king. And here it should be *my* office to pass to other subjects more immediately connected with Table Traits, but I may, perhaps, be pardoned if I add, that the royal corpse, after the copious feeding which its effigy was mocked with, was raised with incredible pomp, and borne into Paris with an attendant mixture of the sublime and the ridiculous. It was preceded by beggars, nobles, cavaliers, and cooks, ("officiers de bouche,") pages, surgeons, and valets de chambre, grooms, heralds, and archbishops. The followers behind the car were of more uniform and exalted rank; and when the procession reached Vaugérard, it was met by the twenty-four town-criers of Paris, who took immediate precedence of the five hundred beggars. The funeral service in the cathedral was conducted with similar magnificence; but what is most singular is the fact, that the solemn ceremony was no sooner concluded, than it was recommenced with all gravity, for the benefit of the waxen effigy that had been served for eleven days with an "omelette fantastique!" and more than this, two of the sons of the deceased king, having been previously interred, but with maimed rites, a newly organized procession and service took place on this occasion, not only for themselves, but for their effigies also! There was an ocean of holy water scattered on these exaggerated dolls; the aspersion, however, was borne with a calmness worthy of their dignity! And at these ceremonies the English ambassador, with other Christian representatives, appeared on horseback, each with a prelate mounted also at his side. The union represented that which ought to exist between church and state everywhere, but which does not even in the Duchy of Baden. When the lengthened solemnities had come to a conclusion, the merry pages, as hungry as they were joyous, scrambled for sweetmeats, and that was the last of the feasting or fasting of Francis I.

All this seems barbarous and antique; it *is* the former rather than the latter. The custom, with some attendant exaggerations, is still prevalent in China, where only two years ago the defunct aunt of the sun and moon, mother to the reigning monarch, was feasted with a solemn parade of magnificent nonsense, the details of which make those of the banquet of the deceased Francis look extremely poor indeed. I believe that the Chinese idea with regard to their poor dead princess was, that she, or the immortal part in her, could not possibly take flight upon the celestial dragon waiting to convey her to the pagoda—paradise of Cathay—until this farewell banquet had been given to her by those who had loved her upon earth.

It is the easiest thing in the world, and perhaps it is the most natural, to smile superciliously at these customs, and dismiss them with the definite remark, that they were heathenish and superstitious. *But* our grandmothers, or *their* mothers rather, saw something very like it in England. In the latter case, it was not the consequence of a law that ruled in such matters, but a spontaneous act of a sublimely ridiculous, or a ridiculously sublime, affection. Henrietta, Duchess of Marlborough, we are told, demonstrated her affection for Congreve in a manner indicative of absolute insanity. "Common fame reports," says Kippis, in the "Biographia Britannica," "that she had his figure made in wax, talked to it as if it had been alive, placed it at table with her, took great care to help it with different sorts of food, had an imaginary sore in its leg regularly dressed, and, to complete all, consulted physicians with regard to its health."

An invitation from the duchess to dinner, to meet her simulative friend, who could hardly be said to have waxed wittier after his metempsychosis, would not have been a lively thing. I am not sure that I would not rather have been in the place of the Hetman of the Zaparogue Cossacks, who was strangely treated and dieted when he was elected to the chief command over his own wild hordes. His followers besmeared (and the fashion is not yet obsolete) his face with mud, placed a symbolic *baton* in his hand, and a saucy-looking crane's feather in his bonnet. They then gave him a cupful of tar (a process that would have delighted Bishop Berkeley), and after pitching greatness into him in this manner, he was allowed a draught of mead by way of purifying his palate. When Shakspere said, "Take physic, pomp," he was little aware of the custom to that effect among the Zaparogues. It was sweetened, indeed, by the conclusive draught of mead, as Berkeley's dissertation on tar-water was wound up by a sermon on the Trinity; but I think I would have preferred swallowing the tar, with nothing to qualify it but the title, rather than have sat down to the most sumptuous of banquets, between the mad duchess and her wax lover with an issue in his leg!

William Howitt tells of an old countrywoman whom he sought to initiate into the simple elements of religion, and to whom he presented a Testament. When the latter had been read through, the worthy teacher asked her what she thought of the solemn record: "Ah, well!" was the graceless comment, "it all happened so long ago, and so far off, that I don't believe a word of it!" Some such witticism may, perhaps, apply to my stories just told, some of which have distant scenes for their locality, and others distant periods for their times of action. But, in the way of barbarous banquets, examples may be cited less open to this objection;

and if the far-off Zaparogue chiefs have a cruelly nasty inauguration into greatness, I do not know if the children in the Scottish Highlands, to whom the wise women there administer a mixture of whisky and earth as their first food, have not a nastier inauguration into life. Having mentioned Scotland, I may, while on the subject of strange banquets, show how they cooked and fed in the days of Edward III. "Nor yet had they," says old Joshua Barnes, "any cauldrons or pans to dress their meat in; for what beasts they found (as they always had good store in those northern parts), they would seethe them in their own (the beasts'!) skins, stretched out bellying on stakes, in the manner of cauldrons; and having thus sodden their meat, they would take out a little plate of metal, which they used to truss somewhere in or under their saddles, and laying it on the fire, take forth some oatmeal (which they carried in little bags behind them for that purpose), and having kneaded and tempered it with water, spread that thereon. This being thus baked they used for bread, to comfort and strengthen their stomachs a little when they eat flesh."

Stomachs that needed no other comforting than this must have belonged to men of irresistible arms. They devoured the bullocks, and afterwards dressed themselves in the cauldrons. They remind us of those nomade people of whom the poet asks,—

> "Was ever Tartar fierce or cruel
> Upon the strength of water-gruel?
> But who shall stand his rage and force,
> If first he rides, then eats his horse?"

And this metrical allusion to ancient banquets, and characteristic prowess connected with them, recalls to my memory the singular story touching the strangest of facts, which has been told in choice verse by Ludwig Uhland. The German poet, in narrating it, has condemned himself to execute a sort of double hornpipe in fetters, having set himself the task to introduce one word, the subject of his poem, into every stanza of his rhymed romance. "Done into English," the legend runs thus:

THE CASTELLAN OF COUCY, OR THE HEART.

"How deeply young De Coucy sigh'd,
  How sad the feeling that came o'er him,
  And smote his heart, when first he saw
  The Lady of Fayal before him!

"How suddenly his song assumed
  The strain of love's impassion'd fire!
  How every measure clearly told
  His heart vibrated with his lyre!

"But vain the sweetness of his song,
  In am'rous cadence softly dying!
  No hope had he to move the heart
  Of her who heeded not his sighing!

"For ever, when beyond his wont
  He fell on some inspired strain,
  The wedded lady's heart scarce moved,—
  It warm'd but to be cold again.

"Then was the Castellan resolved,
  The cross upon his cuirass'd breast,
  'Mid toils in Palestine to seek
  The tumults of his heart to rest.

"And there, in many a hot affray,
  Where perils threat, and dangers thicken,
  He stands till,—'spite his coat of mail,
  His noble heart with death is stricken.

"'Oh! hear'st thou me, my page?' he cried,
  'When this fond heart has ceased its beating,
  To the fair Lady of Fayal
  Bear it, with De Coucy's greeting.'

"In cold and consecrated earth
  The hero's corpse at length reposes;
  But o'er his heart, his broken heart,
  Not so the tomb its portal closes.

TABLE TRAITS.

"The heart within a golden urn
　Was laid; the page received the treasure,
And quickly sped him o'er the main,
　To do his noble master's pleasure.

"Now whirlwinds tear, and waters dash,
　Now lightnings rend, and masts are falling;
All hearts on board are struck with awe,
　One heart alone's beyond appalling!

"Now beams the golden sun again;
　Now France upon the bow's appearing;
All hearts on board with joy are cheer'd;
　One heart alone's beyond all cheering!

"And soon, through Fayal's frowning wood,
　The page and heart their way are making,
When winding sounds the lusty horn,
　With hunters' cries the stillness breaking.

"Then from the thicket bounds a stag,
　Through his heart an arrow flying,
Checks his course, and strikes him dead,—
　At the page's feet he's lying.

"And now the Ritter of Fayal,
　Who first the gallant stag had wounded,
Gallops up with hunting train,
　Who soon the gentle page surrounded.

"The golden urn had quickly fall'n
　To the Ritter's knaves a welcome booty,
Had not the boy stepp'd back a pace,
　And told them of his mournful duty.

"'Heart of a knightly Troubadour,
　Here is a warrior's heart, I say,—
The Castellan of Coucy's heart;
　Let pass this heart its peaceful way!

"'Dying, my gallant master cried,
  When this heart has ceased its beating,
To the fair Lady of Fayal
  Bear it, with De Coucy's greeting.'

"'That dame I know full passing well!'
  Shouted the knight in deadly passion,
As from the trembling page he tore
  The urn, in fierce uncourteous passion.

" And with it, grasp'd beneath his cloak,
  Homeward sped the savage Ritter;
The heart close press'd upon his breast,
  Fill'd it with thoughts of vengeance bitter.

" Scarce at his castle-gate arrived,
  His madden'd thoughts intent on treason,
Than straight his frighted cooks are charged
  The heart with condiments to season.

" 'Tis done! and richly strewn with flow'rs,
  And lain on golden dish withal,
'Tis placed before the Knight and Dame,
  When seated in their banquet-hall.

" The Knight upon the Lady tended,
  Speaking in terms of feign'd delight—
' Of all the produce of my chase,
  This heart is yours, fair dame, by right!'

" But scarcely had the Lady tasted
  Of the dainty placed before her,
When impulse, strong and strange, to weep,
  Irresistibly came o'er her.

" On marking which the Ritter cried,
  With wild and savage laugh unholy,
' Do pigeons' hearts, my faithful Dame,
  Give tendency to melancholy?

"'Then how much more, O Lady mine,
　Must fare like this such passion raise—
　The Castellan of Coucy's heart,
　Whose lyre was wont to sound thy praise?'

"And when the Knight with stern reproof,
　Had ceased thus sneering to upbraid, he
　Stood; while hand on heart too, thus
　With solemn action spoke the Lady:—

"'Thou 'st done me foulest wrong to-day!
　Ne'er false was I, not e'en in thought,
　Till this poor heart I touch'd but now,
　Within my own mutation wrought.

"'The youthful Poet's passion, told
　With sadden'd heart and anxious brow.
　I scorn'd while yet the Poet lived,
　But dead! I yield me to it now.

"'To death devoted, this weak frame,
　To which De Coucy's heart hath lent
　A brief support, shall never more
　Partake of earthly nourishment.

"'May Heav'n its mercy show to all;
　Yes, e'en to thee may Heav'n show it!'
　　*　　*　　*　　*　　*
Such is the story of a heart
That once inspired a youthful Poet."

The above story of the Castellan de Coucy is considered to be one of Uhland's most remarkable poems, as much from its general sweetness, unhappily lost in translation, as from the wit with which he continually keeps before the reader the one word which forms the principal feature in the little romance. The tale is, however, by no means new. There are few nations whose story-tellers do not celebrate a lady who was forced by a jealous husband to eat the heart of her lover. It is common to England, Ireland and

Scotland. In France, the story exists nearly as Uland has told it. In Germany it is to be met with in various forms. In one of these, the lady is shown to have been more kind and less faithful than the Ritter's wife of Fayal. But above all it is, as the mad prince says, "extant and written in very choice Italian," by the at once seductive and repulsive Bocaccio. It is one of the least filthy of a set of stories, told with a beauty of style, a choice of language, a lightness and a grace, which make you forget the matter and risk your morals, for the sake of improving your Italian. In Bocaccio's narrative, the lady is of course very guilty; and the husband also, of course, murders the lover in as brutal and unknightly a fashion as can well be imagined. Nothing else could be expected from that unequalled story-teller, (unequalled as much for the charm of his manner, as for the general uncleanness of his details,) who but seldom has a good word to say for woman, or an honest testimony to give of man. Human nature presented nothing beautiful or estimable to him; and yet it is undeniable that he had an acute perception of beauty and honour. The characters he describes are scurvy, vicious, heartless, debauched wretches; but he dresses them up with such dashing bravery of attire, and endows them with such divinity of beauty, and he writes of their whereabout with such a witchery of pen, that his poor, weak, ensnared readers have nothing for it but to go on in alternate extremes of admiring and condemning. To revert to the German prose story of the Heart, I may say that it is merely a bad translation from the "Decameron," telling in a very matter-of-fact way the history of a Lady von Roussillon, "welche ihres Geliebten Herz zu essen erhält, und sich den Tod gibt."

This strange banquet is not to be set down as positively apocryphal, merely because it has fallen into the possession of the rhymers and romancers. The old German barons were rather inclined to a barbarous species of kitchen—something crude and cannibal of character—if we may so far credit the extravagances of legend as to believe they are founded on fact. But we need not go to Germany and fairy periods for illustrations of extraordinary banquets, or individual dieting.

Among eccentric gastronomists, I do not recollect one more remarkable than Mrs. Jeffreys, the sister of Wilkes. At Bath she slept throughout the year beneath an open window, and the snow sometimes lent her bed an additional counterpane. She never allowed a fire to be kindled in this room, the chief adornment of which was a dozen clocks, no two of which struck the hour at the same moment. She breakfasted frugally enough on chocolate and dry toast, but proceeded daily in a sedan chair, with a bottle of Madeira at her side, to a boarding-house to dine. She invariably sat between two gentlemen, " men having more sinew in mind and body than women," and with these she shared her " London Particular." Warner, in his " Literary Recollections," says that some mighty joint that was especially well-covered with fat, was always prepared for her. She was served with slices of this fat, which she swallowed alternately with pieces of chalk, procured for her especial enjoyment. Neutralizing the *subacid* of the fat with the alkaline principle of the chalk, she " amalgamated, diluted, and assimilated the delicious compound with half-a-dozen glasses of her delicious wine." The diet agreed well with the old lady, and she maintained that such a test authorized use.

We may contrast with the lady who loved lumps of chalk, the people of a less civilized time and place, who had a weakness for a species of animal food, which is not to be found written down in the *menus* of modern dinners. Keating, in his " Narrative of an Expedition to the Source of St. Peter's River," gives some curious details, which may be not inappropriately touched upon here, referring, as they do to a nation of dog-eaters. The custom at first sight strikes us as rather revolting; but the animal in question, to say nothing of our stealthy friend, the cat, is eaten every day in " ragouts," that smoke on the boards of the cheap *gargottes* of Paris and the *banlieux*. After all, custom and prejudice have much to do with the subject. " What do you do with your dead?" once asked a member of a distant Asiatic tribe of a

Roman. "We bury them," answered the latter. "Gracious heaven!" exclaimed the "untutored Indian," with disgust, "what filthy and fiendish impiety!" "Why so?" inquired the other. "What do you and your people with *your* dead?" "We treat them," replied the Indian proudly, "with the decent forms that best become the dead; we *eat* them!" To this day the nobles of Thibe. are honoured after death with a very valuable and enviable privilege. They are reverentially offered to a body of hounds, maintained for the especial purpose of devouring the defunct aristocracy. What remains at the end of the process is cared for, like the ashes which were taken of old from beneath the pile on which a loved corpse had lain. This exclusive honour is never vouchsafed to the commonalty; it is the particular vested right of greatness; and had Hamlet known of it when he traced great Cæsar's clay stopping a bung-hole, it would have afforded him another illustration of the base uses to which mortality may return. Let *us* return to the dog-eaters. Mr. Keating shall tell what he saw amongst them, in his own words: *Sua narret Ulysses.*

"As soon as we had taken our seats, the chief (Wanotan) passed his pipe round; and while we were engaged in smoking, two of the Indians arose, and uncovered the large kettles which were standing over the fire. They emptied their contents into a dozen of wooden dishes which were placed all round the lodge. These consisted of buffalo meat boiled with *tepsin;* also the same vegetable boiled without the meat, in buffalo grease; and, finally, the much-esteemed dog-meat—all which were dressed without salt. In compliance with the established usage of travellers to taste of everything, we all partook of the latter, with a mixed feeling of curiosity and reluctance. Could we have divested ourselves entirely of the prejudices of education, we should, doubtless, unhesitatingly have acknowledged this to be one of the best dishes that we had ever tasted. It was remarkably fat,—was sweet and palatable. It had none of that dry, stringy character which we had expected to find in it; and it was entirely destitute of the strong taste which we had apprehended it must possess. It was not an unusual appetite, or the want of meat to compare with it, which led us to form this favourable opinion of the dog; for we had on our dish the best meat which our prairies afford. But so strongly rooted are the prejudices of education, that though we all unaffectedly admitted the excellence of this food, yet few of us could be induced to eat much of it. We were warned by our trading friends, that the bones of this animal are treated with great respect by the doctors. We therefore took great care to replace them in the dishes; and we are informed that after such a feast is concluded, the bones are carefully collected, the flesh scraped off them, and that after being washed, they are burned on the ground; partly, as it is said, to testify to the dog-species that in feasting on one of their number, no disrespect was meant to the species itself; and partly also from a belief that the bones of the animal will arise and reproduce another. The meat of this animal, as we saw it, was thought to resemble that of the finest Welsh mutton, except that it was of a much darker colour. Having so far overcome our repugnance as to taste it, we no longer wonder that the dog should be considered a dainty dish by those in whom education has not created a prejudice against this flesh. In China it is said that fatted pups are frequently sold in the market-place; and it appears that an invitation to a feast of dog meat is the greatest distinction that can be offered to a stranger by any of the Indian nations east of the Rocky Mountains. That this is not the case among some of the nations on the east of those mountains, appears from the fact that Lewis and Clarke were called in derision by the Indians of Columbia, 'dog-eaters.'"

It may be readily believed that the food above spoken of must be more acceptable to the human appetite than the snails which are fattened for the public markets in the meadows about Ulm. Two Edinburgh doctors did indeed pronounce the prejudice against snails to be absurd, and they showed the strength of their own convictions by sitting down to a charmingly prepared little dish of the particular dainty. The courage of each failed him at the first taste, but neither liked to confess as much to the other. They went on playing with their repast, until one ventured to say in a remarkably faint voice, "Don't you think, doctor, they are a *leetle* green?" "D—d green, Sir! d—d green!" was the hearty confirmatory rejoinder; "they are d—d green! take them away!"

But the Australians do not always exhibit this extreme nicety. If they cannot, or once could not, eat biscuits, they have no such delicate scruples about eating babies, even when those babies are their own. The cannibalism of the Australians appears to be not so obsolete as those who wish well to humanity would fain desire. This is settled by the testimony of Mr. Westgarth, a member of the local parliament, and the latest writer who has touched upon the subject. In his "Victoria, late Australia Felix," he says:— "In their natural state, the aborigines stand out with a species of rude dignity. The precision and acuteness of their observant faculties are not to be surpassed; and they exhibit a surprising tact in their various modes of discovering and securing food. The narrow compass of their minds is concentrated in a few lines of vocation, in which, as in the exhibitions of a Blind Asylum, there are displayed an extraordinary accuracy and skill. But to these barbaric excellences, must be added the most degrading, superstitious, and revolting customs. Civilized nations are still unwilling to believe that infanticide and cannibalism are associated with the customs of any race of human beings, or voluntarily practised, except in those rare cases of necessity which have broken down the barriers of nature alike to the white and the black; but nothing is better affirmed than that cannibalism is a constant habit with this degraded race, who alternately revel in the kidney fat of their slain or captured enemies, and in the entire bodies of their own friends and relatives. Nor can the infant claim any security from the mother who bore it, against some ruthless law, or practice, or superstition, that on frequent occasions consigns the female proportion, and sometimes both sexes, to destruction. On authentic testimony, bodies have been greedily devoured even in a state of obvious and loathsome disease; and a mother has been observed deliberately destroying her youngest child, serving it up as food, and gathering around her the remainder of the family to enjoy the unnatural banquet." It is certainly pleasant to turn from such a spectacle as this to contemplate the wives of the King of Delhi, who pass their time in spoiling, but not killing, their children, and whose chief amusement, after matters of dress, consists in sitting and cracking nutmegs in presence of the Great Mogul!

But there are worse things than these which necessity can render acceptable to the palate. In Australia especially does nature appear to indulge in strange freaks. Many of our salt-water fish there live in fresh-water rivers; and, indeed, more than one inland river is brackish if not salt. Yet of salt itself the natives had never tasted, until the arrival among them of Europeans; they do not take kindly to the condiment even to this day. They prefer their own unadorned cookery; and they would especially have admired the late Dr. Howard, who published quarterly his denunciations against the use of salt. In Australia, the pears are made of wood, and the stones of the cherries grow on the outside, and not within. The aborigines are satisfied with very unsavoury diet. They have one fashion, however, in common with the self-appointed leaders of civilization, the French; they eat frogs. In France it is the pastime of the *bourgeois*, on a summer evening, to resort to some pool with a rod and line, and a piece of red rag or bit of soap for bait, and there catch the little people who could not agree about their king by the dozen. In Australia the native ladies, in their usual scantiness of costume, proceed to the swamps; and there plunging their long arms up to the shoulders into the mud, they draw up the astonished frogs by handfuls. When caught they are cooked over a slow fire of wood-ashes; the hinder parts only are eaten, as in France; and there are worse dishes than the *fricassée* of the edible frog. Indeed, if the Australians devoured nothing more objectionable, their system of diet would almost defy reproof. But, alas! I find upon their bills of fare—grubs, raw and roasted, snakes, lizards, rats, mice and weazels. The mussel is deeply declined by some of the tribes, in consequence of an opinion prevailing that the fish in question is the especial property of sorcerers, whose amiable propensity it is to destroy mankind by means of mussels. If all the world held the same opinion, I have no doubt of great profit therefrom resulting.

One of our earlier captains who visited Australia observing a native devouring some indescribable sort of food, offered him, in exchange for a portion of it, a sound sea-biscuit. The exchange was effected, and then it became a point of courtesy and honour that each should eat what he had acquired by the barter. The trial was a severe one for both parties. The Englishman swallowed slowly, and with a sickening sense of disgust that cannot be told, the odious food of the aboriginal; while the native, nibbling at the biscuit, appeared to grow more horror-stricken at each bit when he tried to swallow. The tears came into his eyes, he grew sick, faint, enraged; and at length, dashing the biscuit on the ground, he as violently seated himself upon it with a bounce that ought to have driven it to the very centre of the earth. The Englishman in the meantime, had flung away the remnant of *his* "*pièce de résistance*," and they remained gazing at each other, with the inward conviction that, as regarded food, each had tasted that day that which deserved to be designated as surprisingly beastly.

Keating's Indians are not the only men of North America who have a delicate fancy for the dog: the Dacotas are also that way given. Their celebrated "dog-dance" is indeed a festival but of rare occurrence, but it is held to show that that highly respectable people would eat the hearts of their enemies with as little reluctance as the heart of a dog. And this is the manner of the feast of "braves;" they cook the heart and liver of a dog, cool them in water, and then hang the dainties on a high pole, around which they assemble as grave and silent as quakers. The spirit is literally supposed to move them, and when one is thus influenced, he begins to bark, and jumps towards the pole. Another follows his example. The jumping backwards and forwards, and the chorus of barking become gradually universal; and the solemn concert is then at its height. Every one does his best, according as nature has gifted him. The children snap like French poodles; the girls yelp like pugs; some snarl, others growl; the women "give tongue" as musically as the Bramham Park hounds; and the fathers of the tribe run through a scale of sounds that would highly astonish Lablache.

And thus, in the midst of it all, one becomes bolder than the rest, looks about him grinningly defiant, and making a run and a leap at the canine dainties suspended from the pole, he generally touches ground again with a piece thereof in his teeth! This good example is also followed universally, until the tempting prize is all consumed, and then there is "a general dance of characters," and the drama is done. The Dacotas have an esteem for diminutive dogs; and, lest my readers should deem the tribe to be wholly unacquainted with civilization and its secrets, I will just mention that these Indians not only drink whisky with as much profusion as it is drunken in godly Glasgow, but they occasionally administer a little of it to their dogs, in order to stunt their growth. Such prayers too as they have, are also marked by a modern and civilized character; for example, they say, "Great Spirit! Father! help us to kill our enemies, and give us plenty of corn!" This is the very spirit of much of the prayer put up by the dwellers in the regions of enlightenment. And the spirit, with its proper motives, is not one to be blamed. These barbarous Indians do not, at all events, insult their Great Spirit, by asking him to give peace in their time, *because* none other fighteth for them but him. This would sound to their ear as though they needed peace, for the reason that their defence in war was not to be relied upon; and, if it had slipped into their formulary, they would at least amend it without delay.

But this is getting critical, and so to become reminds us of authors. Now to treat of *them*, in reference to the table, is generally speaking to fall upon the discussion of their "calamities" and the Encyclopædia of famished writers would be a very heavy work indeed. We have yet time, however, before the chapter of "Supper" opens, to take a cursory glance at a few of the brotherhood of the brain and quill. It can be but of a few, and of *that* few but briefly. "*Tanto meglio!*" says the reader, and I will not dispute the propriety of the exclamation.

AUTHORS AND THEIR DIETETICS.

It is all very well for Mr. Leigh Hunt to write a poem on the "Feast of the Poets," and to show us how Apollo stood "pitching his darts," by way of invitation to the ethereal banquet. This is all very well in graceful poetry, but the account is no more to be received, than the new gospel according to *ditto* is likely to be by the Lord Primate and orthodox Christians. It is far more difficult to tell the matter in plain prose; for, where there are few dinners, many authors cannot well dine. It is easier to tell how they fasted than how they fed; how they died, choked at last by the newly-baked roll that came too late to be swallowed, than how they lived daily,—for the daily life of some would be as impossible of discovery, as the door of the "Cathedral of Immensities," wherein Mr. Carlyle transacts worship. The soul of the poet, says an Eastern proverb, passes into the grasshopper, which sings till it dies of starvation. An apt illustration, but our English grasshoppers must not be used for the illustrative purpose, seeing that they are far too wise to do anything of the sort. A British grasshopper no more sings till he dies, than a British swan dies singing: these foolish habits are left to foreigners and poetry. Let us turn to the more reliable register of our ever-juvenile friend, Mr. Sylvanus Urban.

More than a century ago, Mr. Urban, who is the only original "oldest inhabitant," gave a "Literary Bill of Mortality for 1752," showing the casualties among books as well as among authors. Touching the respective fates of the former, we find the productions of the year set down as, " Abortive, 7000 ; still-born, 3000; old age, 0." Sudden deaths fell upon 320. Three or four thousand perished by trunk-makers, sky-rockets, pastry-cooks, or worms; while more than half that number were privily disposed of. If such were the fortunes of the works, how desperate must have been the diet of the authors! So also was their destiny. As a class, they are fixed, in round numbers, at 3000; and a third of these are registered as dying of lunacy. Some 1200 are entered as "starved." Seventeen were disposed of by "the hangman," and fifteen by hardly more respectable persons, namely *themselves!* Mad dogs, vipers, and mortification, swept off a goodly number. Five pastoral poets, who could not live by the oaten pipe, appropriately died of "fistula." And, as a contrast to the multitude "starved," we find a *zero* indicating the ascertained quantity of authors who had perished by the aldermanic malady of "surfeit."

There is, perhaps, more approximation to truth than appears a first sight in this *jeu d'esprit*. It was only in Pagan days that authors could boast of obesity. They dined with the *tyranni*, as Persian poets get their mouths stuffed with sugar-candy by the Shah Inshah. And yet Pliny speaks of poets feeding sparingly, *ut solent poetæ*. Perhaps this was only an exception, like that of Moore, who smilingly sat down to a broil at home when not dining with "right honourables;" or contentedly thanked Heaven for "salt fish and biscuits" with his mother and sister in Abbey Street, the day after he had supped with the ducal viceroy of Ireland, and half the peerage of the three kingdoms.

Still, in the old times, authors took more liberty with their hosts. In Rome they kept more to the proprieties; for a nod of the head of the imperial entertainer was sufficient to make their own fly from their shoulders. In presence of the Roman emperor of old, an author could only have declared that the famous invasion of Britain, which was productive of ship-loads of spoil, in the shape of sea-shells, was a god-like feat. So, at the table of the czar, all the lyres of Muscovy sing the ode of eternal sameness, to the effect that the dastardly butchery of Sinope was an act that made the angels of God jubilant! The Russian lyres dare not sing to any other tune. It was not so of yore. Witness what is told us of Philoxenus, the ode writer, whose odes, however, are less known than his acts. He was the author of the wish that he had a crane's neck, in order to have prolonged enjoyment in swallowing. This is a poor wish compared with that of Quin, elsewhere recorded, that he might have a swallow as long as from here to Botany Bay, and palate all the way! He was a greedy fellow, this same Philoxenus. He accustomed himself to hold his hands in the hottest water, and to gargle his throat with it scalding; and, by this noble training, he achieved the noble end of being able to swallow the hottest things at table, before the other guests could venture on them. He would have conquered the most accomplished of our country bumpkins in consuming hasty-pudding at a fair. His mouth was as though it was paved, and his fellow-guests used to say of him, that he was an oven and not a man. He once travelled many miles to buy fish at Ephesus; but, when he reached the market-place, he found it all bespoke for a wedding banquet. He was by no means embarrassed; he went uninvited to the feast, kissed the bride, sang an epithalamium that made the guests roar with ecstacy, and afforded such delight by his humour, that the bridegroom invited him to breakfast with him on the morrow. His wit had made amends for his devouring all the best dishes. It is a long way from Philoxenus to Dr. Chalmers forgetting his repast in the outpouring of his wisdom, and entering in his journal the expression of his fear that he had been intolerant in argument. What a contrast, too, between Philoxenus and Byron, who, when dining with a half-score of wits at Rogers's, only opened his mouth to ask for biscuits and soda-water, and not finding any such articles in the bill of fare, silently dining on vegetables and vinegar! The noble poet's fare in Athens was often of the same modest character; but we know what excesses he could commit when his wayward appetite that way prompted, or when he wished to lash his Pegasus into fury, as, after reading the famous attack on his poetry in the Edinburgh Review, when he swallowed three bottles of claret, and then addressed himself to the tomahawking of his reviewers and rivals.

Philoxenus, however, had his counterpart in those abbés and poets who used, in the hearing of Louis XV., to praise Madame de Pompadour. He was writing a poem called "Galatea," in honour of the mistress of Dionysius of Sicily, when he was once dining with that tyrant. There were a couple of barbels on the royal board, a small one near the poet, and a larger near the prince. As the latter saw Philoxenus put his diminutive barbel to his ear, he asked him wherefore, and the poet replied that he was asking news of Nereus, but that he thought the fish he held had been caught too young to give him any. "I think," said Philoxenus, "that the old fish near your sacredness would better suit my purpose." This joke has descended to Joe Miller, in whose collection it is to be found in a modified form. But the story is altogether less neat than the one told of Dominic, the famous Italian harlequin and farce writer. He was standing in presence of Louis XIV. at dinner, when the Grand Monarque observed that his eyes were fixed on a dish of partridges. "Take that dish to Dominic," said the king. "What!" exclaimed the *farceur*, "partridges and all!" "Well," said the monarch, smiling with gravity, "yes, partridges and all!" This reminds me of another anecdote, the hero of which is the Abbé Morallet, whom Miss Edgeworth in her "Ormond" praises so highly, and praises so justly. But Morallet, if he loved good deeds, loved not less good dinners, and he shone in both. His talents as a writer, and his virtues as a man, to say nothing of his appetite, made him especially welcome at the hospitable table of Monsieur Ansu. The abbé had learned to carve expressly that he might appropriate to himself his favourite portions,—a singular instance of selfishness in a man who was selfish in nothing else. It was on one of these occasions that a magnificent pheasant excited the admiration of the guests, and of the abbé in particular, who nevertheless sighed to think that it had not been placed close to him. Some dexterity was required so to carve it, that each of the guests might partake of the oriental bird; and the mistress of the house, remembering the abbé's skill as a carver, directed an attendant to pass the pheasant to M. l'Abbé de Morallet. "What!" exclaimed the latter, "the whole of it? how very kind!" "The whole of it?" repeated the lady; "I have no objection, if these ladies and gentlemen are willing to surrender their rights to you." The entire company gave consent, by reiterating the words, "the whole of it!" and the man, who might have gained the Monthyon prize for virtue, really achieved a piece of gluttony which hardly confers honour on a hungry clown at a fair.

La Fontaine at table was seen in a better light than the Abbé Morallet. A fermier-general once invited him to a dinner of ceremony, in the persuasion that an author who excited such general admiration would create endless delight for the select company, to entertain whom he had been invited. La Fontaine knew it well, during the whole repast ate in silence, and immediately rose, to the consternation of the convives, to take his departure. He was going, he said, to the Academy. The master of the house represented to him that it was by far too early, and that he would find none of the members assembled. "I know that," said the fabulist, with his quiet smile and courteous bow; "I know that, but I will go a long way round." If this seemed a trifle uncourteous—and it was so more in seeming than reality—it was not so much so as in the case of Byron, who used to invite a company to dinner, and then leave them to themselves to enjoy their repast. Noble hosts of the past century used to do something like this when they gave masquerades. Fashion compelled them to adopt a species of amusement which they detested; but they vindicated personal liberty nevertheless, for when their rooms were at their fullest, the noble host, quietly leaving his guests to the care of his wife, would slip away to some neighbouring coffee-house, and over a cool pint of claret enjoy the calm which was not to be had at home. The late Duke of Norfolk used habitually to dine at one of the houses in Covent Garden, out of pure liking to it. He was accustomed to order dinner for five, and to duly eat what he had deliberately ordered; but, as he one day detected a waiter watching him in his gastronomic process, he angrily ordered his bill, and never entered the house again.

It was a common practice with Haydn, like his Grace of Norfolk, to order a dinner for five or six, and then eat the whole himself. He once ordered such a dinner to be ready by a stated hour, at which time he alone appeared, and ordered the repast to be served. "But where is the company?" respectfully inquired the head waiter. "Oh!" exclaimed Haydn, *I am de gompany!*" But if he ate all, he also paid for all. Moore and Bowles, in their visits together to Bath, used sometimes to dine at the White Hart, where, as Moore records, he paid his share of the dinner and pint of Madeira, and then Bowles magnificently "stood" a bottle of claret, at dessert. And a pleasant dinner the two opposite, yet able, poets, made of it—far more pleasant than Coleridge's dinner with a party at Reynold's, when he bowled down the glasses like nine-pins, because they were too small to drink from copiously!

The name of Coleridge's reminds me of Dufresny, an author of the time of Louis XVI., who was full of sentiment and majestic sounds, but who was content to live at the cost of other people, and who never achieved anything like an independence for himself. After the death of his royal patron, he was one day dining with the Regent Duke of Orleans, who expressed a wish to provide for him. Caprice inspired the author to say, "Your royal highness had better leave me poor, as I am, as a monument of the condition of France before the regency." He was not displeased at having his petition refused. A guest at his side did indeed remark, by way of encouragement, that "poverty was no vice." "No," answered Dufresny, sharply, "but it is something very much worse." In act and spirit he was not unlike a prince of wits and punsters among ourselves, who used to set up bottles of champagne on his little lawn and bowl them down for nine pins; and who, of course, left his wife and children pensioners on the charity of the state and the people.

I have spoken of La Fontaine; he was as absent at table as poor Lord Dudley and Ward, whose first aberrations so alarmed Queen Adelaide. La Fontaine was also like Dean Ogle, who, at a friend's table, always thought himself at his own, and if the dinner were indifferent, he would make an apology to the guests, and promise them better treatment next time. So La Fontaine was one day at the table of Despreaux; the conversation turned upon

19*

St. Augustin, and after much serious discourse upon that Christian teacher, La Fontaine, who had till then been perfectly silent, turned to his neighbour, the Abbé Boileau, one of the most pious men of his day, and asked him "if he thought that St. Augustin had as much wit as Rabelais?" The priest blushed scarlet, and then contented himself with remarking, "M. de la Fontaine, you have got on one of your stockings the wrong side out"—which was the fact.

The poet's query to the priest was no doubt as startling as that put by the son of a renowned reverend joker to the then Lord Primate. The anxious parent had informed his somewhat "fast" offspring, that as the archbishop was to dine with him that day, it would be desirable that the young gentleman should eschew sporting subjects, and if he spoke at all, speak only on serious subjects. Accordingly, at dessert, during a moment of silence, the obedient child, looking gravely at his grace, asked him "if he could tell him what sort of condition Nebuchadnezzar was in, when he was taken up from grass?" The Lord Primate readily replied that he should be able to answer the question by the time he who had made it had found out the name of the man whom Samson ordered to tie the torches to the foxes' tails, before they were sent in to destroy the corn of the Philistines!

Moore loved to dine with the great; but there have been many authors who could not appreciate the supposed advantages of such distinction. Lainez was one of these, and there were but few of his countrymen who resembled him. One day the Duke of Orleans met him in the park at Fontainebleau, and did him the honour of inviting him to dinner. "It is really quite impossible," said Lainez; "I am engaged to dine at a tavern with half-a-dozen jolly companions; and what opinion would your royal highness have of me if I were to break my word?" Lainez was not like Madame de Sevigné, who, after having been asked to dance by Louis XIV., declared in her delight that he was the greatest monarch in the world. Bussi, who laughed at her absurd enthusiasm, affirms that the fair authoress of the famous "Letters" was so excited at the supper after the dance, that it was with difficulty she could refrain from shrieking out "Vive le Roi!"

Had the famous "petit père André" kept down his impulses as successfully as Madame de Sevigné did at the supper, where, after all, she did *not* exclaim, "Vive le Roi," it would have been more to his credit, and less to our amusement. The good father, like a better man, St. Vincent de Paul, was excessively fond of cards, but he did not cheat, like the saint, for the sake of winning for the poor. He had been playing at *piquet*, and in one game had won a considerable sum by the lucky intervention of a fourth king. He was in such ecstasy at his luck, that he declared at supper he would introduce his lucky fourth king into his next day's sermon. Bets were laid in consequence of this declaration, and the whole company were present when the discourse was preached. The promise made at the supper was kept in the sermon, though somewhat profanely: "My brethren," said the abbé, "there arrived one king, two kings, three kings; but what were they?—and where should I have been without the fourth king, who saved *me*, and has benefited you? That fourth king was He who lay in the manger, and whom the three royal magi came but to worship!" At the dinner which followed, the author of the sermon was more eulogised than if he had been as grand as Bourdaloue, as touching as Massillon, or as winning as Fenelon.

There was more wit in a curé of Basse Bretagne, who was the author of his diocesan's pastorals, and who happened to hold invitations to dinners for the consecutive days of the week. He could not take advantage of them and perform his duty too, but he hit on a method of accomplishing his desire. He gave out at church, an intimation to this effect:—"in order to avoid confusion, my brethren, I have to announce that to-morrow, Monday, I will receive at confession the liars only; on Tuesday, the misers; on Wednesday, the slanderers; on Thursday, the thieves; Friday, the libertines; and Saturday, the women of evil life." It need not be said that the priest was left during *that* week to enjoy himself without let or hindrance. And it was at such joyous dinners as he was in the habit of attending that most of the sermons, with startling passages in them, like those of Father André, were devised. Thus, the Cordelier Maillard, the author of various pious works, at a dinner of counsellors, announced his intention of preaching against the counsellors' ladies,—that is, against their wives, or such of them that wore embroidery. And well he kept his word, as the following choice flowers from the bouquet of his pulpit oratory will show. "You say," he exclaimed to the ladies in question, "that you are clad according to your conditions; all the devils in hell fly away with your conditions, and you too, my ladies! You will say to me, perhaps, Our husbands do not give us this gorgeous apparel, we earn it by the labours of our bodies. Thirty thousand devils fly away with the labours of your bodies, and you too, my ladies!" And, after diatribes like these against the ladies in question, the Cordelier would dine with their lords, and dine sumptuously too. The dinners of the counsellors of those days were not like the Spanish dinner to which an author was invited, and which consisted of capon and wine, two excellent ingredients, but unfortunately, as at the banquet celebrated by Swift, where there was nothing warm but the ice, and nothing sweet but the vinegar, so here the capon was cold and the wine was hot. Whereupon, the literary guest dips the leg of the capon into the flask of wine, and being asked by his host wherefore he did so, replied, "I am warming the capon in the wine, and cooling the wine with the capon."

The host was not such a judge of wine, apparently, as the archbishops of Salzbourg, who used not indeed to write books, nor indeed read them, but who used to entertain those who did, and then preach against literary vanity from those double-balcony pulpits which some of my readers may recollect in the cathedral of the town where Paracelsus was wont to discourse like Solon, and to drink like Silenus; and before whose tomb I have seen votaries, imploring his aid against maladies, or thanking him for having averted them! It is said of one of these prince primates that when, on the occasion of his death, the municipal officers went to place the seals on his property, they found the library sealed up exactly as it had been done many years before at the time of the decease of his predecessor. Such, however, was not the case with the wine-cellars. What the archiepiscopal wine is at Salzbourg, I do not know, but if it be half as good as that drank by the monks of Mölk, on the Danube, why the archbishops may stand excused. Besides, they only drank it during their leisure hours,—of which, as Hayne remarks, archbishops have generally four and twenty daily.

But to return nearer home, and to our own authors:—Dr. Arne may be reckoned among these, and it is of him, I think, that a pleasant story is told, showing how he wittily procured a dinner in an emergency, which certainly did not promise to allow such a consummation. The doctor was with a party of composers and musicians in a provincial town, where a musical festival was being celebrated, and at which they were prominent performers. They proceeded to an inn to dine; they were accommodated with a room, but were told that every eatable thing in the house was already engaged. All despaired in their hunger, save the "Mus. Doc." who, cutting off two or three ends of catgut, went out upon the stairs, and observing a waiter carrying a joint to a company in an adjacent room, contrived to drop the bits of catgut on the meat, while he addressed two or three questions to the waiter. He then returned to his companions, to whom he intimated that dinner would soon be ready. They smiled grimly at what they thought was a sorry joke, and soon after, some confusion being heard in the room to which the joint which he had ornamented had been conveyed, he reiterated the assurance that dinner was coming, and thereupon he left the room. On the stairs he encountered the waiter bearing away the joint, with a look of disgust in his face. "Whither so fast, friend, with that haunch of mutton?" was the query. "I am taking it back to the kitchen, Sir; the gentlemen cannot touch it. Only look, Sir," said William, with his nose in the direction of the bits of catgut; "it's enough to turn one's stomach!" "William," said Arne gravely, "fiddlers have very strong stomachs; bring the mutton to our room." The thing was done, the haunch was eaten, the hungry guests were delighted, but William had ever afterwards a contempt for musical people; he classed them with those barbarians whom he had heard the company speak of where he waited, who not only ate grubs, but declared that they liked them.

Martial was often as hardly put to it to secure a dinner as any of the authors I have hitherto named. He was fond of a *good* dinner, *ut solent poetæ;* and he knew nothing better than a hare, followed by a dish of thrushes. The thrush appears to have been a favourite bird in the estimation of the poets. The latter may have loved to hear them sing, but they loved them better in a pie. Homer wrote a poem on the thrush; and Horace has said, in a line, as much in its favour as the Chian could have said in his long and lost poem,—"nil melius turdo." Martial was, at all events, a better fed and better weighted man than the poet Philetas of Cos, who was so thin that he walked abroad with leaden balls to his feet, in order that he might not be carried away by the wind. The poet Archestratus, when he was captured by the enemy, was put in a pair of scales, and was found of the weight of an obolus. Perhaps this was the value of his poetry! It was the value of nearly all that was written by a gastronomic authoress in France; I allude to Madame de Genlis, who boasts in her Memoirs, that having been courteously received by a certain German, she returned the courtesy by teaching him how to cook seven different dishes after the French fashion.

The authors of France have exhibited much caprice in their gastronomic practice; often professing in one direction, and acting in its opposite. Thus Lamartine was a vegetarian until he entered his teens. He remains so in opinion, but he does violence to his taste, and eats good dinners for the sake of conforming to the rules of society! This course in an author, who is for the moment rigidly Republican when all the world around him is Monarchical, is singular enough. Lamartine's vegetarian taste was fostered by his mother, who took him when a child to the shambles, and disgusted him with the sight of butchers in activity on slaughtering days. He for a long time led about a pet lamb by a ribbon, and went into strong fits at a hint from his mother's cook, that it was time to turn the said pet into useful purposes, and make *tendrons d'agneau* of him. Lamartine would no more have thought of eating his lamb, than Emily Norton would have dreamed of breakfasting on collops cut from her dear white doe of Rylston. The poet still maintains, that it is cruel and sinful to kill one animal in order that another may dine; but, with a sigh for the victim, he can eat heartily of what *is* killed, and even put his fork into the breast of lamb without compunction,—but all for conformity! He knows that if he were to confine himself to turnips, he should enjoy better health and have a longer tenure of life; but then he thinks of the usages of society, sacrifices himself to custom, and gets an indigestion upon truffled turkey.

Moore, in his early days in London, used to dine somewhere in Marylebone with French refugee priests, for something less than a shilling. Dr. Johnson dined still cheaper, at the "Pine Apple," in New-street, Covent Garden—namely, for eightpence. They who drank wine paid fourpence more for the luxury, but the lexicographer seldom took wine at his own expense; and sixpennyworth of meat, one of bread, and a penny for the waiter, sufficed to purchase viands and comfort for the author of the "Vanity of Human Wishes." Boyce the versifier was of quite another kidney; when he lay in bed, not only starving, but stark naked, a compassionate friend gave him half-a-guinea, which he spent in truffles and mushrooms, eating the same in bed under the blankets. There was something atrociously sublime about Boyce. Famine had pretty well done for him, when some one sent him a slice of roast-beef, but Boyce refused to eat it, because there was no catchup to render it palatable.

It must have been a sight of gastronomic pleasure to have seen Wilkes and Johnson together over a fillet of veal, with abundance of butter, gravy, stuffing, and a squeeze of lemon. The philosopher and the patriot were then on a level with other hungry and appreciating men. Shallow with his short-legged hen, and Sir Roger de Coverley over hasty-pudding, are myths; not so Pope with stewed regicide lampreys, Charles Lamb before roast pig, or Lord Eldon next to liver and bacon, or Theodore Hook bending to vulgar pea-soup. These were rich realities, and the principal performers in them had not the slightest idea of affecting refinement upon such subjects. Goldsmith, when he could get it, had a weakness for haunch of venison; and Dr. Young was so struck with a broiled bladebone on which Pope regaled him, that he concluded it was a foreign dish, and anxiously inquired how it was prepared. Ben Jonson takes his place among the lovers of mutton, while Herrick wandering dinnerless about Westminster, Nahum Tate enduring sanctuary and starvation in the Mint, Savage wantonly incurring hunger, and Otway strangled by it, introduce us to authors with whom "dining with Duke Humphrey," was so frequent a process, that each shadowy meal was but as a station towards death.

When Goldsmith "tramped" it in Italy, his flute ceased to be his bread-winner as it had been in France; the fellow-countrymen of Palestrina were deaf to "Barbara Allen," pierced from memory through the vents of an Irish reed. Goldsmith, therefore, dropped his flute, and took up philosophy; not as a dignity; he played it as he had done his flute, for bread and a pillow. He knocked at the gate of a college instead of at the door of a cottage, made his bow, gave out a thesis, supported it in a Latin which must have set on edge the teeth of his hearers, and, having carried his exhibition to a successful end, was awarded the trifling and customary honorarium, with which he purchased bread and strength for the morrow. No saint in the howling wilderness lived a harder life than Goldsmith during his struggling years in London; the table traits, even of his days of triumph, were sometimes coloured unpleasingly. I am not sure if Goldsmith was present at the supper at Sir Joshua's, when Miss Reynolds, after the repast, was called upon as usual to give a toast, and not readily remembering one, was asked to give the ugliest man of her acquaintance, and thereon she gave "Dr. Goldsmith;" the name was no sooner uttered than Mrs. Cholmondeley rushed across the room, and shook hands with Reynolds by way of approval. What a sample of the manners of the day, and how characteristic the remark of Johnson, who *was* present, and whose wit, at his friend's expense, was rewarded by a roar, that "thus the ancients, on the commencement of their friendships, used to sacrifice a beast between them!" Cuzzoni, when found famishing, spent the guinea given her in charity, in a bottle of tokay and a penny roll. So Goldsmith, according to Mrs. Thrale, was "drinking himself drunk with Madeira," with the guinea sent to rescue him from hunger by Johnson. But let us be just to poor Oliver. If he squandered the eleemosynary guinea of a friend, he refused roast beef and daily pay, offered him by Parson Scott, Lord Sandwich's chaplain, if he would write against his conscience, and in support of government; and he could be generous in his turn to friends who needed the exercise of generosity. When Goldsmith went into the suburban gardens of London to enjoy his "shoemakers' holiday," he generally had Peter Barlow with him. Now Peter's utmost limit of profligacy was the sum of fifteen-pence for his dinner; his share would sometimes amount to five shillings, but Goldsmith always magnificently paid the difference. Perhaps there are few of the sons of song who dined so beggarly, and achieved such richness of fame, as Butler, Otway, Goldsmith, Chatterton, and, in a less degree of reputation, but not of suffering, poor Gerald Griffin, who wrestled with starvation till he began to despair. Chatterton *did* despair, as he sat without food, hope, and humility; and we know what came of it. Butler, the sturdy son of a Worcestershire farmer, after he had astonished his contemporaries by his "Hudibras," lived known but to a few, and upon the charity or at the tables of *them*. But he did not, like the heartless though sorely-tried Savage, slander the good-natured friends at whose tables he drew the support of his life. As for Otway, whether he perished of suffocation by the roll which he devoured too greedily after long fasting, or whether he died of the cold draught of water, drank when he was overheated, it is certain that he died in extreme penury at the "Bull" on Tower Hill,—the coarse frequenters of the low public-house were in noisy revelry round their tables, while the body of the dead poet lay, awaiting the grave, in the room adjacent.

The table life of Peter Pindar was a far more joyous one than that of much greater poets. At Truro he was noted for his frugal fare, and he never departed from the observance of frugality of living throughout his career. He would sometimes, we are told, when visiting country patients, and when he happened to be detained, go into the kitchen and cook his own beefsteak, in order to show a country cook how a steak was done in London,—the only place, he said, where it was properly cooked. He laughed at the faculty as he did at the king, and set the whole profession mad by sanctioning the plentiful use of water, declaring that physic was an uncertain thing, and maintaining that in most cases all that was required on the doctor's part was "to watch nature, and when she was going right, to give her a shove behind." He was accustomed to analyse the drugs which he had prescribed for his patients, before he would allow the latter to swallow them, and he gave a decided county bias against pork by remarking of a certain apothecary that he was too fond of bleeding the patients who resorted to him, and too proud of his large breed of pigs. The inference was certainly not in favour of pork. Peter's practical jokes in connexion with the table were no jokes to the chief object of them. Thus, when a pompous Cornish member of parliament issued invitations for as pompous a dinner to personages of corresponding pomposity, "Peter," recollecting that the senator had an aunt who was a laundress, sent her an invitation in her nephew's name, and the old lady, happy and proud, excited universal surprise, and very particular horror in the bosom of the parliament-man, by making her appearance in the august and hungry assembly, who welcomed her about as warmly as if she had been a "boule asphyxiante" of the new French artillery practice.

It is going a long way back to ascend from "Pindar" to Tasso, but both poets loved roasted chestnuts,—and *there* is the affinity. Peter never drank any thing but old rum; a wine glass, (never beyond a wine glass and a half,) served him for a day, after a dinner of the plainest kind. The doctor eschewed wine altogether, at least in his latter days, as generating acidity. Tasso, however, unlike our satirical friend, was a wine-bibber. During the imprisonment which had been the result of his own arrogance, he wrote to the physician of the Duke of Ferrara, complaining of intestinal pains, of sounds of bells in his ears, of painful mental images and varying apparitions of inanimate things appearing to him, and of his inability to study. The doctor advised him to apply a cautery to his leg, abstain from wine, and confine himself to a diet of broth and gruels. The poet defended the sacredness of his appetite, and declined to abstain from generous wine; but he urged the *medico* to find a remedy for his ills, promising to recompense him for his trouble, by making him immortal in song. At a later period of his life, when he was the guest of his friend Manco, in his gloomy castle of Bisaccio, the illustrious pair were seated together, after dinner, over a dessert of Tasso's favourite chestnuts and some generous wine; and there he affrighted his friend by maintaining that he was constantly attended by a guardian spirit, who was frequently conversing with him, and in proof of the same, he invited Manco to listen to their dialogue. The host replenished his glass and announced himself ready. Tasso fell into a loud rhapsody of mingled folly and beauty, occasionally pausing to give his spirit an opportunity of speaking; but the remarks of this agathodæmon were inaudible to all but the ears of the poet. The imaginary dialogue went on for an hour; and at the end of it, when Tasso asked Manco what he thought of it, Manco, who was the most matter-of-fact man that ever lived, replied that, for his part, he thought Tasso had drunk too much wine and eaten too many chestnuts. And truly I think so too.

The greatest of authors are given to the strangest of freaks.

Thus one of the most popular of the teachers of the people presided at a gay tavern supper the night before the execution of the Mannings. The feast concluded, the party (supplied with brandy and biscuits) proceeded to the disgusting spectacle, where they occupied "reserved seats;" and when all was done, the didactic leader of the revellers and sight seers, thought he compensated for his want of taste, by pronouncing as "execrable" the taste of those who, like George Selwyn, could find pleasure in an execution. But there are few men so inconsistent as didactic authors. Pope taught, in poetry, the excellence of moderation; but he writes to Congreve in 1715, that he sits up till two o'clock over burgundy and champagne; and he adds, "I am become so much of a rake that I shall be ashamed, in a short time, to be thought to do any sort of business." But Pope's table practice, like Swift's, was not always of the same character. The dean, writing to Pope, in the same year, that the latter tells Congreve (a dissolute man at table, by the way) of his sitting over burgundy and champagne till two in the morning, speaks of quite another character of life: "You are to understand that I live in a corner of a vast unfurnished house. My family consists of a steward, a groom, a helper in my stable, a footman, and an old maid, who are all at board wages; and when I do not dine abroad, or make an entertainment,— which last is very rare,—I eat a mutton pie, and drink half a pint of wine." Pope's habit of sleeping after dinner did not incline him to obesity; and it was a habit that the dean approved. Swift told Gay that his wine was bad, and that the clergy did not often call at his house; an admission in which Gay detected cause and effect. In the following year to that last named, Swift wrote a letter to Pope, in which I find a paragraph affording a table trait of some interest: "I remember," he says, "when it grieved your soul to see me pay a penny more than my club, at an inn, when you had maintained me three months at bed and board; for which, if I had dealt with you in the Smithfield way, it would have cost me a hundred pounds, for I live worse here (Dublin) upon more. Did you ever consider that I am, for life, almost twice as rich as you, and pay no rent, and drink French wine twice as cheap as you do port, and have neither coach, chair, nor mother?" Pope illustrates Bolingbroke's way of living as well as his own some years later. The reveller till two in the morning, of the year 1715, is sobered down to the most temperate of table men, in 1728. "My Lord Bolingbroke's great temperance and economy are so signal, that the first is fit for my constitution, and the latter would enable you to lay up so much money as to buy a bishopric in England. As to the return of his health and vigour, were you here, you might inquire of his haymakers. But, as to his temperance, I can answer, that, for one whole day, we have had nothing for dinner but mutton broth, beans and bacon, and a barn-door fowl;" after all, no bad fare either, for peer or poet! Swift too, at this period, boasts no longer of his "French wines." His appetite is affected by the appalling fact, that the national debt amounts to the unheard-of sum of seven millions sterling! and thereupon he says: "I dine alone on half a dish of meat, mix water with my wine, walk ten miles a-day, and read Baronius."

Such was the table and daily life of an author who began to despair of his country! In 1732, however, the dean was again full of hope,—we see it in the condition of his wine matters: "My stint in company," he writes to Gay, "is a pint at noon, and half as much at night; but I often dine at home, like a hermit, and then I drink little or none at all." Was it that he despaired again, when alone; or that he only drank copiously at others' cost? Of his own cellar arrangements, however, he thus speaks: "My one hundred pounds will buy me six hogsheads of wine, which will support me a year, *provisæ frugis in annum copia*, Horace desired no more; for I will construe *frugis* to be wine. How a man who drank little or none at home, and seldom saw company to help him to consume the remainder, could contrive to get through six hogsheads in a year, is a problem that will be solved when the philosophers of Laputa have settled *their* theories." Literature is a pleasant thing when its professors have not to write in order to live. Such was the case in the last century, with poor De Limiers, who was permitted to write in periodicals, on the stipulation that he "never told anybody." It is said of him that he would have been an exceedingly clever person, if he had not always been hungry, but that famine spoiled his powers. This was the bookseller's fault, not his. The same might nearly be said of poor Gerald Griffin; but *he* kept his ability warm even amid cold hunger, and had the courage to write his noble tragedy "Gisippus" on scraps of paper picked up by him in wretched coffee-shops, where he used to take a late breakfast, and cajole himself into the idea that it was dinner.

When Cervantes, with two friends, were travelling from Esquivias, famous for its illustrious wines, towards Toledo, he was overtaken by a "polite student," who added himself and his mule to the company of "the crippled sound one" and his friends, and who gave honest Miguel much fair advice touching the malady which was then swiftly killing him. "This malady is the dropsy," said the student with the neck bands that would *not* keep in their place,—"the dropsy, which all the water in the world would not cure, even if it were not salt; you must drink by rule, and eat more, and this will cure you better than any medicine." "Many have told me so," was the reply of the immortal Miguel, "but I should find it as impossible to leave off drinking, as if I had been born for no other purpose. My life is well-nigh ended, and by the beatings of my pulse, I think next Sunday, at latest, will see the close of my career." The great Spaniard was not very incorrect in his prognostic. I introduce this illustrative incident for a double reason; first, it is "germane to the matter" in hand, and secondly, it reminds me of a fact with the notice of which I will conclude this section of my imperfect narrative: I allude to

THE LIQUOR-LOVING LAUREATES.

It is incontrovertible that, with the exception of two or three, all our laureates have loved a more pleasant distillation than that from bay-leaves. In the early days, the "versificatores regis," were rewarded, as all the minstrels in Teutonic ballads are, with a little money and a full bowl. The nightingales in kings' cages piped all the better for their cake being soaked in wine. From the time of the first patented laureate, Ben Jonson, the rule has borne much the same character, and permanent thirstiness seems generally to have been seated under the laurel. Thus, Ben himself was given to joviality, jolly company, deep drinking, and late hours. His affection for a particular sort of wine acquired for him the nick-name of the Canary-bird; and indeed succeeding laureates who, down to Pye, enjoyed the tierce of Canary, partly owe it to Ben.

Charles I. added the wine to an increase of pay asked for by the bard; and the spontaneous generosity of one king became a rule for those that followed. The next laureate, Davenant, a vintner's son, was far more dissolute in his drinking, for which he did not compensate by being more excellent in his poetry. The third of the patented laureates, Dryden, if he loved convivial nights, loved to spend them as Jonson did, in "noble society." Speaking of the Roman poets of the Augustan age, he says:—" They imitated the best way of living, which was, to pursue an innocent and inoffensive pleasure; that which one of the ancients called 'eruditam voluptatem.' We have, like them, our genial nights, where our discourse is neither too serious nor too light, but always pleasant, and for the most part instructive; the raillery neither too sharp upon the present, nor too censorious on the absent; and the cups only such as will raise the conversation of the night, without disturbing the business of the morrow." The genial nights, however, were not always so delightfully Elysian and æsthetic. When Rochester suspected Dryden of being the author of the "Essay on Satire," which was really written by Lord Mulgrave, and which was offensive to Rochester, the latter took a very unpoetical revenge. As Dryden was returning from his *erudita voluptas* at Wills', and was passing through Rose-street, Covent Garden, to his house in Gerrard street, he was waylaid and severely beaten, by ruffians who were believed to be in the pay of Rochester. The conversation of *that* night certainly *must* have disturbed the business of the morrow!

And next we come to hasty Shadwell, who may be summarily dismissed with the remark that he was addicted to sensual indulgence, and to any company that promised good wine, and plenty of it. Poor Nahum Tate, too, is described as "a free and fuddling companion;" but the miserable man had gone through more fiery trials than genial nights. Of Rowe, the contrary may be said. He was the great diner-out of his day; always vivacious, dashing, gay, good-humoured, and habitually generous, whether drunk or sober. He was but a poor poet, but he was succeeded by one who wrote worse and drank more—Eusden, of whom Gay writes to Mason that he "was a person of great hopes in his youth, though at last he turned out a drunken parson." Cibber loved the bottle quite as intensely as Eusden did, and he was a gambler to boot; but there were some good points about Colley, although Pope has so bemauled him. Posterity has used Cibber as his eccentric daughter did when he went to her fish-stall to remonstrate with her against bringing disgrace upon the family by her adoption of such a course: the affectionate Charlotte caught up a stinking sole, and smacked her sire's face with it; but Colley wiped his cheek, went home, and got drunk to prove that he was a gentleman. With heavy Whitehead we first fall in with indisputable respectability. He sipped his port, a pensioner at Lord Jersey's table, and wrote classical tragedies, for which I heartily forgive him, because they are deservedly forgotten. His successor, slovenly Warton, exulted over his college wine with the gobble of a turkey-cock; and then came Pye, with his pleasant conviviality and his warlike strains, which "roared like a sucking dove," and put to sleep the militia, which it was hoped they would have aroused. Pye was of the time of "Pindar, Pye, and Parvus Pybus;" and it was during his tenure of office that the tierce of Canary was discontinued, and the 27$l.$ substituted. With Southey, a dignity was given to the laureateship, which it had, perhaps, never before enjoyed; and the poetic mantle fell on worthy shoulders, when it covered those of the gentle Wordsworth. Not that Wordsworth never was drunk. The bard of Rydal Mount *was* once in his life "full of the god;" but he was drunk with strong enthusiasm too, and the occasion excused, if it did not sanctify the deed. The story is well told by De Quincey, and it runs thus:—

"For the first time in his life, Wordsworth became inebriated at Cambridge. It is but fair to add, that the first time was also the last time. But perhaps the strangest part of the story is the occasion of this drunkenness, which was the celebration of the first visit to the very rooms at Christ College once occupied by Milton,—intoxication by way of homage to the most temperate of men, and this homage offered by one who has turned out himself to the full as temperate! Every man, in the mean time, who is not a churl, must grant a privilege and charter of large enthusiasm to such an occasion; and an older man than Wordsworth, at that era not fully nineteen, and a man even without a poet's blood in his veins, might have leave to forget his sobriety in such circumstances. Besides which, after all, I have heard from Wordsworth's own lips that he was not too far gone to attend chapel decorously during the very acme of his elevation!"

De Quincey has told how pleasant, and cheerful, and conversational was the tea-time at Wordsworth's table; and there, no doubt, the poet was far more, so to speak, in his element than when in the neighborhood of wine, whose aid was not needed by him to elevate his conversation. But Wordsworth, gentle as he was, had nothing in him of the squire of dames, whom he generally treated with as much indifference as the present laureate, Tennison, was once said to feel for those very poetical little mortals,—children. And here I end the record of a few table traits of the patented laureates, adding no more of the fourteenth and last, that is, the present vice-Apollo to the Queen, than that he has said of his own tastes and locality to enjoy them in, in Will Waterproof's Lyrical Monologue, made at the Cock,—

> "O plump head waiter at 'The Cock,'
> To which I most resort,
> How goes the time? 'Tis five o'clock.
> Go fetch a pint of port.

> "But let it not be such as that
> You set before chance-comers,
> But such whose father-grape grew fat
> On Lusitanian summers."

And now all things must have an end; and the end of pleasure is like the end of life,—weariness, satiety, and regret; and the end of a well-spent day is *not* of that complexion, for its name should be "supper," without which, however, a man had better go to bed, than with it and arise in debt. But, as the moral does not apply to us, you and I, Reader, if you will venture further with so indifferent a companion, will go hand in hand, before we finally separate.

SUPPER.

The supper was the only recognised repast in Rome; if, indeed, we may call that supper which sometimes took place at three in the afternoon. It was then rather a dinner, after which properly educated persons would not, and those who had supped over freely could not, eat again on the same day. The early supper hour was favoured by those who intended to remain long at table. "Imperat extructos frangere nona toros," says Martial. The more frugal, but they must also have been the more hungry, supped, like the Queen of Carthage, at sunset; "labente die convivia quærit." All other repasts than this had no allotted hour; each person followed inclination or necessity, and there was no difference in the *jentaculum*, the *prandium*, or the *merenda*,—the breakfast, dinner, or collation,—save difference of time. Bread, dried fruits, and perhaps honey, were alone eaten at these simple meals; whereat too, some, like Marius, drank before supper time, "the genial hour for drinking." The hosts were, in earlier ages, cooks as well as entertainers. Patroclus was famous for his Olla Podrida, and a Roman general received the Samnite ambassadors in a room where he was boiling turnips for his supper!

Sunset, however, was the *ordinary* supper-time amongst the Romans. "De vespere suo vivere," in Plautus, alludes to this. In the time of Horace, ten o'clock was not an unusual hour, and men of business supped even later. At the period of the decadence of the empire, it was the fashion to go to the baths at eight, and sup at nine. The repasts which commenced earlier than this were called *tempestiva*, as lasting a longer time. Those which began by daylight—*de die*—had a dissolute reputation; "ad amicam de die potare," is a phrase employed in the *Asinaria* to illustrate the great depravity of him to whom it is applied.

There is no doubt, I think, in spite of what critics say, that, however it may have been with the Romans, the Greeks certainly had four repasts every day. There was the breakfast (ἀκφκατισμα), the dinner, (ἄριστον), the collation (ἑσπέρισμα), and the chief of all, despite the term for dinner, the supper (δεῖπνον).

Among the Romans the *Cœna adventitia* was the name given to suppers whereat the return of travellers to their homes was celebrated; the *Cœna popularis* was simply a public repast, given to the people by the government; the *terrestris cœna* was, as Hegio describes it in the *Captivei*, a supper of herbs, *multis oleribus*. The Greeks called such "a bloodless supper." The parasite, in Athenæus, says that when he is going to a house to supper, he does not trouble himself to gaze at the architectural beauties of the mansion, nor the magnificence of the furniture, but at the smoke of the chimney. If it ascends in a thick column, he knows there is certainty of good cheer; but if it is a poor thread of smoke, says he, why then I know that there is no blood in the supper that is preparing: τὸ δεῖπνον ἀλλ' οὐδ' αἷμα ἔχει.

These repasts were gay enough when there was good Chian wine, unmixed with sea-water, to set the wit going. The banquets of Laïs were probably the most brilliant ever seen in Greece, for there was abundance of sprightly intellect at them. It might be said of them, as Sidney Smith says of what used to be in Paris under the ancient regime, when "a few women of brilliant talents violated all the common duties of life, and gave very pleasant little suppers."

It is a well-ascertained fact that when the Greeks gave great entertainments, and got tipsy thereat, it was for pious reasons. They drank deeply in honour of some god. They not only drank deeply, but progressively so; their last cup at parting was the largest, and it went by the terrible name of the Cup of Necessity. There was a headache of twenty-anguish power at the bottom of it. Their pic-nic and conversation suppers were not bad things. Every guest brought his own rations in a basket; but as the rich and the selfish used to shame and tantalise the poorer guests by their savoury displays, Socrates, that dreadfully didactic personage, imperious as Beau Nash in matters of social discipline, insisted that what each guest brought should be common to all. The result was less show and more comfort. But I would not have liked to have supped where Socrates was in the chair, for, in spite of his talents, he was a horrid bore, watching what and how each guest ate, and speaking to or at him whenever his acute eye discovered a rent in the coat of his good manners. If he sometimes said good things, he as frequently said sharp ones; and where he was president, the guests were simply at school.

It is indeed seldom that the sages are desirable associates. "Come and sup with me next Thursday," said a French Amphitryon to a friend. "You shall meet philosophers or literary men; take your choice." "My choice is soon made," was the reply; "I will sup twice with you." It was so arranged, and the supper with the *literati* was incomparably the better banquet of the two.

The supper was the great meal of the Greeks; but neither at this, nor at any other repast, does Homer ever make mention of boiled meat. The Greeks, then, were not like our poor Greenwich pensioners, who, up to the present time, have never been provided with meat cooked in any other way. The result is that the men themselves look as if they were half-boiled. But a new order of things, including ovens and baked joints, has been introduced into the kitchen and refectory of the hospital, and the ancient mariners will soon show the effects of variety in diet and cooking, by a healthier and a happier hue on their solemn and storm-beaten cheeks.

And this matter of boiled meat reminds me of the old Duke of Grafton, who never ate anything else at dinner or supper, (for it was in the days of double meals,) but boiled mutton. Yet every day the cook was solemnly summoned to his grace's side, to listen to orders which he knew by heart, and instructions which wearied while they vexed his spirits. The duke must have been of the saddened constitution which would have entitled him to sup with that nervous Duke of Marlborough, who always joined with his invitation a request that his guest would say or do nothing to make him laugh, as his grace could not bear excitement.

At the supper-table the Romans did not decline the flesh of the ass, nor that of the dog; and they were as fond of finely fatted snails as the southern Germans are, who have inherited their taste. Macrobius, describing the supper given by the epicurean pontiff Lentulus, in honour of his reception, says that the first course was composed of sea hedgehogs, oysters, and asparagus. After these provocatives came a second course, consisting of more oysters, and various other shell-fish, fat pullets, beccaficoes, venison, wild-boar, and sea-nettles,—to digest the marine hedgehogs, I suppose. The third course assumed a more civilized aspect, and the guests were only tempted by fish, fowl, game, and cakes from the Ancona marshes. There is a supper of Lentulus, as described by Becker. The supper was given to Gallus, and the account of it is so little exaggerated as to afford a tolerably correct idea of what those banquets were. Nine guests, two of them "gentlemen from Perusia," occupied the *triclinium*. The pictures around represented satyrs celebrating the joyous vintage; the death of the boar; fruit and provision pieces over the door, and similar designs, calculated to awaken a relish for the banquet, were suspended between the elegant branches occupied by living thrushes. The lowest place in the middle sofa was the seat for the most honoured guest. As soon as all were in a reclining posture, the attendant slaves took off their sandals, and water in silver basins was carried round by good-looking youths, and therewith the visitors performed their brief ablutions. At a nod from the host, two servants deposited the tray bearing the dishes of the first course in the centre of the table. The chief ornament of this tray, which was adorned with tortoiseshell, was a bronze ass, whose panniers were filled with olives, and on whose back rode a Silenus, whose pores exuded a sauce which fell upon the roast breast of a sow that had never fulfilled a mother's duty, below. Sausages on silver gridirons, with Syrian plums and pomegranate seeds beneath them to simulate fire; and dishes, also of silver, containing various vegetables, shell-fish, snails, and a reptile or two, formed the other delicacies of this course. While the guests addressed themselves thereto, they were supplied with a beverage composed of wines and honey scientifically commingled. The glory of the first course was, however, the carved figure of the brooding hen, which was brought in on a separate small tray. The eggs taken from beneath her were offered to the guests, who found the apparent eggs made of dough, on breaking which with the spoon, a fat figpecker was seen lying in the pepper-seasoned yolk, and strongly tempting the beholder to eat. This delicacy, was, of course, readily eaten, and *mulsum*, the mixture of Hymettian honey and Falernian wines, was copiously drunk to aid digestion. A good deal of wine was imbibed, and numerous witch stories told (a favourite supper pastime), between and during the courses, at which the dishes were more and more elaborate and fantastic. A vast swine succeeded to a wild boar at the supper of Lentulus, who affecting to be enraged at his cook for forgetting to disembowel the animal before preparing it for the table, that official feigns to tremble with the energy of his repentance, and forthwith proceeds to perform the office of gutting the animal in presence of the guests. He plunges his knife into its flanks, when there immediately issues from the gaping wound string after string of little sausages. The conclusion of the supper is thus told:—" The eyes of the guest were suddenly attracted to the ceiling by a noise overhead; the ceiling opened, and a large silver hoop, on which were ointment bottles of silver and alabaster, silver garlands with beautifully chiselled leaves, and circlets and other trifles, descended upon the table; and after the dessert, prepared by the new baker, whom Lentulus purchased for a hundred thousand sesterces, had been served up, the party rose, to meet again in the brilliant saloon, the intervening moments being spent, by some in sauntering along the colonnades, and by others in taking a bath."

In the description of the supper given by Siba to celebrate the return of Nero to Rome, we find that the slaves, when they took off the sandals of the guests, supplied them with others of a lighter description, which were fastened by crossed ribands. Those who did not come in "dress," were furnished with variegated woollen vestments to cover their togas. Siba's banquet began to the sound of a hydraulic organ, which, however, was only in place of our dinner-bell. When the lime-wood tables were duly covered and flowered, the guests took their places to the sound of flutes and harps, and said a sort of *grace*, by invoking Jupiter; while a modest libation of wine was cast on the floor in honour of the household gods. The first course consisted of some remarkably strange dishes, but the guests reserved their appetite, or provoked it with pickled radishes, fried grasshoppers, and similar cattle. A master of drinking was then chosen, whose duty it was to regulate how often the guests should drink; and the latter invariably selected the most confirmed toper. *We* leave this office to the master of the house, and in well-regulated families that high official leaves his guests to do according to their good pleasure. The garlands having been duly encircled round the brows of Siba's friends, the trumpets announced the entrance of the second course. The second course was duly discussed, its extraordinary dishes thoroughly consumed, and the four cups were drained to Nero; being the number of letters in his name; and a good deal of jollity began to abound, which was checked a little by the arrival of a present from the emperor, sent to Siba, and which consisted of a silver skeleton. As the guests feared to interpret the meaning of the gift they fell to deeper drinking, and then to singing, and philosophising; and then resumed their eating; and when the force of nature could no further go, they called in the jugglers, and tumblers, and buffoons, and puppets, and having drawn as much amusement from these as they possibly could, they whipped up their flagging sensations by looking at the feats of Spanish dancing girls, and these were succeeded by ten couple of gladiators, who slew one another in the apartment for the pastime of the supremely indifferent personages who lay half asleep and half drunk, and lazily applauded the murderous play. The company were in the very midst of this innocent amusement when the fire was lit up in Rome by Nero, and which did not spare the mansion of Siba. The struggle to escape was not more furious and selfish than that which took place at Prince Schwartzenberg's ball in Paris, at which the devouring flames had as little respect for some of the guests as they had at the terrible supper of Caius Siba.

It may be said that civilization never afforded such examples of deformed appetites as some of those which we find in the records of the olden time. But this is not the case. They are fewer; but they *do* exist. We read in the modern history of Germany, that a man with an uncontrollable appetite for bacon once presented himself at the tent where Charles Gustavus was supping, before Prague, which he was besieging. The man was a boor, and had sought access to the king, to ask permission to perform before him a feat which he boasted of being able to accomplish,—namely, devour a whole hog. General Koenigsmark, who was present, and was very superstitious, warned the king not to listen to a being who, if not the devil, was probably leagued with him. "I'll tell you what it is, and please your Majesty," said the boor, "if you will but make that old gentleman take off his sword and spurs, I'll eat him before I begin with the hog!" The general was no coward; but he took to his heels, as though the man was serious, and left the king to enjoy what pleasure he might from seeing a peasant eat a whole pig.

In Africa, the rustics eat something smaller than pigs for supper. When Caillé was in that quarter of the world, a Bambere woman gave him some yams, and what he thought was gambo sauce, to make them palatable. On dipping his yams therein, however, he saw some little paws, and at once knew that it was the famous mouse-sauce; but he was hungry, and continued his repast. He often subsequently saw the women chopping up mice for their suppers. When the animals were caught, they were singed over a fire, put by for a week, and then cooked. A hungry man *might* eat thereof without loathing. We have all partaken of far less clean animals.

It is commonly said that the time of the evening meal is the very hour for wit. I do not know how this may be, but Souwarow's wit appears to have been uncommonly alert at suppertime. When he returned from his Italian campaign to St. Petersburgh, in 1799, the Emperor Paul sent Count Kontaissow, to compliment him on his arrival. The count had been originally a Circassian slave, and *valet* to Paul, who had successively raised him to the ranks of equerry, baron, and count. The Circassian *parvenu* found the old warrior at supper. "Excuse me," said Souwarow, pausing in his meal, "I cannot recall the origin of your illustrious family. Doubtless your valour in battle procured for you your dignity as count." "Well, no," said the ex-valet "I have never been in battle." "Ah! perhaps you have been attached to an embassy?" "No." "To a ministerial office then?" "That neither." "What important post, *then*, have you occupied?"—"I have been valet-de-chambre to the emperor." "Oh, indeed," said the veteran leader, laying down his spoon, and calling aloud for his own valet, Troschka. "Here, you villain," said he, as the latter appeared, "I tell you daily to leave off drinking and thieving, and you never listen to me. Now, look at this gentleman here. He was a valet like you; but being neither sot nor thief, he is now grand equerry to his majesty, knight of all the Russian orders, and count of the empire. Go, sirrah, follow his example, and you will have more titles than your master; who requires nothing just now, but to be left alone to finish his supper!"

It was at Paris, however, that the evening hour was generally accounted as the peculiar season of wit; but wit, often too daring at such an hour, sometimes got chastised for its over-boldness.

At one of the *petits soupers* of Paris, in this olden time, when wit and philosophy had temporarily dethroned religion, a little abbé, who had the air of a full-grown Cupid in a semi-clerical disguise, or who was like Rose Pomponne in a carnival suit at the Courtille, took upon himself to amuse the assembled company with stories intended to ridicule the old-fashioned faith, (as the philosophers styled Christianity,) and its professors. He was particularly comic on the subject of hell and eternal punishments, upon which questions he dilated with a fulness that would have scarcely edified either Professor Maurice or Dr. Jelf. The whole of the amiable society exploded in inextinguishable laughter at hearing this villainous abbé speak of hell itself as his "feu de joie!" There was, however, one face there that bore upon it no traces of a smile. It was that of an old marechal-de-camp, who might have said, like the old beadle of St. Mary's, Oxford, "I have held this office, sir, for more than thirty years, and, thank heaven, I am a Christian yet!" Well, the old marechal frowned as, looking at the infidel abbé, he remarked, "I see very plainly, sir, by your uniform, to what regiment you belong, but it seems to me that you must be a deserter." "My dear marechal," answered the profligate priest, with a beaming smile, "it may indeed be a little as you say, but then, you see, I do not hold in my troop the rank which you enjoy in yours. I am not a marechal-de-camp!" "Parbleu," rejoined the old soldier, "you never could have reached such a rank, for, to judge by your conduct and sentiment, you would have been hanged long before your chance came for promotion."

At the *soupers* of Paris, however, there were few men who were of the character of our marechal-de-camp. Bungener, in his "Voltaire et son Temps," illustrates the confusion into which men's ideas had got upon the subject of things spiritual and things temporal, by noticing the affair of the Chevalier de la Barre, in 1766. Amid the accusations brought against him was one, according to which it was laid to his charge that he had recited in public a certain filthy ode. He was condemned to be broken on the wheel, on charges of irreligion, of which this was one. But the part of the question that must have made Astræa weep through the bandage with which poets have bound her eyes, was this, namely, that the author of the obscene ode objected to, Piron, was then in the reception of a pension from the court; and this pension had been procured for him by Montesquieu, by way of compensation for his having lost his seat at the Academy, in consequence of his having been the author of this very ode. This confusion of rewards and penalties was enough to make Justice dash her brains out with her own scales. Piron would have been in no wise troubled by such a catastrophe; the pension from the court enabled him to keep a joyous table, and that was enough for him.

Duclos was a contemporary and a co-disciple with Piron, in the temple of philosophy. In 1766, he was at Rome, where he gave such charming little suppers, that the Sacred College gratefully extended to him the privileged permission of reading improper books! The philosophers were then in possession of considerable influence. Marmontel, who was one of them, was sent to the Bastille, on a certain Friday, in the year 1760. Soon after his arrival, he was supplied with an excellent dinner *maigre*, the which he ate without thinking of complaining. His servant was just on the point of addressing himself to the scanty remains, when lo! an admirable but somewhat irreligious repast, of meat and other things which come under the denomination of *gras*, and are therefore forbidden on fast days, was brought in. The unorthodox banquet was intended for Marmontel; the more lenten fare was intended for his servant. For in those days, although philosophers were sent to prison, their appetites were left to their heretical freedom.

This liberty was allowed by the state, but it was neither sanctioned nor practised by the Church. The authority of the latter was great previous to the Revolution. There was then a clerical police, which looked into the dishes as well as the consciences of the people—of all degrees. I have somewhere read of a body of this police coming in collision, during Lent, with the officers of the household of the Prince of Conti, who were conveying through the streets, from a neighboring *rotisseur's* to the ducal palace, a supper, through the covers of which there penetrated an odor which savoured strongly of something succulent and sinful, of gravy and gravity. Thereupon the archbishop's alguazils bade the prince's men stand and deliver. The followers of the house of Conti drew their swords in defence of their rights and sauces.

Much of the latter on the side of Conti, and a little malapert blood on both sides, was spilt, to the edification of the standers by. Finally, the transgressors of the Church law were dragged to prison. The damaged repast remained on the pavé, for the benefit of poor souls who assumed ecclesiastical license to devour it without fear of damnation; and the servants of Conti were left in damp cells to meditate at their leisure upon the argument which Dean Swift at another period had thus cast into verse:—

> "Who can declare, with common sense,
> That bacon fried gives God offence?
> Or that a herring hath the charm
> Almighty vengeance to disarm?
> Wrapt up in Majesty divine,
> Doth He regard on what we dine?"

To pass from cooks and church to courtesy and coachmen, I may here speak of a certain Girard who was known in Paris, during the Terror, for his love of what he called liberty and good living. In his early days he was a very independent coachman, and was just on the point of concluding an engagement with an aristocratic old countess, when he remarked—"Before I finally close with madame, I should like to be informed for whom madame's horses are to make way in the streets." "For every one," said the countess. "On questions of precedence, I am not difficult; if it is yielded to me, I take it; if not, I wait." "In that case," said the aristocratic John, "I shall not suit, madame, as I myself never draw aside except for the princes of the blood!" Now this great personage in livery was no other than the Girard who became, in 1793, the "public accuser," and who sent to the scaffold those same nobles who had not been sufficiently noble for him in 1780.

Upon the matter of what became nobility, however, there was always much confusion in the "aristocratic idea" of the highest continental families. Thus who, in contemplating the famous Princess des Ursins, seated among the most honoured at the table of the King of Spain, would dream of her writing the following sentence in one of her letters to Madame de Maintenon? "It is I who have the honour of taking from his majesty his *robe de chambre*, when he gets into bed; and I am there to give it to him again, with his slippers, when he rises in the morning."

The flattery paid to royalty in France was never more prodigally offered than at the period when " wit and philosophy " were beginning to undermine the throne. We have an instance of this in what happened when the queen of Louis XV. arrived, in 1765, at Ferté-sous-Jouarre, where she intended to sup and sleep. She was met beneath an avenue of trees, outside the town, by the authorities, who offered to her, according to custom, bread and wine. The queen took a portion of the bread, broke it in two, and ate thereof, as well as of some grapes, sipping also the wine; to the delight and edification of the admiring multitude. The authorities were so struck by the act of condescension on the part of the royal personage, that they made record of the fact in the register of the town council. And this they did in such terms as to cause a commentator to remark, that they could hardly have said more, had her majesty been a genuine goddess.

After all, this sort of homage had fallen off, in 1765, from what it had been two centuries before. When Louis XII. encountered his bride, Mary of England, outside Abbeville, he clapped his feeble hands, and wished the devil might seize him (and he *did* die soon after) if she were not more beautiful than report had painted her! At the gates of Abbeville, the ill-assorted pair were met by the bishop of Amiens and the municipal magistrates, to welcome them to the evening banquet ere they betook themselves to repose. The bishop presented the new Queen of France with a piece of the Real Cross. "The *mayeurs* offered a gift, the nature of which brings it within my subject. The gift was usual whenever king and queen appeared at the portals of the old monkish city. It consisted of three tuns of wine, three fat oxen, and fifteen quarters of oats, three pecks of which were presented to the astonished lady on bended knee, and in a measure painted light blue, and covered with golden fleur-de-lys. A complimentary address to the king crowned all. "Sire," said the chief local magistrate, "you may now conclude your marriage in this our good city, without any fear of committing sin thereby; for, in the year 1409 were reformed, as abuses, those synodal statutes by which men in our city were forbidden to live with their wives, during three whole mortal days after the wedding!" The monarch entered and sat down with his consort to a repast which rendered both ill for more than double the period just mentioned. Louis had well-nigh died, like La Matrie, the infidel philosopher at Berlin, of an indigestion. Had he done so, it might have been said of him, as the infidel Prussian king said of La Matrie: "He was a *gourmand*, but he died like a philosopher; let us have no more anxiety about him."

Frederick himself loved philosophy more than faith, and philosophical though profligate kings, more than he did "Most Christian" or "Most Catholic" monarchs. He was wont, therefore, to laugh at the story of the famished beggar who, standing near the statue of Henri IV. on the Pont Neuf, solicited charity of a friend of Voltaire who was passing by. "In the name of God," said the mendicant. The student of philosophy was deaf. "In the name of the Holy Virgin!"—"In the name of the saints!" The appeal was unheeded. "In the name of Henri IV!" exclaimed the petitioner; and forthwith the Voltairean put his hand in his pocket, giving a crown-piece, in the name of a philosophical profligate, while he refused a sou when asked for in the name of God. But, as Frederic used to say, "How divine is philosophy!" In his mouth the exclamation was like the well-known cry of Marcel, the ecstatic dancing-master: "Que de choses dans un minuét!"

There is a story told in connexion with this same great Frederic which is a good table trait in its way. Joachim von Ziethen was one of the bravest of the generals who stood by Frederic the Great in victory or defeat. He was the son of a poor gentleman, and had little education save what he could pick up in barracks, camps, and battle fields, in all of which he figured in early youth. If his head was not over-ballasted with learning, his heart was well freighted with that love for God, of which some portion, as the dismissed lecturer on Ecclesiastical History in King's College tells us, is in almost every individual without exception, and forms the sheet-anchor which shall enable him to ride through the storms which keep him from his desired haven of rest. He became the terror of the foes of Prussia; but among his comrades, he was known only as "good father Ziethen." He was remarkable for his swiftness at once of resolve and execution, and in remembrance as well as illustration thereof, a sudden surprise is spoken of by an astonished Prussian as "falling on one like Ziethen from an ambush."

Now, old Ziethen, after the triumph achieved in the Seven Years' War, was always a welcome guest at the table of Frederic the Second. His place was ever by the side of the royal master whose cause he had more than once saved from ruin; and he only sat lower at table when there happened to be present some foreign royal mediocrity, illustriously obscure. On one occasion, he received a command to dine with the king on Good Friday. Ziethen sent a messenger to his sovereign, stating that it was impossible for him to wait on his majesty, inasmuch as that he made a point of never omitting to take sacrament on that day, and of always spending the subsequent portion of the day in private meditation.

A week elapsed before the scrupulous old soldier was again invited to the royal dinner-table. At length he appeared in his old place, and merry were the guests, the king himself setting an example of uproarious hilarity. The fun was running fast and furious,—it was at its very loudest, when Frederic, turning to Ziethen, smacked him familiarly on the back, and exclaimed, "Well, grave old Ziethen! how did the supper of Good Friday agree with your sanctimonious stomach? Have you properly digested the veritable body and blood?" At this blasphemy, and amid the thunders of pealing laughter, the saluting artillery of the delighted guests, Ziethen leaped to his feet, and after shaking his grey hairs with indignation, and silencing the revellers with a cry, as though they had been dogs, he turned to the godless master of the realm, and said—words, if not precisely these, certainly and exactly to this effect:—

"I shun no danger;—your majesty knows it. My life has been always ready for sacrifice, when my country and the throne required it. What I was, *that* I am; and my head I would place on the block this moment, if the striking of it off could purchase happiness for my king. But there is One who is greater than I, or any one here; and He is a greater sovereign than you who mock Him here from the throne in Berlin. He it is whose precious blood was shed for the salvation of all mankind. On Him, that Holy One, my faith reposes: He is my consoler in life, my hope in presence of death; and I *will not* suffer His name to be derided and attacked where I am by, and have voice to protest against it. Sir, if your soldiers had not been firm in this faith, they would not have gained victories for you. If you mock this faith, and jeer at those who cling to it, you only lend a hand to bury yourself and the state in ruin." After a pause he added, looking the while on the mute king:—"What I have spoken is God's truth; receive it graciously."

Frederic was the patron of Voltaire, who had dared to say at his own table that what it had taken God and the twelve Apostles to build up, one man (Voltaire) would destroy. But Frederic was now, for the moment, more deeply moved by what had been uttered by the unphilosophical Ziethen than by anything that had ever fallen from the brilliant but irreligious Voltaire. He rose, flung his left arm over Ziethen's shoulder, offered his right hand to the brave old Christian general, and exclaimed:—"Ziethen, you are a happy man! Would that I could be like you! Hold fast by your faith; and I will respect even where I cannot believe. What has occurred shall never happen again."

A deep and solemn silence followed, and the dinner was spoiled, according to the guests, to whom the king gave the signal to disperse long before their appetites had been satisfied. Ziethen was preparing to withdraw with the rest, but Frederic, taking him by the hand, whispered:—"You, my friend, come with me to my cabinet."

This anecdote was told by Bishop von Eylert to Frederic William III. That king, who had never heard of the incident, pronounced on it a three-piled eulogium of "excellent, pleasing, and instructive," adding thereto a natural desire to know what passed between the king and Ziethen in the cabinet. It were doubtless well worth knowing, but I have sought for any notice of it, and all in vain. The good bishop, as he deserved, was invited to remain at Sans Souci, to supper. "I excused myself," says the prelate, in his memoir of the king, "as having only a common upper coat on." The king replied, smilingly, "I know very well that you have got a collar and a dress-coat; you are the same in either. I want *you*, not your coat; so, go in."

The Prussian soldiers, in the days of the great Frederic, used to be allowed unlimited liberty in providing themselves with food in an enemy's country. The like permission, but somewhat enlarged, was given to the Croat soldiers, under the name of foraging for "supper;" but in that permission they included every meal. They are as ready at it as Abyssinians; they cut a slice out of the first beast they fall in with, salt it, put it in between the saddle and the horse's back, gallop till it gets warm, and then eat it with Croat appetite. The sportsmen of Dauphiny eat beccaficoes after much the same fashion; they pluck the bird, sprinkle it with pepper and salt, carry it on their hat to dry in the air, and eat it with relish for supper, without any further cooking. They declare it is far better so than when roasted.

Celebrated as the "petits soupers" of the French were during the last century, they were equalled in brilliancy, and perhaps, surpassed in popularity, by those given in Paris by the Duchess of Kingston. The adventures of that very adventurous lady rendered her a favourite with our lively neighbours. When a rustic Devonshire beauty—wayward, capricious, ignorant, and seductive, Elizaberth Chudleigh was suddenly transplanted to the court of the Princess of Wales, as maid of honour. She there captivated the youthful Duke of Hamilton, returned his affections, and accepted the offer of his hand. They loved intensely, quarrelled furiously and were reconciled warmly; the enemies of both toiled incessantly to prevent the marriage, and each was daily told of the alleged infidelities of the other. One of these stories excited the ardent beauty to such a rage that she dismissed her ducal lover, and in the whirlwind of her wrath gave her hand to Captain Hervey, brother of the Earl of Bristol. She married in haste, and repented quite as hastily. She hated her husband before they left the church together; and after six months of the most active domestic warfare, the ill-sorted pair separated by mutual consent. She went abroad to find solace for her disappointment, and was heartily welcomed at the courts of St. Petersburg, Prussia, and Saxony; she was the favoured guest of Catherine II., and of the great Frederic, at Berlin; and no electoral banquet took place at Dresden without being enlivened by her presence and her wit. When she accepted the invitation to resume her place at the English court, the reception she met with was enthusiastic: she played whist with the men, and she drove four-in-hand as if she had been the born daughter of a charioteer, brought up to her father's business. Her accomplishments won the heart of the simplest of dukes and the gentlest of men, his grace of Kingston, and as an ecclesiastical court, in 1769, pronounced her marriage with Captain Hervey (now Earl of Bristol) null and void, she speedily espoused her ducal admirer, while her former husband bestowed an earl's coronet on a second wife. The duke's property was not entailed, and the duchess spent it with such reckless prodigality, that his grace was fairly frightened into consumption and death; and in 1773 she was a beautiful widow, with a large remnant of the duke's fortune in her possession—as long as she did not marry again. Away she went to Rome, sailed up the Tiber in her own yacht, entertained the pope (Ganganelli) Clement XIV. at breakfast, dinner, and supper, and kept up such a state that the world had never beheld such extravagant splendour since the days of the most profuse and profligate of queens: the heirs of the duke, seeing their inheritance fast melting away, instituted against her the famous suit for bigamy, on the ground that the ecclesiastical court which broke her first marriage had no power to do so. To meet her accusers she hurried to England, where she considerably startled the modest among our grandmothers by her Sunday amusements, and the daily display afforded by the very lowest of dresses. But as she gave most splendid dinners she had no lack of friends, and few men could find it in their hearts to abandon a woman in distress, whose kitchen fires were never extinguished, who gave her guests green peas at Christmas, and whose commonest beverage was imperial tokay. The House of Lords judged her case, heard her defence, and pronounced her second marriage bigamy, by overthrowing the decree of the ecclesiastical court with regard to her first union. To avoid the vulgar penalty she immediately fled, crossed the Channel in a storm, and proceeded to Munich, where she was royally entertained, especially as the law could not touch the property bequeathed her by the Duke of Kingston. The courtesy title of duchess was still allowed her, and the Elector of Bavaria added to it that of Countess of Warth. Great nobles gave entertainments in her honour, which lasted for days, and ended with a ball, a banquet, and, instead of commonplace fireworks, the storming of a town at midnight. Poor nobles vied with each other for her smiles and the life-interest of her possessions; but as she had once been nearly entrapped by a Greek Prince Warta, who turned out to be the son of an ass-driver in Trebizond, and who committed suicide in prison, she made and kept her resolution to be her own mistress for the future, and not that of either count or kaiser.

In France, where she ultimately resided, she purchased the estate of St. Assize au Porte, which had formerly belonged to the Duke of Orleans, the father of "Egalité." She paid down a million and a half of francs for it, and sold seven thousand francs' worth of rabbits from it, during the first week of her residence there. A fricassee of the duchess's rabbits was, for a long time, the chief dish at all the *guinguettes* round Paris. Her own great suppers were famous for their refinement and luxury. She was a lover of good living, a *gourmet* rather than a *gourmande;* an epicure of taste, but not a glutton; and the gastronomic art never could boast of a more liberal patronage than that she bestowed upon it, especially in her Paris residence, where her table, her wit, her dinners, and her diamonds, made of her, for a time, the most remarkable personage in the capital. She died suddenly, of the rupture of a blood-vessel, in 1788, and was completely forgotten before that year had also expired.

I have mentioned that our eccentric country-woman had purchased the property of the Duke of Orleans; and that reminds me how fatal the table, and particularly the supper-table, has been to the dukes of that house. Thus Philippe, the brother of Louis XIV., quarrelled with the latter touching the marriage which the king wished to conclude between one of his own natural daughters and the duke's son. Orleans, fevered and flushed, went to sup "with the ladies of St. Cloud." He had not long before eaten heavily and drunk deeply at dinner; and at this second meal he was fatally stricken with apoplexy. The king said he was sorry, and having thus far given way to his grief, he sat down with Madame de Maintenon to rehearse the overture of an opera. This duke's son and successor gave suppers, at which his infamous daughter, the Duchess de Berri, presided, and admission to which was purchased by the candidate making simple denial of his belief in a God! The fate of both had something retributive in it. The Duchess de Berri, who had privately married a profligate and ugly officer of her guards, named De Riou, sought to overcome her father's wrathful refusal to acknowledge the union, by giving him a splendid supper *al fresco* on the terrace of Meudon, on the 13th May, 1709. The evening proved cold and damp, and the duchess caught there a fever brought on by a chill, over feeding, and deep drinking, of which she died. Fourteen years afterwards, the sire who, at sixteen, had all the experience in vice of a man of sixty, was dining with the Duchess of Phalaria, his last mistress, when he was taken ill. The physician who was summoned enjoined abstinence immediate and complete. "Wait till to-morrow," said the duke, "I will enjoy myself to-night." And accordingly, the exemplary pair supped together, and the lady was in the act of telling the duke one of her lively stories. As she went on, the glass slid from his hand, and his head sank upon her shoulder. She thought he was asleep, and went on her story; but he to whom she was telling it was stone-dead. The son of the regent duke was in every respect unlike his father. He ate *his* last supper with the Jansenist fathers of the Geneviève—symbol of his general habits and the society he kept. *His* son was the father of *Egalité*, and at the time of his death (1785) was popular with the lower classes at Paris for the nightly suppers which he distributed to them, and which consisted of bread and wine, with medicine for those who needed it. It was a distribution made not charitably, but politically. Of the last meal of Egalité, before he went to execution, I only know that it was a breakfast, and not a supper, and that he both ate and drank heartily. Misfortune quite as little disturbed the appetite of the Louis Philippe of our own days. During his flight from Paris he never forgot the hour of supper or dinner; and when "William Smith" landed at Newhaven, the first thing he asked for was—something to eat. I notice these table traits, simply because the Orleanist historians always speak contemptuously of Louis XVI. eating, with appetite, in open court during his trial. The stomach of Orleans was ever as ready as that of Bourbon.

The supper has been called the conversational meal, but to make it so in perfection it requires a thorough professor of the science of conversation—one who knows that its very spirit consists less in being a good talker himself than in flinging about suggestive matter to induce others to converse upon. The host who understands the science will so do this that his guests will be satisfied with themselves. Some French writer has said, in reference to this after-supper gossip, that it should be like a game at cards, at which each player does his best,—but I do not endorse this sentiment to its fullest extent, although I allow that there is something in it. The wise generally, and dyspeptics especially, will do well to avoid political subjects after supper; and perhaps there is no more comprehensive remark to be made on this matter than one advanced by a follower of La Bruyère, a minor moralist, who has said that "la confiance fournit plus à la conversation que l'esprit ou l'érudition."

I recollect once seeing the dullest of evenings made suddenly bright by an apt query modestly put by one who needed not to inquire, but who quietly asked if any one present could name the author of the line:—

"Fine by degrees, and beautifully less,"

Many a wide guess was fired off prior to the successful naming. The general opinion was in favour of Pope, and Pope has indeed written a line very like it:—

"Fine by defect, and delicately weak."

The falling upon such coincidences are the very explosives of after-supper discussions: thus, the very familar line—

"Rides in the whirlwind, and directs the storm."

may be the text for a pretty dispute. It occurs in Addison's "Campaign," and also in Pope's "Dunciad." The latter poet too has said—

"Ye little stars, hide your diminish'd rays;"

but Milton, before him, had written—

"At whose sight all the stars
Hide their diminish'd heads."

Schiller's "Thekla" warbles melodiously her melancholy assurance—

"Ich habe gelebt und geliebet;"

and Byron's "Sardanapalus," equally used up, mutters with a faint sigh the same words—

"I have lived and loved."

We all know who tells us that

"Gospel light first beam'd from Boleyn's eyes;"

and Horace Walpole harped on the same tune, when he said—

"From Catherine's wrongs a nation's bliss was spread,
And Luther's light from Henry's lawless bed."

Gray and Moss, too, afford instances of like coincidences of sound or sentiment, or both. The first, in his "Elegy," has—

"And leaves the world to darkness and to me."

The second, in his "Beggar's Petition," sings to the same air—

"And left the world to wretchedness and me,"

I have noticed, in a former page, how Gray's line of

"Dear as the light that visits these sad eyes,"

must necessarily remind one of Shakespeare's words, in the mouth of Brutus—

"Dear as the drops that visit this sad heart."

Demosthenes has truly said—

Ἀνὴρ ὁ φεύγων καὶ πάλιν μαχήσεται,

so that Sir John Minnes is not even the original author of the Hudibrastically sounding assertion—

"He who fights and runs away.
May live to fight another day."

The lines in Hudibras are as the perfecting and comment on the above, remarking as they do—

"For he that runs may fight again,
Which he can never do that's slain."

These coincidences are, no doubt, unintentional. For my own part, I do not believe that Shakespeare, when he spoke in Hamlet, of

"The undiscover'd country, from whose bourne
No traveller returns,"

necessarily had in his mind the

> "Qui nunc it per iter tenebricosum
> Illuc unde negant redire quemquam."

of Catullus; although the latter lines were quoted by Seneca the philosopher, and were as familiar as household words among the verse-loving ancients. Dr. Johnson's remark on the similarity between Caliban's desire to sleep again, and the πάλιν ἤθελον καθεύδειν of Anacreon, may apply to nearly all the passages in our national poet which appear to have been derived from the ancients. If we judged them by any other rule than that the ideas presented themselves naturally to Shakespeare's mind, without consideration whether any one before him had sung to the self-same tune, we might soon turn *his*, and indeed any poet's works, into a thing of shreds and patches. For instance, again, when the young Dane describes Osric as "spacious in the possession of dirt," we might accuse the author, yet wrongfully, perhaps, of having stolen the idea from the "multa dives tellure" of Horace. We might imagine that the "Id in summa fortuna æquius quod validius," of Tacitus, gave birth to

> "That in the captain's but a choleric word,
> Which in the soldier is flat blasphemy,"

of Shakespeare, who would have been very much surprised had he been told as much. Again, Corneille, because he said,

> "Qui commence bien ne fait rien s'il n'achève,"

is not to be accused of having written a pendant to the assertion of Flaccus—

> "Dimidium facti qui cœpit habet."

Neither has Beaumarchais rifled Otway, because "Desirer du bien à une femme est ce vouloir du mal à son mari," has a close resemblance to—

> "I hope a man may wish his friend's wife well,
> **And no harm done.**"

If mere close resemblance establish a charge of plagiarism, then Chaucer, when in speaking of maidens dark or fair he said—

"Blake or white, I toke no kepe,"

stole the thought from the ancient Irish bard, who said—

"Bohumileen a coolen dhuv no baun;"

a line which Chaucer could not have read, though his own is a literal translation of it. Examples like these I might go on citing *ad infinitum*. As Rosalind says, "I could quote you so eight years together, dinners, and suppers, and sleeping hours excepted." But I will conclude with one more case in point between a well-known English author and the French dramatist Molière. Thus writes the one—

> "What woful stuff this madrigal would be,
> In some starved, hackney'd sonneteer, or me!
> But let a lord once own the happy lines,
> How the wit brightens and the style refines!"

And thus sung the other—

> "Tous les discours sont des sottises,
> Partout, d'un homme sans éclat.
> Ce seraient paroles exquises,
> Si c'était un grand qui parla."

If this be digressing, it is because after-supper conversation *does* take a discursive character. In the last century, in Paris, the majestic nonentities were invited to dinner; the talkers, be they who they might, to supper. "La Robe dine; Finance soupe," was another of these distinctions; and it was found that the supper was by far the most agreeable meal of the day. The Duchess of Kingston, as I have said, was especially celebrated for her Paris suppers. They were infinitely more splendid than her English breakfasts, so pleasantly sneered at by Horace Walpole. The wits assembled round her in gay clusters, and they and the poets cudgelled their brains to prove one another plagiarists; while the peers stood by, and marvelled at the extent and elasticity of the human understanding. Nothing could well surpass the hilarity and magnificence of these entertainments, where the philosophers were voted as dull as the nobles, and no aristocracy was acknowledged but the aristocracy of intellect. Another lady, remarkable for the elegance of the little suppers over which she presided, was Madame Tronchin: but the Reign of Terror came on, and her friends and relatives were daily dragged from her to the guillotine; and Madame Tronchin, who had a most feeling heart, used to say, that she never could have gone through such horrors had it not been for her little cup of café à la crème. The courtiers used to joke in like fashion, at the suppers of Versailles, at national disgrace. When the Count d'Artois returned from the siege of Gibraltar, to which he had gone with much boasting, and began to talk of his batteries, the courtiers used to smile, and to whisper to one another that he meant his "batterie de cuisine."

With regard to the dietetics of supper, it may be taken for granted that late, heavy meals are dangerous, and to be avoided. Chymification and sleep may go on tolerably together after it; but when the time comes for chylification and sanguification, feverish wakefulness will accompany the process. Dyspeptic patients, however, are authorized to take a light supper before going to bed. It is said that the idle man is the devil's man; and it may also be said of the stomach, that if it has nothing to do it will be doing mischief. It is especially so with persons of weak digestion; for whom an egg, lightly boiled, or dry toast and a little white-wine negus, is a supper *selon l'ordinance*. But a wise man will hardly want a guide in this matter. Breakfast may be the meal of friendship; dinner, of etiquette; and supper, the feast of wit;—but, generally speaking, he will show most wit who takes the least supper. Common sense should teach him the exact measure of his capacity.

A whale swollows at a gulp more shrimps than would be required to make sauce for the universe. That gentle songster, the canary, is like the celebrated contralto songstress, who eats daily half a peck of saffron salad;—the bird consumes nearly his own bulk weight of food. But he is delicate compared with the caterpillar, which consumes five hundred times its own weight before it lies down, to rise a butterfly. As for the hyæna, he is popularly said, when hungry, and other food not presenting itself, to eat himself; and probably, like Dr. Kitchener, he carries his own sauce-box about him! But the stomach of man is not made to perform such feats as those accomplished by the whale, the canary, or the caterpillar. He is especially to remember, that though an animal, he is not a beast.

Man, it must be remembered, began with refinement. He was made perfect, upright, and to him was given "every herb bearing seed, which is on the face of all the earth, and every tree in which is the fruit of a tree, yielding seed; to you it shall be for meat." Here food is used as a symbol of celestial blessings; as in the passage, "He should have fed them also with the finest of the wheat, and with honey out of the rock should I have satisfied them." With the fall, civilization and innocence also fell, and barbarism was the offspring of disobedience. There was a time when men had sunk so low that they were like the Troglodytes described by Pomponius Mela—"Troglodytæ nullarum opum domini, strident magis quam loquuntur, specus subeunt, alunturque serpentibus"—they had no property, shrieked rather than spoke, lived in caves, and devoured serpents for food. The fine wheat and the honey from the rock was not theirs. The Fenns, painted by Tacitus, were only a shade less barbarous: "Mira feritas," says the graphic Caius Cornelius, "fœda paupertas; non arma, non equi, non penates; victui herba, vestui pelles, cubili humus"—wonderful for their wildness, their poverty filthy; they had neither horses, nor gods; the grass was their food, skins their raiment, and the ground their couch. The Helvetii were *progressistas* in the race for the prize of civilization; and, when planning an emigration project, they took two years to thoroughly perfect the plan, laying up stores of provisions the while. Whoever

Ceres may have really been, it is clear that in her is to be recognized the benefactress of mankind:—

> "Prima Ceres unco glebam dimovit aratro,
> Prima dedit fruges, alimentaque mitia terris,
> Prima dedit leges;"

she who taught them the uses of the plough, of agriculture, and of fixed laws, and who gave them what God had intended for civilized and innocent man, "the finest wheat,"—she must have been the renovator of the earth, and of beauty upon it. Man, like the rudest saints of the desert—so near may savagery be to undisciplined sanctity—had been "feeding on ashes;" but now the finest wheat was again there to give him strength and delight,— wheat, where golden grain had, perhaps, first yielded its abundance beneath the shade of the primeval tree of knowledge.

The era of wheat, of the ploughshare, and of iron, was the era of the second civilization. Man was no longer generally a wild savage, or a cunning hunter. God again vouchsafed to him "the finest of the wheat;" and, as civilization progressed, so also was widened the circle of supply, upon which indeed much of civilization depends.

The subject of "Man and his Food," with regard to the future, has been ably discussed by Dr. Leonard Withington, of Newbury, Massachusetts. He has moved the question, whether we have reached the terminus of all our stores or not? He holds, that the forest, the field, the river, and the sea may yield contributions to our table, in addition to the known abundance for which our as abundant gratitude is now due. We have not reached the line of our last inventions; and, doubtless, new articles are to be discovered, which will have an equal influence on virtue and happiness. "Boundless nature," says Dr. Withington, "lies before us, and undeveloped skill is wrapt up in the human breast. The exuberance of our system is not exhausted,—her beasts, her birds, her fishes, her plants, her growing trees and her copious grasses, her pastures, her valleys, her lofty mountains, and her rolling streams, are all spread out to the hungry world. Nature is an image of God, and she echoes, though she does not originate the words, 'In my Father's house is bread enough, and to spare.' 'Thou visitest the earth, and waterest it; thou greatly enrichest it with the river of of God, which is full of water; thou preparedst them corn when thou hadst so provided for it. Thou waterest the ridges thereof abundantly; thou settlest the furrows thereof; thou makest it soft with showers; thou blessest the springing thereof.'"

Dr. Cumming holds, not only that death is the most unnatural of conditions, but that when the era of heavenly, everlasting life shall be established, the heaven of man will be here upon earth. So Doctor Withington thinks that the earth will not only be made more heavenly beautiful than it now is, before the period of the new paradise, but more abundant also. "The manna," he says, "which is hereafter to be provided, will not be rained down from heaven, but will spring up from the earth." And there is common sense in this last assertion, for in it is implied that abundance will come by the proper application of knowledge and labour, without which the earth, ever wise and prudent, will yield but little. The increasing populations of that earth have two objects before them which are of no small importance, and which are thus defined by Dr. Withington:—"One is, to impart from the open field of nature all those good and wholesome things which our Father has laid up for us; and secondly, to train our taste and habits for the using of those things which are nutritive and sweet, and which may have the best influence on our moral character and social happiness." The training should begin from early childhood,—and early childhood requires delicate training.

An American writer on dietetics is half afraid that people will smile if he, in connexion with the subject, introduces dainty children; and yet, as he justly remarks, "there is a mystery about this subject, on which we may well bestow a passing thought." There are children in all the various classes of life who are "very difficult about their food." "These little connoisseurs," says Dr. Withington, "cannot eat with the rest of the family, and the mother and the son are often at issue in an interminable controversy. The mother often says it is all whim and caprice; and some severe matrons tell their children that they shall not eat a morsel until the given lump is devoured. But the son would say, if he could quote Shakespeare, 'You cram these things into mine ear against the stomach of my sense. I know I do n't love it. I can't eat it; it is not fit to be eaten.'" The doctor proceeds to inquire if this turn of the appetite be a matter of caprice or necessity. He examines whether the mother, or the boy be right. He acknowledges the antiquity of a controversy which has been carried on for ages, and he has no doubt "that Eve had it with Cain and Abel, the first supper she gave them after they were weaned. We offer it," he adds, "as a profound conjecture, that Cain was a dainty boy, and probably doubled up his fist at his mother." With regard to the controversy itself, he appears to think that it has much of the quality of that which marked the dispute about the colour of the chameleon, and that "both parties are partly wrong." It is likely, as he remarks, that much depends on the training, and volition, and also on original nature and temperament. "There are some things we were never made for, and they were never made for us. There are some kinds of food which, though they may suit the race, were never made for the *individual*. But this blinded appetite, partly natural, partly artificial, follows through life." And this is leaving the controversy very much where the worthy doctor found it.

Finally, let them who fancy that man was made merely to enjoy, learn truth from contemplating the portrait of one whose sole philosophy was gastronomic enjoyment. If ever there was a man who had a gay celebrity, and who taught in the porch, that life was only life at the tables in the "salon," it was the editor of the Almanach des Gourmands." He taught not that *bibere est vivere*, but that *bibere* was only the half of *vivere*, and that to *live* was emphatically to eat and drink. He was a practical philosopher, it should be observed, and here is the portrait of the man at the end of his philosophical practice :—" The author of the Almanack is still in the land of the living. He eats, digests, and sleeps, in the charming valley of Longpons.... But how is he changed! At eight o'clock, he rings for his servants, scolds them, cries *Extravagantes!* calls for his *soupe aux ficules*, and swallows it. Digestion now commences: the labour of the stomach reacts upon the brain, the gloomy ideas of the fasting man disappear, calmness resumes her sway, he no longer wishes to die. He speaks, converses tranquilly, asks for Paris news, and inquires for the old gourmands still living. When digestion is finished, he becomes silent, and sleeps for some hours. On awaking, complaints recommence; he weeps, he sighs, he becomes angry, he wishes to die, he calls eagerly for death. The hour for dinner comes; he sits himself down to table, dinner is served, he eats abundantly of every dish, although he says he has no want of anything, as his last hour is approaching. At dessert, his face becomes animated; his eyes, sunk in their orbits, sparkle brightly 'How is Marquis de Coussy, dear doctor?' he exclaims: 'how long will he last? They say he has a terrible disease. Doubtless they have not put him on regimen. You would never have suffered that, for one must eat to live,—ah!' At length, he rises from table. Behold him in an immense arm-chair. He crosses his legs, supports his stumps upon his knees (for he has no hands, but something resembling the flap of a goose), and continues his conversation, which always runs on eating. 'The rains have been abundant,' he cries, 'we shall have plenty of mushrooms this autumn. What a pity, dear doctor, that I cannot accompany you in your walks to St. Genevieve! How fine our vines are! what a delicious perfume!' And then he falls asleep, and dreams of what he will eat on the following day!"

Fancy, if the theory of guardian angels be a beautiful truth, what the winged watcher of this animal, staggering over the supper of life, must feel at contemplating the ward committed to his care. For our own profit such examples may be employed, as the ancients showed their slaves drunk in presence of their sons, that the latter might be disgusted with inebriety. And this tailpiece should be engraved at the end of every work professing to teach that there is even in this world, a paradise for *gourmands*. The old heathen Socrates knew better, when he said, " Beware of such food as persuades a man, though he be not hungry, to eat; and those liquors that will prevail with a man to drink them when he is not thirsty." In the same spirit, the pious Dodsley taught, that health sat on the brow of him only who had temperance for a companion—temperance, which Sir William Temple styled as "that virtue without pride and fortune without envy, which gives health of body and tranquillity of mind, the best guardian of youth, and support of old age." So Jeremy Collier says, " Temperance keeps the senses clear and unembarrassed, and makes them seize the object with more keenness and satisfaction. It appears with life in the face, and decorum in the person; it gives you the command of your head, secures your health, and preserves you in a condition for business." What comment can I add to texts of such philosophy, but to bid wise men welcome to the feast of reason, where

> " May good digestion wait on appetite,
> And health on both!"

THE END.

www.ingramcontent.com/pod-product-compliance
Lightning Source LLC
Chambersburg PA
CBHW051239300426
44114CB00011B/806